To Eleanor.

The Barlinnie Special Unit

Art, Punishment and Innovation

The Barlinnie Special Unit: Art, Punishment and Innovation

ISBN 978-1-914603-46-4 (Paperback)
ISBN 978-1-914603-47-1 (EPUB ebook)
ISBN 978-1-914603-48-8 (PDF ebook)

Published 2024 by Waterside Press Ltd
www.WatersidePress.co.uk

A catalogue record for this book can be obtained from the British Library.

Ebook *The Barlinnie Special Unit: Art, Punishment and Innovation* is available as an ebook including through library models.

Printed and bound by CPI Antony Rowe.

The Barlinnie Special Unit

Art, Punishment and Innovation

Edited by Kirstin Anderson

Editorial Team

Bill Beech
Claire Coia
Mike Nellis
Sara Trevelyan
Rupert Wolfe Murray

Foreword Baroness Helena Kennedy KC

WATERSIDE PRESS

Royalties from this work will be paid to the Gateway Exchange Fund, which is listed on the Foundation Scotland website, to support projects that offer arts in Scottish prisons as well as services which benefit prisoners and ex-prisoners.

Contents

Acronyms and Abbreviations

ACEs Adverse Childhood Experiences
BSU/Special Unit/the unit Barlinnie Special Unit
Cages ('The Cages') Barred segregation cells
CAPP Comprehensive Assessment of Psychopathic Personality
CPT European Committee for the Prevention of Torture and Inhuman or Degrading Treatment or Punishment
GMRC Glasgow Museums Resource Centre
HMP Her/His Majesty's Prison
RCS Royal Conservatoire of Scotland
RSAMD Royal Scottish Academy of Music and Drama (now the RCS above)
SACRO Scottish Association for Care and Resettlement of Offenders
PRISM Promoting Risk Intervention by Situational Management
SPOA Scottish Prison Officers' Association
SPS Scottish Prison Service

Foreword

Baroness Helena Kennedy LT KC

When I began my legal practice at the English Bar in the seventies, I was a frequent visitor to prisons. The whole prison system filled me with gloom. It was a way of warehousing offenders and any ideas of rehabilitation were hotly contested. The death penalty had been suspended in 1965 and finally abandoned in 1969, so less than a decade earlier, leaving a large part of the population still disgruntled that the country was going soft on crime. There was an overwhelming belief that a prison sentence should mean more than loss of freedom. It had to be harsh and punishing. While there were pockets of enlightenment in certain prisons with training and literacy programmes and there was, and continues to be, the unique HM Prison Grendon, a prison in England with a psychiatric component for prisoners with antisocial personality disorders, places that placed a premium on rehabilitation were rare. It was therefore incredible to read in the press about the Barlinnie Special Unit (BSU) which had been set up in my own home city of Glasgow. I stumbled upon an article about it and then learned more from an English lawyer called Anthony Lester (later the Liberal Democrat Peer Lord Lester QC) who had visited and been greatly impressed.

Amongst convicted prisoners, Scotland's prisons were considered the toughest in the country. I remember a Scots client telling me there was 'no place Sooth o' the Border as bad as Peterhead.' Relations between prisoners and prison staff there were so toxic that there was escalating violence and a serious risk of death of either a prisoner or a prison officer. Out of the desperate impasse at Porterfield Prison Inverness, where violent prisoners were kept in cages so that their every move could be monitored, came a truly extraordinary and innovative idea of placing some of the most difficult prisoners who were serving life sentences into a Special Unit at Barlinnie. The idea was to see whether there was anything to be learnt from HMP Grendon which ran along 'therapeutic community' lines and research studies showed that there were lower levels of internal violence and of reoffending on release as a result.

From the start at the BSU the formalities of prison were dispensed with and staff and prisoners called each other by their first names and a uniform was unnecessary. The original concept was that the unit would be psychiatrically orientated with an in-house Forensic Psychiatrist and specially trained staff including specialist nurses. However, the men who were given places on the unit soon showed a reluctance to bare their souls, but other ways were found to resocialise these very institutionalised men.

Years later, I was presenting the BBC programme *Heart of the Matter* and interviewed Jimmy Boyle, who had been one of the prisoners in the unit. It was on the subject of Redemption. Can a person change and lead a very different life? If so, what makes the difference? He was very insightful about the unit and what had mattered to him. He had not been prepared or ready to take part in the intimate exposure involved in group therapy and nor had the other hard bitten prisoners, but he found an incredible emotional outlet in sculpture which was encouraged by an amazing art therapist, Joyce Laing, who developed the creativity of the individual prisoners. His sculptures became an expression of his anger and need for survival and their raw, visceral quality was recognised by art experts and, on his release, it was also recognised by art dealers who sold many of his pieces. He felt valued. He explained that his previous prison treatment had made him rage against the system and all its rules, whereas in the unit decisions were made in meetings where every voice was heard and complaints were taken seriously and not dismissed. An important element was being treated with respect as a human being by fellow prisoners, not because they feared you but because they heard you, and by staff because they did not see you as an animal.

What he was describing was a form of therapy through a living process: learning the give and take of living in a community. The acquiring of social skills, like mutual respect. The preparation for life in the outside world. And through his wife Sara Trevelyan,[1] a psychiatrist whom he met when she visited the unit, he learned what it really meant to love and be loved—one of the fundamental

1. Sara Trevelyan spelled her name 'Sarah' at this time. For consistency, she is referred to as 'Sara' throughout this book.

human drivers. And I would say that he was also learning about human rights. As did the staff and those who came to see the project for themselves.

There was progress within the prison system in the years that followed with many education and training programmes introduced, including rehab for drugs and alcohol addiction, as well as programmes addressing the impact on victims of crime. There was much talk about alternatives to prison and restorative justice but the trajectory did not continue to bend towards progress. Prison reform was not helped by the arrival of an economic crisis and austerity policies which greatly reduced funding for criminal justice and subsequent challenges like the pandemic and a new economic downturn.

Here we are 50 years later and our prisons, up and down the nation, are in total crisis, crammed to bursting point, full of drug use, underfunded and understaffed so that prisoners are kept in cells for most of their waking hours. Instead of looking at ways to reduce the prison population, the political parties are busy promising to build yet more prisons at huge cost when the money could be used to better ends.

From the 1990s onwards Law and Order became a Dutch auction between the political parties. Who could be tougher on crime? As a result, we have seen the ratcheting up of prison sentences and an impoverished public debate on how to respond to crime. 'Lock them up' is the easy answer when looking for a soundbite. In reality most people commit crime and end up in prison because of trauma, dysfunctional family life, abusive experiences, violence in childhood and consequent addictions, an impoverished existence and a good lathering of greed and self-interest which underpins the contemporary values of our society as a whole. Of course, there are offenders who commit terrible crimes and need to be imprisoned for the protection of the public and to mark society's abhorrence but what is also needed are good rehabilitative programmes in prisons, including education and training, mental health support, anger management and preparation for a return to society.

The Probation Service, a vital part of criminal justice, is on its knees through underfunding and staff shortages. Alternatives to prison require good community support (as does release from gaol and oversight of those on parole) but it means employing experienced well-trained social workers, who are capable of recognising and managing risk.

Looking again at the BSU is a reminder that we have to reform the prison system. It means treating people in a humane way, even those who have committed serious crime, and by inventing creative projects which restore a person's self-worth as a better route to redemption than mere punishment. This is in all our interests if we want to live in decent societies.

This book tells the stories of people involved in the BSU from wide-ranging, but also intimate, perspectives. The edited collection introduces a conversation that is diverse, and reawakens the spirit of the unit where a radically different approach, that included creativity and the arts, opened new doorways of possibility. I used to think that by this time in my life we would have solved so many of the world's problems. Now I know that moving forward is not always linear and that there can be serious setbacks. However, I still believe we can get to a better place—if we set our minds to it.

April 2024

The author of the Foreword

Baroness Helena Kennedy of The Shaws, LT, KC, FRSA, FRSE(Hon) is a Scottish lawyer, broadcaster, Labour member of the House of Lords and former Master of Mansfield College, University of Oxford. A barrister and member of Doughty Street Chambers, her publications include *Eve Was Framed* and *Just Law*. She is President of Justice, the law reform think tank, and of the Helena Kennedy Foundation as well as being Director of the Human Rights Institute of the Bar Association.

The Editor, Editorial Team and Contributors

The Editor

Kirstin Anderson has taught for 22 years in schools, universities and prisons. She has a PhD from the University of Edinburgh, and led the first empirical study to look at Music Education and Music Making in Scottish prisons. She has written about education and arts in prisons, public health and criminal justice, prison overcrowding, and prison abolition. Kirstin is currently working on a research project about prisoner made magazines in Scotland including *The Key* and *STIR*. She is a Lecturer in Criminology at Edinburgh Napier University.

Editorial Team

Bill Beech is an artist filmmaker and was a visitor from 1974 to 1982 to the BSU who worked closely with the community, particularly Larry Winters and Jimmy Boyle in collaboration with the American artist and writer Michael K Meyers. Bill curated exhibitions and contributed to conferences and festivals including in America and Japan. The work with Winters led directly to Beech creating the screenplay for the feature film *Silent Scream*. His association with the unit continues through his work managing the Special Unit Coyote Fund Archives with Caroline Tisdall and Danny Pope.

Claire Coia is a curator for the Open Museum, which is the outreach branch for Glasgow Museums. Her passion lies in making art accessible to people who are traditionally excluded, creating dynamic opportunities for engagement through facilitating community curated exhibitions and projects. Claire has developed her portfolio of expertise in 'spaces of confinement' which involves taking museum objects beyond the walls of the museum to work in partnership with people in prisons and psychiatric hospitals. Claire has an MA (Hons) in

History of Art, an MRes in Human Geography, and is currently undertaking a PhD with the University of Glasgow researching the art of resistance and the role of women in the BSU.

Mike Nellis is Emeritus Professor of Criminal and Community Justice in the Centre for Law Crime and Justice, University of Strathclyde. Whilst doing social work with young offenders in London he was inspired by *A Sense of Freedom* to improve his practice and become involved in penal reform. He has a PhD from the Institute of Criminology in Cambridge and was long involved in the training of probation officers at the University of Birmingham. Mostly he has written about probation, electronic monitoring and prison movies.

Sara Trevelyan trained as a medical doctor and began a career in psychiatry. She met and married Jimmy Boyle when he was imprisoned in the BSU. She left medicine shortly afterwards and, following his release, they worked together to establish and direct The Gateway Exchange Centre in Edinburgh. Subsequently she trained in psychotherapy and continues to work in private practice. Their marriage ended in 2004, they have two children and two grandchildren. Sara published a memoir *Freedom Found* with Scotland Street Press in 2017.

Rupert Wolfe Murray is a travel writer, editor and project manager. He has published books on Bosnia, Romania and Tibet and his latest is a description of doing 12 jobs in 12 months.

Contributors

Irvine Allan is a Lecturer in Drama and Performance at Queen Margaret University and a multi award-winning theatre and film Director.

Jimmy Boyle is a sculptor and writer. He was one of the first prisoners in the BSU. His publications include the autobiographical *A Sense of Freedom* (1977), *The Pain of Confinement: Prison Diaries* (1985) and a novel, *Hero of the Underworld* (1999).

Graeme Brooks was born in Yorkshire where drawing, skateboarding, pop art and punk stimulated his alternative thinking, iconoclastic rebellion and independent experimentation. Art is his constant, holistic lifestyle companion, compass, entertainment, language, passion, motivator and drug, which he has shared with students, children and now grandchildren. He taught Art in prisons for 21 years and was Head of Art at HMP Humber's Graft Studio.

David J Cooke was the Consulting Psychologist for the BSU for ten years. He is a Fellow of the Royal Society of Edinburgh and a Fellow of the British Psychological Society. He has held chairs at Glasgow, Glasgow Caledonian and Bergen Universities. He is currently an Adjunct Professor in the Department of Law at the Australian Catholic University.

Andrew Coyle is Emeritus Professor of Prison Studies at the University of London and was founding director of the International Centre for Prison Studies in the School of Law at King's College London. He has a PhD from the School of Law at the University of Edinburgh and was elected a Fellow of King's College London in 2004. During his time in the Scottish Prison Service he was Governor of Greenock, Peterhead and Shotts prisons and had frequent contact with the BSU.

Johnny Steele was born into a criminal dynasty in the East end of Glasgow's tough ghettos. He spent most of his life in-and-out of delinquent homes and young offender institutions and went on to spend years in most of Scotland's prisons. His first real break in life was when he was transferred to the BSU having spent many years in solitary confinement in various punishment blocks throughout the country; for him, the unit was a matter of life and death. He now lives in the Scottish Borders with his partner and two beautiful daughters.

Jane Whitaker is a poet, performance artist and was a visitor to the BSU in 1974. Jane is currently a part time Senior Lecturer in Fine Art Critical Studies at the University of Brighton. She was a researcher and co-writer on the feature film *Silent Scream*, and has contributed to exhibitions including the UK City of Culture Exhibition in Hull in 2019. She currently supports the Special Unit Coyote Fund Archives.

Brian Wilson is a former politician and journalist who founded the *West Highland Free Press*. Elected to Parliament in 1987, he became Minister of State at the Scottish Office, with responsibility for Education and Industry in the Labour Government of 1997. He went on to become UK Trade Minister and UK Energy Minister. He is a Visiting Professor at the University of Strathclyde and writes for various newspapers.

In Memory of Ken Murray and Joyce Laing.

This book is dedicated to the pioneering men and women who had an alternative vision of what prison could be, the passion to persist, and the courage to create change.

We also remember the people whose stories are not explored within these pages, whose labours hold the narratives together with invisible glue.

Introduction

Kirstin Anderson, Sara Trevelyan, Mike Nellis,
Bill Beech, Claire Coia and Rupert Wolfe Murray

In 2016, a group of prisoners in HMP Barlinnie in Glasgow worked together to curate an exhibition 'A Way Out of a Dark Time' on the Barlinnie Special Unit (BSU) to be displayed in HMP Barlinnie and at the Kelvingrove Art Gallery and Museum in Glasgow. The BSU, abhorred and admired almost in equal measure, was a small therapeutic unit that was created specifically to hold violent men in the Scottish Prison System who had become unmanageable despite, or in response to, the increasingly punitive methods which failed to control them. Claire Coia, who writes in this collection on the project, reflects that, despite the efforts of the men to research the unit, to read autobiographies of former BSU prisoners, to speak to people who worked in the unit and to read the small number of academic papers that have been published on the unit, 'huge parts of the story were missing'. This edited collection of chapters written by people who lived in the unit as prisoners, who worked in the unit as prison officers, managers and psychologists, who visited the unit as artists and other professions, is an offering to fill in some of those missing pieces of the story.

The compilation of this book has been undertaken in the spirit of Christopher Carrell and Joyce Laing's 1982 publication *The Special Unit Barlinnie Prison: Its Evolution Through Its Art*, a multi-voice, illustrated publication which itself commemorated the first major exhibition of the unit's artworks at Glasgow's Third Eye Centre in 1980. The voices compiled by Carrell and Laing were selected from retired staff, visitors and prisoners in the unit, although the editors discuss in the preface of the text the restrictions placed by the then

Scottish Prisons Department[1] including that prisoners could only comment on their art; no discussion of their experience in prison before the unit was allowed. Perhaps surprisingly, 50 years on from its opening in 1973, that book remains the single most comprehensive record of what the Special Unit's early days were like. Kirstin Anderson, editor of this collection, was ecstatic to find a copy in a second-hand bookstore as a graduate student in Edinburgh, as the manuscript is now out of print.

Like Carrell and Laing's volume, this book is an edited collection of essays and reflections from people involved in the BSU. However, this collection is different in that it contains reflections on the life of the unit throughout almost 22 years of operation including the closing of the BSU and reflections on its role in the Scottish Prison Service (SPS). It contains personal reflections, photographs, memories, as well as academic research on the BSU. We hope that this book becomes a catalyst for questions and conversations. Fifty years on, with the benefit of hindsight, it brings together not only recollections from the people who experienced the BSU first-hand, but explores its potential to inspire reform with new insights from people who work within the current criminal justice system. In preparing this introduction to the volume, we found ourselves connecting storylines, seeing the environment from different perspectives, and thinking about the experiences of people who lived, worked and visited the Special Unit. We think this edited collection presents the BSU in an honest light; one that recognises the unique environment it presented for some people, but also acknowledges that it was not perfect and, even with its incredible freedoms (freedoms that were also not offered to other people imprisoned in Scotland's gaols at the time), it was still very much an experience of imprisonment.

There are a number of themes that run through the chapters. You will hear people's reflections on the sounds heard in the unit, the closeness of its walls (it really was very small) and the visual memories that stick in people's minds; the 'hot seat' at community meetings, children visiting and playing, decorations in cells and sculptures in the garden. We hope that you come away from these chapters knowing more about how the BSU came to exist, its connection to HMP Peterhead and 'The Cages' at HMP Inverness, and the Working Party

1. As the service was known before its current organizational form as an Executive Agency of the Scottish Government in 1993.

that gave it its 'experimental' label that never went away. The Special Unit is often remembered alongside the role art played for many in the early days of the unit, however, these chapters also emphasise the importance of the therapeutic element of community meetings and the significance of prisoners and prison staff talking to each other and making decisions about the running of the unit as a community.

This collection is divided into three parts. In Part I we present the 'Origins and Early Days' of the BSU. First, Sara Trevelyan discusses how the unit developed as a therapeutic community and the role art and artists played in sustaining the community in the early days of the unit. Joyce Laing, Scotland's first accredited art therapist, is the subject of Claire Coia's contribution; in this chapter she shares Laing's reflections on the how the arts almost did not feature as part of the regime of the unit. Bill Beech, who went to the BSU as a visiting artist in the early days of its operation, discusses how the artist Joseph Beuys came to play a significant role in the unit, supporting the development of art there and in the community. He reflects on his life in Edinburgh and his life's work with Edinburgh Arts. One of the defining texts to come out of the unit is *A Sense of Freedom* by Jimmy Boyle who was imprisoned in the BSU. Rupert Wolfe Murray presents a chapter about the role his mother played in the publication of that book. The final two chapters of this part are interviews; firstly, with the artist Richard Demarco and his reflections on how the Scottish arts community supported the BSU and, secondly, with David Croft, on his experience as a prison officer in the unit.

Part II 'Voices From Within the Unit', focuses on the reflections and experiences of individuals in the BSU throughout its existence. To begin, Johnny Steele shares his experiences of imprisonment in establishments compared to the BSU followed by a chapter where Jimmy Boyle and Bill Beech share their memories of Ken Murray, principal officer when the BSU first opened. Former Scottish prison Governor Dan Gunn shares his experiences of working in the BSU as a governor and Irvine Allan, co-founder of Cat A Theatre Company, discusses the role of art in the later years of the unit. Sara Trevelyan writes about the development of The Gateway Exchange, a multi-purpose centre in the Edinburgh community that took inspiration from the work and lessons learned in the BSU. Psychologist David Cooke shares his experience of working in the BSU for ten years and his work on the particular environment and regime of the BSU to reduce violent behaviour. The part ends with an interview with Professor Richard Sparks and his reflections on his SPS commissioned research on the Special Unit and the subsequent closure of the unit.

Part III of this volume, 'Legacies and Lessons', brings together a number of contributions that consider how the BSU has been remembered, and in some ways, pushed aside and forgotten. Professor Andrew Coyle traces the creation of the BSU as a response to what he describes as the endemic violence in HMP Peterhead and describes the sometimes fraught relationship between the unit and the rest of the SPS. Next, journalist and former politician Brian Wilson looks at the role of the Scottish press in reporting on the BSU, before Professor Mike Nellis discusses how Jimmy Boyle and the unit have been remembered, and misremembered, in popular culture. Following this, two chapters outline how the Special Unit is being archived and commemorated, the first by Claire Coia detailing the work of Glasgow Life Museums, and second, Bill Beech and Jane Whitaker discuss their work with the Special Unit Coyote Fund Archive. The penultimate chapter highlights the work of Graeme Brooks and the Graft Studio, an arts intervention programme in HMP Hull. The section closes with Kirstin Anderson's reflection on the role of arts in prisons in Scotland and around the world today.

As with any edited collection, the work to complete this volume has been a labour of love. The editorial team, made up of people that worked in or visited the unit during its operation and people who have studied it over the years, have contributed chapters to the book and helped shape the collection as a whole through their contacts with people who worked and lived in the unit; we are grateful for everyone's contribution to this edited volume. It has been no mean feat of perseverance and persistence to bring these collected voices together to reflect on the achievements of this bold experiment in the Scottish Prison System, which was eventually closed in 1994. This process was supported by some extraordinary synchronicities that have allowed us to connect with people who were involved in the BSU 30 to 40 years ago. The 2016 'A Way Out of a Dark Time' exhibition, mentioned at the beginning of this Introduction, enabled the original spirit of the BSU to come roaring back into life in a way which felt surprising after such a long passage of time since it was officially closed. The remarkable degree of interest that this exhibition held, which took place inside the walls of HMP Barlinnie, attracted prisoners involved in curating it, as well as those outside the prison walls. The Scottish media showed that, despite having apparently been laid to rest in the nineties, interest in the BSU was still very much alive. The embers of the Special Unit 'experiment' started to glow with life again. This was further reinforced through a subsequent exhibition in 2019 in Hull, 'I Am The Coyote', curated by Bill Beech, which again attracted considerable interest from those attending as well as from the media. In the aftermath of these successes, a group of us who were loosely connected through our different involvements in the BSU and its story, decided to gather the strands together and give them substance in the form of a book to celebrate our memories and bring these hidden histories to those who would not otherwise be able to access them. The histories presented in these chapters are not definitive; these are the stories of people who can speak of their own experiences. We suggest there are many stories that are not told in this book, and we hope this collection will inspire more stories of the BSU to be shared.

As 2023 marked the fiftieth anniversary of the opening of the BSU, we care that the unit is not forgotten and that there is a discussion of its legacy. Whether experienced by the people who lived, worked or visited the unit, or encountered it second-hand in the tabloids, prisoner autobiographies or through the artwork produced, the BSU was both success and failure combined. We must ask why unease surrounded, and continues to surround, the experiment, given that this unease provoked both empathetic support and condemnation. To do this, we must call into question the wider themes of crime and justice, rehabilitation and punishment. This book aims to commemorate the work, legacies and lessons of the BSU because, although it remains a unique penal development in Scotland, its significance has still not been properly acknowledged, nor all its lessons learned.

PART I

ORIGINS AND EARLY DAYS

CHAPTER 1

The Barlinnie Special Unit as a Therapeutic Community

Sara Trevelyan

Why the Barlinnie Special Unit was Created

The Barlinnie Special Unit (BSU) was an unexpected innovation in the Scottish Prison System, aptly described by Kay Carmichael as 'a lily in a turnip field' (Carrell and Laing, 1982). It came into existence in 1973 as an attempt to find a better way to deal with a group of violent and difficult prisoners who were proving unmanageable. The abolition of capital punishment in 1969 in Britain created a challenging situation. The Scottish Prison System found itself having to deal with a small number of very long-term prisoners who felt they had nothing to lose. Easily provoked by the harsh discipline which they encountered, their frustrations were often expressed through fighting and violence. The hardline response of prison officers only fuelled the hatred amongst these resistant and hostile prisoners, resulting in riots and escalating tension in the system.

The methods adopted to assert control resulted in the most troublesome individuals being dispersed to remote prisons in the North of Scotland, such as HMP Peterhead and HMP Inverness. The regimes in these prisons at that time were particularly harsh. Discipline was imposed increasingly by isolating prisoners who were challenging a system they considered to be brutalising them. The culture of meeting resistance with force, the 'iron fist' approach, merely exacerbated the problems. In 1966 in Inverness Prison a special segregation unit was established, which came to be known as The Cages. This infamous unit which was described by Jimmy Boyle as 'The Siberia for prisoners in the Scottish Prison System' was a place of extreme isolation, degradation and minimal human contact; a prison within a prison, a desperate and barbaric way of attempting to achieve control. Even with these extreme measures, prisoners continued to riot, attack staff or engage in dirty protests—covering themselves in their own excrement. In a graphic way, this symbolised the hopelessness of the whole situation.

It required courage to explore the possibility of a different approach. In 1970 a working party under the chairmanship of Alex Stephen was set up by the then Scottish Prisons Department to consider the 'Treatment of Certain Male Long-Term Prisoners and Potentially Violent Prisoners'. The working party included senior Prison Service officials, a consultant psychiatrist, two prison governors and representatives of the Scottish Prison Officers' Association (SPOA). They visited units in England and gathered evidence from prisons, as well as specialised psychiatric units which had experience in working with offenders, including Grendon Underwood.[1] The report was published in 1971 and implemented in 1973 with the opening of the BSU.

The initial aim of the unit was to reduce the general level of violence in Scottish prisons by removing a small number of the most violent and troublesome prisoners. It was the particular inspiration of Ken Murray, a Scottish prison officer, and Ian Stephen, who worked for the Scottish Prison Service (SPS) as a forensic psychologist. Dr Peter Whatmore a consultant psychiatrist from the Douglas Inch Clinic Glasgow was also involved. The unit was staffed by prison officers—with it being felt desirable that a number of the staff should have hospital training and that a Chief Nurse Officer should be included as a senior member of the uniformed staff. The Governor of the unit was to be independent of the main prison and supported closely by a consultant psychiatrist. The working party report recommended that the unit staff should be recruited only from those who had volunteered, and stressed the importance of good training, with help for staff to acquire new skills, encouraging a sense of teamwork between staff at all levels. They were expected to build positive relationships with prisoners while at the same time maintaining 'a keen vigilance

1. The establishments visited are listed in the report as (in Scotland) Perth Prison, Peterhead Prison, Inverness Prison and the State Hospital Carstairs, and (in England) Parkhurst Prison, Grendon Underwood Prison and Broadmoor Hospital.

and realistic appreciation of the dangers involved.' The Scottish Office Working Party believed that the Special Unit concept would require a change in the attitudes of the staff as well as a fundamental change in the approach to working with prisoners.

Formative Influences

When the initial concept of the Special Unit was announced by the working party and the Secretary of State, the unit was to have a strong psychiatric orientation. The regime envisaged by the working party was one in which the element of discipline would be maintained while the traditional officer/prisoner relationship would be modified to one of a therapist/patient. In addition to a psychiatric or psychological approach, it was intended that the unit would use group therapy or counselling and that there would be numerous joint meetings between staff and prisoners. This was the early vision. The reality on the ground resulted in a blurring of some of this original blueprint, although the basic intention to establish a small unit with a regime radically different from the mainstream remained. Maxwell Jones, one of the founders of the therapeutic community movement, had an important influence on the development of the original vision of the Special Unit.

Jones was brought up in Edinburgh and graduated from Edinburgh Medical School in 1931. He worked at the Maudsley Hospital in London, where he became involved in treating traumatic stress disorders in military personnel caused by combat experience in the Second World War. Subsequently he became responsible for establishing the Henderson Unit which worked with patients who had psychopathic disorders. He used unconventional methods, such as staff not wearing uniforms, and became skilled at promoting dialogue within the peer group, harnessing forces which surfaced amongst the patients to produce emotional learning and behavioural change. He continued his therapeutic community work in the United States becoming a visiting professor at Harvard University before returning to the UK in 1962 where he stepped into the role of Physician Superintendent at Dingleton Hospital in the Scottish Borders.

Over a period of seven years, he transformed the traditionally run community psychiatric hospital into a democratic social system where across the board, patients, as well as staff participated in community meetings. The approach which he established was based on principles of listening and learning, with two-way communication of content and feelings at all levels of the hierarchy. He was widely known as an inspirational and visionary leader, whose thinking and experience had a significant influence on those involved in establishing the BSU.

When the BSU opened in 1973, in the former women's wing of Barlinnie Prison, there was uncertainty among all those in charge as to what the daily routine would involve. Inevitably at the start there was an atmosphere of mistrust and suspicion. Despite the commitment to trying something new, both staff as well as prisoners, carried into the new situation deeply conditioned attitudes that they had acquired in the mainstream prison system. For the first prisoners in the unit, some of whom were arriving from the brutalising conditions of The Cages in Inverness, and who had participated in violence which erupted in riots, the informal, relaxed regime was a complete anathema—disturbing and disorientating. They were full of suspicion and mistrust.

Very early on the prisoners voiced their concerns about the use of psychiatric methods in the unit. They were convinced that the system was using the unit as a 'launching pad' for the dreaded state mental hospital Carstairs. To counterbalance this view and to alleviate their fears, the unit's staff supported instead the adoption of the democratic therapeutic community model proposed by Maxwell Jones. Central to this was the use of meetings to facilitate regular ongoing communication between inmates and staff. According to Ian Stephen, the unit's psychologist, four main types of meeting evolved over the years: formal community meetings, special meetings, those of four people (known as 'four groups') and informal meetings.

The community meeting held every week on Tuesdays became the formal meeting of the community, everyone was expected to attend and participate in it. The meeting was structured, with a chairman elected by the group and formal minutes of the meeting were kept. The chairman led the meeting and ensured each person, staff and prisoners, were asked if they wanted to raise any topics of discussion. General issues, including the development of the unit, were also discussed by all present.

Special meetings could be called by any member of the unit if there was an issue which caused concern. It was considered important that the group should be allowed sufficient time to attain the satisfactory resolution of any conflict, big or small. On several occasions in the unit these special meetings ran for several hours to achieve this end. Small group meetings could also be called to help in particular situations and informal meetings were held on Fridays where staff and prisoners could meet with the psychologist to discuss issues in general as well as individual and group behaviour.

In the early days there was a question of how the men were to be occupied through the day, as due to their reputations for making trouble, they were deemed unsuited for participating in work programmes taking place across the walls in the mainstream Barlinnie Prison. One of the aspects of the Special Unit which was unusual was that visits from families, friends and other outside contacts were encouraged. This was seen as a way to support the re-socialisation of prisoners who, because of the way they had been imprisoned by the SPS, had become radically and dangerously disconnected from all humanising relationships and were institutionalised to a debilitating degree.

In the initial planning of the Special Unit, the arts had not been considered. Making art was alien to most prisoners' education and life experience. However, through the prison Governor reaching out and inviting the involvement of the art therapist Joyce Laing, the arts were to become an integral part of daily living in the unit. This resulted in a regime in which self-expression flourished and gave rise to an extraordinary range of creativity where the arts played a vital role in unleashing previously untapped talents in prisoners, offering a way to express and release pent up feelings. It is possible that had any attempt been made to introduce a structured programme of arts education, the natural emergence and growth of arts activity would have been unlikely to have succeeded.

A basic concept of the BSU was the involvement of each prisoner not only in their own 'treatment' but in that of their fellow prisoners through communication and confrontation. The involvement of the staff and prisoners developed to the extent that they came to regard themselves as a single community with mutually accepted aims and responsibility for internal domestic matters (e.g. cleaning, and cooking meals). All members of the community were accountable to the weekly meeting—if someone did something detrimental, they were answerable to the whole community. The unit, lacking any clearly specified remit at the beginning, evolved through the creation of its own internal structures into a therapeutic community.

The key that opened the door for the unit's early success was the mere fact that prisoners and staff talked to each other. The environment was secure, being based as it was within an existing prison, but within these secure surrounds the regime in the unit was markedly more relaxed than that which existed in the mainstream prison system. Although fraught with difficulty in the early stages, gradually a degree of trust was built amongst staff and prisoners that allowed the previously high walls of defensiveness and mistrust on both sides to break down. In essence, this was an environment which attempted to restore to these seriously institutionalised prisoners, a degree of respect and human dignity. This was an extraordinary achievement in itself, and would not have happened without a radical transformation of the traditional top-down hierarchical model of control, discipline and punishment that existed in Scottish prisons, as well as most penal establishments in the UK, at the time.

My introduction to the BSU and Experience of Working at Dingleton Hospital

I first visited the BSU in 1977 at the suggestion of a mutual contact involved in a prison reform organization in London. Along with other medical students and doctors, I had taken part in a campaign in the early 1970s to seek to end the use of Control Units in English prisons. These were units designed to control and subdue troublesome and potentially violent prisoners through the use of solitary confinement and sensory deprivation—lights were to be kept on 24 hours a day and the units were heavily soundproofed. Doctors working in prisons were involved in certifying inmates as physically and mentally fit to be sent to these units—a practice we felt was unethical given the damaging consequences to prisoners' physical and mental health of confinement in such extreme conditions. The Special Unit represented, as I have explained, a completely different approach to changing the behaviour of violent and disruptive prisoners, and one which was very much more in line with my own beliefs and values.

Clearly this had a positive impact on Jimmy Boyle, who had formerly been considered to be Scotland's most violent prisoner, but who had flourished in the Special Unit environment, discovering a talent for sculpture as well as writing his autobiography *A Sense of Freedom*, which became a best seller. While I was working as a junior doctor in a hospital in Inverness, I bought a paperback copy with a striking red and black cover off a bookstand in Inverness Railway Station. Like many others I found it compelling reading. Prompted by my friend's recommendation, I wrote to him requesting a visit, something I normally wouldn't have done, but her encouragement persuaded me. I received from Jimmy Boyle a visitor's pass to present at the prison gates of Barlinnie. Having passed through the grim fortified entrance of this Victorian era prison, I was then conducted across a yard to a small door in a high internal wall, which opened into the Special Unit. It was a prison within a prison, with its own courtyard where there were pieces of sculpture, and a small garden, both of which humanised the environment.

The environment felt relaxed, more like a hostel than a prison. I was escorted by a prison officer through a communal area which contained a pool table and a small kitchen, then upstairs past a colourful painted mural to Jimmy's cell. Jimmy, casually dressed in dungarees greeted me warmly at his door. The walls of his cell were attractively decorated with William Morris wallpaper. On one side was his bed, in the middle there was a small coffee table with a meal laid out and on the other side a set of bookshelves which lined the walls. Being able to decorate and personalise their own space was another important aspect for the men in the Special Unit.

Prisoners were also able to prepare their own food—memorably Jimmy had prepared for me what he called a 'Gorbals salad'. He had even baked his own bread! All of this was unexpected and demonstrated a completely new approach to confinement. Leaving Jimmy's cell, he pointed out the mural which had been painted on the downstairs wall with help from the American artist Beth Shadur. All of this was impressive, but I was aware when it came to say goodbye, and an officer came to unlock the small door, that I was free to leave whereas Jimmy and the other prisoners were clearly not able to. In the relaxed atmosphere of the unit, it was possible to forget, or overlook, that confinement in itself is a punishment that causes a lot of emotional stress.

My own experience of the therapeutic community approach began a short time later in Dingleton Hospital. I was attracted by its reputation for offering a radical alternative to the hierarchical structure and organization that existed in other traditional psychiatric hospitals in Scotland at that time. I was inspired by Dr Maxwell Jones's reputation, and in 1977, sometime after this first meeting with Jimmy, I applied for a post as a junior hospital doctor. The hospital had been transformed through Dr Jones's charismatic leadership into a therapeutic community. His philosophy was that everyone should participate in patient care—which led to frequent meetings that included the entire hospital staff—doctors, nurses, social workers, secretaries and even hospital porters and cleaners. It was a radical approach, ahead of its time, which extended to its multidisciplinary outpatient programme where we were able to visit patients in their own homes and assess the underlying causes of disturbance at a grass roots level. This proved an effective way to reduce admissions into the main hospital.

An important aspect of the Special Unit as a therapeutic community was the inclusion of families and outside visitors—which made it possible for a group of us—nurses, doctors and social workers, to visit from Dingleton Hospital for a shared discussion about therapeutic communities. This visit took place a year or so after my initial meeting with Jimmy. He took a leading role in this encounter as he was one of the most actively involved prisoners in the unit, but from memory it was a lively discussion with staff and others contributing as we compared experiences of therapeutic communities in these two very different settings.

I started visiting Jimmy regularly after this hospital visit, which led up to us getting married in January 1980. My visits to the unit continued up until the time when Jimmy was transferred to HMP Edinburgh about seven months later.

Reflections

There is no doubt that the groundbreaking therapeutic community approach of the BSU proved successful in terms of the small number of violent incidents which took place in the unit over the years. It also demonstrated on many different occasions the wealth of talent amongst the prisoners—exhibitions and performances took place, there was even an art festival. Personal creativity can be expressed in many different ways. Some prisoners wrote poetry or plays—while others built pigeon houses.

There were limitations to the unit as well. The extremely liberal visiting policy had the potential to allow inmates to 'hide', isolating themselves with their visitors in their cells rather than participating in the active life of the community. Visitors were not included in meetings and brought with them the culture and values which they were familiar with, which tended to be more in line with the traditional prison inmate culture, where such practices as group meetings were alien and unfamiliar. On some occasions the trust was exploited to find ways to subvert the system. The relaxed regime was vulnerable to drugs and alcohol being smuggled in, as well as making sexual relations possible behind closed doors. These developments, which unfortunately gave rise to sensationalist stories in the press, undermined the official, as well as the public image of the Special Unit.

The daily visits with family and friends, which took place unsupervised in prisoners' cells, allowed prisoners to engage in relationships which would not have been possible, or would have been much more difficult, in the restricted visiting conditions afforded by the mainstream prison system. These visits played an important part in the re-socialisation of individuals who had previously become institutionalised. They were an essential part of the life of the Special Unit and helped to ease the stresses of long-term confinement, which despite the opportunities afforded by the Special Unit were considerable. The relaxed and open regime of the Special Unit however was challenging for some prisoners. One prisoner found it so difficult that they asked to be transferred back to the mainstream. He later regretted this choice, but it showed that the regime which the Special Unit offered was not suitable for all prisoners.

The training of staff and skilful leadership of the community was extremely important. Ken Murray, the Chief Nursing Officer in the Special Unit was instrumental in its early success. Unfortunately, rather than being promoted for his outstanding service, he was transferred to HMP Low Moss, a short-term prison, in what would be hard to interpret as anything other than an intent to curb the international acclaim and successes of the Special Unit. The innovative new regime had become too much of a challenge for the more orthodox tradition bound bureaucracy to handle.

In Ken Murray's words, 'In the early days the authorities would have been happy if the prisoners in the BSU had been fed ice cream six times a day—they just wanted the troublemakers removed from the system.' They achieved considerably more than this in the unit, with a major downside being that the experiment was never properly researched. There were many important lessons to be learned from the experience in the unit in terms of how the behaviour of previously difficult prisoners was altered and changed for the better.

The therapeutic community approach which evolved from Maxwell Jones's innovative work was central to the successes of the Special Unit and has much to contribute to an important question which underlies the raison d'etre of prisons, which is how to support deep-seated behavioural change. The need for innovative thinking in this direction is as relevant as ever for a system where recidivism rates remain unacceptably high. The experience of the BSU clearly showed the potential of the therapeutic community model. This contrasts with the well-known debilitating impact on prisoners of institutionalised top-down regimes that continue to be used in most traditional penal establishments today. The BSU became an internationally recognised beacon of hope for a more enlightened approach to imprisonment as a whole.

Relentless punishment has been shown to be ineffective in changing human behaviour. Restoring human relationships is the key to transformation and needs to be at the heart of all future planning for the prison system. The Special Unit shone a light on how the experience of imprisonment could facilitate change and transformation in a group of prisoners previously considered to be beyond the pale, and who might otherwise have never regained their freedom. This surely is worth taking serious account of, as it offers hope for all those who believe that the true purpose of imprisonment is to show that better choices of behaviour are possible, and can lead in the direction of creatively fulfilling and purposeful lives which benefit not just the individual but their family and whole community.

References

Carrell, C and Laing, J (eds) (1982), *The Special Unit Barlinnie Prison: Its Evolution Through Its Art,* Glasgow: Third Eye Centre.

Hall P (1983), The Process of Change by Professor Maxwell Jones, *International Journal of Social Psychiatry,* 29(2):156–156, London: Routledge & Kegan Paul Ltd. doi:10.1177/002076408302900214

Smith, R (1984), Grendon, The Barlinnie Special Unit, And the Wormwood Scrubs Annexe: Experiments in Penology, *British Medical Journal* (Clinical Research Edn), 288(6415): 472–475. http://www.jstor.org/stable/29514040

Stephen, I (1988), The Barlinnie Special Unit: A Penal Experiment. In Backett, S, McNeill, J, Yellowlees, A (eds), *Imprisonment Today*, London: Palgrave Macmillan. https://doi.org/10.1007/978-1-349-08897-3_8

Wilson D, Brookes M (2020), A Failed Success: The Barlinnie Special Unit, *International Journal of Prison Health*, Aug 17: 17(1):31–41. doi: 10.1108/IJPH-12-2019-0070. PMID: 33634655

CHAPTER 2

Joyce Laing: The Development of Art in the BSU

Interviews with Joyce Laing by Claire Coia

Joyce Laing at the exhibition launch of 'Barlinnie Special Unit—A Way Out of a Dark Time' in Kelvingrove Art Gallery and Museum, 2017. © CSG CIC Glasgow Museums Collection.

Pioneering art therapist Joyce Laing was a catalyst in transforming the lives of individuals in the Barlinnie Special Unit (BSU) by offering opportunities to engage with the arts. This helped enable rehabilitation by providing a safe outlet for these men to channel and express their thoughts and emotions, rather than expressing these through violence. Unexpectedly, this engagement uncovered latent talent, with individuals from the unit emerging as artists and authors, generating public interest and unprecedented support from the art world. The Special Unit is mostly encountered by contemporary audiences through the autobiographies of its former prisoners, but the recent resurfacing of art and archives from the unit hints at largely forgotten tales. Many threads weave together the story of the BSU; this chapter explores the birth of the arts there, drawing from my interviews with Laing in 2016 and 2021, together with autobiographies, publications, archival fragments, and prisoner testimonies.

The story of the BSU is a unique synchronicity of situation, opportunity, and passionate individuals, and Laing herself puts her role as the unit's art therapist down to 'chance'. Sifting through the archives in the Reading Room of the National Records of Scotland in Edinburgh, however, it becomes apparent that the art produced in Barlinnie did not emerge from completely untilled soil. As early as 1970, Laing was paving the way for art provision in Scottish prisons to be valued as something more than a rewarding hobby for well-behaved prisoners. A pioneer in the field, she broke barriers and created new pathways to thinking about art as a therapeutic tool in prisoner rehabilitation.

Laing was Scotland's first psychiatric art therapist, and the first art therapist to work in prisons. An alumnus of Gray's School of Art, Aberdeen, she began her career in the tuberculosis wards of Glen O'Dee Sanatorium in Banchory in the 1950s. Little was known at that time about the impact that art can have on mental health and there was no real definition of 'art therapy'. Laing was told to, 'Go in and do what you do.'[1] Working on the wards, she discovered a pattern between patients' artwork and their health, whereby oncoming episodes of illness could be predicted by changes in their art. In the 1960s, Laing was invited to join a dynamic team of medical staff at the new Ross Clinic in Aberdeen which focused on the benefits of psychiatry and psychotherapy. She was given a large art studio and every patient admitted was invited to use it as part of their treatment. Laing recalls that the doctors had never seen the visual side of illness: art could be used to communicate where traditional talking

1. Hutchison, 2011: 115.

therapies had failed. During these staff discussions, the question arose, 'If you can get patients to paint, why can't you get prisoners to paint?'[2]

Laing joined the Scottish Prisons Department in 1970 as a self-styled art therapist, working with young offenders in Polmont Prison and YOI near Falkirk. She was self-employed, receiving the equivalent of an art teacher's pay. The role of an art therapist in prison did not yet exist, and her early campaign to embed the arts in prison resulted in both cautious support and scathing responses. 'I must say,' wrote the Deputy Governor of HMP Perth, 'that she falls into the same trap as many other experts in that she sees a minor success in specified areas as offering a panacea for all areas.'[3] Art was very much considered as a relaxing pastime alongside craft work, and usually offered as an evening class for well-behaved prisoners. In response to Laing's petition, The Governor of HMP Penninghame added: 'Art has its place in prison as a hobby and I feel we should concentrate along these lines.'[4] To set the context, it was not until 1979 that a full-time art teacher was employed in Scottish prisons, which gives an indication of the marginal status accorded to art provision. By that time, the art and artistic community of the BSU had become world famous.

Back to Barlinnie: Remembering the Special Unit

It's August 2016. After the usual security checks at HMP Barlinnie, I introduce Joyce Laing to a group of prisoners who are curating a temporary exhibition on the BSU for Glasgow Life Museums. This is the first time that Laing has been in Barlinnie Prison since her time as an art therapist there. The men are in awe of such an esteemed guest; they have researched what they can from the available archives and compiled their list of interview questions. Until this project, there has been little interest in the art of the Special Unit, since its last public exhibition 'The Special Unit, Barlinnie Prison: Its Evolution Through Its Art' by the Third Eye Centre in 1980 and the publication of a book of the same title in 1982. For many, perceptions of the BSU are shaped by memories of tabloid headlines and recollections of gangsters who were seen to have

2. Interview with Joyce Laing by Claire Coia and Sara Trevelyan, 2021.
3. (1974), National Records of Scotland, HH57/1912.
4. Ibid.

'beaten the system'. For many, it has become a part of history best forgotten. The prisoners meeting Laing are keen to hear stories of the Special Unit from the people who directly experienced it. The kettle goes on, tea and biscuits are shared, then a quiet comes over the room as prisoners and staff gather round to hear Laing's story of how the arts came to shape the BSU.

> 'My reason for being there was chance. I had worked in Polmont Young Offenders Prison. And I was also trained and worked in an Aberdeen psychiatric clinic. So, my background was sort of known. And I was aware, as I say, as everybody in Scotland was, there was trouble in the prisons. That these riots were going on. Then I got a phone call from the Governor of the Special Unit saying, "I know you're working at Polmont, could you come and visit us at this unit? I feel the guys have nothing to do." Because they weren't allowed to work with other prisoners in Barlinnie and they weren't allowed to meet other prisoners in Barlinnie, and there was no work for them. So, there were whole days and days in front of them with nothing and he thought, "Maybe if I could get them to paint"—as he said—"some little pictures, we will help you to frame them." And I thought, *the one thing we're NOT going to do is little pictures in frames.* But I said I would look in and see what I felt about it and what it was.'[5]

George Duncan, the first Governor for the BSU, was aware of Laing's successes with young offenders and was supportive of her work. She had introduced a precedent for art therapy with her work in Polmont, collaborating with prison psychologist Ian Stephen. Even if the concept of art therapy was little understood, Laing was obviously doing something right, something new, and something that might be a good fit for the people in the BSU. Ian Stephen would become the psychologist for the Special Unit, with Laing joining him soon after it opened.

As discussed in the previous chapter, the Special Unit was one of several segregation units, but in combination with the broad philosophies of a 'therapeutic community', this removal from the main prison population allowed the prisoners an opportunity to develop away from the accepted codes of prison culture.

5. Joyce Laing, interview with Claire Coia, 2016.

The staff and prisoners of the unit had been given almost free rein to shape the space; however, there were few opportunities immediately available to these prisoners for self-development. Unlike the traditional 'therapeutic community' model, no work or formal education programme was in place. Art therapy in the unit was not part of its original conception but introduced to fill a 'gap'.

> 'I think in many ways it happened...luckily. There was panic. And so I don't think there was any great thinking of what they could put in place but their main jump in thinking was, "We'll not just have another senior prison officer who's come through the system, we'll take a psychiatrist in." I mean, that was a big jump, you know, a psychiatrist responsible for these seven men, and the psychologist and myself coming in from a different area—art therapy. I mean that immediately sets up a different ambience.'[6]

Laing was met with deep suspicion when she first encountered the group, most of whom had come directly from The Cages of the Inverness small unit, known for its extreme measures of solitary confinement. After several unsuccessful weeks of trying to engage the first five men in art, she became frustrated. Drawing on her psychotherapy training, she changed tactics.

> 'So, the governor opened the door of this sitting room, and the guys were all sitting there looking, wondering what's happening next. And he said this, "This is the artist" and he shut the door. And there I was, five guys and I'm the artist. And they looked at me and I looked at them and I said, "Well, I presume I'm here to try and get you to paint, or make things or do things." They didn't want anything to do with it. And so I would turn up—if you take the first six weeks—I turned up every week, and I brought with me on my first week a polythene bag full of paper, paint, pencils and all the things you need to do something, anything. When we finished chatting just about anything, I put them down and said, "Now, it's yours. You can do anything you like with it. It cannot be wrong, whatever you do, if you tear it up that's okay, do anything you want with it. But it's yours." For every week that I went after that, I would turn up and that polythene bag with the

6. Ibid.

artwork materials was sitting in the same spot. They were even hoovering around it, they never moved it, they never touched it. I said, "Do you not feel like painting or doing something?" Nothing. By the fifth week, I was getting worried as [there was] a real block and I hadn't hit it before. I'd been working with patients, and the guys in Polmont had all been quite happy to paint. This strange block of five guys, just asking quite a lot of questions, strange questions. I got worried about what was happening, and thought to myself, and one of my own trainings in psychotherapy, if you're not getting anywhere with your clients, what about yourself. What's wrong with you? So I began to think, I'm very angry, I mean, I feel like God's gift to these guys! Coming here and offering them art materials, and one of the answers is: well, why don't you do something about it, if you can? I thought, next time I went in I brought with me also a bag of clay. I said, "If you guys are going to waste your lives sitting doing nothing every week, I'm going to go on with my art." And I sat on the floor because there wasn't even a table, I sat on the floor and started making a little relief head in clay. They watched, like foxes, they watched every movement. I was aware of them being quite intrigued by what I was doing. But nobody asked about it. And I said, "Right, I'll leave the clay as well. There's a whole lot of art materials there for you, do what you like." The next time I went in several of them had made things [...] They were put in front of me when I went in on that sixth week wondering what was happening. In fact, I'll show you [this photograph] ... as you can see, you see, the little figure was called "Solitary—Inverness".'[7]

Jimmy Boyle remembers their motivations slightly differently, given that they had little contact with women and that Laing was a 'good-looking bird', they wanted her to keep coming back! Had this first group of prisoners not engaged, the Special Unit would have turned out very differently. Regardless of the men's motivations, this moment of creation catalysed the birth of the arts in the BSU. Boyle recalls:

'One day she brought in a 7lb bag of clay for us to mess around with and the five of us sat there humouring her and having a good laugh till such time

7. Ibid.

> as she had to leave. When Joyce left, the clay was abandoned by the others but I kept working on it. I felt great pleasure in creating the sculptures and knew that I had stumbled onto something within myself.'[8]

Starkly different to the traditional prison regime, staff and prisoners moved freely in the space, and were not constrained by timetables. 'This relaxed approach on how the inmates used their time was an important one, for it protected the precarious first steps of creativity.'[9] Just as importantly, the arts provided a key to the mental lock of criminal identity, crystalised through years of navigating cultural expectations both within and without the prison walls. Inspired by Laing's description of 'Outsider Art' and the way in which artists in spaces of confinement would use 'found' materials that were available to them, Boyle had taken the clay and supplemented it with mixed media. Building work was underway in the unit and he salvaged a small piece of wood and some copper piping from the rubbish to create a cage for his small clay figure.

'Solitary—Inverness' (1974) by Jimmy Boyle. Wood, metal and plaster. Reproduced courtesy of the artist. Photograph taken at the 'I Am The Coyote' exhibition, University of Hull, 2019. © Clare Coia.

8. Boyle, J (1977).
9. Laing, J (1982): 58.

> 'The bars in this piece are not in perimeter formation, as to my mind the visible bars in any prison are not the ones that count. The bars here are actually entangling the figure. These are the bars that matter.'[10]

'Solitary—Inverness' can be seen to represent the past, present, and future. It encompasses Boyle's painful memories of solitary confinement in the Inverness cages, embodies the act of creation, and unconsciously heralded the birth of the arts in the BSU. Given the deprived areas from which many of the inmates came and the need to present a hard 'front' to survive (or succeed) in a masculinist gang culture, the arts were derogatively seen as 'poofy stuff',[11] a sentiment expressed by several in the unit throughout its lifespan. More insightfully, Laing suggests that 'the pursuit of artistic activities is regarded as belonging to the people with education, authority and consequently, power... There is also the representation of feelings, the denial of emotion and sensitivity.'[12] The prisoners' affinity with Laing's 'Outsider Artists' whose artmaking practices engendered personal agency even within highly controlled spaces appears to have inspired artmaking in the unit, enabled by her careful facilitation of a space in which to experiment with the inner self through art.

Boyle expressed a strong desire to work with stone carving soon thereafter. Given that the tools required for stone sculpting could be weaponised, granting access to these can be seen as a full commitment to the unit philosophy by both prisoners and staff. Most symbolic of this, however, was the removal of the reinforced steel door of the punishment cell to create a sculpture studio for inmates. Although the arts had not been considered in the planning of the BSU, artmaking came to replace traditional work concepts and communal spaces were repurposed for the production or exhibition of art. The unit Governor was keen to bring inspirational speakers into the unit as a way of preventing boredom and tension during the cold and cooped up winter months, and it soon became a busy hive of people and activity. Laing offered to bring in people from the art world, and Jimmy Boyle recalls his first encounter with the contemporary art scene, inspired by the 'one-man tornado' Richard Demarco, or Ricky:

10. Boyle, 1982.
11. Boyle, 1977: 250.
12. Carrell and Laing, 1982: 56.

> 'He was a small man with a strong personality and a tremendous amount of energy, a one-man tornado. Coming in he moved around, never standing still, always talking. Joyce Laing, Alex Stephen and another departmental official Tom Melville brought him in. Ricky then took over. He walked around my sculptures that were on display, examined and discussed them using words I was ignorant of. He said, there and then, that he would like to put my work on show at his gallery during the Edinburgh Festival. [...] I had been doing these sculptures and putting them on shelves in the unit and now had a good collection. The next logical step was an exhibition but as it was all new to me there hadn't seemed to be a next step, until now.'[13]

Art quickly became part of the unit's collective identity in the early years of its existence, integral to daily life as a focus for individual development and in shaping the community around artistic activity. The BSU encouraged a steady stream of visitors from all walks of life—from family members to politicians, researchers, celebrities, and artists—many of whom would never have had the opportunity or even inclination to meet in 'real' life. This catalysed it as an artistic hub, inspiring public exhibitions of prisoner art and in-house arts festivals. The arts became entwined with the identity of the unit, giving many of the inmates a sense of purpose and an opportunity for personal and community development. Bringing together this unusual mix of people played a huge part in its success, and many prisoners made strong connections with people and organizations who would come to support them on the outside. The public exhibitions and performances which ensued—fuelled by dynamic figures in the art world such as Richard Demarco, and Giles Havergal of the Citizens Theatre—enabled a platform for creative dialogue which was pivotal in communicating the value of the BSU beyond the walls of the prison.

Acclaim for Jimmy Boyle's sculpture in the contemporary art world, however, threatened to overshadow others in the unit. Not everyone was artistically gifted, and this had to be carefully managed. 'From these beginnings of artistic creativity in the Special Unit grew the concern to ease the way for the others to discover creativity within themselves,' wrote Laing in 1982, 'yet if the first creative works are almost too successful and too highly acclaimed they can

13. Boyle, 1984: 24–25.

hamper the endeavours of others by their very success, discouraging them into believing they could never match such a high standard.' Laing's aim was to encourage self-expression and personal growth, emphasising that 'No matter how artistically unskilled, the art productions of inmates will be an expression of the self, an attempt to find their place in the world... and should be seen as an ongoing rehabilitative medium for *all inmates* at *all times*.'[14]

She often tried several approaches before a prisoner found an activity that was a 'fit' for them and would then bring in materials and experts in that area. Emphasis on a wide range of art forms meant that inmates would not feel inhibited by the highly skilled outputs of a few members of the community. Although public exhibitions were curtailed after 1980 for complex reasons, the first annual in-house arts festival was facilitated by Laing and launched in 1979. These festivals were to form the backbone of creative activity for many years, sustained by forward-thinking governors and staff after Laing's retirement in 1986, resulting in community partnerships and enabling prisoners to participate in various ways, regardless of artistic ability.

The Rehabilitative Role of Art in Prison

'By all means use the arts but keep them in their place, this would be a very small place I think'[15] was among the responses by prison officials in response to Laing's early attempts to promote the rehabilitative potential of the arts in prison. 'Now that it has happened it is difficult to imagine a prison unit of this nature functioning without the arts,' wrote Laing in 1982. She had a very clear idea of the role that the arts could play in the wider Prison Service and had a clear agenda from the outset. Throughout her career she continued to try and change the status and purpose of art provision in prisons: her goal was not only provision for the Special Unit but a wider agenda for change.

Art in prisons was, and is, nothing new. Prisoners often illicitly create art with whatever materials they can find; burnt material can be used to create charcoal, ink can be extracted from magazines, matchsticks and bars of soap can be used to create small sculptures. At HMP Barlinnie, the tradition of creating highly

14. 1979, National Records of Scotland, HH57/1912.
15. Charlton, Prison Governor, April 1974. National Records of Scotland, HH57/1912.

decorated scrolls to send to loved ones persists to this day. Art found in cells, however, is often confiscated. Evening art classes in the past, and current art classes as part of the education curriculum, have always played a crucial role in creating a protected space for prisoners to channel their energies into art. However, state-approved art is censored in terms of subject matter and often self-censored by the prisoner wishing to fit in with the system. Technically skilled copies of art or photographs, for example, are much admired and often commissioned, forming part of the prison economy. Laing was highly critical of 'copy art', while accepting that the technical skill developed by this work had merit, but it was not an art form which encouraged expression and an exploration of the self, and consequently held little or no value for true rehabilitation. Furthermore, she emphasised that art should never be seen as a 'reward' for good behaviour or withheld from troublesome prisoners.

Laing fought her battles, creatively navigating the individual needs of the prisoner within the rules and regulations of the Prison Service. For Laing, 'rehabilitation' was not a means to create a model prisoner or docile citizen, but to engender meaningful self-transformation. Prisoners are not only physically kept in place, but psychologically imprisoned within its cultural micro-climate. Issues of autonomy, access, choice, power—and perhaps most importantly—personhood, are often broken in prison, and resistance can manifest in harmful ways ranging from anger to apathy. Art therapy was used as a tool for uncensored expression, experimentation and an exploration of space and their place within it: an aesthetic, engaged approach, as opposed to the anaesthetic coping mechanisms often used to survive imprisonment. As such, art for the men of the unit became a positive method of resistance and force for transformative change.

Had it not been for Joyce Laing, the art for which the BSU is famously known would never have happened. How art is valued as a tool for rehabilitation in Scottish prisons today echoes her groundbreaking work, and her persistence in the face of scepticism reminds us of the difference that the individual can make within even the most forbidding of environments.

References and selected bibliography

Boyle, J (1977), *A Sense of Freedom*. Edinburgh: Canongate Publishing.

Boyle, J in Carrell, C and Laing, J (eds.) (1982), *The Special Unit Barlinnie Prison: Its Evolution Through Its Art*, Glasgow: Third Eye Centre.

Boyle, J (1984), *The Pain of Confinement: Prison Diaries*, London: Pan Books.

Carrell, C and Laing, J (eds.) (1982), *The Special Unit Barlinnie Prison: Its Evolution Through Its Art*, Glasgow: Third Eye Centre.

Coia, C (2016), Barlinnie Special Unit—A Way Out of a Dark Time, exhibition in HMP Barlinnie (2016), Kelvingrove Art Gallery and Museum (2017), and Tramway (2017), Glasgow. Exhibition leaflet published by Glasgow Life Museums, 2017.

Collins, H (1998), *Autobiography of a Murderer*, London: Pan Books.

Collins, H (2000), *Walking Away*, Edinburgh: Rebel Inc.

Gussak, D E (2020), *Art and Art Therapy With the Imprisoned: Re-creating Identity*, New York: Routledge.

Hutchison (2011), *The Silent Weaver: The Extraordinary Life and Work of Angus McPhee*, Edinburgh: Birlinn Ltd: 115.

Kornfeld, P (1997), *Cellblock Visions: Prison Art in America*, New Jersey: Princeton University Press.

Laing, J (1980), Scrapbook, Glasgow Life Museums Collection, accession number GMA.2012.1.1.261.

Laing, J in C and Laing, J (eds.) (1982), *The Special Unit Barlinnie Prison: Its Evolution Through Its Art*, Glasgow: Third Eye Centre: 58.

Laing, J (2016), Interview transcript from Coia, C 2016. Barlinnie Special Unit—A Way Out of a Dark Time Exhibition, Glasgow Museums.

Laing, J (2021), 'Development of Art in the Unit'. Interview with Joyce Laing by C Coia and S Trevelyan.

McGeachan, C (2019), 'A Prison Within a Prison'? Examining the Enfolding Spatialities of Care and Control in the Barlinnie Special Unit, *Area*, 51:2: 200–207.

National Records of Scotland, HH57/1912.

Nellis, M (2010), Creative Arts and the Cultural Politics of Penal Reform: The Early Years of the Barlinnie Special Unit, 1973–1981, *Journal of Scottish Criminal Justice Studies*, 20: 118–22.

Oliver, V M (2017), Understanding Historical Changes in Social and Penal Arts Programs, *Journal of Offender Rehabilitation*, 56:8: 511–33.

Steele, J (2002), *The Bird That Never Flew*, Edinburgh: Mainstream Publishing.

CHAPTER 3

Joseph Beuys, Richard Demarco and Social Sculpture

Bill Beech

In the book *The Special Unit Barlinnie Prison: Its Evolution Through Its Art,* effectively the catalogue for the exhibition at the Third Eye Gallery in Glasgow in 1982, there is a list of the 45 artists; visitors from diverse cultural backgrounds who made a connection with the prisoners and staff of the Barlinnie Special Unit (BSU). Whilst the book gives seminal personal accounts of the effect the arts had on the evolving ideology of the unit, it is worth looking closer at the work inspired by Richard Demarco during August 1974 that was created by the prisoners with Edinburgh Arts participants, including the German artist, Joseph Beuys.

In 1974, having set out to challenge the role of the artist and art students in the Edinburgh International Festival, Demarco invited a whole host of willing participants from art schools in the UK and the United States to join him on a journey of self-discovery to the Celtic World. He called the project 'On the Road to Meikle Seggie'. This involved excursions through Scotland and 'the landscape of Stirling, Argyll and the ancient Kingdom of Dalriada, to the Western Isles' (Demarco, 1974). Demarco's aim was that having witnessed, debated and exchanged ideas on what was discovered, the participants would then make work which would, help 'define, disrupt and inspire new thinking within the Edinburgh Festival itself' (Demarco, 2023). To this end, Demarco had recruited the likes of Buckminster Fuller, Paolo Soleri, Roland Penrose and Joseph Beuys as contributors to this process.

Joseph Beuys had lost his post as Professor of Monumental Sculpture at the *Kunstakademie* Düsseldorf in 1972 (for abandoning any entry requirements to his classes) and since this time had been working on plans for a Free International University. The idea was aimed at stimulating interdisciplinary research and an extended definition of Art, acknowledging 'creativity is not limited to people practising one of the traditional forms of art' but also had capacity 'to shape material which could be extended to other socially relevant spheres' (Beuys, 1975). These ideas coincided with Demarco's thinking which in parallel formed the driving force, underpinning the Edinburgh Arts programme and leading to Demarco viewing his gallery itself as an experimental University of All the Arts.

In the early 1970s, Demarco was also challenging what he saw as the conservative thinking in UK art schools and was proselytising the introduction of a socio-cultural dimension to creative education. Though Fine Art courses were no longer focused simply on teaching painting and sculpture and a new approach to teaching in the studio was emerging through the ideas of Tom Hudson, Harry Thubron and Victor Pasmore, the wider influences internationally of the Bauhaus and the Black Mountain School had largely been ignored.

Art schools were still relatively conservative places. Coming together as international participants on Edinburgh Arts 1974 we were soon to realise that whether we were from art schools in Sheffield, Kansas City or Chicago we were all caught in the momentum for change. Drawing, painting and sculpture were still central to thinking in Fine Art but now a plurality of means and ends in the approach was possible, utilising photography, film and video. Artists like Joseph Beuys, who was building a reputation as one of the most important artists of the later part of the 20th century, were also using discourse in the newly emerging area of Performance Art to express ideas.

During the 1974 Edinburgh Arts, with incredible foresight, Demarco had decided to lay down two challenges. The first centred on a debate in what he called 'The Black and White Oil Show', which focused on the environmental implications of the discovery of oil in the North Sea. In the second debate, he focused on the work of the revolutionary BSU, recognising it as a proof of concept of the impact art can make on society.

A few years before, Demarco had been involved with a remarkable theatre project in San Quentin Prison in the USA that focused on Samuel Beckett's

Waiting for Godot. On his return to Scotland, he worked with young offenders in HMP Young Offender Institution Polmont, and subsequently was invited to the Special Unit, to mentor the notoriously reviled prisoners, Jimmy Boyle and Larry Winters. Demarco's complimentary influence to the work of Joyce Laing, the unit's inspirational Art Therapist, resulted in Boyle and Winter's work being included as part of the 1974 exhibition called 'Art from Scottish Prisons'. Demarco then extended an invitation to the Special Unit prisoners to contribute to the Edinburgh Arts debate from their cells.

This led to him enabling a small group of Edinburgh Arts participants with diverse Fine Art interests being able to visit Barlinnie and begin a dialogue. Phil Hitchcock from Chicago Art Institute was to make the initial visit, he invited Michael K Meyers and Steven Whitacre from Kansas City Art Institute to accompany him. JoAnn Baker was to make still photographs, Jane Whitaker and I were invited to make a video record to enable the discourse to continue with Demarco and the rest of the Edinburgh Arts participants when we returned each evening to Edinburgh and the old medieval Poorhouse in Forrest Hill.

I Like America and America Likes Me

Demarco provided the Poorhouse in the heart of Edinburgh as a place for this kind of exchange, to consolidate thinking, to make and show work. It was also a venue in the 1974 Edinburgh Arts which, significantly, housed only one permanent exhibition, and the day before we entered the BSU it was there Richard introduced us to Joseph Beuys. Beuys was supervising the hanging of Caroline Tisdall's resonant photographic documentation of 'I Like America and America Likes Me', the performance installation Beuys had made only weeks before in the René Block Gallery in New York. In this piece, Beuys spent five days locked up with a coyote, the most reviled living creature in America. Beuys said of this, 'I believe I made contact with the psychological trauma point of the United States energy constellation: the whole American trauma with the Indian, the Red Man. This is where the figure of the coyote appears respected and venerated by the Red Man, despised and persecuted by the White Man, a polarity, a gulf. Somehow the trauma has to be reversed and amends made.

You could say that a reckoning has to be made with the coyote, and only then can the trauma be lifted' (Tisdall, 1998).

'I like America and America Likes Me'. Photo and © Caroline Tisdall.

Beuys was to regard the confines of the physical body spiritually as a 'form of prison', but he said, 'no prison could hold the body of perception of feeling, the body of thinking, the body of consciousness in the way it holds the physical body' (Tisdall, 1988). Beuys and the 'Coyote' consumed our discussion as the six of us made our way from Edinburgh to the dark underbelly of Glasgow.

Behind the Green Door

Before entering 'Bar-L', we were briefed by Alex Stephen, the Controller of the Scottish Prison Service (SPS), who told us about the risks the Prison Service and the Scottish Prison Officers' Association were taking in establishing the highly controversial Special Unit experiment. Crossing the bleak yard behind the prison's main gate, we were left in no doubt about Stephen's commitment to its cause and belief that whilst the effects of crimes perpetuated by the five individuals we were about to meet were devastating and could not be changed, the aim was to reduce offender recidivism. The Special Unit experiment was intended to lay new ground for this, so the victims of violence and their families and the families of the offenders, who in their lives outside the prison were serving their own kind of sentences, were less likely to be subjected to such trauma again.

Despite Alex Stephen's briefing, approaching the small green door in the massive desolate walls of this prison within a prison we were nonetheless unprepared for what we found on the other side. The impact was completely unexpected, it was like going into an art school studio, there was work everywhere, but with one distinction, the primary focus here was not on the aesthetic but a mixed iconography of anguish, violence and contrition in sculptures that had been made in an abandoned punishment cell.

The Special Unit Gallery. Photo and © Bill Beech.

Inspired by Demarco and Laing, and without recourse to anything but a fleeting understanding of art history, prisoners had discovered the latent ability to express themselves through poetry, drawing and sculpture. The idea of what drove the making of such work exercised our collective interest in teaching, we wanted to understand how the pedagogy of mentoring and learning in this extreme environment could produce such remarkable results. The effect, as Laing (1974) suggests, 'surpassed anything that had been anticipated' either by the prisoners themselves or those who were encouraging them. No mimesis here, just a brutal honesty in the works that seemed to emerge from deep down in the psyche of men caught up in violence and physical depravity, which they confessed meant at times they had found themselves on the edge of madness.

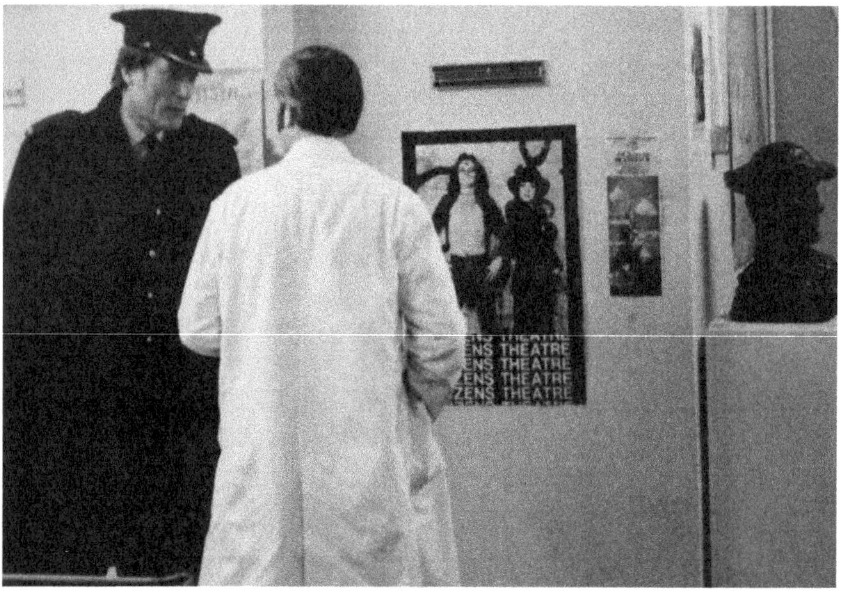

Nursing officers Ken Murray and Walter Davidson. Photo and © Tony Riley 1975.

There was surprising unanimity between the prisoners and Ken Murray, the Chief Nursing Officer, and the other staff on how the Special Unit had been created. We learned that the setting up of the unit was a direct result of devastating injuries sustained by both prison officers and prisoners alike during the 1972 riot when Boyle, Winters and three others protested the conditions they suffered in the notorious solitary cages of Inverness Prison.

The Special Unit was seen as a last resort, a response to counter brutality surrounding this small group of lifers who had been caged in solitary confinement, marginalised, excluded losing all hope, paying for their crimes with further years piled onto their sentences because of their violent reaction to their treatment. With the abolition of capital punishment in the UK, violence, it seemed, refused to be neatly caged, entombed in concrete, clamped like a pearl of disturbance too horrific to be confronted by society at large. Attempts at brutal control, and the regular submersion of the psyche through the use of tranquillising drugs metered out to long-term prisoners like Larry Winters, only temporarily plugged the problem and the institutionalised system regularly blew, exploding in sporadic eruptions of aggression.

A stuttering rendition of 'All Along the Watch Tower' bounced around the walls of the exercise hall as Larry Winters played his guitar. JC and Rab prepared a Gorbals salad. After we had eaten, Larry read selected poems from his HMP notebooks. He talked animatedly about Jack Kerouac and the beat poets, told us he was studying Zen and yoga, reading the *Bhagavad Gita,* the novels of Hermann Hesse and Tolkien.

Jimmy Boyle's work had a raw power and the titles told their own story, 'Solitary', 'Survivor', 'The Clenched Fist' and 'Knucklehead'. Though self-taught, he found he had a real talent for modelling and carving, he describes making his sculpture eloquently 'as a result of free expression between my hands and my inner self.' He has characterised the dynamic of the stone carvings 'as the muscles flex then tense to wield the hammer that hits the chisel which chips the stone and back again. I find myself becoming magically fused with the solid mass before me. What is this miracle? ... And so the creative process raises unanswerable questions, all of which are irrelevant, the experience being the all important issue ... You see, there is something almost neurotic about it; the actual physical reality has a functional derangement in that I stand before a block of stone chipping thousands, sometimes millions of small pieces off it ... each small chip on its own makes a difference, therefore the action has to possess some fundamental force to motivate me' (Boyle, 1979).

Jimmy Boyle's stone carvings. Photo and © Caroline Tisdall, 1976.

Was there a paradox Demarco had foreseen? On the one hand here were individuals for whom violence had so often represented their human condition now seizing the possibilities offered by the perceptual elements of visual expression, a way to say something about their emotions and experience, and be heard. On the other hand, here were artist visitors transported so far out of their comfort zone and shocked at what they were being presented with, they had to find new ways to express their feelings. In the weeks of Edinburgh Arts, just as Richard planned, the collision of these two elements led to an extraordinary creative impetus.

The significance of Beuys' work on our discussions was not lost on Jimmy Boyle who had made such progress since the opening of the Special Unit that he was given a day's parole to see his own sculpture in the Edinburgh Festival show. This was to be his first sense of freedom in ten years, so it was significant he chose to give up precious time to see for himself what Beuys' 'Coyote' was all about. Jane Whitaker and I filmed Jimmy when he crossed the threshold in the great oak doors of the Poorhouse and saw the Caroline Tisdall photographs, analogue black and white, incongruously strung out on a clothesline.

Having seen these iconic images, when Richard introduced Jimmy to Beuys in the unit, Jimmy famously proclaimed 'Joseph, I Am The Coyote'.

The Special Unit had become an example of reform because mentoring and learning was overcoming the negative conditioning of individuals on both sides of the issue. The most impressive thing was the recognition of a state of mutual dependency, with those necessarily held captive and those who held them captive able to realign their actions in a radical leap of faith and progressive thinking. The results for both sides created trust and communication and the proof that this was working was the reduction of the levels of violence. The Special Unit raised the obvious question if this could be achieved within an environment thought to be one of the most restrictive and punitive in Scotland, wasn't there an implication for wider radical reform? Prisoners, staff and visitors also saw that art could enable this positive thinking to escape over the wire so the lessons could impact on the politics that control the wider prison system. Laing said the visits from professional artists were strategically important to the Special Unit's education opportunities, suggesting this went beyond therapy, giving a new 'creative dimension both to the lives of the prisoners and the expansion of the arts' (Laing, 1974). Murray and Boyle saw building these relationships also as a way of sustaining outside support for the unit experiment as it came under increasing political threat. This was to have a major impact on Beuys.

Video Documentation: 'You Can Film Them, But You Can't Show Their Faces'

Importantly, when Alex Stephen gave permission in 1974 for our Edinburgh Arts group to enter Barlinnie, he allowed us to take in a Sony Portapak video camera, which enabled instant playback. There was a condition however that we could not show any of the faces of the prisoners to a wider audience because of a regulation aimed at protecting victims and their families from the public showing of any recognisable portraits of serving prisoners.

The recent rediscovery of the artist proof of the recordings shows the symbiosis that occurred quite naturally with the staff and prisoners in respecting this editorial directive. In the first instance, we simply held newspapers in front of the faces of prisoners when they were on camera to show we were having to work with a hierarchal canvas. As the only distinguishing feature between us all was the white coats of the staff, we all dressed in white coats. We then went through a ritualistic painting of faces, reducing everyone to anonymity. Alex Stephen had said nothing forbidding drawing, so visitors, prisoners and staff alike made collaborative portraits of each other.

In 'Mirror Mirror' Steven Whitacre created a sculptural kaleidoscopic merging of faces, symbolic of reconciliation between two groups, who a year before had been fighting each other.

Steve Whitacre's 'Mirror Mirror'. Photo and © JoAnn Baker, 1974.

The recent printing of JoAnn Baker's extraordinary photographs overcoming issues of censorship, show prisoners, staff and visitors sharing identities and their experience.

Art practice was providing the means to make tangible emotions that could not be made tangible in any other way. In *We Go This Way*, Caroline Tisdall (1988) presents a view held generally by Joseph Beuys that art held the key to healing what he called 'the wound of society'. There can be no greater wound inflicted by an individual on society than murder, and there were few greater wounds inflicted by society in 1974 than the solitary punishment cages of Inverness Prison. How do you say something about what it must be like, the profound experience of being held naked in solitary confinement with nothing but your own body to proclaim any idea of self-representation? Caroline Tisdall's (1998) affirmation of Beuys' understanding of the 'self' is useful here, 'Beuys developed the idea of the self as icon, away from the self-representation of the portrait to the self-representation of the self, the artists own body and persona as the vehicle of expression.' Jimmy Boyle's first piece of sculpture revealed that in solitary confinement it was as though the very bars of the solitary cage were piercing his body.

'Solitary—Inverness' by Jimmy Boyle, 1974. Photo and © Bill Beech.

Throughout those weeks in 1974 we tried to find visual metaphors to explain our understanding of confinement. In the performance piece 'Metaphors for Restraint', one of the collaborative installations we took back to the Poorhouse for discussion, the performance was based on other descriptions Jimmy and Larry shared with us concerning 'solitary' where the extremities of the body became the entire confines of their internalised world.

'Metaphors for Restraint'. Photo and © JoAnn Baker, 1974.

We didn't realise it at the time, but being able to instantly replay the discourse surrounding the art works that emerged in coming to terms with the censorship helped politicise the Special Unit community. Being able to see the impact of our visits each day through the video tapes, they decided to refuse to collaborate in any subsequent documentaries unless the prisoners could appear in front of the camera. It was because of this that the programmes made later that summer by World in Action and BBC Scotland were the first ever to broadcast portrait images of serving prisoners in Scotland's prisons.

What typified Demarco and Joseph Beuys' work throughout their lives was the creation of discourse in the face of ideologies that were questionable. This was the reason Richard had thought it important to introduce Beuys to the

BSU in the first place. The 1974 video shows the moment Demarco introduced Beuys to Jimmy Boyle's work for the first time and he identified instantly with Boyle's plight which he considered epitomised his famous proclamation 'Everyone is an Artist'.

Beuys was to make two further visits to Scotland that had an impact on the Special Unit and his own work. In August 1980, Demarco gave over his gallery for Beuys to return and present a Free University Event and make his historic lecture 'Art = Kapital' together with Heiner Bastian and Robert McDowell. During this visit, Beuys also learnt that the very future of the Special Unit was under threat and decided he would take legal action against the Secretary of State for Scotland and stage a hunger strike in support of the Special Unit and because the authorities had made plans to transfer Boyle back into the traditional prison regime. It was during this event Beuys also made the work that became known as the 'Jimmy Boyle Days' blackboards. These are now in the *Hamburger Bahnhof* Gallery Berlin. Demarco in turn put the whole future of his gallery on the line, committing himself to organizing a petition of support for Boyle and the Special Unit. As a consequence he was forever marginalised, never again receiving any financial subsidy from the Scottish Arts Council because they said Demarco's actions brought 'dishonour to the meaning of Art' (Demarco and Martine, 2023).

The video we made also offers an intriguing insight into why the Poorhouse became such a significant place for us all. It was where we were able to present ideas, and where Jimmy Boyle saw the 'Coyote' photographs. During Beuys' 1974 visit it became so important to him he recognised a need to consecrate the space with his 'Three Pots' performance. This work, symbolic of the human psyche in terms of 'thinking, feeling and will', paid homage to the misery and suffering of those who had been held captive by their poverty. Beuys proclaimed, then celebrated the resurrection and reconsecration of the space as a place for ideas.

Joseph Beuys and the Poorhouse, 1974.
Photo and © Demarco Digital Archive, University of Dundee.

Stepping across the thresholds of the doors to Barlinnie and the Poorhouse for prisoners, staff, artists and audiences alike challenged by Demarco's invitation to 'join a journey of self-discovery', had a profound effect on us all. For Joseph Beuys, the space became so important to him that he returned in 1981 and claimed the great doors as an art work, they are now in the *Staditsche Museum* Monchengladbach, titled 'New Beginnings are in the Offing'.

Throughout the 1970s, new beginnings had been made possible for prisoners and visitors alike by Alex Stephen, Ken Murray, Joyce Laing and the rest of the Special Unit staff. What followed was extraordinarily creative and productive, Jimmy Boyle wrote his autobiographical play *The Hard Man* with Tom McGrath and began writing *A Sense of Freedom,* which entered the best seller lists on its publication and was recommended on the A-Level reading lists for schools. Jeremy Isaacs and Peter McDougall turned the book into a feature film with David Hayman playing Boyle. Larry Winters had his poems published. Demarco staged further Edinburgh Arts with Jimmy Boyle contributing directly each day to the 1976 dialogue from his cell. Jimmy then went on to make 'Gulliver', a huge play sculpture with the Craigmillar community on their estate in Edinburgh.

In 1982 there was the collaboration with The Third Eye Centre and Christopher Carell on 'The Evolution of the Special Unit Through its Art'. This included the work of other prisoners, Bobby Brodie and the extraordinary drawings and sculpture of Hugh Collins. Collins, who Demarco proclaimed as the most visually talented artist prisoner from the unit, was to go on to write two honest books about his life of crime and gaol, and two other works of crime fiction. Collins always acknowledged the debt he owed the Special Unit; he said it saved his life.

Through the latter part of the 1970s the message of the BSU was getting out as visitors with interests across all aspects of the visual and performing arts became involved. We took an exhibition and made a presentation about the unit's work to the National Conference on Deviance in Cardiff. This seemed to have little impact on criminologists in England who at the time were much more focused on 'Control Units', the alternative and highly controversial English solution for treating the equivalent long-term prisoners. Ken Murray and I made a presentation to the Association of Art Therapists in Leeds. The Scottish Office became concerned when the media coverage reached a nationwide audience on TV through the BBC live lunchtime programme *Pebble Mill at One*. The message of the Special Unit was lauded by some but caused deep concern to others, and the success and relative freedom of the unit's radical operation was to become a real threat to its very existence.

The End of an Era

Events in 1977 were to have a devastating effect. Larry Winters, despite the progress that had been made, was proving the most difficult prisoner. Winters had been convicted of the murder of a barman in London (whilst going AWOL from the army trying to get back home to Scotland). This was reduced to manslaughter because he was found to be suffering from a temporal lobe condition. Winters was sentenced to life imprisonment, but the drugs initially prescribed to him were subsequently also used to control his behaviour. Winters struggled with addiction, one that had been developed with the support of the prison system, and the Special Unit had been helping him fight his battle.

Daphne Brook, another regular visitor to the BSU, helped significantly in this context by working with Winters on a collection of his poetry and prose for a book he called *The Silent Scream*. I had also worked closely with Winters and made a series of drawings with him based on his writing. We were developing an idea for a piece of theatre called 'Leopold Walsh' when things took a dramatic change for the worse.

Ken Murray, in his role as Chief Nursing Officer, had been central to the support given to Winters and indeed to the story of the unit. He and I became great friends, and I stayed with Murray and his wife on my visits to Glasgow, on occasion he would take me to the Prison Officers' Club so I had a good idea of the pressure he was under. Murray was also the secretary of the SPOA and there was resentment from staff outside the unit concerning the way it was working. One morning in September 1977, Ken phoned me to tell me that Winters had been found dead in his cell from an overdose of barbiturates that had been smuggled in to him. The events had a devastating effect on everyone who had worked with Winters, and threatened the very future of the unit.

'I Am The Coyote'

The idea of contrition and the impact on victims and prisoners' families was acknowledged in the Special Unit. There was a great deal of discussion over these issues and they were at the very heart of Winters' writing. Alex Stephen's original affirmation that whilst crimes perpetrated by individuals could not be changed, the most important thing was to try and reduce the possibility of offender recidivism, thus preventing more victims in the future. In 2019, in this context, Jimmy Boyle and Larry Winters' stories had a particular resonance on a wider, more diverse group of prisoner learners when we started working with Graeme Brooks and Lisa Fielding in a collaboration with HMP Humber's Graft Studio. This was in the lead up to the 'I Am The Coyote' exhibition staged in the Brynmor Jones Gallery at the University of Hull as part of the Hull Freedom Festival and the Hull UK City of Culture programme.

'I Am The Coyote': Graft Studio HMP Humber.
Photo and © Graeme Brooks, 2019.

Graeme Brooks and Lisa Fielding had identified with the work of the Special Unit and because the most difficult problems being faced by staff and prisoners today are inevitably drug related, Larry Winters' writing in particular had a strong contemporary connection through his book *The Silent Scream* and the feature film of the same title we made based on his life and writing in 1989. The British Film Institute and Channel 4 enabled this award-winning production, which came directly out of the script Winters and I were developing for the performance piece Leopold Walsh. The film, made with talented Glasgow filmmakers, was directed by David Hayman with Iain Glenn winning a Silver Bear at the 1990 Berlin Film Festival for his role in playing Winters.

In these challenging times within our penal system, evidence that can be gathered from initiatives that have engendered a positive legacy, or examples of best practice, have to be worth consideration. The Special Unit closed but the legacy of a highly successful educational programme remains in HMP Barlinnie including the radical prisoners' radio project, 'Barbed Wireless'. The Citizens Theatre continue their work with projects like 'A Family Sentence', written and developed in collaboration with prisoners and their families. The exhibition in Hull in 2019, and the parallel project in Glasgow organized by Claire Coia, 'Barlinnie Special Unit—A Way Out of a Dark Time', shows how artist visitors and prisoners continue to learn from each other in ways that mutually improve their understanding and lives. Inspired by Ken Murray, Richard Demarco and Joyce Laing, the Hull University and Glasgow Kelvingrove exhibitions illustrated how the arts can play a unique part in penal reform and can offer insight to support society's understanding of the causes of violence resulting from incarceration, drug abuse and physical deprivation. The progressive context set through the work of HMP Barlinnie and HMP Humber's Graft Studio in finding creative solutions through the transformative possibilities of art, can be seen to reflect the Beuysian ideas of 'Social Sculpture' and those at the heart of Richard Demarco's extraordinary Edinburgh Arts experiment.

References

Boyle, J (1979), Jimmy Boyle Sculpture Exhibition Catalogue, Hull College of Higher Education.

Beech, B (1975), You Can Film Them But You Can't Show Their Faces, Video shown at the Serpentine Gallery, London.

Beuys, J (1975), Report to the European Economic Community—Founding Concept and Manifesto of the Free University.

Demarco, R (1974), The 1974 Edinburgh Arts Exhibition and Events Catalogue, Richard Demarco Gallery.

Demarco, R and Martine, R (2023), *Demarco's Edinburgh*, Edinburgh: Luath Press.

Laing, J (1974), The 1974 Edinburgh Arts Exhibition and Events Catalogue, Richard Demarco Gallery.

Tisdall, C (1998), *Joseph Beuys: We Go This Way*, London: Violette Editions.

Winters, L (1974–1976), Notebooks 1974–1975, Special Unit Coyote Archive.

CHAPTER 4

The Publication of *A Sense of Freedom*

Rupert Wolfe Murray

One day in 1975 Jimmy Boyle gave Anne Goring a manuscript. She put it in her bag, left the Barlinnie Special Unit and went home. The next day Anne went to see Stephanie Wolfe Murray, the editor at Canongate Books in Edinburgh, and handed it over. Less than two years later *A Sense of Freedom* was published, unleashing a media storm of controversy, outrage, praise, and delight. Over the years, a certain amount of mystery has built up about how *A Sense of Freedom* was 'smuggled' out of HMP Barlinnie, a harsh, disciplinarian prison that had, at its heart, a little island of creativity—the Special Unit.

Anne Goring was key to the story of this book's publication, but who was she? Anne worked for the Richard Demarco Gallery in Edinburgh in the early 1970s and she frequently visited the Special Unit because of the art being produced there. Most people I have talked to assume the manuscript was smuggled out at great risk, and even Boyle described the event with a certain glamour when he said, 'Annie got it out by hiding it under her jumper.' But when I spoke to Anne Goring about this in 2021, she made it sound very ordinary, 'I just put it in my bag,' she said, as if there were no risks involved. And, in a way, she was right as the liberal regime of the Special Unit actively encouraged self-expression. Quite unlike the strict visiting rules for the main prison, guests of the unit were free to come and go whenever they liked and, unlike visitors to the main prison, they were not searched by the strict and disapproving guards at the main gates.

Not only did *A Sense of Freedom* bring fame to Jimmy Boyle and the Special Unit, but it was one of Canongate's first commercial successes. Now, almost 50 years later, the book is still in print longer than any other UK prison autobiography according to Mike Nellis, Emeritus Professor of Criminal and Community Justice at the University of Strathclyde. Prison writing is a vast genre but very few of these stories of struggle and redemption remain in print for more than a few years even though some of them are excellent, such as *Autobiography of a Murderer* by Hugh Collins, another former prisoner of the Special Unit. Those few that have remained in print, such as *Papillon* by Henri Charrier, *Darkness at Noon* by Arthur Koestler and *A Day in the Life of Ivan Denisovich* by Alexander Solzhenitsyn can be seen in all good bookshops with cutting-edge covers and modern introductions. These are the classics of the genre.

For me the most remarkable part of this story is how *A Sense of Freedom* came to be written in the first place. I have spent the last 30 years struggling to write books and I can't imagine a less creative environment than a prison. I take my hat off to all those who managed to write their stories in the toxic atmosphere of a gaol.

My mother Stephanie was the main editor at Canongate Books and, although she had a soft heart, she was tough when it came to selecting books for publication. She would ignore, reject and even lose the manuscripts that were sent to her door on a daily basis. Publishing a book is an investment in editing, design, production and publicity and it is always a risk. Each new book is unique in its own way as there is no guarantee anyone will buy copies. Stephanie never would have published *A Sense of Freedom* had it not been so good: detailed, interesting, honest and unsentimental. The opening chapters on the poverty, atmosphere and community in the Gorbals, a district in Glasgow, are on a par with George Orwell's description of working-class life in *The Road to Wigan Pier*. When it comes to his life of crime, I think that Jimmy Boyle takes responsibility for his actions and does not blame others. I know some people in Scotland don't agree with this view.

Boyle wrote a fluent, coherent and gripping story because of his own intelligence and energy, unleashed by the unique atmosphere of trust in the Special Unit. But that doesn't account for his crisp literary style nor his phenomenal self-discipline. In *A Sense of Freedom*, Boyle mentions in passing that he had read Fyodor Dostoevsky's *Crime and Punishment*, a book that describes in extensive detail the torture of conscience the main character goes through after murdering two women in St Petersburg. I wonder if some of Dostoevsky's style and self-discipline rubbed off on Jimmy Boyle, and that reading books in prison gave him the confidence to search for his own voice.

A further insight can be found in a conversation between Jimmy Boyle and Richard Demarco, the Edinburgh-based impresario who connected the Special Unit with the world of international art. One of their conversations was filmed in 2019 many years after the book's publication, and is available on YouTube.[1] Towards the end of their talk Boyle explains that he got into writing long before the Special Unit was set up, from the very beginning of his incarceration in the late 1960s. He would get hold of a scrap of paper, write in miniature words and, presumably, defuse some of the anger he must have felt. Somehow, he managed to hold onto these scraps of paper as he was moved from one establishment to another within the prison system and now, many decades later, they are tightly rolled up, covered in wax and preserved as artworks in his home in France. At the time of his incarceration in the Special Unit he also wrote articles for the unofficial prison magazine *The Key*.

Scotland's education system also deserves a mention here. According to Professor Mike Nellis, who lives in Glasgow, *A Sense of Freedom* is a massive indictment of the Scottish education system as Boyle and other working-class boys, or boys from criminal families, experienced it. But, despite this disadvantage, Boyle did learn the essential skills that enabled his prolific reading and writing when incarcerated. My own view is that he was a beneficiary of Scotland's educational system which, for all its failings, has long been considered of a better quality than in other parts of the UK.

Sometimes I wonder what Jimmy Boyle would have published if he had continued to write over the long term. Although he wrote prolifically when at the Special Unit and for some years afterwards, and there were rumours in Scotland that he was working on a novel about the theft of the Mona Lisa, he ended up moving to France where he continues his art, but not his writing. I can relate to his desire to leave Scotland, especially when one considers the level of hatred so many Scottish people seem to hold against him for making the transition from crime to art.

1. See 'Demarco and Boyle in coversation' [sic], https://www.youtube.com/watch?v=FkImrmSIAdE

The one piece of fiction he did publish, *Hero of the Underworld*, is unpolished, but fascinating. The main character is sexually abused in gaol by sadistic guards, then released and assigned to a slaughterhouse where he is beaten and exploited mercilessly. Despite this grim backdrop, the novel has a light touch and a fairytale quality as our hero assembles a team of misfits and organizes a satisfying revenge. I think this novel represented Boyle's fears of what could happen to him upon release from gaol. It also reminds me of the work of the great Ukrainian-born writer Nikolai Gogol who, like Boyle, never really fitted in. Gogol was a satirical writer and he was known as a champion of the little man as a literary hero. The *Encyclopaedia Britannica* describes Gogol's style as 'aggressive realism' and that he could 'neither adapt himself to the world nor escape from it, and is therefore all the more anxious to expose its vulgarity and evil.' After the publication of *The Inspector* in 1840, a biting satire on the bureaucracy of the Russian Empire, there was such an outcry among Moscow's reactionary press that he fled to Rome for two years.

As well as being part of the vast body of prison writing, *A Sense of Freedom* has a place in the pantheon of Scottish literature. It can be described as a rare working-class voice within the tradition of Scottish romantic fiction. People still remember Sir Walter Scott, who died in 1832, and the later gritty realism of Ian Rankin, James Kelman, Darren 'Loki' McGarvey and Irvine Welsh. It can also be argued that Boyle's work has a place within the Angry Young Men literary movement, which dates back to the 1950s and, as Luc Gilleman writes, was characterised by 'impatience with the status quo, refusal to be co-opted by a bankrupt society, an instinctive solidarity with the lower classes.'

Several references about his own writing can be found in Jimmy Boyle's second publication, his prison diaries, *The Pain of Confinement*, published by Canongate in 1984. Although he does not go into much detail about *A Sense of Freedom*, Boyle does mention his daily writing routine and it is clear that everyone in the Special Unit knew he was working on a book. Boyle's diaries reveal that he was engaged in various discussions with high level officials about *A Sense of Freedom*, asking for their help in getting it published. He expressed some wariness about publishing at all as he was afraid of the negative impact it would have on the unit, but his outrage at what was happening to others in the prison system spurred him on.

The top officials in the Prisons Department of the Scottish Office knew about Boyle's manuscript and yet they made no attempt to confiscate it, censor it or impede its publication. Neither did they reply to his respectful letters about how he might get it published. I wonder if they had any idea how controversial it would become? Perhaps they knew how difficult it is to get a book published at the best of times, and assumed Boyle would have no chance of being taken seriously by the highbrow literary world. I think this situation reflects the paradox within the Prisons Department at the time. On the one hand they were running a system that was based on colonial-era military discipline, where self-expression and creativity were stifled. On the other hand, they had set up the Special Unit where trust and creativity was the norm. Despite the harsh nature of its regime, I am impressed that the Prisons Department had the decency to respect the rules by which the unit governed itself. But, like a glitch in a machine, it could not last.

There is a good reason why Jimmy Boyle says *A Sense of Freedom* was smuggled out of HMP Barlinnie. He did not trust the Prisons Department. Jimmy had given them a copy and they had asked if it was the only one. Suspicious that the manuscript would mysteriously be lost, or they would try to censor it, he managed to get some copies made. My view is that the Prisons Department had no policy on the publication of prison memoirs and there were probably deep divisions about what to do with it, hence their silence on the issue.

It would be reasonable to ask why Anne Goring took the manuscript to Canongate Books. Why did she not offer it to literary agents or other publishers in Scotland? There are two points to explain here, a family connection and the state of publishing in Scotland at the time. The family element is that Anne Goring was related to my mother and it just so happened that she, my mother, was really interested in Jimmy Boyle's story to the extent that she would take us, her four sons, to visit Boyle in the unit. Both of these women believed in the redemption of Boyle, and I believe she took us to see him in the hope that we would learn not to judge people by their past actions. But, these cosy family connections only explain a small part of the story. The fact is that *A Sense of Freedom* could not have been published in Scotland as, in the early 1970s, there was virtually no Scottish publishing industry at all. Alasdair Gray, the late author of *Lanark*, explained this context when he wrote a statement in remembrance of my late mother: 'Till the 1840s Scotland was the main centre of British publishing, but not after Collins, Constable and other big presses moved their headquarters to London a century later.'

The element of timing is remarkable. Canongate Books was established in 1973, the same year the Special Unit was established, and for the first time in a generation it was possible to publish books in Scotland that were risky, innovative and international in their appeal. My mother attended the great international book fairs, the biggest of which is at Frankfurt, where publishers buy and sell rights to books from other countries. I remember her proudly telling me that she had sold the rights to *A Sense of Freedom* to one of the biggest paperback publishers in the world, Pan Books, now Pan MacMillan, thus ensuring its place in the mainstream. There was such an outcry after the launch of *A Sense of Freedom* that the offices of Canongate were attacked, windows were smashed and someone broke in and defecated on the floor. To the tabloid press it was unthinkable that a convicted murderer could transform himself into a writer and artist, and this resonated with many people in Scotland who still do not believe in Boyle's redemption. The tabloids pumped out regular headlines about 'The Most Dangerous Man in Scotland' and ran lurid tales, based on half-truths, of unheard of luxury, sex and drug abuse while the rest of Scotland's prison population suffered in silence. This put the authorities under pressure to crack down, close the unit and reinstate military-style discipline. The broadsheets, on the other hand, were interested in the Special Unit experiment and the *Guardian, Times, The Scotsman* and *Herald*, as well as the Scottish TV and radio stations, were supportive. Many insightful articles were written about the unit, some asking if it still makes sense to lock prisoners up based on a nineteenth century philosophy of Christian redemption.

One of the first editors hired by Canongate in the 1970s was Charles Wild. Wild contributed to a book I put together about my mother. He offered some insights into the Scottish publishing scene at the time. He told the story of Southside Press, a small Scottish publisher that had failed and was taken over by Canongate in the 1970s. The man behind Southside was Robin Lorimer, whose life's work, *The New Testament in Scots,* was eventually published by Canongate. 'Lorimer's vision,' wrote Wild, 'was the revival of general publishing in Scotland (abandoned in the 1950s and 1960s) and he believed that books by Scotland-based authors should enjoy the same high editorial and production standards as those published in London or New York.'

Until my mother's death in 2017, and the tributes started pouring in, I did not appreciate what an impact my mother had had on Scottish publishing. One tends to take one's parents for granted. Alexander McCall Smith, whose early children's books she had published, described her 'achievement in inspiring and nurturing a publishing renaissance.' This was the woman who had the courage to publish *A Sense of Freedom*.

CHAPTER 5

The Barlinnie Special Unit and Edinburgh Arts: 'An Experiment in Education'

Interview with Richard Demarco by Kirstin Anderson

Richard Demarco is an artist, teacher and promoter of all the arts. He collaborated with artists in the Barlinnie Special Unit (BSU) alongside artists in Edinburgh Arts for the Edinburgh International Festival. The interview with him in this chapter took place on 2 February 2024.

Preface

Richard Demarco, at 93-years-of-age, was energetic and prolific in his recollections when I interviewed him for this book. I came with a list of questions that I had carefully prepared to ask about his involvement with the Special Unit. After 45 minutes from asking my first question, Richard began to speak of the Special Unit specifically. I was reminded, as an interviewer, how important it is that people can situate themselves in the story. Richard Demarco did not just find himself working in the BSU one day, and it was not only due to his connection with Rick Cluchey whose theatre production, 'The Cage', he premiered in HMP and YOI Polmont during the 1973 Edinburgh Festival, or his long friendship and collaboration with Joseph Beuys. In our interview, Richard described to me his experiences growing up as an Italian boy in Edinburgh at a time when his name, Riccardo, was enough to ensure he would be assaulted by his fellow peers at school, in the local baths and Portobello Promenade. Richard told me of his experiences of meeting with artists that led to his life's total art work, his *Gesamtkunstwerk*. He spoke of living during times of war, of entire countries feeling like a prison. These experiences were central to what he referred to as his preparation for the Special Unit, and his development of an experiment in education as a response to Joseph Beuys' concept of the Free International University.

The Interview

Below is an edited version of our conversation. Many thanks to Terry Ann Newman for supporting this interview. Newman is an artist and, since 1999, has worked with Demarco as a collaborator and an outstanding patron.

Kirstin Anderson (KA): Thank you so much for meeting with me today, Richard. I've read a lot about your work as a teacher, and the incredible role that you played in connecting artists and people in custody together. One thing I've never been able to find is your experience of going into the BSU for the first time. How did it feel? What did it sound like?

Richard Demarco (RD): You must go back to 1947. In 1947, I experienced the Edinburgh Festival for the first time as a schoolboy at Holy Cross Academy; the only Roman Catholic secondary school in Edinburgh. This academy introduced me to the Edinburgh Festival. I was just 17, I think. I attended the Edinburgh International Festival, and it changed my life. Because what I got in full force, no holds barred, was the world's greatest manifestations of art in [the] form of the greatest orchestra in the world, which had been banned by Hitler in 1933 because it contained many Jewish musicians. It was the Vienna Philharmonic. You understand this?

KA: Yes.

RD: But long before that, I had spent my life as someone who was the British equivalent of the German Jew because I was part of a physical presence of something which was not entirely kosher in terms of the British way of life, that includes the Scottish way of life. As a primary school child, I had experienced the war. The war ended in '45, but it didn't end, because it produced the world's largest prison, the Cold War. My father said you can't walk out the door of this house with the name on your birth certificate, Riccardo Demarco (it was in 1940, I was ten), because Mussolini has just declared war against the Allies. And you, on your birth certificate, are clearly Riccardo Demarco. That's why my mother and father, and my uncles and aunts, called me Rico; it's the diminutive of Riccardo. My father said you'll have to invent a British name. I think the nearest to Riccardo is Richard, so you'll have to become Richard. You can't leave this house, you'll be attacked.

And I was certainly attacked. Stones were thrown at me as a child as I walked along the promenade at Portobello. And when I went to swim in the public baths at Portobello and afterwards when I had a shower, I was attacked so that blood was running down my face. A small group of 15-year-old thugs simply saw this strange bronze looking creature, a little boy. And I went home, my face was covered in blood. My parents said you must never go to the public baths again. And at that time, anything Italian, referred to as an 'Eyetie', was a kind of swear word. So, it wasn't a good idea to be an Italo-Scot because you knew you were never going to be trusted and you couldn't become part of the British Empire, the imperial powerhouse.

So, you've got to understand that these were my experiences in my childhood and my teenage years when I began my secondary education at Holy Cross Academy. So, I got used to being ... not quite acceptable. Europe had been taken over by the horror of Communism. There was no sense of freedom. So, if Jimmy Boyle was here, I'd be saying to him, I was born into a prison. That's why I became the Director of the Edinburgh International Festival's programme of contemporary avant-garde visual art. It was on one condition — that I didn't want to deal only with artists who are in the art world, but artists who identify with the word 'outsider' and that includes all those artists in prison.

KA: This was a condition that you made to them, that you would be able to work with people in prison?

RD: Peter Diamond was the perfect director of the Edinburgh International Festival, having been the Director of the Holland Festival. Unfortunately, he did admit to me that he was not particularly interested in the visual arts. Music was the dominant language he identified with, not the international visual art world, but he had to put on the programme that Lord Harewood, his predecessor, had planned for the 1967 festival. There was no time to create a new programme. So, I'll not forget his words, I can hear his words now in his Jewish Dutch accent, 'Ricky, you can do it!' But, on one condition, and he pointed at me, he said, 'You pay for it.' Meaning I would be unpaid. I did the job for 25 years, unpaid. And I had to raise £7 million from the Governments of Canada, France, Italy, Ireland, Spain, the Baltic States, Poland, Romania, the former Yugoslavia, Croatia, Slovenia, Serbia and Georgia. It's about time people knew this because I am not *in* the Scottish art world, OK, I never have been from 1947 onwards. In 1967, my first major exhibition giving the Edinburgh International Festival the full energy of the avant-garde was entitled The Edinburgh 100. It attracted 2,000 artists from all over the British Isles. I wanted to liberate the Scottish art world from the concept of Scottish art. I found the money to present three first prizes of £1,000 each, in today's money this would be the equivalent of over £15,000. So, think about all of this and think about my mind whirling around, how to make sense of the Edinburgh Festival involving the spirit of the international avant-garde?

And then in 1968 there was the impact on my life of the Canadian Government in the form of the Canada Council inviting me to travel the length and breadth of Canada to decide on an exhibition titled Canada 101 at the Edinburgh International Festival. I travelled coast-to-coast, and the American Government noted this. They thought if Richard Demarco is inviting Canadian artists to the Edinburgh Festival, it's about time he invited American artists. So, in 1970, I received a letter from the United States Government saying I was to be the first ever British citizen to be invited to travel the length and breadth of America. So, I got used to being flown here, there and everywhere, meeting the Director of the Metropolitan Museum in New York, the Director of the Chicago Art Institute, the Director of the Los Angeles County Museum of Art. I also lectured in all the top universities.

In 1970, I turned the whole Edinburgh College of Art into one great *Gesamtkunstwerk. Gesamt* means energy released [makes whooshing sound], *kunst* is art and *werk* means work. *Gesamt*! I love that word. *Gesamtkunstwerk*. I turned the whole building, every staircase, every floor, every corridor, every room into an art experience. The exhibition had a palindromic title, called Strategy: Get Arts. And it was not just German art. It was artists attracted to Düsseldorf as the alternative to New York. It was the European soul somehow reborn. However, it was not welcomed by the Board of Governors of Edinburgh College of Art. But, in fact, it was regarded by the international art critics as the moment when the Edinburgh Festival embraced the spirit of the international avant-garde. There were 100 films, unfortunately they were all confiscated by the police.

So, I was never allowed to show them. There were six concerts of avant-garde, modern music. There were performances and there was one sculptural piece, a masterpiece, by Joseph Beuys, called 'The Pack', about global warming.

When I was invited to the Philadelphia Museum in 1970, I was introduced to one of my top patrons, Acey Wolgin; she was the chairman of the Board of Governors of the Philadelphia Museum Board. So, Acey made a point of saying to me, 'I have a friend that I'd like you to meet. I think you'll find him interesting. He should be on Death Row in San Quentin, the notorious prison in California.' How then did I meet Rick Cluchey, because without my meeting with Rick Cluchey, I would never have gone through the door of the Special Unit. He was possessed of the same kind of mindset as Jimmy. He knew he was about to be electrocuted but he was an artist and he founded a theatre company. And he deserves to be put into the spotlight in terms of the history of Jimmy Boyle and the Special Unit just after it was founded. Cluchey said to me—'I decided to have a theatre company of my fellow death row friends. And we decided that the one play that would make sense is "Waiting for Godot". And that would be performed for the benefit of my death row prisoners.'

But then he did something quite amazing. He found it difficult to get to grips with the essence of the play, so he wrote to Samuel Beckett, and said 'Can you help us direct the play?' Samuel Beckett wrote back and said, 'Of Course, I'd be delighted.' Can you imagine what that meant? The world's greatest living dramatist was prepared to work with people on Death Row. So, I said to him, you must come to the Edinburgh Festival. He said, 'Well, I've got a play called "The Cage".' And I knew there was something between Glasgow and Edinburgh. Guess where it is?

KA: Polmont Young Offender Institution.

RD: Polmont. In 1972, I therefore invited Rick Cluchey to present 'The Cage'. It's all about how life is impossible in such a place where you suddenly realise you're being simply educated to go to the real prison. The young offenders, as an audience, recognised that the play was all about their lives. The production of 'The Cage' was made possible because the Governor of Polmont Young Offenders, George Duncan, understood the importance of the play. He became the vitally important first Governor of the Special Unit. Meeting with this extraordinary person changed my life. It was natural for him to invite me to experience the

Special Unit when he became the Governor of what was to question the nature of penal reform in Scotland.

KA: So, this was before you went into the Special Unit?

RD: I'll never forget that first meeting I had in the Special Unit where I introduced them all. I've got photographs somewhere I took of all of them. I was suddenly aware of two human beings there. One of them was Jimmy, who I could see was the leader, the driving force. I could see his face alight. He could see that he was dealing with someone who understood how to use the language of arts. What did I know then? Well, I had met Beuys and I knew that he believed that everyone is an artist. If you teach in a primary school, you will see that every child will play, sing, dance. You give them a piece of paper; they will make marks on it. Everyone is naturally creative. It's only at secondary education level that the dunderheads say we don't want to know about creativity. We simply want to know about your capacity to remember, use your memory and pass exams. Information, information, information. We don't need information; we certainly do need imagination.

I could see from my own experience as an underdog, an outsider, that there was something very sick about British society dominated by the spirit of the British Empire and I was born into the dying years of British Empire. I immediately made contact with Jimmy. In that first meeting, I said to him, 'Don't worry, I'm going to find a way, because I know who you are.'

KA: Was he already making art when you went into the unit? Did you see his art?

RD: Of course, every word that he spoke in our conversation was the language of a true artist.

KA: You said there were two people the first time you went to the Barlinnie Special Unit who you remember. Jimmy and …?

RD: Jimmy Boyle and Larry Winters. I could see in their faces, in their eyes, that they were a part of my life. There was no separation between them and me. Larry Winters' poetry showed his profound concern for the future of humanity.

KA: It's really helpful to understand the context. How can we understand your role in the BSU without understanding, as you've described, how you grew up and what was happening in the world. What were your hopes for the Special Unit at that time?

RD: I didn't want Jimmy Boyle or anyone connected with the Special Unit, but especially Jimmy, to be thought of as anything else but a powerful, living, breathing artist. So, who did I bring into the Special Unit? The world's most controversial artist...JB met JB.

KA: It's such a lovely exchange.

RD: In 1976, in the Demarco Gallery on the Royal Mile, Joseph Beuys was prepared to open Jimmy Boyle's exhibition titled 'In Defence of the Innocent'. In his introduction to the exhibition, Joseph Beuys took off his hat and said, 'I am Jimmy Boyle.'

KA: Oh, I've never heard that. I've heard of Jimmy in conversation with Beuys saying 'I Am The Coyote' the first time they met.

RD: But why did Jimmy say that? Because during the Edinburgh Festival in 1974, when I first introduced Jimmy Boyle to Joseph Beuys, there was an exhibition of photographs taken by Caroline Tisdall in New York of the three-day visit that Beuys made to New York, where he said 'I don't want to talk to the President of the United States. I don't want to talk to the Director of the Museum of Modern Art. I want to talk only to the most despised animal, the animal that you should, as soon as you see it, throw stones at it.' It's a sacred animal to the American Indians but it is the coyote and to the newcomers to America, the first settlers, it was a despised animal.

KA: You talk about this mutual understanding that the men in the Special Unit and artists, like Beuys and other artists that you were bringing in, had of each other. Not, these are the prisoners and these are the artists...

RD: I knew that Jimmy would be able to give and take with the world's greatest artists. He was already an artist. This was also the case with Hugh Collins. He wasn't there in the beginning of the Special Unit, but when I met him, he already had a fully-fledged artistic soul. As soon as I saw his drawings, paintings, and, most importantly, his sculptures, I knew he was a master of fine art. I use that phrase knowing that there's no such thing as a process of education that can confer that title upon any human being.

KA: How did the collaboration between artists and men in prison impact the art world?

RD: The art world on its own was not ready for it. Joseph Beuys, as a result of the war, became a prisoner of the British army in Cuxaven and there he nearly died of starvation. He suffered mental and physical wounds that eventually ended his life at the age of 64. He knew exactly what it was to be a despised prisoner.

KA: Did people in Scotland start to see what you saw? Did the people coming to the Poorhouse to attend these exhibitions start to care about prisons?

RD: I don't think so. However, from my lecture tours of America the majority of the visitors I introduced to the Special Unit were my Edinburgh Arts students from universities such as Yale and Harvard. Some were studying Medicine, English Literature, some were students of History. They weren't all artists.

KA: When reflecting on the Edinburgh Arts 1975 project, 'On the Road to Meikle Seggie', you wrote, 'The Special Unit extends the space of the Demarco Gallery in the right direction. Edinburgh Arts is inconceivable without it.' How did the experience of the project influence you and the artists who were communicating with the men in the Special Unit while navigating Scotland's landscape?

RD: The prisoners weren't allowed to experience the physical reality of Scotland. That's why the postcards were used by the Edinburgh Arts students and teachers, to share their reactions to the wind and weather, the smells of vegetation of flowers, the sight and sound of animals, especially birds in flight. The movement of trees withstanding the powerful winds blown from the Atlantic. There are the lines of a famous Scottish folk song, 'If it's thinkin' in your inner heart the braggart's in my step, you've never smelled the tangle o' the Isles.' It's 'The Road to the Isles'. I took all my students on the road to the Isles, but I couldn't take the men in the unit. But with the postcards, we were sharing our experiences with the men in the unit. The postcards were talismans. They were messages of hope, not just communication. And, as far as I know, this kind of use of postal communication to give the much-needed signals of hope has never been done since. Mother Nature calls but you can hardly see her in a prison. Most of the postcards expressed the elemental splendour of nature; for example, some of [the] postcards contained images of the famous sunsets over the Cuillin Mountains on the Isle of Skye.

Can I just say that it was a problem for me, certain artists didn't understand it was a fruitful experiment in education. And it was an experiment using the Special Unit as the extreme situation. It was a daily reminder to the Edinburgh Arts students of their capacity to freely experience the gifts of Mother Nature, which the men in the Special Unit could not experience within the confines of the encircling walls of HMP Barlinnie. The Demarco Gallery published an edited collection of writings, postcards, drawings and photographs revealing the importance of the complex dialogue between the community of the Special

Unit and the Edinburgh Arts students and teachers, and on the final page there is a potent reflection by Jimmy Boyle, 'The journey that the Edinburgh Arts artists were about to embark on was shrouded in a mist of hidden qualities that embraced Time, Space, Art and Society, each of which must be clarified in relation to people, and this was the main point of the exercise—involving human beings as artists.'

KA: Who was this experiment for? Was it for the artists? Was it for society?

RD: For society in general. I remember saying to Beuys when you say everyone was an artist, does that include people in prison? Ja! Does that include people serving life imprisonment. Oh, ja. Does it include murderers? Ja! OK, I'm not going to waste your time visiting Scotland's museums and galleries. I'm going to take you to a kind of vision of hell on earth, which is Barlinnie. And inside HMP Barlinnie, there is a special experiment taking place, and it's called the Special Unit. And I want you to meet Jimmy Boyle. I had confidence in Jimmy's artistic soul. Art is often misused as a form of entertainment. It is about the need to confront life and death.

KA: Maybe that's it. We are talking about life and death. And who better to understand life and death than a group of men who are in prison and people who have lived through war time.

RD: Can I just say, the basic thing is that when I asked Beuys, 'What is the nature, the quintessential nature of your art?' he said, 'It's very simple. My art is my teaching.' He doesn't make art the way most artists do, to sell. That's why he used blackboards. He was teaching. He then explained that he had wanted to become a doctor, be involved in medical science and then he decided that being a doctor wasn't good enough because he believed in something he called 'Social Sculpture'. He said, I believe that the role of the artist is to reshape society so it's doing the right thing. He said, 'You must understand that every 24 hours, if you take the Lord's prayer seriously, particularly "give us this day our daily bread." Not the week, not the month, the day, because everything will go wrong in 24 hours. And the job of the artist is to put things right.'

KA: If you were talking to someone who had never heard of the Special Unit. And they said, what was this? What was the role of art in the Special Unit? What would your response to that be?

RD: Well, I believed that the dialogue between an inmate of the unit and a highly regarded, respected artist was the proof needed to reshape a society misshapen by the forces of Mammon.

KA: Did it reshape society?

RD: No. I wanted to help reshape British society. I wanted to help reshape Polish society because I didn't think the Cold War would end. I thought it would go on forever. There was no proof that it would end and so I crossed the Iron Curtain 60 times. That meant that I was going in the opposite direction to where all the artists who wished to achieve fame within the art world were going.

I realised that I needed Beuys in my life but also, I needed to become what I really have never escaped from; the world of teaching. I am, in the depth of my being, a born teacher. I didn't want to be involved in an exhibition programme or a theatre programme or programme of films or whatever. I wanted to use the language of art as the language of healing. The language of love. The language of reconciliation. Of forgiveness. Art is not an industry. It's not to do with sport. It's not to do with the leisure industry. It's a matter of life and death.

On the 10th anniversary of Strategy: Get Arts, which was in 1980, I went back to Germany. And I said to the West German Government, I'm looking for artists who can help me celebrate this 10th anniversary of Strategy: Get Arts. And when I had lunch with Joseph Beuys, set up by Dorothee Bouchard, he decided that things had changed, the situation is not the same as it was in 1970, so you can't replicate that spirit. But, he said, 'What I'm prepared to do is to come to Edinburgh and we will have a symposium and I will make something for you, which will be about the structure of society and why the language of the arts is not the language of politics, not the language of big business. The language of the arts is the one language we have got to focus on.' I said, 'Of course.' This was music to my ears.

But on the day, when he arrived, I said to him, 'I think you should go straight to Barlinnie, to the Special Unit.' And he did so, and he found Jimmy. Jimmy had been in the Special Unit for several years. Jimmy was facing the fact that in a few days' time he was going to have handcuffs put on his wrists again. He was in a state of tears. He was very upset. He said 'They're going to move me from the Special Unit.' Joseph couldn't understand how this could possibly be because Jimmy was the perfect example of the unit's success.

Joseph Beuys then said, 'I must go on a hunger strike and protest this ridiculous decision. I must now write a letter to the Secretary of State for Scotland because he is the Queen's representative. I want it to go to the highest authority in Scotland and my letter must state that I think Scotland's Prison Service is a disgrace. Something should be done and you should consider the success of the Special Unit in producing both Jimmy Boyle and his fellow inmate, Hugh Collins.' And so, Joseph Beuys posted the letter under the address of the Richard Demarco Gallery. It caused a knee jerk reaction and resulted in the Arts Council of Scotland requesting a meeting with me immediately in the middle of the Edinburgh Festival and while Jimmy was waiting to be transferred. Beuys said, 'I'm cutting down my stay from five days to two-and-a-half days, and I'm going on hunger strike.' He had just returned from New York, where he had a most fantastic success at the Guggenheim Museum with a solo exhibition.

At the meeting, I was offered a cup of coffee and a biscuit. And then the Director of the Visual Arts of the Scottish Arts Council said something I cannot ever forget. He sat opposite me. He had two senior Arts Council officials beside him. I noted only one member of his visual arts committee was present as the meeting had been called at great speed. The Director of Visual Arts was obviously furious. He said, 'We must now discuss the fact that a foreign artist has taken a court action against the Secretary of State in support of an inmate of the Special Unit. The letter has come from your gallery's address.' After this short introduction, I listened to the unforgettable words, 'You have brought dishonour to the meaning of art, you have brought dishonour to the meaning of art in Scotland.' And I said, 'If I've brought dishonour to the meaning of art, my heavens, what an achievement.'

His final words were, 'You have brought dishonour to the meaning of the Richard Demarco Gallery!' And then he said, 'And from now on,' and we're in the middle of the festival, 'you do not deserve to have any arts council annual funding, so therefore we are removing all funding immediately.' I could not believe this decision. And then he thumped the table and said, 'I don't want to discuss this any longer. You're finished.' I then replied, 'I think you have brought dishonour to the meaning of the Scottish Arts Council.'

KA: What was the response of the artists who you worked with?

RD: Well, I've always believed that art originates in the meetings of friends and their shared value systems and their shared hopes and aspirations, and they use the language of art as the way of communicating with each other. So, I decided to write a letter to 1,000 of my personal friends. And the result was that I received from my friends financial support, in some cases £100, in these days that was quite a lot of money. But usually £25 from poets, from writers, from ordinary people and from people who had been in charge of the Arts Council in previous years. Joseph Beuys himself put in something like nearly £20,000. And so I got rid of the immediate problem, but from that day onwards I have never had the benefit of national, government support in the form an annual grant.

So, now at the age of 93, I don't have a five-year plan [laughs]. However, I am heartened that you are editing a book on the Barlinnie Special Unit. I want to stress the fact that I am simply an artist who continues to paint watercolours and make pen drawings and prints. But none of these works were ever seen as a one-off. They were all manifestations of what I call my life's journey and my linking up with fellow artists, because I realised to achieve what I have to do, I have to consider my role as a teacher using the language of all the arts. And I realise with my instinct as a teacher that everyone I would meet on my journey through life had to be regarded as a creative human being.

My main decisions were not aesthetic ones, they were moral decisions. I had no choice. I had to help Beuys make that decision, using the Richard Demarco Gallery address.

KA: You were ready for him?

RD: Yeah, exactly. But I said, 'I'm going to test you to the breaking point.'

KA: I'm sure he was up for it.

RD: He was certainly up for the challenge I offered. And now we've got to celebrate 1974. What happened in 1974? Well, that was the year when I decided on the one day that Jimmy was released from prison where precisely he would experience his freedom. I had rented from Edinburgh University a disused building without electric light, with no toilet facilities and a leaking roof. It had been, in its history, a medieval madhouse. Indeed, the Scottish equivalent of London's Bedlam. It had long been known in Edinburgh as The Poorhouse. This poorhouse was linked to the medieval graveyard and church associated [with] the Franciscan order of monks who tended to the poor and underprivileged of Edinburgh. Beuys loved it. And I loved it because it was not a gallery. Jimmy came accompanied by two prison guards and I introduced him to Joseph Beuys, and it's on a little clip of film, Jimmy introduces himself, 'Hello, Joseph. I Am The Coyote.'

KA: And what was Joseph's response?

RD: He did not show anything else than acceptance. Being the genius that he was, he understood exactly what this other human being was saying to him.

Jimmy Boyle was, of course, moved against his will to Saughton Prison in Edinburgh. Whilst there I introduced him to Helen Crummy who founded and directed what I consider to be an alternative arts festival in Edinburgh. It was not to be found in the city centre but in a working-class district known as Craigmillar. It was at the centre of the mining industry, which dominated the lives of a significant part of Edinburgh's population. Helen Crummy commissioned Jimmy to make a gigantic sculpture in concrete, it was made for the children of Craigmillar. This great sculpture was living proof that despite the fact he'd been moved out of the Special Unit, he was still making meaningful art. I've realised Jimmy doesn't want to be forever associated with the Special Unit. He is also firmly linked to that of the Craigmillar Festival.

KA: Yes, this is something that often happens with people who've experienced custody. They don't want to be associated with prison after they leave.

RD: He had to leave Edinburgh and indeed, Scotland. He managed to leave behind him the most remarkable experiment that he created with his then wife, Sara Trevelyan, this was known as the Gateway Exchange, an institution that Edinburgh needed to help all those experiencing the shock of being released from prison. I still to this day regret the fact that he had to leave Edinburgh.

KA: What do you think about when remembering the Special Unit today?

RD: My friendship with Jimmy Boyle continues to enrich my life. When I think of the Special Unit, I automatically think of his life as an artist, but also the lives of his fellow artists who benefitted from the environment of the Special Unit. I cannot think of Jimmy Boyle without thinking of his fellow inmate, Hugh Collins, who, like Jimmy, enjoyed a fruitful dialogue with Joseph Beuys. Hugh Collins famously sent Beuys a portrait he made of him entitled 'The Revolution is Us'. Nor can I think of Jimmy Boyle without thinking of the poetry of Larry Winters. It inspired the award-winning film that was directed by Bill Beech entitled *The Silent Scream.*

I've now reached that stage in my life where I regard each day of my nonagenarian life as a blessing and a challenge. I am living in the constant presence of artists, who like Jimmy Boyle, are still alive as well as those who, like Hugh Collins, Larry Winters and Joseph Beuys, still dominate my thoughts because although they are no longer alive, their art has given them the gift of immortality. They personify the enduring creative spirit of the Special Unit.

Richard Demarco and Kirstin Anderson in 2024 © Terry Ann Newman.

CHAPTER 6

'It Was a Community'

Interview with David Croft by Kirstin Anderson

David Croft joined the Scottish Prison Service (SPS) as a prison officer in 1968 at 22 years old. He worked in the Barlinnie Special Unit (BSU) from 1980 to 1984 as a Principal Officer. The following interview with him took place on 17 March 2023.

When did you first go to the BSU?

I went in 1979 for a week from Shotts Prison. Staff used to be able to apply to go for a week on a trial basis. At the end of the trial, I decided that I just didn't have enough understanding of what was going on and I thought to myself, they're pretty sophisticated guys in there, prisoners and staff, and I think I need a bit more experience with the long-term prisoners I'm with now before going ahead with an application. A year later I applied for promotion to an 'Opportunity Post' there and was accepted. The condition of the promotion was that I had to remain in post for at least two years or I would be returned to my previous rank—talk about 'Golden Handcuffs'! That was in 1980 and I stayed for four years until 1984.

For training we went to Dingleton Hospital in Melrose and Grendon Underwood Prison which operated a regime based on secure therapeutic communities. Yes, I think we spent one week at Dingleton and two at Grendon. We spent time with the staff, not really working with them, but observing how they engaged with patients and how they handled difficult issues. They took the time to explain what they were doing and what the issues were for them.

The training was a worthy attempt to prepare us for working in the BSU but in terms of our actual needs, what we would do today, it was miles away from ideal preparation. You see, as far as I am concerned even today, almost everyone being interviewed for the job as a prison officer is asked, 'Why do you want to be a prison officer?' The answer is usually 'Because I want to help people.' I said exactly the same thing. Naïvely, we think we are smarter and better than the prisoners and that we know more than we really do about life. It doesn't take long before you realise that prisoners are much smarter than we thought they would be and as far as the Special Unit was concerned multiply that by ten!

What was the training like?

The training made me feel as though I was entering a very special field of work. I didn't feel important, but I felt an effort was being made to help me prepare for working in a unique environment. Unfortunately, as a relatively inexperienced person who had no academic background, or great experience, life experience, I had no real idea what I was taking on. It was therefore difficult to properly prepare for what lay ahead. However, compared to any other training that was going on in the Prison Service at that time, this was a genuine attempt to try to prepare people for dealing with the very challenging and difficult prisoners in the Special Unit. Remember, in the early days of the unit almost all of the staff, at all ranks except the Governor, were trained nurses. As was Ken Murray, a Principal Nurse Officer, who in my opinion was about the most significant and influential staff member ever to work there.

Although the training was intended to prepare me for working in the unit, in reality, it was what I learned on the ground that equipped me. You have peaks and troughs of experiences and feelings the whole time you are working there. The Special Unit was certainly the place throughout my career, and I worked in many prisons, that developed me most as a person and as a prison professional. The social dynamics were wide ranging and challenging and consequently my enthusiasm, confidence, inner strength and my learning ebbed and flowed constantly. It was an absolute emotional rollercoaster which with hindsight, every minute was worth experiencing. As time passes and you leave it all behind, you can rationalise it much easier than when you are operating in it.

So, you've done the training, you're going into the unit. Tell me a bit about being a prison officer at that time.

I was a principal officer, there were two of us, one on each shift, in charge of the shift. There were four staff on a shift at a time, two officers, a senior officer and a principal officer. And there was a daytime chief officer and a Governor; the latter being the only person working in the unit who was not a volunteer, they were appointed by the Prisons Board.

The thing about the Special Unit is you've no idea what you're facing until you're in it. When you first go in on your trial week, when you go and visit, it's surreal. Staff and prisoners are playing snooker, others are sitting in the sun or playing badminton outdoors. Some might just be sitting watching a film with the lights out. It was just like being in a community centre. In the early days working there I thought, this is a breeze, it could actually become quite enjoyable. Although I also had feelings of guilt, spending so much time playing games. This sense of guilt would often be exacerbated when going on and off duty and having to pass a large group of staff from the main prison who, in the early days, were pretty hostile towards unit staff.

Going on duty, mainstream Barlinnie staff would all first assemble inside the fairly crammed gate area until the chief officer shouted, 'Right!' and together staff would all enter the prison. The Special Unit staff, under a different management structure independent of the main prison, would come in and walk right through them heading up to our separate unit. Many of the Barlinnie staff could not tolerate the thought of the Special Unit staff coming together as a 'community' with prisoners, many of whom had seriously injured their colleagues in conflicts of the past. The prisoner/staff culture in most prisons at the time was still one of 'us and them'. It wasn't like it is in so many places now, where staff seek to create a positive environment with opportunities for prisoners to improve their lives.

It was clear, that neither side would fully understand the other's point of view unless we spoke with each other and shared our perspectives. The subsequent creation of 'Special Unit Awareness' slots into all levels of the SPS national staff training programme, allowed us to dispel many of the myths that surrounded people's views of what the unit was trying to achieve. I genuinely believe that the lessons learned from the life of the unit on the part of prisoners and staff, have contributed to the operational stability that has lasted for so long now right across the SPS.

In terms of relationships with colleagues outside the unit, I suppose I was fortunate in that I played in the Prison Officers' Football League and had many opportunities to spend social time with staff across the service and that led to friendships. So, I was part of all of it. But at the same time, you have to be your own person to retain your self-respect and you had to have the courage of your convictions. I genuinely believed that I was doing something that was far and away more valuable than anything I'd done before in terms of the purpose for which I joined the Prison Service. I suspect most of us who worked in the unit thought the same or they wouldn't have gone there in the first place.

Can you explain what it felt like to walk into the Special Unit compared to walking into a residential hall?

One of the features was that you already knew the names of every prisoner in the place as most of them had notorious reputations. They were all well known and most had received a great deal of publicity by the time I got there. As a result, I was intrigued to see if they were as described—I was in for a surprise! On first walking in I was apprehensive but at the same time inquisitive. I had wondered if the 'community' concept they kept throwing in every visitor's face really existed. I was hit by the realisation that I never had the communication skills that everybody else seemed to have. As a community, they had a sort of cultural language they would use to talk about corporate responsibility and commitment to the 'community' and its 'norms'. It was a community, a very close community, one in which everyone who lived, and most of them who worked within it, were anxious for it to succeed.

Look, at that time, if you went into any other prison, the prisoners and the staff would speak only of what was wrong in their prison and the people and prisoners within it. This was less common in the Special Unit because of the demands of the community. Anyone, staff or prisoner, who was speaking or acting contrary to the interests of the unit, would be taken to task at the weekly community meeting. If the matter was a serious one then it could not wait and a meeting of the community would be called without delay. To have observed or heard of anyone acting or speaking about something contrary to the unit's best interests and not having called a meeting, was likely to result in that person being the subject of a community meeting. It happened often! At the end of the day we were all, staff and prisoners alike, subject to an unwritten contract.

Being called to account at a meeting was often considered as having been in the 'hot seat' and could be quite a challenging experience. You'd be in a room, maybe twice the size of this room with everyone sitting round the wall. Minutes were taken at all meetings by either a prisoner or a member of staff. If on duty, the Governor would chair the meetings. In the early months working there you would often feel apprehensive, concerned that you might become the subject of a complaint or challenge. Apprehensive, not because you were physically scared but because never before in our careers would we have tolerated being verbally attacked by a prisoner in the presence of other prisoners or staff. I'm talking about being challenged about your performance or perhaps about the extent of your commitment to the success of the Special Unit. The same would apply equally to prisoners being verbally challenged about the same things by their peers or a member of staff. Depending upon the mood within the unit at any one time, meetings could be over in under ten minutes whist others could take several hours.

When you went on shift into the unit the mood somehow was normally instantly evident. It did not take long to assess whether all was well or whether conflicts of one sort or another were rumbling under the surface. On the early shift we would open up at 6 am after checking all prisoners were alive and well. The staff would then sit in the muster room drinking coffee awaiting the first prisoners to rise and join us, this would probably happen within about 15 minutes. There we would relax and chat about the world in general and often the Prison Service more widely. We would never get into discussions about anyone not present, the outcome of such 'gossip' would be likely to become the subject of a special meeting further down the line! It didn't take long to work out the meeting 'trigger points'.

On the late shift, going on duty at 1 pm, the unit was halfway through its day and it would take a little bit longer to assess the general mood within both staff and prisoner groups. The problems that might emerge were never traditional 'security' type matters but rather under the surface interpersonal issues that inevitably arise between people working and living together in such close surroundings. Indeed unthinkingly, I am sure that I would sometimes have been the 'problem' and would have had to face up to that too! Once you learned about the place, you understood the rules and 'norms' with which we were all required to comply. This again was challenging, I was in uniform and wearing pips and had braid on my cap, anywhere else I would be a figure of authority.

What kinds of supports were in place for you as officers working in the BSU? Were their official supports or did you have to kind of form your own?

That's a difficult one as in these times letting anyone know you needed support, especially psychological support, was not something you would want to admit. At times one would feel very lonely and occasionally vulnerable, especially in the early days of your attachment. It was such an unnatural working environment compared to what we had experienced before. This is hardly surprising given how physically close together staff and prisoners always were in such a small building. As leader of a shift, I considered it my duty to observe, support and guide staff who may be struggling in one way or another. But given that we all had different reactions to different events, and we had not received relative previous training in this area, it took me some time to become an effective support to staff.

We were really lucky with the chief officer we had. Given his natural discipline orientated personality he was not one you might have expected would fit in at the unit. As it happened, this trait turned out to be an asset and a comfort to all. He didn't spend as much time with individual prisoners or staff as we did but I know I personally found his presence to be reassuring, as I did the Governor who was even less close to everyday matters in the unit.

The unit was well served by a part time psychologist and a psychiatrist. They attended I think weekly, usually on the day of the weekly community meeting. Their primary purpose was to work with the prisoners but they both always made themselves available to staff for any purpose.

Was it important to have someone to decompress with after a day's work?

It definitely was, more than in any other setting I have worked. Some staff found it all too much and left the unit well before their due date. The human dynamics were in many ways very intense and they affected staff and prisoners equally. Remember, everyone living and working there was accountable to the community for their performance, commitment and contributions. Anyone wavering from those requirements would soon be found out and be taken to task at a community meeting. Although the meetings themselves were not threatening, staff being openly confronted by prisoners or their colleagues in the presence of prisoners and colleagues was a completely new experience, one that in the early days could make one feel humiliated and weak. This was all so contrary to our previous experiences where in my judgement most prisoners and staff acted in accordance with what strengths they were expected to have, rather than what they actually possessed. It was their way of coping and being accepted by their peers.

Everyone therefore needed someone with whom they could share their feelings. I suspect that prisoners achieved this through chosen visitors. For staff that person needed to have had experience of the unit. I had a couple of colleagues with whom I could confide and share my feelings and uncertainties.

You are in a couple of pictures in the Third Eye book. When you look at this photo right now, what does it make you think about? Can you remember the moment?

That photo was taken on a Press Open Day. The Special Unit had been constantly the focus of press attention, some of the stories printed were ridiculous and others were true. Through the media we just wanted the public to get a glimpse of what it was really like. It was at the time an extremely innovative and brave initiative from which, in my opinion, much could be and has been, learned and introduced into prisons more generally. Mainly issues around mutual respect for each other, being transparently accountable for your actions and offering an environment and opportunities for the personal development of everyone involved, prisoners and staff. I thought that my willingness to be photographed would perhaps in some small way, project to the public a more positive image of staff who work in the Scottish Prison Service.

Some people would look at this and be quite surprised that this is considered a cell; to have all of these things, and the decorations.

All of the furniture and decorations that were in that cell were either passed on from a previous prisoner or paid for by the prisoner himself. They would gather scraps of wood and make themselves a table, chair etc. A family member might have provided the wallpaper and curtains or they may have been left behind, again by the previous prisoner who occupied the cell. There was no cost to the Prison Service. Creating their personal cell design was considered to be helpful to a prisoner settling into life in the Special Unit—nothing was as easy as it looks!

And this is the Muster Room. I see lots of coffee cups?

As much as anything, the muster room served as a hub for early morning or evening chat with those around just after unlocking cells in the morning or just before lock up in the evening. Symbolically, it reflected much about the special nature of the unit's regime and how much staff and prisoners shared their spare time and spaces together exchanging views, stories and discussing widely, general issues of mutual interest. Over coffee in the muster room, I personally learned a very great deal about the various lives, opinions and evolving values of staff and prisoners. This learning contributed greatly to my approach to management at a more senior level throughout the rest of my career.

It says 'Special Unit staff relaxing in the unit muster room' [both laugh].

Yes, it could have been a tea time or night time when the prisoners were locked up. Other than break times, staff rarely spent lengthy times there without prisoners being present. Staff spending time chatting together in the muster room was always a comfortable opportunity for staff to have 'downtime'. However, it had to be managed in a way that did not lend itself to being an escape hideaway for staff. Indeed, I recall at least one occasion when a prisoner called a meeting and asked those from the muster room, 'Tell me, is there anything you're all meant to be doing in there? Is anyone available to speak to someone like me out here? You've been in there for hours talking when you get paid to work with us—we don't get paid, we've got to be here.' A hot exchange of views followed!

Did any of the men feel that they should have been able to not be locked up at night?

I can't recall such an issue being raised. Security was about the only matter that we never consulted prisoners about. We may have occasionally needed to advise them of what our intention was in relation to any change and let them know the reason why. I suspect in the early days of the unit there would have been emerging security matters that needed to be addressed but things had settled down by the time I went there.

Was there a mechanism for addressing behavioural matters on the part of prisoners?

Yes, and it was not uncommon for prisoners to be 'punished' by having various sanctions imposed on their levels of freedom within the unit. This would happen at a meeting of the whole community, recorded and reviewed at set periods. Unacceptable behaviour would include being found with items of property the prisoner was not allowed to have, or threatening another prisoner or staff member with violence. It might have been that he was just refusing to participate fully in the life of the Special Unit. Any prisoner who broke or disrespected the unit's norms, for example not attending community meetings, would also be sanctioned.

The sanctions would be reviewed at periods set by the community and might last about a month. They could include a loss of access to visits, closely supervised visits or even terminating his stay in the unit. Whilst subject to sanctions the affected prisoner might be required to participate in 'four groups', whereby two staff members and another prisoner would meet with the prisoner, sometimes daily, to discuss his conduct and how he was progressing towards a return to full regime access. Four groups might also be used when relations between any two people had become so strained that they might have escalated into something more serious or were negatively affecting the smooth running of the unit. Whilst much of the content of the four groups was confidential, updates on progress would be fed into the weekly community meeting.

Art, as you know, played an important role in the Special Unit. What opportunities did people have inside the unit compared to other prisoners to make art?

All of the prisoners in the Special Unit had the opportunity to engage in art compared to a very small percentage of people in other prisons. When I went to the BSU in 1980 almost all of the prisoners were progressing art projects of one kind or another. It was already well established and maintained, overseen by Art Therapist Joyce Laing. Joyce's influence on the prisoners through art was considerable and she did so almost independent of the formal staff group. We would encourage them, pass on positive compliments but rarely be involved. However, even I could tell that some prisoners were clearly producing art to a very high standard and others to a good standard.

That was clear in* The Key*?

The internal magazine *The Key* had stopped just as I got there and there was never any talk in my time of doing another. My unfortunate experience of these initiatives in other prisons is that once the initial innovators move on, the project invariably dies.

When you think about the men that you were working with in the unit; were they artists when they came in or did the unit provide something that enabled people to create and to think about art?

The Special Unit provided every prisoner with the opportunity to spend as much time as they wished doing art. It also provided them with an expert Art Therapist to advise and guide them along with the materials with which to explore their artistic interests. No prisoners in any other prison had artistic opportunities to anything like that degree. The unit provided the environment, culture and time conducive to concentrated learning, so the prisoners there clearly had an advantage over their peers elsewhere.

In my time, almost every prisoner who came to the unit tried art and the ones who didn't do well quickly moved on to handicraft type work, things like for example, plaster models, chess boards and pieces, and things like that.

A host of prominent artists from the local community took a great interest in the prisoners' art work and regularly visited the unit. This resulted in art and creativity becoming embedded into the BSU's culture. Allowing prisoners to mix with these artists and to build different relationships in my opinion widened further the social skills of us all.

Nobody could argue that for the majority of prisoners, art was something that they would benefit from getting involved in and many seemed to have a talent for. Maybe they just had creative minds, perhaps that's part of being a prisoner or why you become a prisoner, because you have a creative mind and can't express yourself in any other way? Either way, I have always thought art was positive for those who wanted to engage.

Did the officers in the unit ever make art?

Not often, but on a small number of occasions as an outdoor activity. It often took place when engaging with prisoners who were creating their own art and where it felt appropriate to the engagement as part of the community. You're having a laugh and people are having a laugh at your dubious art skills.

You made a piece of sculpture?

I remember I used to pick up individual's tools and say, 'Can I borrow that?', 'Can I borrow this?' I watched them and how they used the tools. Speaking to individuals and understanding how the creative side of them allowed them to express themselves helped my understanding of art. One individual said to me, 'Sandstone's the easiest stone, the chisel just crawls over it. It's a great feeling.' I enjoyed it and would have liked to do it again.

Thinking about the BSU in the 1980s and that's when you went into it. What was the kind of collective thinking about the BSU at that time compared to its initial years? Did people in the organization just see it as part of the operation of the Prison Service?

For several years since its opening there was significant resistance across the SPS to the regime that was developing. Staff's first thoughts were naturally ones of loyalty to those colleagues who had over previous years been assaulted, some very seriously, by some of the prisoners now in the unit. How, they wondered, could former colleagues sit and have coffee with such prisoners and engage in dialogue with them on equal terms? I have to admit that I understood their concerns and that prior to working in the unit I had some similar concerns. However, the unit had been in operation for seven years before I went there and not one violent incident had yet occurred. Something special had to be taking place for that to happen and I wanted be part of it.

I admired Ken Murray greatly; he had tremendous courage. He came out and spoke about what needs to be done with these guys and the Prison Service wasn't ready for that. It needed to be said or we might have been waiting today still for it. The story about him and Jimmy and the scissors;[1] it's one of the most powerful stories I know in terms of management of prisoners and what it tells you; the whole thing about trust, and that carried on right through the unit. That's his legacy. Trust.

The staff turnover in the unit was very high, mostly due to some staff finding it difficult to adapt to the regime, others because of the claustrophobic environment and others the incessant interface with prisoners. Although expensive in terms of manpower wastage and specialist experience, I believe that the level of turnover is what allowed the unit eventually to becoming a valued part of the SPS strategy for managing difficult prisoners. The high number of staff moving back into the mainstream led to them sharing experiences and demonstrating their newly developed skills back in the system. In addition, becoming more transparent about the unit's purpose and regime and sharing that across the SPS staff training programme eventually led to the Special Unit being accepted by staff across the service.

1. The 'scissors story' is described in other chapters, including by Sara Trevelyan in *Chapter 1* and Jimmy Boyle in *Chapter 8*.

Was it difficult to go back to a traditional prison environment?

Not at all, I was a completely different person upon my return, better equipped to effectively manage prisoners and staff. I was much more resilient and had learned so much particularly in how to communicate with staff and prisoners in potentially volatile situations. Most importantly, I had learned the importance of saying and doing the right thing irrespective of how unpopular it might make me. I became more confident in standing up for what I believed to be in the best interests of staff and prisoners and to challenge what I considered to be non-progressive thinking.

A good example of this happened about six weeks after my transfer from the Special Unit to HMP Edinburgh. It had what was known as a 'top end' called Pentland Hall where life sentence prisoners were located towards the end of their sentence. Along with other principal officers, I was asked to attend a meeting with the Governor. The meeting's theme was about raising standards and what he wanted to be addressed. He turned his attention to Pentland Hall and raised significant concerns about the untidy state of the prisoners' cells and that we should expect more from prisoners soon to be released. He said that from now onwards he wanted prisoners located there to build 'bed blocks' every morning before going to work. 'Bed blocks' are what at the time soldiers used to make up by folding the blankets into neat squares and placing them on top of each other in a 'box shaped' orderly way. He then pointed to the two principal officers in charge of Pentland Hall and said, 'You're in charge of Pentland Hall, it's your responsibility to get this done now.' He then asked if anyone present had any questions and I put my hand up. He never even knew my name. I said, 'Tell me Governor, if whilst at a party in a friend's home you went upstairs to the toilet and when passing an open bedroom door, you saw a "bed block" at the end of the bed, would you not think it very strange? Just saying…'

That's an amazing story. What did he say?

He was livid! He said, 'It's nothing to do with you when I go to a party.' He then asked if anyone else had questions and nobody said anything. Afterwards I was called into the chief's office, I should have known I shouldn't be contradicting the Governor. I would never have dreamt of saying that had I not worked in the BSU.

What lessons do you think the SPS learned during the almost 22 years that the BSU was in operation?

I think the Special Unit was absolutely necessary at the time of its conception and up until the 1990s when we saw the culmination of a decade of chaos and disruption in Scottish prisons. Whether by accident or intention, the lessons learned from the life of the BSU have now become embedded in the culture of the Scottish Prison System. Regimes are now built around the quality of relationships between staff and prisoners, based upon mutual respect, opportunities for personal development and most importantly making a difference to the lives of those within their care. Even when things do break down and a prisoner needs to be removed from mainstream circulation, every effort is made to reintegrate them as soon as possible.

What did you think when you heard that the BSU was closing? How did you find out about it?

A Small Units Steering Group had been set up to consider the ongoing benefits of small units for difficult prisoners. I was a member of a group of senior managers with which the Steering Group was consulting. I was aware of the direction in which things were going and so the BSU's discontinuance came as no surprise. Aside from the fact that prison regimes had improved beyond measure, and the need for special arrangements for only a few prisoners had receded, special units were very staff intensive and expensive to operate. They could only cope with a single figure number of prisoners at a time and over a lengthy period, so very few prisoners have access to them. Whilst it was right for its time, I no longer believe there is a need for special units like that which existed at Barlinnie. I think it was like any experiment, it eventually runs out of steam. Therefore, we needed a decision made; is it right to keep it or should it go? It was ready to close, but the BSU was remarkable when you look back at it.

PART II
VOICES FROM WITHIN THE UNIT

CHAPTER 7

Port in the Storm

Johnny Steele

I was sentenced at the Glasgow High Court to 12 years in prison for a couple of botched robberies along with three other accomplices. When I heard the judge sentence me to 12 years in prison, I felt something inside me die. My three co-accused received five years, but I was seen to be, by the judge, the ringleader, which was far from the truth. I heard a mournful wail come from my mother at the back of the court as this sentence was passed on me, which would haunt and torment me for the rest of my days. How I would manage to get through this act of self-destruction, I had no clue. I felt that life for me was worthless; I had let all those that I loved dearly down, including myself. With all these regrets on top of the pain of long-term confinement, I had to try to find a way through this.

To my surprise the authorities at Barlinnie Prison informed me that I was soon to be transferred to the most dangerous prison in Scotland, HMP Peterhead. This Victorian prison was built in the 1880s and had a fearsome reputation throughout Britain for its brutal and inhumane regime and punishments, one could cut through the atmosphere and tension with a knife. It was a system void of all humanity and geared to break the spirit to stop re-offending. It was nothing other than a 'hate factory'. This was my first impression the day I arrived nigh on 23 years old and looking much younger than my age.

I learned in the coming days that most of the prisoners were very bitter and angry and would talk of mutiny and escapes, as well as hunger strikes and work strikes. This sort of attitude was 'music' to my ears and it was much easier for me to rebel against such a system than to accept it. The daily routine had us up in the morning at six o'clock to empty our chamber pots, often overflowing with urine and shit as hundreds of prisoners made their way to the Victorian ablutions to empty their pots. Half an hour later, breakfast was brought into the halls and every prisoner was fed in their cells amongst the stench and filth. We were sent out to work at 8 am for less than £1 sterling a week. We were sent back into the cells for lunch at 12 noon, then out to the exercise yard for one hour with as many as 100 cons playing football in a small yard with warders watching every move. There were many fights and stabbings, and oftentimes suicides and prisoners being transferred to the state mental hospital. After each witless work day there was a recreation period for a spell where prisoners would sit in cells, some playing poker or just generally talking or reminiscing, while others were plotting and planning riots and escapes. Once a week we were allowed to send a letter to family or friends, this left a lot of prisoners feeling frustrated and angry. There were no phone calls back then so all communication was done by mail, and all outgoing or incoming mail was censored by warders. To break any rules meant being taken to the punishment block for however long was deemed necessary by the Governor or Visiting Committee.

I had been in and out of institutions all my life, so punishments were nothing new to me. My first spell in the punishment block was for attempting to escape down a tunnel in the prison football field for which I received 28 days in solitary confinement and forfeiture of 60 days remission. In the punishment block there were rules to be adhered to and one of those was 'NO TALKING'. I would pace the floor most of the day whilst reminiscing about home, family and friends. Being left alone with my thoughts was the most painful part of the punishment. I found it hard to escape from inside my own head, so I started to sing out loud to entertain myself and my fellow cons. There were occasions when the warders would use brute force to try to restore good order but this didn't work, neither did continuous punishments resulting in more time in solitary confinement.

I had been involved in two serious riots and managed to escape which resulted in me getting a further three year sentence to run consecutively with my 12 years. In a short period of time, I had lost all four years' remission from my 12 year sentence. Although it was painful to have to live like this, it never really deterred me. If anything, it made me more determined to fight on. On many occasions I was sent to Porterfield Prison (HMP Inverness) to be detained in a cage which was built inside of a prison cell. On the wall facing the metal bars of The Cage there was a fairly large mirror so that any time you looked in the mirror you would see yourself in this cage like an animal. There was really no purpose for the mirror to be there other than to have a damaging psychological effect. We fought back by any means—through assault, trying to cut through bars, throwing our own urine and shit at the guards and smearing it all over ourselves, locks, walls and windows. The conditions were brutal. So many years had somehow flown by with so many punishments, and additional prison sentences. In the eight years of my time at Peterhead Prison the Governor informed me that I was 'on record' as the most punished and disruptive prisoner in the penal history of Scotland.

Then one day in 1986, my cage gate opened and I was taken into a room. There were five men sitting there in plain clothes with no table between us. I felt very on edge because I could not understand why there wasn't anything between us. They saw the expression on my face as I was wondering why there was no table and they told me that they had removed the table deliberately to try to make me feel more comfortable. I was offered a seat and I sat down. The way that they spoke to me made me feel at ease. There were no prison officers from The Cages present at that meeting. They told me to relax because they had a lot to talk to me about. They had come to tell me about a prison unit that they thought that I could benefit from. At that point my mind was more focused on thinking that it might be much easier to escape from such a place, than trying to make sense of the regime and ethos they were describing to me.

They told me they were concerned about me coming from such a hostile environment and the way that I had been living since the start of my 12 year sentence (which by then had been increased to 16 years). They told me that they had never seen a prison record like mine. What they articulated to me about the Barlinnie Special Unit (BSU) had me confused. I was already confused just sitting there in front of them being spoken to and treated like a normal human being. After the meeting with the BSU team and the psychiatrist, I was confronted with the Inverness Prison guards who escorted me back to my cage and left me there, where I tried to make sense of what I'd been told. It seemed to me that I was being offered a chance to escape from this old prison system to another more humane one—one which would offer me sanctuary from this hell hole. The BSU seemed like a port in the storm.

I thought long and hard about what was on offer there—family visits every day and night, the trust which they said would be given to me to run my own affairs, and other opportunities which seemed endless. As I was struggling to come to terms with this opportunity, weighing up the pros and cons, a voice in my head was telling me to tell them all to go to hell and stay put! I didn't realise how damaged my head was until trying to make a rational and comprehensive decision. I wondered at times if I were mentally ill.

Four weeks later I was taken to the BSU. I was taken to a part of Barlinnie that I'd never seen before, this part was separated from the rest of the prison and no guards from the main prison were allowed entry. This unit had its own prison rules and regulations, and no member of staff in the BSU had access to the main prison. There were only ever seven prisoners kept in this small cell block. I was greeted at the door leading to a small exercise yard by a couple of guards and prisoners who welcomed me in as if I was visiting them. Someone called a special meeting and, within minutes, all the staff and prisoners made an appearance to welcome me to the Special Unit. I knew all of the prisoners there and was surprised to see how healthy they looked. They were also all wearing civilian clothes.

I was officially welcomed into the BSU community by everyone there. It was a strange feeling being among my old friends from the punishment block where we so often rebelled and rioted, going on dirty protests and throwing our excrement at the guards. I noticed a couple of Peterhead Prison guards there who I had a few run-ins with during my time there. Ironically, they were now part of the Barlinnie special experiment. All the prison guards were volunteers in this regime which was like no other in the UK. The visits took place in our own cells where we could sit with our families, wives or girlfriends. The unit ran on trust. If there was ever an issue between any prisoners or staff someone would have to call a special meeting to hopefully help resolve the matter. From where I was sitting at the meeting, I could hear children laughing and playing in the cells area. It turned out to be some of the prisoners' children. No violence could ever take place here as it meant instant removal for anyone, and that went for both prisoners and staff.

I was told that should I feel uncomfortable for any reason I should talk to someone or call a meeting to help resolve any problems. I was amazed to discover that so much help was at hand here with everyone eager to help. I wasn't used to this kind of dignity and it messed with my emotions. I was shown my cell and told to make it as homely and comfortable as possible and try to relax and get used to my new environment. When my fellow gaol pals brought their families and friends and introduced me to them, it crossed my mind that I could be hallucinating. I began to feel a desire to crawl back into my cage at Inverness Gaol as this new way of life felt uncomfortable.

None of our visitors were searched before or after visits, which took place from 8 am to 10 pm. It was all down to being discreet, though not everyone was and to be caught resulted in being put on sanctions which meant that instead of having visits in one's prison cell, visits would take place in the TV room with no privacy. As time went by, I began to feel more settled in my new environment. I was getting visits from my family on a daily basis; seeing cousins I'd never met before and aunts and uncles I'd not seen for a long time. I began to build up my confidence. The fight in me never seemed to go away but I had learned to use my tongue as a weapon. Often at the weekly meetings I would raise the subject of the brutal regime back in The Cages and punishment blocks, advocating for change and challenging the old regime to change.

There were people from all walks of life visiting the Special Unit. Many were from all over the world: penal psychologists, psychiatrists, penologists, guards from prisons in Canada, Australia, America and Germany—probation officials, law students, nurses, police and on and on. It was mentioned at many of the meetings that I was quite articulate when debating the prison regime, hence when most of these visitors came to the Special Unit, I was always asked if I could make myself available as their guide. Visitors couldn't turn up as they pleased, they had to write in to get permission and it would be put to the community. A vote would then take place. I don't know of anyone who was ever rejected.

One day the Governor read out a letter at the weekly meeting from the Scottish Debating Society who wanted to challenge the prisoners and staff to a penal reform debate. The Glasgow and Strathclyde University debating teams joined forces to challenge us. They were holders of the Observer Mace (later known as the John Smith Observer Mace) and champions in Scotland. There was a vote to see who was going to take part in the debate. No prisoners rose to the challenge, but the Governor and the unit's psychologist, David Cooke did. They needed a prisoner on board but still no-one rose to the challenge.

The Governor looked at me and said, 'Come on Johnnyboy, you can do this.' Everyone agreed with him so I put myself forward somewhat reluctantly. On the evening of the debate my family and friends turned up to watch me take part in the biggest challenge until then in my lifetime. The debating society turned up with many of their friends and followers. There were dozens of spectators all excited to take part in this historical moment inside Barlinnie Prison. Each of us had to give a three minute speech on the theme of 'Hang them and flog them or rehabilitate them?' I was for rehabilitation with my team. I had weeks to think about this evening knowing that I was going to be representing my fellow prisoners and society.

For years whilst in solitary confinement I often wrote my own songs and verse and would entertain my fellow prisoners at my cell window. On the evening of the debate, I was hit not by 'writer's blank' but by 'thinker's blank'. As I took the floor, I was aware of an eerie silence. I almost panicked and wanted to jump straight into a self-induced coma! Then out of nowhere, I started to recite a bit of verse which I wrote in the punishment block in Peterhead so many years ago:

'Ladies and gentlemen ...
There stands a gaol by the sea and some say it's reekin mad with sin ...
Some say it was the devil's den that erupted outta hell ...
And others say in their philosophical way
"Ah but it serves its purpose well!"
Now I'd likt tell a story, and facts I promise too,
That these gaols are full of decent guys ... but I'll leave that up to you ...
And should you find my judgement sound
Then I guess it says a lot,
For all the men who are in there, for any good in them to rot.'

I went on to tell them that there was no rehabilitation, and that as taxpayers they were being robbed by a system that was geared to break the spirit, a system that would fail in whatever it hoped to achieve, a system that was cruel beyond belief. As a result many prisoners were released back into society having become institutionalised, and soon ended up back inside again. I remember hearing everyone cheering and clapping. It felt great to realise that I was getting respect for once, for all the right reasons! We won the debate.

There were many opportunities at the Special Unit available to help the prisoners fulfil their day and commit themselves to something constructive—and perhaps alien to them. I tried many things to pass the time away exploring and discovering hidden and raw talents. There were some professional art students who volunteered to come to the Special Unit to work with us at least twice a week. The environment was ecstatic and healthy. It was easy to lose yourself in a world with so many opportunities. I met a friend, Barney Platts-Mills, a filmmaker from London who would visit me on an almost daily basis. He was interested in my past lifestyle in prison and wanted me to use my songs and verse to produce a prison musical at the BSU. I raised the matter at the following community meeting asking if there were any objections to me being allowed a super VHS camera into the unit to use in putting together my prison musical. It was unprecedented, and I believe a first in British penal history, for me to have access to my own video-recording equipment. I also took up some sculpting. I worked on a piece called 'The Burden'. It was a strange feeling for me to have known that I created this almost life size image of a figure on bended knee with a very, very large ball and chain on its shoulders and chain and bracelet attached to a leg. I was quite bewildered when studying the finished results and remember asking myself, 'Where did this come from?' The truth of the matter is it was more likely an image that had lain dormant within me for a very long time.

Sometime later I was visited by a young man called Tommy Sheridan. Tommy was a household name in Scotland. He was the common man's choice. He fought vigorously against the 'poll tax' and also attended and disrupted warrant sales. He was a champion to the people and also spent time in prison. During his sentence he was elected as a member of the Scottish Parliament. One day he came to visit me and as I was showing him around the Special Unit, he saw my sculpture and asked me about it. As he was studying it, I told him the story behind it. Then to my surprise he asked if he could borrow it to take to George Square in Glasgow! They organized a hunger strike where he and six others took part in the protest against the poll tax in Scotland. For seven days they slept in a small tent on a grassy verge as thousands of sympathetic members of the public and friends signed a petition against the poll tax.

Tommy had organized a flatbed lorry to come to the prison to collect and borrow my sculpture which I re-named 'The Burden of the Poll Tax'. It took six of us to get it onto the lorry. I was quite chuffed to know that my sculpture, which also represented me, was part of the fight against the poll tax. After the last day of the seven day hunger strike, the seven of them came to visit me at the Special Unit with a lorry carrying my sculpture following behind. I immediately congratulated them on their fight and began preparing a good old fashioned Scottish meal of minced meat, potatoes and vegetables.

I guess I owe my life to the prison officers and friends at the BSU for all their help without which I know I'd be dead. My life had been restored to me in instalments whereas in other parts of the system our lives were taken away from us in one go. For me, the BSU was the only port in the storm.

CHAPTER 8

Remembering Ken Murray

Jimmy Boyle and Bill Beech

Ken Murray and Jimmy Boyle in the Special Unit © Tony Riley 1975.

Ken Murray (1931–2007) was central to the creation and development of the Barlinnie Special Unit (BSU) in its early years until his transfer out of the unit to another establishment in 1979. This chapter shares the reflections of two men who worked closely with Murray in the BSU; Jimmy Boyle, who was a prisoner in the unit, and Bill Beech, an artist who worked in the unit in the early 1970s to support the men incarcerated there.

Jimmy Boyle

My first meeting with Ken Murray was memorable for the kind gesture he made. I had been transferred from The Cages in Inverness Prison to the BSU. Escorted into an office, Ken told me to have a seat then handed me a pair of scissors to cut open a brown paper parcel tied with string that held my worldly possessions. The previous six years of my confinement had been so strict that anything that could be used as a weapon was prohibited. My passive aggressive posture at that point registered the gesture while simultaneously dismissing it. He was the enemy. He wore the uniform, therefore, was one of them. It was as simple and straightforward as that. Years of such indoctrination defined who and what was authority. One of them will have a good day when a colleague is having a bad day, regardless, the prisoner will always be on the wrong end of whoever's bad day it is. It was him today, somebody else tomorrow. I've no doubt the staff's view was a mirror image of ours. Simply put, we lived as combustible, pent-up coils primed for instantaneous violence.

Two of the other prisoners already there were old friends. Ben and Larry had been in juvenile detention institutions with me since our teens. We had never known each other on the streets, but enjoyed camaraderie as prison pals. They had been transferred here a few weeks before, so tried to give me a breakdown on the place. There were two other prisoners, unknowns, which meant their purpose was to dilute the intensity we brought to the occasion. First off, my vocal cords were trashed after years of being unused by being in solitary confinement. This was indicative of where I was currently, emotionally, and psychologically. Animalised. No other word for it. I would need time to exercise my voice to hold a conversation, much longer to rectify what else was going on within. The big question for me and Larry was, could we be arsed? Both of us in our twenties, serving life sentences with further prison sentences for attacking prison officers. On top of that we were both awaiting trial for the attempted murder of six prison officers during a riot in The Cages. Both of us had a mind-set of never again being released. In the end, we were each sentenced to a further six and a half years for the Inverness riot and attempted murder of the prison officers.

Although all the staff in the BSU were volunteers and had some training on how to handle difficult individuals, it was obvious to us that the theory of dealing with us when in training fell flat when faced with the real thing. No surprises there. During the first tentative conversations between individuals, it was clear that Ken's interpretation of what we were doing here was different to that of a colleague whose ranking was equal to his. Whilst Ken's approach was a more cohesive humane version, his colleagues' were far from it. This added to our wariness and paranoia fearing that Ken was trying to lull us into a false sense of security. The less humane version espoused by his colleague simply reinforced our view of how we saw them anyway.

Ken stood out by being the Deputy Chairman of the Scottish Prison Officers' Association (SPOA). The history of this lot as far as we were concerned was that they tried to improve the members conditions at the prisoners' expense. It was incumbent on them to make us more dangerous, desperate, and violent to the media and anyone else that would listen. Never in their history had a guard ever been held responsible for bad behaviour against a prisoner. Never. They'd been held to account for assaulting a colleague, fraudulent behaviour within the administration but even then, it's settled within so that rarely does it go to a criminal court. The prison system is so loaded against the prisoner that for me, Ben and Larry, who spent our childhoods locked in these institutions, we lived by our own set of rules developed over the years of living here. Being rebellious was an integral part of that. In our own inarticulate way, we had found our true voice even though when expressing that voice, we were doubly damned. The only reason we were here in this building was because we demanded to be heard. As far as Larry and I were concerned, we had forsaken our freedom to do so. That was the price we had paid to be here. Larry had a further debilitating scourge in that over the years of his being rebellious he had become hooked on large doses of prescribed drugs. Ben, unlike us, had a determinate sentence of seven years so knew his release date. Having said that, he still put his neck on the line. It was thus we found ourselves in this place wondering what its real purpose was.

The gaps in the screws' training were obvious to us from the beginning. In trying to understand why we hated cops and screws so much, someone suggested we hated uniforms which brought them to wearing white medical coats as a cover. We had an equal distrust of psychiatric abuse, but no-one seemed to consider this. However, the one genius stroke they did get right was a weekly forum where all of us sat to discuss whatever was the issue of the moment. Hence our finding out about the reason for the white coats. I know that in the beginning most of us couldn't see the point of these meetings. It was a new concept that felt threatening. The fact that they had agreed to call the prisoners by their first names was awkward. We three did carry a wall of hate with us and in a strange sort of way Ben's hate was much more severe than that of me or Larry. Over the years in my conversations with them, from bits and pieces, I realised that they both had serious issues that related to their childhoods. Whilst my background included poverty and losing my Dad at four years old, I had a Ma that gave me lots of love. They, on the other hand, would let slip some awful family issues that reminded me how lucky I was. Having this intimate knowledge of them I understood why they were so impulsively aggressive which added to the fear the screws had. My violence was more calculated and was a means to an end. Although the building itself was small by traditional prison standards, it was much bigger than The Cages where we had been. There were 14 cells, seven on the ground floor, seven directly on top. There was a kitchen, a meeting/TV room, a space with a mini pool table and several offices for various people, including the prison Governor. There was also an outside yard whose walls were covered with razor wire and CCTV cameras. It's hard to describe how difficult it was for each of us to accept the Special Unit. The cell doors were unlocked at 6 am till 9 pm when we were again locked up. There was no structure to the day which in a way made it easier for me, Ben, and Larry as we were used to being in solitary confinement where we had nothing to do all day. The downside being that we had unlimited daily access to each other during this unlocked period which was unnerving. This degree of freedom was something we weren't used to. I can only guess that the intention was to encourage staff and prisoners to get to know each other, and in a strange way this did work.

At our first weekly meeting the unit Governor (the only one in civilian clothing) read out a prepared statement about the rules that would be put in place. We would each be given a spending allowance of two pounds a week to buy toiletries, etc. If we didn't take a shower once a week, we would be fined 20 pence, if we didn't keep our cell clean, we would be fined 20 pence. If our attitude towards prison staff was bad, 50 pence fine. These rules offended me, Ben, and Larry. We got up and walked out of the meeting as it struck at the core of our prison grievances. Because we came from the backgrounds we did, the assumption of the authorities was that we were from a low class who were incapable of keeping ourselves and our place of habitation clean. The truth is we wanted unlimited showers a day and access to proper disinfected cleaning materials to prevent cockroaches and vermin. This initial rupture created a stand-off between the two sides. In trying to ease the tension we were approached by a staff member of equal seniority to Ken. This guy had as bad a reputation amongst the prisoners as we had amongst the staff. He explained to us that they were aware that in the past batons made no impression on us, explaining that he and his colleagues were volunteers for the Special Unit and were trained to do things in a better way. Telling us that if we 'act' up they are trained to hold us down, giving us an injection that will put us out till we calm down and that on revival there will be no disciplinary measures. This served to heighten our paranoia and reinforce our views on the white medical coats. It simply enhanced our suspicions. The two other prisoners were excluded directly from these high-wire tensions, though it must have been scary for them being in the middle of it. In these early weeks the high levels of testosterone swirling around were unwieldy to say the least. It was an all-male environment devoid of any softness. An indication of the pressure we were under at that time which witnessed me, Larry, and Ben retreat to a cell where we would spend hours brooding. Larry sitting on the floor full of his prescribed drugs was in a state of oblivion, Ben and I sitting on the bed facing each other. The two of us would never do drugs, so we were clear headed, but suddenly out of nowhere we got into a crazy fight, attacking each other, drawing blood. No sooner had it started, we finished looking at each other asking how that had happened. It shocked both of us. It was down to the pressure of being here.

Although the Governor was the official leader, he had in reality become the invisible man. It was at this point Ken entered the picture. His entrance was timely as all of us were so adrift to a degree that was dangerous. He gave us his interpretation of how he viewed the unit and its potential. Although this was fairytale stuff to us at the time, what hit home was him being very honest and believable. He had obviously made a personal decision to be upfront with us regardless of the consequences. He explained how our past violence against prison staff meant officers resigned, creating a recruitment problem. He wanted to bring the violence to an end and, so with the consent of politicians and senior bureaucrats in the Prisons Department, this unit was the result. Ironically, this was during a Tory Government. The Scottish Minister in charge of prisons was Alick Buchanan-Smith, from a well-known Scottish wealthy family. The senior civil servant was Alex Stephen, and it was these two whom Ken negotiated with on behalf of the SPOA. He reassured us that they had our back, but we were all in at the deep end and should try to make it work. This meeting didn't resolve matters, but it did identify Ken as more thoughtful and substantive than some of his colleagues. In this way, he was our first contact of significance. Ken was very tall and slim with a craggy warm face, his eyes always registering interest. His authority was unlike that of his colleagues in that it had a very clear soft edge. When engaging with us prisoners, there was no sense of a stand-off, it was more of a welcoming embrace and done without looking over his shoulder. This surefootedness was a shining example to his peers, bringing the best out in them. He relished being in the thick of discussions between prisoners and staff, playing the role of instigator. He wasn't out to please anybody and in doing so was setting a tone that was non-threatening.

As an individual, I was having to get to grips with my many years of solitary and violence whilst at the same time making sense of what was going on here. I felt I had to have some continuity from what had gone before to where I was now. I abhorred the luxury of having a pillow, blankets, and a mattress so I put them out, retaining a blanket and a board on my bed which was bolted to the floor. I threw out my table and chair. I had been allowed one book a week so kept one book in my cell, the only difference now was that I could chose it myself. The fact that I could retreat to my cell to curl up alone was a life saver as I needed to get away from the others. I couldn't speak to anyone about it and didn't want to. That was respected. There were occasional acts of kindness. In my solitary years, I hadn't drunk tea and had never in my life tasted coffee. One day, Ben made me a coffee (my first ever) by boiling milk and putting in Nescafé (milky coffee) and I really liked it. Larry, with his misplaced judgement, would offer me some sleeping tablets, which of course I refused. In this way everyone during the first few months was struggling to adapt. All of this came to a head when a group of us happened to be in the main area. I have no idea how this began but suddenly Larry had a prison officer pinned to the wall with a pair of scissors pressed to his throat. Everyone froze except me and Ben who instinctively grabbed Larry, taking the scissors from him. It was a moment of silence with everyone looking at each other, no-one knowing what to do. Ken, who had emerged from the Governor's office took in the situation suggesting that we assemble in the meeting room. I handed the scissors to a prison officer. Once seated Ken asked what had brought this about? There was a long silence finally broken by the threatened staff member. He burst out crying, telling everyone his wife had a baby girl three weeks previously and he thought he would never see her again. This put a lump in everyone's throat, especially us prisoners who had never seen the other side of the offence. It also managed to penetrate Larry's drug fog. Thus began a dialogue about trust and the lack of it between us. This led to a frank discussion about how much we disliked each other as opposing groups. Ben and I expressed how badly we felt betraying Larry by taking the scissors from him. This was not normal behaviour for us. This meeting went on for the best part of five hours, with everyone exhausted.

I had suggested to the group that perhaps a good idea would be to invite outsiders to visit so that there would be independent voices amongst us. Ken agreed that this would be a good idea but that he would have to take it higher up the chain. This suggestion did have legs leading to further discussions about the sort of people we should invite and, after much debate, we settled on those from the art world thinking they would be more inclined to accept such an invitation. Our reputations were so bad that we were on tenterhooks about acceptance. I can't remember who it was, but someone had come across Joyce Laing, a practising Art Therapist working in a Glasgow Clinic. We, the prisoners, were wary of the therapy label but on her first visit we all got on well though it did raise issues for some of the staff. The idea of a woman mixing with us presented security issues for them. This inevitably brought tensions between the two groups. Disagreements like this were now being discussed in our meetings which by now had become the acceptable forum for resolving matters. It was during such an occasion that we as prisoners were recognising that some prison staff were struggling to come to terms with the place. Although, in the beginning we were dismissive, the fact is we were becoming more empathetic as time went on meaning relationships between us were starting to form.

Once Joyce was settled as a visitor, we tasked her with approaching other individuals or groups to visit. One of the first was the Director of The Citizens Theatre of my old district in the Gorbals. He was Giles Havergal, highly intelligent and perceptive. Having introduced himself he worked out that whenever there were gaps in his theatre schedule, he would bring members of the cast to visit. They did, working with us on improvisation, voice sessions and acting. These meetings were bringing home the message, telling us, don't take yourselves so seriously guys. Exactly what the doctor ordered. The volume of outsiders visiting the unit grew substantially. This coincided with the relaxation of prison rules. We were now allowed to wear our own clothing, have musical instruments. Larry, being an accomplished guitarist, poet and writer was able to have sessions with other visiting musicians. It was during this period that Joyce left a package of clay and, after some days, I opened it, doing two portraits, one of Larry, the other of Ben. It was like a creative dam burst open inside me. This moment changed my life forever being the first creative thing I had ever done. I was encouraged to take this further and did. I threw myself into studying art by reading everything and anything related to it, searching for art materials. I turned a vacant cell into an art studio. I had a sculpture stand in the prison yard where I could carve stone. An established Liverpool sculptor sent welding equipment to me as a gift which initially caused a great deal of anxiety in the hierarchy, but they allowed its safe passage.

These were tumultuous days for the BSU. Another important early visitor was the irrepressible Richard Demarco, art entrepreneur and gallerist. His role was very important, giving the unit an international platform introducing Joseph Beuys, the iconic German sculptor and artist. I had read about Joseph performing a piece in a New York Gallery. He spent one week in a cage with a coyote (America's most reviled animal) where they worked out a system of cohabiting throughout that week. Having spent so much time in a cage this piece resonated very powerfully with me. He introduced others such as Marina Abramovic, performance artist, and Tadeusz Kantor, an extraordinary Polish theatre director. Although some of these people were famous names in the art world, we hadn't a clue who they were, but we were learning fast. Richard offered to exhibit my sculptures in his gallery at the next Edinburgh Festival. True to his word he did. Lo and behold, against all my expectations, I was allowed a day out for the opening. I spent an afternoon of that day at a Joseph Beuys lecture where afterwards I introduced myself to him, 'Joseph, I Am The Coyote.' On that day my two escorting officers let me spend most of the day on my own, with a girlfriend and Richard. The level of trust we had built between us meant that I would not breach that, even though I had no future release date. The speed and diversity of change was exhilarating. We had community groups visit from deprived areas in Glasgow and Edinburgh. As community activists, they were trying to improve the quality of life for people living in the areas we came from. This was an invaluable connection as it kept us informed of changes within our communities. Whilst we had been destructive forces while there, these groups were instruments for good, a lesson we badly needed to learn, and did. They encouraged me to use my newly found creativity to benefit kids in the area commissioning a sculpture for Craigmillar Community Festival. Taking the theme of Gulliver's Travels, I designed a version of Gulliver lying on his back with various play features to climb or slide down, envisaging the children playing on the figure as the Lilliputians. Once built by members of the local community it became the largest sculpture in Europe. In this sense, the unit became a focal point for groups and individuals internationally.

We had a visit from the Prisons Minister, Buchanan-Smith accompanied by Alex Stephen and an entourage of officials. The one thing that struck me about Buchanan-Smith was his leadership qualities. He wasn't being led by obfuscating officials. He took charge of the visit from beginning to end. Heading straight for me and Ken, he introduced himself to me, asking us both to show him around the place whilst simultaneously telling his officials not to come. Once alone in the cell area he stopped. Looking us both in the eye he made it clear that he was hanging his political hat on this place succeeding. Turning to me he said that we now had an international platform, 'Alex's [Stephen's] worry is that the prisoners may mess it up. I'm depending on you to ensure that won't be the case.' I assured him that I'd play my part. To have this degree of political backing was so important for the place and solidified the leadership role of me and Ken. I have to qualify this by clarifying that Ken had vast experience as a negotiator and, so for me, it was a masterclass in how to deal with problems without getting too deeply involved emotionally. The unit seemed to have a strong cultural gravitational force in that having brought in the art world, then the community activists we now seemed to be in the political phase. Soon after the meeting with Buchanan-Smith, an unassuming woman called Kay Carmichael was introduced. She was the Head of Social Services for Glasgow. A calm, quiet spoken person, one arm afflicted by polio in her childhood, she was married to Neil Carmichael MP. Her brother-in-law was also an MP, both Labour Party. It was obvious that Kay was a force to be reckoned with in her own right. Just after the first anniversary of the Special Unit the Labour Party came to power under the leadership of Harold Wilson. Ken was an active member of the party so between him and Kay we assumed things could only get better. What we didn't realise is that with a change of Government it brings tremendous upheaval in the Civil Service. This meant losing our two most powerful supporters in one fell swoop, Buchanan-Smith, and Alex Stephen. Initially this didn't mean much with a newly elected, and hopefully, sympathetic Labour Party. Little did we know.

Although the Special Unit as a community was making great strides in so many areas, our reality was that we were a small forward-thinking unit surrounded by a large traditional prison. This did create friction, especially between the two sets of staff. Although the unit staff worked in a separate place, both shared housing quarters and the officers' social club where they lived cheek by jowl. The dynamics of this are no different from that of the prisoners in that the loudest voices hold sway. The resentment of the traditionalists was growing. This first manifested itself by Ken being dismissed as the Deputy Chairman of the SPOA. The very people who pleaded with him to find a solution to our violence were the same ones who voted him off. The demise of his influential status as a union rep was another example of his knowledge and understanding of process. We were more upset than he was. His great strength was his principles and the value of debate, something he strongly emphasised to junior staff. The real issue for them was how it was affecting their families. Although the prisoners were encouraged to follow pursuits in the arts or education, or like Larry with his music, the staff were also encouraged to pursue university degrees on a part-time basis and a few of them did so. Over time those who went into further education were more resilient to the traditional staff pressures than those who were immersed in the prison infrastructure. Ken was a formidable protector of these junior staff, but regardless the challenges of adjusting to living and working here were difficult. All of us were tested, no one was immune. Amidst this upheaval we found Larry dead in his cell because of the drugs he was being prescribed. I am firmly of the view that it was accidental and not suicide. This was something that I had always feared would happen and now that day had arrived. His death brought the predictable tabloid headlines of sex and drugs in the Special Unit. There was one MP, Teddy Taylor, a Tory, who was forever calling for our closure and that was expected. However, it did provoke a visit from the new Prisons Minister from the new Labour administration, Harry Ewing MP. His visit was straightforward and friendly enough. He was not the sort to set the heather on fire, that's for sure. We were all taken aback the next day; the tabloid headlines of him being quoted as saying 'Boyle is running the place' suggesting that the unit was out of control and that he would implement severe measures. Alick Buchanan-Smith he was not. The truth is, and as a Labour supporter I hate saying so, but they were absolute cowards and an embarrassment when it came to supporting the place. It was almost inevitable when bending to the hardliners' will that Ken was transferred back to the main prison. He had long been a target of those who resented progress. Being the sort of person he was, he simply shrugged in that calm determined way. There is no doubt that he was the prime motivator in the Special Unit being in existence, therefore, we all knew that being removed must have been a serious blow to him. He never once showed any negative reaction. Instead, he spoke of what we had achieved and could go on to do. He made it clear that he would remain a staunch supporter, and he did. He was ever vigilant even from a distance.

There was now a clear shift in thinking from the top. The BSU had to be reined in. I had been told in no uncertain terms that the day release I had (about three days in total) were things of the past. Being a serial diarist with an ancient Olivetti typewriter I wrote about life in the place as I lived it. I wrote my autobiography *A Sense of Freedom,* which sold successfully and became a movie. All the proceeds I gave to a charity to help underprivileged kids. I co-authored a play *The Hard Man*, which toured internationally. My sculptures were exhibited in galleries around the country. Despite all of this when given a liberation date for 1 November 1982, I was ordered to serve the last 30 months in a traditional prison to be 'tested', just to be sure I wasn't conning everyone.

The synchronicity of that period of the early 1970s is worth considering. Getting together with Giles Havergal and his crew at The Citizens Theatre, whose whole artistic thrust was to deconstruct traditional plays by presenting modern interpretations creating philistine tabloids to headline them 'sodomy, nudity, queer shagathons', and the Richard Demarco Gallery whose visionary director understood that art only had relevance if it benefited society as a whole. To accomplish this endeavour Richard created art in war zones and prisons. He was breaking the mould, moving art from its elitist platform into troubled zones which it serves better. In response, his grant from the Scottish Arts Council was removed. It's no coincidence that we turn up, trying to shift a failed prison system into something that will benefit society by healing people, not destroying them. They closed the unit.

On my release from prison, I saw Ken on a regular basis. Still as positive a force for change, he was elected a Labour councillor in Glasgow, and even here he stood head and shoulders above the rest. I continued a friendship with Ken until he died. There is no doubt in my mind that had it not been for Ken Murray's courage and integrity, I would not have survived my prison sentence. He kept apart from the pack regardless of the pressure and that must have been considerable. My life has taken many a bizarre twist and turn, but none more so than to proclaim that a prison officer saved my life. I had infrequent contact with Joyce, speaking to her days prior to her death. Both have been immeasurable influences in my life and that of many others. I write this now coming into my eightieth year having since my release from prison made a reasonable contribution to the wider society. Simply put, the BSU was a gaol that brought out the best in people.

Bill Beech

To put it simply, Ken Murray was one of the most decent human beings I have had the privilege to know. Most people who worked with him for any length of time would, I believe, say the same thing. I first met Ken on my first ever visit to the Special Unit in June 1974. I'd never been in a prison before, so crossing the threshold of the Barlinnie main gate was a big deal for me. I was struggling, coming to terms with the environment. I didn't take anything at first from the fact Ken was dressed in a white coat, until I learnt this distinguished the Special Unit staff as nursing officers from the rest of the prison. That was the difference, as the Chief Nurse Officer, Ken accepted a heightened responsibility of care and mentoring, always as an advocate of reform and championing the need for a redemptive penal system.

I soon discovered Ken was also giving support beyond the wire in areas of social justice. A committed Labour Party member, he took his political views into his role as vice chair of the Social Committee of Strathclyde Regional

Council. Eventually he also worked with the Glasgow Association for Mental Health and the Scottish, and UK, Drugs Forum.

Ken cared, he was a true socialist through and through. He was at his very best when he was helping people, on the side of the underdog, dealing with problems where the existing system had simply failed. This was certainly the case in the early 1970s with five prisoners who had earned the reputation as the most violent in Scottish prisons. Ken realised the system couldn't handle them, and it had run out of ideas; they were reduced to holding human beings like animals in solitary confinement in the notorious cages of Porterfield Prison for two and a half years.

Ken knew there had to be better ways of treating violent offenders. The background story is well known, there was a meeting of minds, Ken, Secretary of the SPOA, together with Alex Stephen, the Controller of the Scottish Prisons where they agreed to a solution that was to define their whole careers in the Prison Service. Violent prisoners like Boyle and Winters should be kept out of the mainstream, yes, but in a maximum-security community with a diametrically different approach to anything else in the system. The idea was prisoners, as well as staff, would be given a voice in making decisions and setting the agenda. It was an extraordinary proposition.

Risky? Of course. It was famously illustrated when Ken offered Jimmy Boyle a pair of scissors to cut the string as he opened his parcel of belongings on his first day in the new unit. Did it work? Well, for Boyle, yes, it did spectacularly. Ken said right at the start he had to make a gesture of trust, defining the new regime and placing the onus on the inmates in a way they had to respond. Ken then had an even more difficult problem of encouraging the proposal within the membership of the SPOA, arguing such change was long overdue and was just as important to his members as the offenders. Radical stuff indeed but it proved a very difficult idea for the majority of the SPOA to accept, as it was for the right-wing Tory Government of Margaret Thatcher and the Minister for Scotland, Teddy Taylor.

What Ken and Alex Stephen determined in Scotland stood in sharp contrast to the position South of the border. In England the solution to dealing with violence amongst lifers with no hope of release was to introduce the notorious Control Units.

Even more controversial in the Special Unit was Ken's idea to shift the focus onto the creative potential of inmates, an idea which would never have worked without Alex Stephen giving institutional support bringing in the Art Therapist Joyce Laing, encouraging the move to a relaxed approach to family visits, and encouraging other visitors from diverse cultural backgrounds. Ken was forced to protect the idea every day on every front, the most difficult battle internally with his own union members who understandably were concerned so much licence was given, and trust expected of, inmates with records of violence like Boyle and Winters. You could feel the resentment every time you entered the main gate of Barlinnie, I felt it in the evenings when I went with Ken for a drink in the Prison Officers' Club, but Ken was always there, tirelessly defending the idea that the deprivation of liberty was the punishment for the offence, the only hope to head off more violence and reoffending was to place an emphasis on rehabilitation, not further physical punishment.

You only have to read, or to listen to what prisoners had to say about Ken to understand how much his commitment, understanding and the political skill on the ground was central to the experiment. Ken was essentially a practitioner and there is a great irony in the fact that unlike Boyle, Winters and Hugh Collins, the experience he gained and shared with them was never set down in print. Ken's way was always immediate, if there was a problem, then get to the bottom of it and solve it. Ken took every opportunity to take advantage of any platform offered to him to proselytise or defend the Special Unit experiment. He made frequent excursions South across the border to talk at conferences, to students where I was working in Sheffield, Hull or Brighton, to meet the British Association of Art Therapists in Leeds, or appear on the panel at the premier of *Silent Scream* at the Brighton Festival. Ken's great skill was making a direct connection with people and bringing clarity and understanding to complex arguments, and this skill was tested to the limit at times in the Special Unit community meetings.

Ken, together with Boyle, representing the prisoners, held the whole thing together. This is not to say the governors were sidelined, but they were always in a difficult situation. Given the democratic management of the Special Unit, the governors had to steer a difficult path between the interests expressed in the community meetings and what they could expect to be accepted within the demands made by the main prison system. Ken could point to the drop in violence in the system, clear evidence he would say, in support of a redemptive penal system. On the other hand he recognised that some considered the prisoners were just exploiting what was a cushy number, a waste of precious taxpayers money that ought to be better spent on more urgent and deserving social needs such as supporting victims of violence.

Ken's life became increasingly dominated by the Special Unit and the political battle for reform of the prison system. Knowing just how much Ken was taking on was a constant worry to Meg, his wife, who would voice concern when I stayed with the family on my trips from Brighton. Meg saw the toll and cost mounting on the health of her husband as the system inexorably moved against him. The calls for the Special Unit's closure became more strident the more it challenged the orthodoxies. Ken realised the unit was becoming a victim of its own success and the death of Larry Winters from a drug overdose in 1977 was a body blow to everything in terms of the unit's future. It was Ken who said I should do something with the work Larry and I had done over the years to help counter the awful publicity that emerged. Ken and I understood that Larry had an addiction, but his addiction was produced by the system, drugs had been used not only for his medical condition but also as a means of controlling him. He had come a long way in the Special Unit but the damage had been done long before.

I remember, it was half time at a Partick Thistle game when Ken was watching his beloved team, that he told me the Prison Service were moving him and Jimmy Boyle out of the Special Unit. Ken knew it was because they were the outspoken public face of the Special Unit and sure enough Boyle was transferred back into the main prison system, despite much protest from the growing list of supporters. It even made the international art press with the great German artist philosopher Joseph Beuys going on hunger strike in 1981, even making a work of art about it called 'Jimmy Boyle Days', which can still be seen hanging in the great *Hamburger Bahnhof* gallery in Berlin. Ken's transfer followed and with it the flame in Ken grew dimmer. On his retirement Ken held a celebratory dinner for a small group of us and toward the end of the evening Ken turned the topic of conversation to how the script I was working on was going. By that time, I'd been commissioned by Alan Fountain at C4 to develop the screenplay for a film about Larry Winters' life. It was there that David Hayman offered help and, together with the wonderful Glasgow filmmakers, we went on the make *Silent Scream*.

Some time after Ken's death, Meg came to stay with us in Lewes and I realised how little recognition Ken had been given for championing one of the most important radical developments in British penal history. It is why I have devoted considerable time and energy to preserving the archive of material Ken entrusted to me and have been duty bound to curate exhibitions celebrating his work and the achievements of the Special Unit over the years. The archive dedicated to Ken Murray is considerable and deserves to be developed with a priority for an appropriate venue and space for an exhibition in Scotland.

CHAPTER 9

What Happened in the Later Years of the Barlinnie Special Unit?

Interview with Dan Gunn by Mike Nellis

Dan Gunn was Governor of the BSU from 1988 to 1991 (towards the end of its life). The following interview took place in February 2024.

What had been your background prior to becoming Governor of the BSU?

The summer of 1988 saw me receive what was only my second promotion — to the BSU — in a career which had started in 1975. My first had only been three years earlier. Those three years had been very dramatic both for the Scottish Prison Service (SPS) and for myself. The SPS had been rocked by conflict on a massive scale, involving losing control in various halls in many prisons, including Peterhead. The organizational consequences of these unparalleled events were to prove massive and immediate. One specific change was a shift to promotion supposedly on merit rather than, in the past, on seniority. In 1985, following my first promotion, I had been sent to what was then Wakefield Staff College in England to oversee the training of assistant governors, with an expectation I would be there for five years. But a mere two years later, I was seconded to the team in SPS opening up HMP Shotts Phase 2, and within six months of that I was tasked with setting up a Training and Development Unit at the SPS College. Less than a year later, I was saying goodbye to the college, having overseen the first course, based on a radically different format and content, for training prison officers, and walking through the door in Barlinnie marked 'Special Unit', as the new Governor.

How well prepared were you for the role of BSU Governor?

I was arguably well-prepared compared to my nine somewhat unenthusiastic predecessors. Early in my career, I had been involved in putting prisoners forward for the unit. My role was very low level but, nevertheless, I had been introduced to the process and complexities of selection because for four eventful years I had been C Hall governor in HM Prison Perth, which had had more than its fair share of Scotland's 'problematic' prisoners. Following my transfer to HM Prison Dungavel (now an Immigration Centre, formerly a pioneering low security prison) in 1981, I was again involved in considering prisoners but this time in taking them back from it. Generally, transfers went smoothly, although one transferee subsequently mounted a brief rooftop protest. Given that it was peaceful, with no damage to the building, it perhaps suggests his experience in the unit was a success. My other source of preparation was a colleague, David Croft, who had worked in the unit for several years in the 1970s. I had the immediate benefit of working with him prior to my promotion, and he shared his insights into what was involved. In addition to my extensive casework knowledge, I was in effect the first *volunteer* Governor of the BSU. It had been something of a talking point in SPS over the previous 15 years that everyone in the unit was a 'volunteer', except the Governor—they were simply ordered to take up the post as, in fact, all governors were. But the days of going in to work to be given a brown envelope containing the dreaded letter beginning 'Dear [surname only], it has been decided to transfer you to...' were coming to an end. SPS Human Resources brought in a new scheme to involve governors more in their moves, asking them to give three preferences, from which one would be selected. I included the BSU as one of mine. I suspect I was the only one to do so, because this post had not been remotely popular with my colleagues.

What did the SPS expect of you as BSU Governor?

I had expected a briefing of some sort from my line management—notably Operations, in HQ—which had itself recently experienced far-reaching change at every level from the top down. However, nothing came. I did then receive an invitation to meet the Head of Policy instead, which included casework.

That entailed an informal chat, instigated by a career civil servant with whom I had previously had very little contact. The most memorable moment came at the end: he wished me well and advised me that, if I left the unit with my integrity and reputation intact, I would be doing better than most of my predecessors. This downbeat line was a suitable antidote to any excessive idealism still lingering in me. As for Operations, I learned slowly that what they wanted was never to hear of, or from, me while in post.

Were there any early incidents in your time as Governor?

At the end of a quick, verbal handover in the unit, my predecessor casually mentioned, 'Oh, by the way, you have a royal visit coming up'–HRH The Princess Royal, in her capacity as Patron of the Butler Trust. Alas, alarm bells did not ring, and I made the mistake of assuming that everything was already in place, especially given the tight timescale. However, I soon found that prisoners, who expected, at the very least, to be consulted on everything pertaining to the unit, had not been briefed as to what was involved and were unwilling to accept extensive security searches by the police. Much difficult discussion followed: it was touch and go, but eventually the prisoners acquiesced. The visit itself went smoothly, with the only unexpected moment—bordering on crisis—being a prisoner's visitor trying to lobby the Princess Royal about a health issue of a family member. While I was immediately taken aback, the Princess Royal did not seem concerned at all, handling the matter with skill and sensitivity and moving on adroitly. The legacy of the royal visit, for me, was a deeper insight into decision-making in the unit, the need to involve everyone, and—just in case I had any doubt—recognising the severe limits to my 'power' as Governor. The unit had been deeply divided between management and prisoners over the visit, and while it did seem to come together quite quickly afterwards, I was unsure for a time how adverse my personal legacy was. I was perceived by some prisoners as not having stood up for the unit (over the searches), thus betraying its principles of independence and personal trust. I became part of 'them', not 'us'. At HQ, the visit was deemed to have been a marked success without anyone knowing, or probably caring, about the acrimonious lead-up and the numerous potential pitfalls. My credibility externally was intact and conceivably enhanced, but among the prisoners I was someone who had quickly exhausted any honeymoon *goodwill*, and was viewed with suspicion.

Who was in the BSU at the time you went there?

I inherited a mere five prisoners in summer 1988, which historically was only a little on the low side. Two prisoners had been ejected before my arrival for possession of illegal alcohol. In practice, the unit had existed with a norm of five to seven prisoners, although the residential area contained ten cells, two rows of five. I asked HQ if I could review the waiting list, but was told—for the first time—there was no waiting list. This seemed to be surprising, given the levels of violence in the prison estate over the previous three years. I made it clear to all and sundry that I wanted more prisoners and therefore many more referrals. I thought this would be both good for the unit and help us to make a bigger contribution to the mainstream adult long-term prison. But there was clearly a reluctance by governors to nominate candidates. I had to reflect carefully on what I might do to change this, and how quickly. The ethos of the unit was supposedly about managing violent prisoners—prisoners who had either been violent during their sentence to date or were perceived as an extreme threat to good order. However, on looking at the population I had inherited, I found that the entry criteria had been interpreted very liberally. Only three had been violent, and not recently. Another one had been a troublesome somewhat infamous prisoner decades earlier, but he was at this point simply marking time. The fifth was an enigmatic individual who claimed to have an eating disorder which stopped him eating prison food. Even today there is no consensus as to whether this was genuine or an elaborately sustained deception. This individual became unique in another sense, when he was given parole and released directly from the unit, which had not previously been allowed or even remotely considered good practice.

Did you manage to increase prisoner numbers over your time in the unit?

My attempts to increase the numbers led initially to an unexpected challenge. I was asked by HQ to take back a prisoner who had earlier been moved out of the unit. My senior staff protested vehemently, claiming a longstanding policy of 'once out never back'. There was nothing actually written to that effect anywhere, so I agreed we would consider him in the normal way. The prisoner concerned was someone I had known from my Perth days. Ultimately, our assessment team did not see any value in bringing him back for 'more of the same'. My report was accepted at HQ without any comeback, much to my surprise.

Eventually my strategy for increasing numbers worked, but eight came to be our absolute maximum. This was a success for me, but I had the nagging question as to whether or not this was the right eight who should actually be there, both in terms of their personal needs, and the system's needs. One undoubtedly met our 'official' criteria, and continued to be extremely aggressive: he was frequently challenged, but with seemingly limited effect. Much later, I was asked to consider a prisoner with a high profile in the media who was not in any way proving violent in custody, but was causing the system acute management difficulties because he was protesting his innocence and not accepting prison food. We assessed him in the normal way and decided to take him, a decision appreciated by headquarters as a problem which, if not totally solved, was at least parked elsewhere and therefore helpful in managing the mainstream population. The prisoner's greater opportunities to promote his case while in the unit were viewed by HQ as less of a problem than the need to prevent his death via a high profile hunger strike. I did not see his case out. A month after his admission in 1991, I was summoned to the Human Resources Director's office to be told I was being transferred. The earlier, more liberal consultation process about transfers prevailing three years earlier had been discontinued. As I was, by then, the second longest serving Governor of the BSU, I was now keen to move and offered no protest—which would, of course, have been pointless. There was an immediate 'conspiracy theory' among the unit staff that my transfer was the quid pro quo for me having delivered this latest controversial admission because it wasn't popular with staff or prisoners. From my point of view, there was no link. There was perhaps a legitimate staff concern that somehow the admission rules and eligibility criteria had been, if not broken, then tweaked. But the usual process of a joint staff management interview team had been followed and there was a unanimous agreement to admit the prisoner. The transfer did undoubtedly help him cope with his imprisonment and ensured the SPS's ability to manage him safely—and the unit in fact took its increase to a record population in its stride.

How did the staff group function in the BSU while you were there?

I inherited a staff group who had been in the unit for some considerable time. One member had enjoyed two promotions in situ and become my acting Deputy Governor, which allowed him to claim that he had held every post in the unit. Experience, I was told repeatedly, was critical for a smooth functioning unit. While this was a tenable argument, what concerned me was staff complacency, and the danger of seeing any crisis that arose not on its own merits but through the prism of the past, 'the way things used to be done'. My opportunity for changing this situation came quickly. Several staff applied for promotion. I offered them all a mock board, which was novel and accepted with alacrity. Everyone who applied was successful. This was very good for the unit's profile and reputation as well as further proof of the changing criteria of promotion. Unit staff had considerable skill and expertise in prisoner interaction, case work and conflict prevention, capabilities which were arguably unique to them and staff in HMP Dungavel, where the concept of group officer—which required these skills—had been pioneered since the mid-1970s. However, not all unit staff demonstrated their expertise and commitment in the preferred fashion. One officer, not noted for his level of activity, seemed to sit on 'his chair' for most of his shifts and did eventually leave. A prisoner told me he 'missed' him. I explained that he had been transferred, to which his response was, 'Did he take his chair with him?'

So, with the benefit of a new enthusiastic senior management team, and significant inputs from our psychologist and psychiatrist, new staff selection criteria were devised and a much more rapid turnover achieved. A two year tour of duty was optimal in my view, and I hoped that ex-BSU staff could be successful catalysts for change wherever they moved on to serve. Creating these changes in the unit overlapped with an external commitment I had been allowed to retain from my Staff College time, which was to devise and deliver what became the Higher National Certificate in Prison Studies. This was to run for eleven years.

How would you characterise the BSU 'regime' while you were Governor?

The term 'regime' has military overtones and has never been a favourite of mine. However, prison practitioners and policy-makers have yet to come up with a more acceptable label to describe the full range of prisoner activity. So, what of the BSU regime? The early years undoubtedly were heavily influenced, if not dominated, by art and, in particular, sculpture. The unit did 'discover' and develop at least two prisoners, who had considerable, if not exceptional, talent. Other forms of cultural activity were pursued at different times and by different inmates. These are all documented elsewhere. In retrospect, the retiral (before my time) of Joyce Laing, the unit's remarkable Art Therapist, saw the emphasis on such activities diminish appreciably. During my time, we were only able to keep the making of art going in small ways. At a later unit event, I had the privilege of meeting Joyce and, for my sins, she soundly and emphatically upbraided me for not doing nearly enough to promote the 'artistic' scene.

We did pioneer a project making Tolkien's characters. This aroused some interest, including from some visitors. It would be hard to argue that it had much impact on any prisoner's attitude to, or expertise in 'art', but it did finish, to an exemplary standard, which were both considerable achievements. Subsequently, it went on a tour of Glasgow city libraries. One prisoner in the unit during my time did claim to write several plays. It was easy to mock, given his dubious writing skills, but to his credit he was trying his best. Among his interests was understanding his upbringing in a mixed religious household, Catholic and Protestant. This was topical at the time but it was a theme well worth exploring from 'the inside'. As it happened, on my last working day as Governor I attended a production of one of his plays in Cumbernauld. Some unit inmates wrote their autobiographies, with or without permission. At least one was largely, if not totally, written during his time in the unit and this caused me no end of problems. Glasnost had not yet reached the inner recesses of the SPS, although it was coming. I did indulge in somewhat topical banter, for want of a better term with the then Governor of HMP Barlinnie, suggesting that while he was pursuing glasnost, I was focused on perestroika, topical terms at the time. He was doing a remarkable job at the time in trying to change the overall Barlinnie culture which included a very proactive approach to media involvement. I was conscious that he and his deputy were very supportive of me in general and as a result I was able to draw on support from many departments and managers.

What were the visiting arrangements that prevailed in your time as Governor?

One of the key features of the unit's regime had always been open visiting. Any prisoner could invite anyone at any time. Visits were unsupervised and often took place in the prisoner's cell, although the door was meant to be open. For 'official' visitors who wanted to come, I had to go to the community meeting for approval. This was usually routine but occasionally questions were asked and obstacles presented. Official visitors, in my view, brought many benefits. The then new Chief Executive of the SPS used to visit regularly, simply to talk and listen to the prisoners' views. He just turned up without giving notice! Clearly he saw this as useful to him, helping to develop his knowledge and perhaps improving his credibility as someone who wanted to be seen as 'hands on'. The Secretary to the Scottish Home Department participated in a passionate discussion about AIDS in prison, with prisoners offering markedly different views without personal rancour. I said to him afterwards this was very rare, if not unique, for prisoners to disagree with each other in public and to comment on and even debate on such an emotive issue. This he readily acknowledged. On the downside, the retiring chair of the Parole Board on her last (of many) visits announced to everyone she had changed her mind and now thought prisoners should be released directly from the unit. I was aghast, indeed apoplectic.

One perennial source of division among the prisoners themselves was any media visit request. Some enjoyed and arguably thrived on what might be deemed media attention, while others were strongly opposed, fearful of drawing attention to themselves, reminding the public of their horrific crimes and the relative 'freedom' they enjoyed. Staff tended to be neutral on the value of such visits, but they rarely engaged with the media. Debates over access like this were on the whole good, bringing points of difference into the open but, remarkably, always producing an agreed decision which was then accepted without complaint. Children did visit with families on occasion, much to the annoyance of one prisoner, who was often angry with the noise they made. Occasional high-profile visitors would turn up, occasionally under the influence, creating one of many sources of conflict with staff on the main Barlinnie gate, requiring tactful diplomacy and, if that failed, escalation of the issue to senior Barlinnie management.

Were the community meetings still important?

The weekly community meeting of everyone in the unit on a Tuesday at one o'clock (of which minutes were taken) was — in theory at least — the highlight of the week. It was notionally democracy in action, involving prisoners, officers and the Governor. Every decision was minuted. Everything else would stop. Attendance was compulsory. Everyone sat in a circle with a different chairman every week, alternating between staff and prisoners. Having perhaps had excessive expectations of these meetings, I found them disappointing when I first arrived as they were often over in a few minutes with nothing of substance discussed — this was rather democracy 'inaction'. Given that these meetings were vital to the traditional purpose of the unit, it was obvious to me that I had to do 'something' about this, but exactly what? I tried a variety of techniques. I discovered relatively quickly that the objective for many participants was to sit on the right-hand side of the chair, as this would mean being the last one called to speak. Invariably, the chair went round the room clockwise, asking for questions or issues. So, I encouraged sometimes changing the order to counter-clockwise. Another lesson I learned about seating was this: it is much more difficult to disagree with someone who is sitting right beside you than sitting opposite you. Group work skills were literally learned 'on the floor'.

Staff were no longer as used to this democracy as they might once have been. Some complained about the prisoners coming prepared with an agreed line about how issues should be resolved, but staff were often the same. Gently, but steadily, I tried to steer staff to disagree with each other in public. This was a big step for them, and for some a step too far, but to my mind it was the essence of the unit. I had tried to recruit staff who had a level of confidence around speaking up and finding themselves in a minority. As the prisoners grew in numbers, they found keeping a united approach among themselves more difficult. On my part this was a deliberate and calculated version of divide and — if not rule — then divide and open up and talk. I had one situation where an officer raised a concern and felt he was not supported by anyone. He took this personally and eventually decided to leave. A sad outcome, but the officer did progress into management.

I still vividly remember the longest and most divisive community meeting that occurred in my time as Governor. The SPS had announced publicly the introduction of drug dogs. An officer said to me in passing, 'They won't be coming in here, will they?' My answer of 'Absolutely, yes' visibly shocked him. The officer's response was then 'The prisoners don't know that' and I in turn said, 'Bring it up at the community meeting.' I did wonder if the officer would, but to his credit he did as promised. The response to this at the community meeting was uproar, if not bedlam. Once the sense of shock had dissipated, various arguments emerged. The most salient was a sense of not being trusted and that I, as Governor, had betrayed the unit and all it stood for. As the meeting progressed, tempers calmed, but opposition remained vigorous and virulent. More debate followed but eventually the penny was dropping with the prisoners that the dogs were coming in regardless and there was no convincing argument against.

One small but important learning point for the prisoners was how it would look externally, if they were in some way exempted. At the risk of generalising, and perhaps even being somewhat patronising, prisoners of all persuasions in my experience did tend to look at any issue from a strictly personal point of view. The idea of identifying the big picture or recognising the need to step back and reflect on a variety of views, often conflicting, is not something that comes readily or easily. However, back to the community meeting and by 5.15 pm, having had earlier a brief adjournment for everyone to reflect privately, unanimity was reached and an agreement to the dogs coming in accepted and minuted. My view was, and remains, that the unit was functioning at its best in situations like these.

The Tuesday meeting was occasionally complemented by others that anyone could call at any time for any reason. There were also other types of meetings, such as 'two by twos', consisting of two staff and two prisoners meeting to address a matter of common interest. Regrettably, this was rare in my time, but I did participate in one. Our task was to agree a unit response to the then latest policy document flowing from HQ, called 'Assessment and Control'. Unlike its predecessors and immediate successors, this one was not well received, internally or externally. Ultimately our group produced a submission which was ratified by the community meeting and duly forwarded. I believe this was the only response which included a prisoners' perspective. In a small way, by doing this, the unit was helping prepare the ground for what became known as the 'Climate Survey' (initially an annual questionnaire open to all prisoners), and also the first ever conference held in a prison (HMP Peterhead). Both were firsts for the SPS.

How did the late period BSU fit in with emerging policy in the SPS more generally?

My time as Governor coincided with the highest level of Prison Service interest both North and South of the border in the idea of Small Units addressing various good order problems in a positive and constructive way, designed to effect personal change. England operated a small number of units, essentially focused on control. Ironically, this proved not to be a good time for the BSU. The SPS decided to replace it with a purpose-built unit at HMP Shotts, followed by another such Unit in HMP Peterhead. A small part of HMP Perth also became a unit, although it was never national or independent of the main institution (i.e. having its own dedicated staff management and Governor). Later, the Shotts Unit and the BSU were run together, before the latter was eventually decommissioned as planned.

My successor in the BSU was certainly not a 'volunteer' governor; his job was to wind it down. During the 1990s, with no obvious champion, interest in small units in Scotland waned. The only fresh thinking was the design of a new segregation unit in HMP Edinburgh, which was to become the standard for the new builds starting in the noughties. The Shotts Unit, latterly only semi-independent, closed chaotically and violently in 2002. I personally did not give up on the special units and prior to my retirement, when Acting Director of Operations in SPS, I floated the idea of a unit to manage the small, but exceptionally powerful and divisive organized crime 'graduates' who were clearly intent on running their empires from inside. The SPS did not pursue this and continues to prioritise keeping them in circulation rather than segregating them, which is arguably to its credit. That said, I think too little is actually known about the criminality and suffering perpetrated by organized crime from inside, as well as outside, prison. Despite the absence of serious incidents with them in the mainstream, there were individuals who did not cope and one who successfully took his case to Europe. This case had a racial dimension. I wonder if such a person could have benefited from a unit like the BSU.

How do you look back on your time as BSU Governor?

I left the BSU as I had entered, a strong advocate for such units as a way of developing a meaningful regime for a disparate group of 'extreme' disturbed individuals. I was alert to such units' risks and weaknesses, such as inconsistent entry and exit criteria, and the admittedly horrendous cost per prisoner place. However, the system allowed no actual costing of the benefits of preventing violence or sustaining prisoners' human rights in the mainstream. The BSU had, during its entire existence, created and sustained a safe space to enable and support personal change, which the peer group somehow accepted as authentic. This outcome benefited the prisoners selected, the mainstream and society. A win, win, win. It also helped to develop in staff a range of transferable skills, which were to become embedded in the SPS of the 1990s and beyond. Not every prisoner sustained his progress, either in the mainstream or community, but there are no certainties in the world of personal change and ultimate rehabilitation is a matter for society, not the criminal justice system. No initiative can ever deliver 100 per cent success. Whatever successes attributed to the unit can and should be debated, but fundamentally in my opinion its success was substantial. In my case, I had tried to take the unit back, if not to its roots, then to rediscovering and re-enacting at least some of its fundamental principles. Perhaps I should have looked forward and created a new 'regime' in its widest sense. The Shotts Unit tried this but lasted only a decade, including a temporary closure for a re-think. Thankfully, interest in assessing the legacy of the BSU does continue, and deserves to continue. Perhaps this interest is more external than internal, but the SPS ignores the lessons of its past at its peril. While many critical observers were, and still are, reluctant to view any part of any prison as a success, Scottish society should remember favourably the imagination, the creativity, the commitment of a select number of different people who, working collaboratively 50 years ago, designed a unique penal setting which delivered, for two decades, a pioneering means of tackling the curse of Scotland—violence. This work carries on with equally far-reaching thinking and radical initiatives, such as this century's multi-agency Violence Reduction Unit. Every generation needs to re-think violence on its own terms and, above all, continue the direction of travel to making a 'Safer Scotland for all'.

CHAPTER 10

Arts in the Later Years of the Barlinnie Special Unit

Irvine Allan

I was a mature first-year student at the Royal Scottish Academy of Music and Drama (RSAMD) (now the Royal Conservatoire of Scotland (RCS)) looking for a poem written by Larry Winters, a prisoner of the Barlinnie Special Unit (BSU), which I had heard recited in David Hayman's excellent Scottish film, *Silent Scream* (1990). Looking for that poem changed my life. When I called David Hayman, who was at that time Director of 7.84 Scotland Theatre Company, he directed me to the BSU, where he thought there might be an archive of Larry's poetry. I called the unit and a prison officer passed the phone to Dr Willy Maley, who was working part-time as writer-in-residence there.

Willy was a working-class, radical intellectual. His father, James Maley, had fought with the International Brigades in the Spanish Civil War. Willy was fired from the same mettle; a tough, extremely clever, young Glaswegian academic and community artist who had shone at Strathclyde University before going on to do his doctorate at Cambridge, where he was a major intellectual force within the student body. Willy would later move to teach at Goldsmiths, University in London, before taking up a post at the University of Glasgow where he is currently Professor of Renaissance Studies. Willy suggested I come up to the unit to hear a reading of some creative writing the prisoners were presenting the following evening. I jumped at the chance.

Entering the prison was a harrowing experience, the smell hit you as you went inside. It stank like weak disinfectant disguising stale urine. I checked in at reception and waited with another group of folk on one side of the waiting room. Looking around, some people were smoking cigarettes, many had that look you too often see around Glasgow; if people can wear poverty and class, you will see it on the faces of the people in the prison waiting room. A prison officer arrived to escort us all through the numerous locked gates and I was relieved when I walked into the unit to meet a group of smiling faces and receive a warm welcome. People were playing pool. Children were running wild in the place, having fun. It felt more like a crèche than a prison except there were bars on the windows. The prisoners involved in reading their creative writing were William Porter Elliott (aka 'Billy', or more commonly and notoriously, 'Toe'), Tommy 'TC' Campbell and John Galloway.

I watched and listened to the presentation of poems and songs, written by the prisoners, some put to music by singer songwriter, Derek Lang, of the Glasgow band, The Basement. Willy suggested I get involved in a presentation of creative writing for Glasgow's Mayfest, an annual arts festival launched in 1983 with a strong city-wide community programme. Tommy, John and Toe were enthusiastic about the idea. That was how Cat A Theatre Company was born. The company would go on to produce a trilogy of important plays, win awards and receive accolades on both sides of the Scottish order—including a Fringe First for Outstanding New Production at the Edinburgh Festival Fringe 1992, and a stunning review in *The Stage* for the company's debut drama, *No Mean Fighter*. The plays would bring voices from inside prison outside and voices from outside the prison inside. The company was committed to performing in mainstream and non-mainstream venues, playing in nearly every Scottish prison, young offender institution, and children's secure unit.

No Mean Fighter explores the situation that led to the riots in Peterhead Prison in the 1980s where most of the men in the unit had served time. The play used the trope of a fictitious diary found in a prisoner's cell to link the present with the past through the life and times of Scottish radical John Maclean, who served four years in Peterhead for sedition during the First World War, and was released in 1918. Maclean died in 1923. The play explored issues of class, and the effects of prison on inmates and their families. One of the real revelations in the play were the voices of the female characters exploring how imprisonment affects the whole family. There were a series of visiting scenes, some of which focused solely on the women by presenting only their side of the conversation. This convention was particularly powerful in telescoping and isolating the issues faced by the women on the outside.

The play was episodic, using a mix of short scenes, poems and songs. Some scenes were written by the prisoners with contributions from their wives and girlfriends. Other material was created taking a verbatim approach by using extracts from the inquiry into the Peterhead riots. Other scenes were written by the students involved from the RSAMD and Willy Maley himself contributed a major part of the script. It was a truly collaborative process where all the materials were workshopped in rehearsals and we literally cut and pasted scenes into an order to create a logical narrative. I was at once director, editor, creator, and collaborator, bringing together a diverse group of individuals with different skillsets and outlooks and talents, as well as distinct understandings of what was possible with theatre—drama students and inmates sharing innovative ideas.

The creative space and freedoms offered by the open door policy of the BSU allowed us to involve the prisoners as often, and as much, as possible in the process of making the play. As well as the creative writing contributions, I arranged auditions for fellow students at the unit where prisoners helped to cast the play. We held rehearsals in the unit so the prisoners could give feedback and input ideas. The material we created held a significant weight of authenticity and it was remarkable that the prisoners, along with a dedicated group of first- and second-year drama students, would go on to be awarded a *Scotsman* newspaper Fringe First Award for outstanding new production at the Edinburgh Festival Fringe in 1992.

After the success at the Fringe, we were encouraged by the Scottish Arts Council drama officer, Charlie Bell, to apply for funding to tour the work and were successful in our application, raising over £45,000 from various sources, including Strathclyde Region Social Work Arts Unit and Glasgow City Council. We went on to tour the play across Scotland, playing mainstream theatre venues such as The Tron, The Traverse, The Lemon Tree, community theatre circuits in both Edinburgh and Glasgow, and nearly all of the Scottish Prisons. Everything went well until our last two shows, which were planned for HMP Craiginches, in Aberdeen, with the last performance to be in Peterhead Prison itself, where the play was set. The Governor of HMP Craiginches, Bill Rattray, cancelled our performance in the prison because he felt the play could cause a riot. I tried to explain that we had played nearly every prison in Scotland without incident.

Even more disappointing, Frances O'Boyle, Education Officer at Peterhead, called to say our performance there was to be cancelled too. Instead, we could only perform some scenes to the prison drama group followed by a discussion.

What we discovered from the drama group in Peterhead was that one scene from the play, based on a scenario from Perth Prison, involved a prison officer currently working at Peterhead. To my amazement, as the prison drama group helped us out with our theatre set late that night, there he was. One of the prisoners whispered to me, 'That's him—that's Sid Vicious.' Now we understood the sensitivities around our performance. The event we had enacted was infamous throughout the prison system. This is indictive of why the Prison Service had, in previous years, tried to limit the freedom of what could be said. The Third Eye Centre published a book in the late 1980s about the unit in which prisoners were permitted to talk only about their art, not their time in the mainstream prison system.

The interesting and powerful aspects of the work we were presenting through Cat A Theatre Company was that through the plays we could say things that the prisoners could not. We could take their voices and experiences onto the public stage. We also provided a portal for drama students into another world. For several of those who acted in *No Mean Fighter*—including Tony Curran and Kate Dickie—it was a launchpad to a stellar acting career. The BSU provided a creative space from where the prisoners could connect to the wider community through the arts focusing on vital social issues. Dr Willy Maley provided an important note to our theatre programme leaflet stating:

> '...the present setting is used as a site from which the company can question confinement and prejudice in the culture at large, opening up the genre to create a new form of political theatre based on the premise that wherever liberty is curtailed, which is to say, almost everywhere, then all drama is prison drama. This is not to belittle or ignore the specific experiences of those serving time within the present system, but to link experiences to a bigger picture in which revenge rather than justice determines the course of human life, where punishment is as much a cause as the consequence of crime.'

The second part of the trilogy to emanate from the unit, *Dirt Enters at the Heart* (1993), was to be just as controversial as the first and decidedly more embarrassing for the Scottish Prison Service (SPS). This was a play about AIDS, and highlighted how prisons had become a nodal point for the spread of the disease. The sharing of needles inside prison was a major factor in the spread of the disease in Scotland, with Edinburgh known as the AIDS capital of Europe. The prison policies of putting AIDS sufferers and drug users together on the same floors led to a rapid increase in those infected. One such floor in Perth Prison was dubbed 'Death Row' by staff. The issues were telescoped in the play by choosing three characters: the gay man, the intravenous drug user, and the heterosexual hard man.

The play brought a significant amount of publicity to the issue, and Dr David Goldberg, Head of Transmissible Diseases at Ruchill Hospital, wrote to thank us, stating that the play was of vital importance and was in fact an international issue. The media attention brought to the issue by the play helped in accelerating the move to have needle exchanges and condoms available inside prison. Sometimes art really is a matter of life and death. We played in most Scottish prisons, and I believe we had the whole prison population, as well as those in power at SPS headquarters, discussing this issue. I suspect this play could have saved some lives.

It was clear we had hit a nerve. The TV and press piled in with extensive previews, reviews and articles. The momentum was with us and voices from inside the BSU were out there making waves, big ones. Willy's brother, John Maley, had joined the writing team. A talented poet and writer, as well as being a social worker, he added significant quality to the playwriting. *Doing Bird* was to attract the attention of Andy Senior, a talent scout for English director Jude Kelly at the West Yorkshire Playhouse, which led to us being invited to play there at a Criminal Justice Conference the following year with the final part of the 'Take No Prisoners Trilogy', *Doing Bird.*

Doing Bird was about women in prison. We again telescoped issues through the choice of three characters: the prostitute, the shoplifter, and the black widow who had killed her husband after years of abuse. The issue of violence against women had been a recurrent thread in all the plays. Direct discrimination against women in the criminal justice system was brutally exposed in the play. This was a time before there was a legal defence for women like Margaret, the character in the play who had killed her husband after years of abuse. A time when women who broke the law were seen by the courts as bad, as well as mad. A time when women were pushed up the criminal justice tariff by judges faster than men. A time when women were imprisoned after committing fewer crimes than men. A time when no Training For Freedom (TFI) was available in women's prison as there was in men's prisons.

I attended a conference for the Scottish Association for Care and Resettlement of Offenders (SACRO) that focused on women in prison. There was a Q&A and I asked the question that, as we had seen and heard clear evidence of direct discrimination against women in Scottish prisons, should someone take a legal case against Eddie Frizzell, Chief Executive of the SPS. Margo MacDonald was chairing the panel and looked around for someone to field the question. There were no takers. Suddenly, from the audience, Helena Kennedy QC (now KC) stood up and said that legal action does make them get off their backsides, and promptly sat down again. You could hear a pin drop.

Willy Maley again provides a clear insight to the relevance of the work in his programme notes for *Doing Bird*:

> 'The play examines the loss of self, guilt, blame, pain, humiliation, suffering, denial and strategies of survival that come with custody, official and "domestic", through the pain of confinement and the politics of control—sexual moral and spiritual. Eschewing neat solutions, *Doing Bird* juxtaposes survival with loss, "living on" with grief and death. The questions can be asked on-stage—the answers have to come from elsewhere. Beyond the fatal opposition of victim and perpetrator, beyond the law of revenge, lies the possibility of justice, justice without revenge. Finally, there is the implicit suggestion that we are all "doing bird" and that as well as looking for alternatives to custody, we should be looking at alternatives to the incriminating culture we inhabit.'

Doing Bird toured extensively in Scotland, also playing the West Yorkshire Playhouse and five prisons in Yorkshire. The play opened a major conference on criminal justice. Again, the press interest in the work was off the scale.

After the unit closed in 1994 it became very difficult to continue our collaboration with the prisoners, as they were moved to other prisons across Scotland.

However, Annie George (actor and administrator), along with writer John Maley and I, continued to produce plays for Cat A Theatre Company, and worked in both prison and probation settings. We produced three other full-length plays, *Witchdoctor*, *Daylight Robbery* and *Greenock Central*. These are not considered part of the 'Take No Prisoners Trilogy' as they were not part of the collaboration with the BSU prisoners. Some people have suggested that towards the end of the unit's existence in the early nineties, there was little art produced, and that interest in the arts produced in the unit had waned. I do not think that is a fair analysis, because this was a vibrant and productive period for artistic output, particularly for the voices coming out of the unit and truly making an impact on the Scottish Prison System and wider society.

CHAPTER 11

The Gateway Exchange

Sara Trevelyan

Where It All Started

On 1 November 1982, after 20 years imprisonment, Jimmy Boyle was released from Saughton Prison. This was a moment of triumph for us both, and for Jimmy, a moment of long-awaited homecoming. It was also a moment of incredible tension as he waited in the early morning for the gates of Saughton Prison to finally open. He describes this moment in the final paragraph of his prison diaries, *The Pain of Confinement* (1985: 303).

> 'I was taken to the gate where I waited for Sara. These were the longest moments of all. The gate officer said Mr Hills (the Governor) had called to say he was coming in. I stood on edge. Mr Hills drove in the gate. He didn't look at me. He didn't speak. Sara arrived. Mr Hills gave the signal and the duty officer opened the gate. I stepped over into Freedom.'

This abrupt and unceremonious ending of his 20-year sentence contrasts with how he was welcomed into the Special Unit by staff calling him by his first name and giving him a pair of scissors to open a parcel. Being only too aware of the difficulties that so many ex-prisoners face when they re-enter society, we decided to establish a place of safety and welcome, a centre in Edinburgh which came to be called the Gateway Exchange. 'Gateway' expressed the passage which Jimmy had stepped through, on his first day of freedom—'Exchange' was because we wanted to put the emphasis on the positive creative potential which exists in each one of us.

Jimmy and I had married in January 1980 while he was still incarcerated in the Special Unit. Our unlikely marriage, I was working as a psychiatrist in Glasgow at the time, although not in any way professionally involved in the Special Unit, attracted a great deal of press attention and would not have been possible had he not been fortunate enough to be placed in the Special Unit, where he was able to have contact with many visitors from the outside world. In what felt like a reaction of embarrassment caused by our widely publicised wedding, the Prisons Department decided that he should spend a further two years and two months in the mainstream prison system being 'prepared' for release back into the outside world. In the Special Unit he had regained his sense of personal worth, the floodgates of his creativity had burst open. He had discovered a natural ability to sculpt and had unleashed pent-up feelings by chipping away at massive blocks of sandstone, as well as creating figures in clay, allowing forms to emerge which had an extraordinary power and presence. He had also become an author while he was in the Special Unit, writing his personal biography, *A Sense of Freedom*, which became a groundbreaking book after it was published in 1977.

The Special Unit offered an environment where prisoners were encouraged to take responsibility, to articulate their grievances and to resolve conflicts through dialogue, rather than resorting to violence. The men in the unit began to relearn the skills of relating to others. They had unrestricted access to their family members, partners, friends, and the diverse assortment of individuals who ended up visiting the unit. This was in complete contrast to the tightly controlled visiting facilities in existence in the mainstream prison system at that time. In the Special Unit, visits could take place seven days a week, mornings or afternoons, with prisoners able to invite visitors into their personally decorated cells. Our relationship, which began with me reading Jimmy's bestselling book *A Sense of Freedom*, was made possible by these relaxed visiting conditions. This is something which I will always be grateful for, but these arrangements were also controversial. This was a grey area which could be exploited, and unfortunately contributed to the eventual demise of the Special Unit.

When we married, Jimmy did not have a release date but we were hopeful that our choice to make a commitment to each other would pave the way for his return to society. The question of how an individual should be released from the Special Unit though was never fully addressed. The Prisons Department's policy was that he should be returned to the mainstream prison system for his pre-release programme. Given all that he had been through, this was absurd, and we challenged it vociferously at the time. To be, in effect, re-socialised, then to be returned to a system where all decision-making authority was to be taken away again with every aspect of life controlled was a change in circumstances equally dramatic to his arrival at the Special Unit in 1973, from the Inverness cages, only in reverse.

'Preparation' for Release

Unlike the relatively unrestricted visiting conditions of the Special Unit, where I was able to meet with Jimmy in his cell seven days a week, our visits were suddenly reduced to an hour a month when he moved back into the mainstream prison population. We sat at a small table in a crowded, noisy visiting hall, supervised by prison staff. Fortunately, soon after his transfer, Jimmy was placed on a two day a week pre-release work programme with the Wester Hailes Community Workshop. This was achieved with the assistance of the manager, Lawrence Demarco. Meanwhile, within the prison, Jimmy had to manage a slow progression through different halls with minimally increased freedoms, but all within a pervasive culture of petty rules and restrictions. It was a situation of bizarre contrast with him being out and about on the days when he was on community placement, fully trusted as a responsible member of the team, helping other people with their problems, while each evening he was plunged back into the dispiriting conditions of mainstream life within the prison.

There are positives in any situation, so despite the slow trawl through the pre-release programme, as well as a two year separation for both of us in terms of our marriage, it was an opportunity for Jimmy to become aware of one of the greatest deficiencies of the prison system, the lack of preparation or support for prisoners being released. At the same time, I had my middle-class frame of reference expanded by being introduced to the realities of life on a peripheral housing estate.

Despite being the newest of Edinburgh's housing schemes, I learned that Wester Hailes was the area with the highest overdose rate in the city. I was able to get a job with the Scottish Association for Mental Health to explore the reasons for this and in the process learned a lot about the mental health problems heavily present in communities of this kind. Newly created with the emphasis purely on housing in relatively sterile tower blocks, there was an absence of the most basic of community facilities, bus services, shops, schools or health services, these environments became breeding grounds for loneliness, depression, overdoses, drug abuse, alcoholism, family breakdown and violence. In these kinds of circumstances children are particularly vulnerable to neglect and abuse, a concerning reality that is now officially recognised as Adverse Childhood Experiences (ACEs). Through his placement in the community, Jimmy became involved in supporting young kids experiencing homelessness settle into flats and teaching them basic social skills. He used his charisma, experience and talents to divert them from drug addiction or violence.

People released from prison face numerous challenges in many ways. Jimmy was fortunate to have the full backing and support of the team in the Wester Hailes Community Workshop, as well as his relationship with me and other friends. He also had his own plentiful inner store of creative resources to draw on, a wellspring which never failed him. The others in the TFF hostel where he was eventually transferred to had far fewer resources, and a scarcity of support. They were sent out to work in places such as Dalton's Scrap Yard and the Fruitmarket where they were open to abuse through being called 'prisoner' or picked on as they struggled to learn basic skills of survival in the outside world. Their experiences only reinforced the stigma, and undermined their self-esteem.

Creating the Gateway Exchange

These are the experiences which on Jimmy's release led to us creating Gateway Exchange. What was foremost in our minds was establishing a place where individuals could come when returning to the community, whether being released from prison, as Jimmy had been, discharged from a psychiatric hospital, or recovering from alcohol or drug addiction. We wanted to combine our different experiences and talents to support others. We kept our remit broad as we did not want to exclude anyone. We were aware that in many institutions the individual is reduced to a problem, a diagnosis, a label, a set of behaviours and is seen almost exclusively through an anti-social lens. We had a vision of creating a centre where those who came along could be encouraged to become part of a dynamic community, where their uniqueness and talents would be recognised and welcomed.

We were determined to demonstrate the philosophy which had been at the heart of the Special Unit, that those with backgrounds of offending, mental illness or addiction have hidden reserves of potential. Our intention was to create a radical alternative to what we saw as the prevailing culture in the voluntary sector of offering care, but often without anything which might encourage personal expression or tap into the creative side of an individual.

We began by putting our own resources into this project. I was fortunate to have sufficient finance to start things off and we fundraised energetically amongst family, friends, and trust funds for the rest. We purchased a building in Abbeymount, Edinburgh, which was close to the less salubrious area of Easter Road, but which was bizarrely a stone's throw up the hill from Holyrood House. The premises had a double shop front with a central hallway leading through to a large, cavernous warehouse at the back divided by a mezzanine floor. This allowed space to develop creative workshops, with the area above eventually becoming the Mandela Theatre. The first task we tackled was to clean out, paint and refurbish the building beginning with the front office spaces. It was a mammoth undertaking, and it was bitterly cold winter weather, but our enthusiasm kept us in high spirits. A pair of close friends, Sebastian and Evlynn Horsley, joined us as committed early members of our team. They were both artists whose different backgrounds mirrored that of Jimmy and myself. Together we were the lynchpins of this fledgling project which was to occupy all of our energies through the 1980s.

As the word spread about this new project people from all walks of life came along to join us. Nobody was paid for their hard work, but the camaraderie created a melting pot of human experience and an atmosphere of authenticity and integrity which attracted others. Some of those who came along would have been considered 'write-offs', individuals who the system had labelled as failures, but we recognised and encouraged whatever skills they had and there were always tasks on the go which people could help with.

The emphasis was on getting to know each other by working together and creating a community that we could all feel a part of. The moving force was the energy and enthusiasm of the assortment of people who threw themselves into the heave and thrust of everyday life. The building would open at 9 am and work would begin with the ritual of cleaning the toilets and hoovering the floors. There was a phone which needed to be answered, correspondence to be attended to, creative projects to be pursued, exhibitions which needed hanging, lunchtime soups which needed to be prepared—the day was not structured and work would continue until the doors closed at 6 pm, with activities sometimes continuing into the evenings. The only fixed point was a weekly meeting for all involved in the centre after lunch on Fridays. We had a stream of visitors from all walks of life—journalists, social workers, ex-prisoners, prisoner's wives, people who had struggled with addiction, former sex-workers, as well as some of the young people Jimmy had worked with in Wester Hailes, curious to learn what was happening as the word spread about the centre.

Early on we staged an exhibition called 'New Beginnings'. The sculptures, paintings and collages had all been produced by untrained people. We were keen to challenge the elitist definitions of Art... for us it was ALL art. The building was as much an evolving piece of art for us as the exhibitions, which we put on in the front office. We wanted to redefine the whole concept of art and place it at the heart of life. This was similar to the Special Unit where the process of transformation which occurred in the individual through making a piece of art was viewed as having as much, if not more importance, than the finished product. We started to have visits from community groups who made their way across from Glasgow. Heroin was starting to flood into the housing schemes at this time. The rising tide of drug addiction, especially amongst young people, resulted in parents starting to get together in some of the communities worst affected to find ways of providing help and support to those affected by these problems. They looked to us as a source of expertise in terms of how to go about establishing these rudimentary services.

Creative work started to take place in the studio spaces developed at the back of the Gateway. The area underneath the main hall was transformed into a sculpture workshop which became known as 'The Underworld'. Over the summer the whirlwind of work was directed towards preparing for the official opening which took place on 12 August 1984. Jimmy devised a stunt for the opening which consisted of Billy Connolly, who we were extremely grateful to for accepting our invitation to do the honours for us, being presented with welding equipment and asked to break his way into a painted casket—which would open to reveal a powerful bronze cast logo for the front gates that Sebastian had made. The team of helpers, many of whom had relapses, visits from the police, or other such crises happening in their lives, held up remarkably well. The opening night was a fitting extravaganza, attended by a throng of different folk. Billy was the star of the show, bringing his own unique brand of humour to the occasion, as well as introducing a more serious note as he linked what we were doing to the striking miners and the Campaign for Nuclear Disarmament (CND). Hot on the heels of this event we turned our premises over to become a venue in the Edinburgh Festival—this was a way for us to earn some much-needed funds. Various theatre groups gave powerful performances tackling controversial issues which we felt a strong affinity with.

All of this activity had a shadow side which was that with a lack of formal supervision, some people started to abuse aspects of the project—money was taken, a cassette recorder disappeared, and people were taking advantage of the phone. We put the emphasis on learning from our mistakes by talking things through in community meetings. We created a management committee which consisted of individuals who were willing to accept additional responsibilities for overseeing the running of the centre. The weekly meetings provided opportunities for people to sit down together as a group to discuss and review our progress. Our model for this was clearly based on the community meetings which had taken place in the Special Unit. The therapeutic community style of approach fitted equally well in our community-based facility. We wanted to create a model that was based on open communication and honest sharing, addressing interpersonal issues as well as the work agenda.

The Gateway Exchange through the years 1984–86 became a hub of activity and place of connection for the diverse group of individuals who made up our core team, as well as for a number of emerging community groups. It defied all conventional attempts to typecast or label it. We resisted approaching the local authority for funding in the early days because of Jimmy's background and were fortunate to manage to attract generous support from trust funds as well as certain individuals. We became an expression of a new approach to rehabilitation which went beyond anything happening in the social services at that time. It was also an early attempt at social enterprise—brave, controversial, idealistic and groundbreaking. It was also anarchic at times, lacking in clear focus, all-consuming of our energies and ultimately unsustainable—but it took us until the end of the decade to recognise this. Openness and transparency were important values which we held so we never tried to hide the difficulties—we confronted them in the weekly meetings, which were dynamic, challenging and, at times, frustrating, but honest and authentic.

Engagement with Social Issues

As well as developing different creative facilities including the sculpture underworld, a darkroom, a pottery, a video department, a kitchen, and the Mandela Theatre, we were also active in tackling social issues. We were aware that the prison authorities did not seem to be interested in what happened to people after release, all too often the problems would rebound on the communities the offenders came from. The high recidivism statistics showed where the prison system was failing. The lessons that emerged from the Special Unit experience suggested that changing the conditions and approach could help the individual to break free of cycles of offending and re-offending which were causing such misery. We suggested that a change in approach within the prison system was needed to address some of these problems and, in particular, advocated for an increase in dialogue with community representatives. This is now starting to be addressed more in the Scottish Prison Service (SPS) through what are called community facing prisons, prisons which have active links with communities. At the time when we were working there was an absence of this more enlightened thinking or approach.

As word spread about our existence, a number of prisoners sent letters to us. We would respond encouraging them to express their thoughts, feelings and experiences through the written word. One of many publications which we produced was a small booklet called *Poetry from Prison*. This contains some moving contributions. Creativity offers a way to break down barriers, external as well as internal ones. The writing opens windows to aspects of a prisoner usually suppressed and buried by a system which denies any possibility of expressing true feelings. This is poignantly expressed in the opening lines of one of the poems that we received from Fraser MacDowell, a prisoner in HMP Peterhead, which we included in this collection titled 'Almost Died':

A hard man some call me
But that's the only part they see
Don't they know I have a soft heart
Why can't they see that part
You're tough, your solid they atone
Some even say I have a heart of stone
I know myself this isn't true
And you my family know it too
None of them have been near
When I have shed many a tear
Yes, I admit I have sat and cried
I opened my heart and almost died
You see my hardness is only a charade
I sneer and keep up my evil facade
You are to blame, you Peterhead
You took my heart and left it for dead…

We organized public meetings taking place in response to the worrying number of suicides in Glenochil Complex for Young Offenders, and in the process of this, connected with those who we called 'the human face of the system'. We were in touch with staff who, like us, questioned the unremitting punishment ethos and who agreed that there was an urgent need for improvement in attitudes and conditions throughout the prison system. We campaigned on the issue of drugs and had a lot of contact with the parents of drug users as well as people who had struggled with addiction. We gave out a clear message that the Gateway Exchange was a drugs free area and emphasised that the individual needed to take the first step by expressing a willingness to stop taking drugs. We supported the work being done by rehabilitation centres that were active in Scotland at that time and preferred to advocate withdrawal as opposed to the prescribing of maintenance scripts, which was becoming the prevailing statutory response. We were somewhat out on a limb in this respect but we established excellent links with the Calton Athletic Support Group from Glasgow, who were an inspiring example of energy and commitment. They succeeded in getting a number of young people from the East End of Glasgow off drugs by creating a local football team and encouraging their members to run marathons.

Looking at our achievements from a distance now, what we did was extraordinary for that time. For a short while we were able to function as a kind of beacon for those who felt alienated from the mainstream or who were seeking to address these difficult social problems in their own communities. I am proud of the contribution that we were able to make, even though the realities of trying to tackle so much meant that we ended up finding ourselves overstretched and under-resourced. We tried very hard to find successful and sustainable ways for the Gateway Exchange to stand on its own feet. We experimented with renting out the café, and the theatre, as well as creating a band rehearsal area in the Washhouse, a premises which we had acquired next door, as we were keenly motivated to try to find commercial ways to remain in existence. Finally, through necessity, we started to seek statutory sources of funding. We also began to consider the possibility of fundraising for salaries for core members of staff. One of the thorny questions which we faced was how we could balance earning income in these ways, while at the same time supporting people with difficult personal issues.

One of the more remarkable achievements of this time was that Jimmy and Sebastian succeeded in establishing a bronze casting foundry in the Washhouse, where along with a group of willing others, they created a public sculpture which was commissioned by one of our wealthy supporters in Hull. The sculpture was a larger-than-life size seated figure with a bowed head, sitting in the middle of a cluster of four steel bars. Called 'Imprisoned Mankind' (representing imprisoned minds), it was similar in its conception to the iconic small sculpture 'Solitary—Inverness' which Jimmy had created in the early days in the Special Unit, which was so expressive of his lost years in The Cages in Inverness. Making this sculpture which had to be cut into 25 pieces for the casting process was a marathon achievement for an inexperienced team.

We put our problems to one side when there was a rooftop protest with a hostage taken at Peterhead Prison, followed by a similar incident at Perth Prison. Jimmy became frantically busy dealing with media enquiries. We held a public meeting on 4 December 1986, chaired by Donald Macaulay QC, which led to the expression of dissatisfaction with the limited and partisan investigation to be mounted by the Prison Inspectorate and demanded unanimously an independent inquiry. A committee was appointed which included Ken Murray, who on his retirement from the SPS had become a Strathclyde Councillor, Alistair Duff, a solicitor, Phil Scraton and Joe Sim, both criminologists. Jimmy represented the Gateway. Together they managed to compile a substantial report on the crisis, with a foreword by Ludovic Kennedy, titled 'The Roof Comes Off', which Gateway Exchange published in November 1987. The report made recommendations pertaining to a number of issues including food, hygiene and sanitation, health and safety, work and education, medical care, discipline and complaints processes.

Crisis and Change

The pressures on us personally to keep the Gateway Exchange running were unrelenting. Exacerbated by our rapidly diminishing funds we were at a point of crisis. As 1987 drew to a close we were facing a situation where closure was imminent unless new funds materialised. At this same time another crisis arose, this one was to affect the whole city, and indeed it eventually spread around the world. This was due to the arrival of HIV, the virus that causes AIDS. At first it seemed that this deadly epidemic was happening a long way away from us, as reports appeared of the infection spreading amongst the gay community in the United States. In the Gateway, we worked with many young kids who Jimmy had initially met when he was involved in the homeless flats project in Wester Hailes. We had seen these young people through different crises through the years and some of them became regular participants in the Gateway. One of these was a young man, who like many in this group, was unemployed and who had ended up injecting heroin in the 1980s. The other people struggling with addiction tended to be family members or close friends who, due to knowing each other well, thought that it was fine to share needles. Tragically this led to a situation where these conditions, which were replicated in other large housing schemes in Edinburgh and Glasgow, gave rise to the rapid wildfire spread of the HIV virus in Scotland.

We started to hold workshops and a public meeting to inform ourselves better. Reality struck home to us that it was on our own doorstep when this same young man went for an HIV test and tested positive. We were all devastated. It was all the more upsetting as, paradoxically, he was playing the lead role in two Gateway Exchange Theatre productions staged in the Mandela Theatre. In one of these he played the part of Jimmy in the play about his life *The Hard Man*. Tragically, we were at the start of a time when a devastating number of these young people were to die from this condition. Suddenly we found ourselves facing stigma, illness and bereavement on an unprecedented scale. As always there were gifts and opportunities to be found in facing this inconceivable crisis. One of these was the emergence of a number of front line support services which we had strong links with as they represented marginalised groups, and were operating outwith the mainstream services.

Unexpectedly, the crisis of providing support for the many infected with HIV created a way for us to transform our difficulties. The building, which in the beginning had seemed to offer so much creative scope and potential, had started to feel like an albatross around our necks. This unprecedented situation gave rise to newly formed groups who were needing space to meet—we had the space but found ourselves stretched to the limit to raise the funds we needed to run it. Word reached us that the idea of an AIDS Resource Centre had come up at a working together day for AIDS held by Lothian Region. At this point we decided to approach both social work and the health board to offer the use of our building for these purposes. Suddenly things turned from an outlook which had seemed increasingly bleak, to putting forward an exciting new vision and getting positive responses. Although it was hard for those of us who had been involved full-time in the running of the Gateway Exchange over the past five years to let go, it was clearly time for change. It helped to know that our legacy could continue in the form of a new and much needed facility for the community impacted by HIV.

We had given our all to making the Gateway the unique and special place that it was. Many people in all sorts of different capacities had come through our doors. Individuals had blossomed as a result of crossing the threshold and becoming part of the vibrant energy of the place. Many discovered previously hidden talents throwing themselves into the unpredictable life and work of the centre in impressive and courageous ways. We had our failures and our limitations, but we tried to be honest about these, and knew that what we offered, despite the range of ways for people to get involved, was not for everybody.

The Gateway Exchange was an experiment which arose out of the unique set of circumstances which followed on from Jimmy's release from his 20 year prison sentence. In some senses it allowed us to work through and integrate the experience of the Special Unit, as well as his arduously slow-release programme. The lessons learned in the Special Unit had implications which spread far beyond the prison walls. We saw creativity and the arts as a catalyst for both individual, as well as collective change. Art provided a way to expand horizons and transform people's experience of themselves.

The Gateway Exchange was unquestionably part of the legacy of the BSU and demonstrated how these same principles of approach could be applied in a community setting. In common with the Special Unit the lifespan of our project was limited, but we punched well above our weight in terms of achievements and offered a pioneering vision for employing the arts as a potent resource for personal change and growth, as well as showing the importance of collaboration between different groups in the community. The waves which we succeeded in creating, were part of a much bigger movement which saw the development of a thriving community-based arts scene, which brought a new spirit of dynamism and hope to communities across Scotland. The lesson, as was demonstrated so convincingly by the Special Unit, is that extraordinary talents will continue to emerge anywhere where individuals find themselves in environments which nurture, encourage and celebrate them.

Postscript

The legacy of the Gateway Exchange continued in the form of SOLAS which was the name first given to the AIDS Resource Centre. SOLAS, which suggests the radiant light and warmth of the sun, felt very appropriate at this dark time. A couple of years later the name was changed to Waverley Care. This organization has continued to the present day, although it moved on from the premises in Abbeymount, which we rented at low cost to the council for this purpose for 20 years. The building was eventually sold and the funds were used to support the refurbishment and upgrading of the Salisbury Centre, a unique place supporting personal and spiritual growth in Edinburgh which is approaching its 50th anniversary. A Gateway Exchange trust fund was formed which continues to support community groups as well as individuals under the umbrella of Foundation Scotland.

Reference

Boyle, J (1985), *The Pain of Confinement: Prison Diaries,* Edinburgh: Canongate.

CHAPTER 12

Evaluating Violence Reduction in the Unit

David J Cooke

In the distance I could hear loud hammering—steel on stone. An officer opened the small door in the high wall, I entered the prison within a prison and was confronted by a long-haired, lean and muscular prisoner—stripped to the waist—dwarfed by an eight-foot-high lump of sandstone. He grunted, he sweated, he swore as he hammered. Gradually over many weeks a figure was emerging—a figure of Christ. In another part of the yard, hamsters and rabbits were petted by pre-school children, pigeons tumbled from their coop and couples sunbathed. This was a prison yard, but not any prison, this was the yard of the Barlinnie Special Unit (BSU).

Some 18 months before I had been appointed head of the Forensic Clinical Psychology Service in Glasgow; one part of my job was to be the consulting psychologist for the unit. My experiences in the unit were to have profound effects on my professional career. It became my university of crime and criminality. It shaped the direction and focus of my research and practice for decades to come. I was not alone in this; it became clear to me, over my ten-year association with the unit, that it affected staff as much as the prisoners.

Joining the unit had been a shock. I had progressed through a conventional clinical psychologist's training. I had spent the last seven years treating people in the West End of Glasgow—the posh part—treating people suffering from depression, anxiety and phobias. Thus, working with unit prisoners was not a steep learning curve, it was a vertiginous curve. My naïvety must have been plain for all to see— prisoners and staff alike. The prisoners in the BSU were very different from my previous patients. The majority of men had killed someone, at least once, however, murder was only one element in their pattern of persistent and serious violence. They had been brought up in a sub-culture where violence was normal—if not celebrated—starting at an early age they had graduated though diverse and prolific criminal careers to serve long prison sentences. They caused mayhem in other prisons across the estate. They suffered from many known risk factors of violence: severe personality pathology, substance misuse, and in some cases, major mental illness. Despite this concentration of risk, little violence occurred in the unit. The prisoners as a whole were dominant, forceful, challenging, impulsive, suspicious and reckless—yet their violence was curbed. That was the mystery of the unit.

Scottish prisons in the 1980s were tough, harsh and bleak places. Prisoners were housed in buildings built while Victoria reigned; prison wings were dim, airless and smelly (the unit was no different). Staff learned to manage prisoners by watching their elders, and thereby a harsh approach persisted. Psychologists are used to being viewed with suspicion; in the mid-1980s the Prisons Department of the Scottish Office had little psychological input, psychologists were seen as unnecessary, or worse.

In the simple days of the 1980s, there were no job-descriptions, no job plans, the role of the unit psychologist was unclear. I eased into a pattern of seeing individual prisoners in their cells at the back of the unit. We would talk about their tensions, anxieties or whatever their current preoccupations were. I would act as a sounding post and suggest strategies that they might try to relieve their pains of confinement. I was conscious, even then, that it was only possible to provide psychological first aid when really major surgery was required. These men had so many problems, and problems were deeply rooted. Over a decade my role evolved from providing direct support to prisoners and to the preparation of parole reports, through the selection of new prisoners and staff, to the provision of training and support for staff. It was always a challenge, stimulating and, I would say, a privilege.

The early months were not easy; I was put to the test. It was four-fifty in the afternoon when I left a prisoner's cell to be confronted by a locked gate between the cell area and the main unit, and importantly, the door out of the prison. Every evening the keys from the unit had to be taken to a central point in the main prison so that prisoners could not grab keys from the remaining staff and escape. I called through the grill gate and the two officers told me that the keys had been sent to the main prison. I was on the wrong side of the gate with the 'seven most dangerous men' in Scotland. The officers said they could not get me out for an hour; it was a serious breach of security so they could not let anybody know. The prisoners thought this was hilarious and laughed and joked, saying come in and have a wee dram—I never discovered if they were joking or not. Likewise, I never discovered whether this was a deliberate test by the prison officers, but it certainly was a right of passage. Fortunately, I did not panic, I joked with the prisoners and I did not 'grass' the officers who had breached security. I think that this was a pivotal moment; I became more accepted by prisoners and staff. Of course, some remained understandably wary.

One of the reasons that I was given the job of psychologist was my research record. Dr Peter Whatmore, the founding father of the BSU, encouraged and supported the notion that the unit should be evaluated. I am sure he recognised that this would be politically sensitive but he felt an evidence-based approach was important. Peter encouraged me to apply for a Cropwood Fellowship at the Institute of Criminology based at the University of Cambridge. Cropwood Fellowships were designed to allow practitioners to take time from their usual jobs to concentrate on a focused piece of research.

The library in the Institute was probably the best criminology library in the UK at the time. It is hard to recall how important libraries were, now that we are in the age where any published paper can be downloaded to your desk in the twinkling of an eye. One of the joys of browsing bound volumes of articles is that while searching for one article you discover another by chance. This is how I came across an article by Robert Hare, a psychologist in Vancouver, Canada, in which he described 'A research scale for the assessment of psychopathy in criminal populations' (Hare, 1980). I wrote to Professor Hare and some six weeks later I was excited to receive a package covered in Canadian stamps containing a manual explaining how to decide whether someone was psychopathic or not. This opened my eyes; many of the unit prisoners fitted his description of being psychopathic.

One of the first steps in my research was to describe the prisoners; as I have already outlined the vast majority had convictions for homicide, some were known to have killed more than once, and several were suspected of killings for which they were not convicted. The pattern of homicide was unusual; most of their victims were male, many of their victims were strangers rather than acquaintances. Apart from homicide they had long criminal records, they committed violence both outside and inside prison. They had convictions for assaults, mobbing and rioting and hostage taking in prison which resulted in extra prison time. They presented major control problems for the prison staff. I used Hare's method to determine whether the prisoners suffered from psychopathy: 72 per cent fitted his description of 'psychopath';[1] another 25 per cent had significant elements of the disorder. This was a remarkable finding given that a few years later I carried out a study across the whole of the Scottish Prison System and showed that only between three to five per cent of prisoners in Scottish prisons could be described as psychopaths. The prevailing wisdom at the time was that people with this disorder could not be treated. The reasons for this are not hard to discern. Psychopathic people are contemptuous of social norms and social controls; they reject authority and discipline because they feel entitled, superior, and special. Their behaviour is impervious to punishment, they don't learn from experience. They suffer from suspiciousness; they believe others are out to get them and they often have short fuses. They get bored easily and often get pleasure by playing mind games to disturb others. In short, the BSU prisoners were not a good bet for treatment, they were not a good bet for change. But they did change.

I carefully reviewed all the prisoner's records (25 while I was in Cambridge; an additional eleven after the unit closed). I was looking for some way of measuring the prisoners' disturbed and disruptive behaviour. First, I counted up all the people the prisoners had assaulted during their prison sentence before coming to the unit; this inevitably was an underestimate because a lot of prison violence is hidden. Second, I counted up seriously disruptive incidents that didn't entail direct physical assaults: escaping, fire-raising, barricading, dirty protests, 'smashing up' and hostage-takings. The findings were stark. The cohort of prisoners carried out 181 assaults in their current sentence before being transferred to the unit (they had many, many more in previous sentences). Two assaults occurred in the unit. There was a problem, of course, that the prisoners spent different time periods in their original prison and in the unit. I calculated expected rates adjusting for these different time periods. This calculation revealed that

1. The term 'psychopath' was commonly used. It is now recognised as unacceptable to describe people in that way in the same way it is no longer acceptable to describe someone as a schizophrenic as compared with someone who suffers from schizophrenia. The individual is more than their disorder.

131 would be expected while only two occurred. Serious incidents showed a similar marked decline (Cooke, 1989; 1997).

Something seemed to be happening but of course the unit was unique—and the prisoners extraordinary. Without a control group, and random allocation to either treatment or control conditions, it is harder to argue that the unit as such produced the reduction in assaults. But in reality, sometimes real-world research cannot be squeezed into rigorous experimental designs. This was a case in point. Fortunately, there are other methods—quasi-experimental methods—based on logic and analysis that can evaluate other competing explanations for the observed reduction in assaults. I applied these methods; it was possible to exclude other explanations.

The unit seemed to work. Being young and enthusiastic I wrote up the results thinking that the Prisons Department would be pleased. I was still naïve. I wanted to submit a paper to an academic journal—the *British Journal of Criminology*. Although I was not employed by the Prisons Department, I sought permission to publish. I was subjected to a torturous, protracted process which culminated in me seeking a meeting with a senior civil servant. He told me, with his mandarin's insouciance, that if I wanted a quick decision, I could have it—it would be no. Somehow, we worked through the impasse and the paper was accepted by the journal without amendments, a very unusual occurrence in my experience. I can only imagine the reluctance to grant permission was because the success of the unit cast a shadow on other aspects of the prison system; a system that was being wracked by a series of riots and hostage takings that were underpinned by systemic failures in mainstream prisons.

So why did the unit have this effect on its prisoners? It should be self-evident—but it wasn't—that disturbed, distressed and disordered people are not violent merely because of who they are, but also, because of where they are—and how they are treated. There was no silver bullet, no simple explanation. Rather there was a mosaic of situational factors that promoted this change of behaviour. Context matters. Supermarkets know this. That is why expensive wine is placed at eye level, slow music is played to encourage lingering, the smell of baked bread is diffused to trigger pleasant memories and, of course, chocolate bars are located at the check-outs to entice.

When it comes to understanding violence, unfortunately, context tends to be ignored at the expense of the individual. This is a fundamental attribution bias; that is, when we explain the behaviour of others we focus on their personal characteristics and peccadillos and downplay the impact of their circumstances; this is the opposite of what we do when explaining our own behaviour. Ultimately, individuals make decisions to be violent. This may be a bad decision, or a decision made badly. In an all-embracing environment such as a prison the decision is influenced by situational risk factors which—amongst other things—engender a sense of injustice, a sense of disrespect, a sense of uncertainty, loss of agency, loss of trust, or fear.

Clearly individual risk factors and situational risk factors interact; what were the situational risk factors within the unit that affected violent outcomes? It is difficult to identify and rank the specific ingredients that impacted behaviour, indeed, different aspects would be influential for different prisoners and at different times. Some factors do stand out. There can be little doubt that conscious attempts to change staff-inmate relationships were critical. Right from the beginning attempts were made to break the us-and-them culture, officers called prisoners by their first name, and vice-versa—a then unheard-of practice. A charismatic and influential prisoner, Jimmy Boyle, was clear: 'What made the Unit unlike any other place was the way staff and prisoners were allowed and encouraged to sit down and talk together. This was the single most important factor of the Unit' (Boyle, 1977: 11). And he was probably right.

Working in the BSU could be a tough experience for prison staff. Many were remarkable people. In those days being a prison officer required little training, but many had natural skills for dealing with people. The unit gave them the opportunity to exercise and hone these skills. They learned how to cajole, to negotiate, to reason rather than to impose their will by the application of rigid rules. It was a finishing school for staff who wanted new ways of working. I always thought that the unit should be judged as much for what it did for staff as for what it did for prisoners. There could be costs to pay. Colleagues in the mainstream prisons would deride unit staff as being 'care bears'; while, in fact the challenges of dealing with prisoners in new ways was anything but easy. Maintaining staff morale was important; this was a fundamental task for the unit Governor. It is noteworthy that the only significant act of violence during my ten year tenure at the BSU occurred when morale was at a particular low as a consequence a threat of disciplinary action hanging over staff. Staff were confused, they were demoralised, and the prisoners were infected by the anxiety that 'their staff' would be removed and hostile staff imposed upon them. Staff, fearful for their job, stopped focusing on their job. They weren't managing the violent men. Senior prison management knew about the problem; but despite my prompting, they failed to act.

While staff were critical, so were visitors. The greatest privilege in the unit was prisoners' access to visitors. Peter Whatmore was clear in his writings that personal visitors provided a control over violent and disruptive behaviour and an impetus towards change in social behaviour (Whatmore, 1987). Mothers, wives and girlfriends could assert control and influence. They did not want their sons or their partners to be shipped back to Peterhead Prison. This provided powerful control. But access to visitors could be a two-edged sword. They could bring in unacceptable goods and practices into the unit. In the latter days of the unit, certain prisoners avoided meaningful interactions with other members of the community by hiding behind their visitors.

Much has been made in some quarters about the quality of the regime: 'Porridge with Cream: a life of luxury behind bars in the Barlinnie Special Unit' read one of the headlines in the paper. To be frank, the physical conditions of the prison were grim; a dark, dank, cramped Victorian prison with little access to facilities in the main prison. Prisoners were encouraged and resourced to pursue their own interests; many engaged in constructive activities; some languished. Much emphasis has been placed on the artwork of the unit; this is quite right, some was remarkable. However, artwork was relevant to only a small proportion of prisoners. I suspect that the emphasis on art may reflect the existence of physical artifacts and powerful advocates for that work. In retrospect, while the laissez-faire approach to activities worked for a minority of prisoners, a more structured regime might have assisted the majority of the men.

The BSU prisoners arrived from conditions of high security and control, yet, perhaps contrary to expectations, the less overt and more diffuse control of the unit did not result in violence. The contrary was the case. This may seem paradoxical, but it is now clear that high levels of overt security and control can be the trigger for violence, not the solution for violence. This is particularly true when managing prisoners who are domineering, antagonistic, self-aggrandizing, entitled and reckless. The need to 'save face' can be critical; aggression escalating in a trial of strength.

In the unit, the nexus of control was shifted from the Governor and his other staff towards the community. Community meetings of various types and sizes were used to deal with everything from the mundane—why the video repair was taking so long—to the serious—a prisoner going absent while on day-leave. Community meetings depended on challenging the inappropriate behaviour of staff and prisoners alike. I recall being challenged and it was not comfortable! Attempts were made to resolve conflicts or crises through discussion and debate, rather than through violence. Often resolutions would not be achieved but the process would take the heat out of the issue.

As I said, the BSU served as my university of crime and criminals. So, what did I learn from my time served with the unit? I can identify three themes that influenced my subsequent research and professional experience. First, I became aware of the concept of psychopathic personality disorder. I also became aware of practical and theoretical problems with the standard measure of the disorder. Thus, together with colleagues from Canada and England, I developed a more comprehensive and clinically nuanced description of the disorder—the Comprehensive Assessment of Psychopathic Personality (CAPP)(Cooke, Hart, Logan, Michie, 2012). This measure was designed to measure change, should change occur, either through therapeutic intervention or maturation. The CAPP has now been translated into over 28 different languages and is widely used (Cooke, 2018). Second, the unit highlighted the importance of context when it comes to understanding institutional violence. Together, with another colleague, we developed PRISM. This delivers an evidence-based risk assessment process designed to identify the situational risk factors that promote violence in institutions (Cooke, 2020; Johnstone and Cooke, 2008). The approach has been used to understand and modify practices in prisons and high-security hospitals, across England, Scandinavia, Singapore, New Zealand, California and Barbados. Third, the unit taught me the folly of simplistic risk assessment. People are violent for many different reasons; they may come to the same destination along many different pathways. I have railed against these simplistic approaches and promoted evidence-based structured professional judgement approaches (Cooke and Michie, 2014). I can trace the origins of these three themes of research directly to the unit. I am very conscious of how privileged I was to have had the opportunity to work with the staff and prisoners in this historic, stimulating and influential prison experiment—the BSU.

References

Boyle, J (1977), *A Sense of Freedom*, London: Handbooks.

Cooke, D J (1989), Containing Violent Prisoners: An Analysis of the Barlinnie Special Unit, *British Journal of Criminology*, 29: 129–143.

Cooke, D J (1997), The Barlinnie Special Unit: The Rise and Fall of a Therapeutic Experiment. In *Therapeutic Communities for Offenders*, E Cullen, L Jones and R Woodward, London: Wiley: 101–120.

Cooke, D J (2018), Psychopathic Personality Disorder: Capturing an Elusive Concept, *European Journal of Analytic Philosophy*, 14(1): 15–32.

Cooke, D J (2019), Violence and the Pains of Confinement: PRISM as a Promising Paradigm for Violence Prevention. In D Polaschek, A Day and C R Hollin (eds), *The Wiley International Handbook of Correctional Psychology*, 78–93. London: Wiley.

Cooke, D J, et al (2012), Explicating the Construct of Psychopathy: Development and Validation of a Conceptual Model, the Comprehensive Assessment of Psychopathic Personality (CAPP), *International Journal of Forensic Mental Health*, 11(4): 242–252.

Cooke, D J and Michie, C (2014), The Generalizability of the Risk Matrix 2000: On Model Shrinkage and the Misinterpretation of the Area Under the Curve, *Journal of Threat Assessment and Management*, 1(1): 42.

Hare, R D (1980), A Research Scale for the Assessment of Psychopathy in Criminal Populations, *Personality and Individual Differences*, 1: 111–119.

Johnstone, L and Cooke D J (2008), Promoting Risk Intervention by Situational Management: Structured Professional Guidelines for Assessing Situational Risk Factors for Violence in Institutions. See https://prism-network.no/

Whatmore, P B (1987), Barlinnie Special Unit: An Insider's View. In *Problems of Long-term Imprisonment*, A E Bottoms and R Light, Aldershot: Gower.

CHAPTER 13

'The whole thing felt like the hot seat in some respect'

Interview with Richard Sparks by Kirstin Anderson

Richard Sparks is Professor of Criminology at the University of Edinburgh. He co-authored the 1994 Scottish Prison Service (SPS) commissioned report 'Barlinnie Special Unit and Shotts Unit: An Assessment' with Keith Bottomley and Alison Liebling. He has worked extensively on questions of power and control in prisons before, and since, his work on the BSU. The following interview took place on 3 April 2023.

To begin, can you tell me a bit about your professional career, your studies as a student and then your development as a researcher?

I became a Criminology student in 1983 when I enrolled on the MPhil course in Criminology at Cambridge like many others before and since. I guess my specific interest in the subject had been aroused by a series of lectures given by Colin Sumner, who later became my PhD supervisor, when I was an undergraduate studying sociology and social psychology, also in Cambridge. Unlike many people who enter the criminological field from some area of practice, it was very much an academic trajectory for me. Originally, when I began my own PhD studies, they had nothing to do at all with prisons. I was working on representations of crime and media and I wrote a book on that subject. And for a long time, I didn't know whether I was a criminology person or a media studies person, and indeed some of the first jobs I applied for were in media and journalism rather than criminology or penology.

Intellectually, it seemed to matter less to me after a while that I somehow needed to resolve a dilemma about being or not being a criminologist. I became very relaxed about that; and I still think that—which is easy for me to say, because you know I've had secure jobs in criminology for a long time. So, I was thinking about it from a fairly privileged standpoint. However, I still think it's important that one can become much too preoccupied by those kinds of disciplinary definitional questions that actually just get in the way of doing what you would most like to do, that's most useful to do.

What interested you in studying prisons and have those interests changed over your career?

As with many things, I do think there was there was an element of chance and luck about how I wound up studying prisons. Tony Bottoms, who was the Wolfson Professor in Cambridge and Director of the Institute of Criminology at that time, was starting a research project about control problems in long-term prisons in England and Wales that fed into all kinds of debates that were going on in and around the Home Office—as it was at the time, the Prisons Department of the Home Office—about the persistence of that particular set of problems. Tony wanted a couple of people to work on this project and he fingered me and my colleague Will Hay as being what he conceived as being a sort of 'Dream Team'. If I use that term, it's not a boast, but it's what I think Tony felt about the disparate pairing of quite a young person in me with quite a strong academic history and an interest in theory, and Will, who had lots of those things too, but he also had a completely different set of life experiences. He was a probation officer who had been around the scene in a practical sense for a long time. He had been in and out of prisons a lot as a probation officer. Before he was a probation officer, he was a betting shop manager. He was the kind of old hand, as it were.

And Tony thought that we somehow might complement one another in an interesting way. And we like to think that proved to be the case because that group, I mean the group of the three of us, I think really did feel a lot of affinity with one another and interest in what each other brought to the project. And we're still friends now, nearly 40 years later. So, I've been lucky. Whenever

I get interviewed about these kinds of questions that is what I tell people. I've been very lucky.

It didn't take me long to work out as soon as I started going into prisons that on a kind of personal and emotional, as well as intellectual level, it was challenging and involving in a way that other things I was doing, or might have gone on to do, weren't. So, the realness, but at the same time the puzzling peculiarity and kind of enigmatic nature of the prison as an institution, made a very forceful impact upon me from a very early point. Once I was involved in that world, it soon became something that preoccupied me greatly. I managed to finish my PhD and to maintain an interest in those subjects for a while, but that kind of fell away because I became much more interested in what I encountered doing the prisons research and thinking about all of the multitude of moral, philosophical, sociological and personal problems that they present.

I don't know if I should mention this because it didn't strike me at the time as being particularly relevant, but it's hard to say without it becoming apparent that it is actually relevant, that my father was for some period of time, a prison chaplain. Most of my young life, he was actually working as a teacher and subsequently a psychotherapist. But first he was a Church of England minister, and he was the chaplain at Lancaster Prison when I was a teenager.

That's a whole other interview, thinking about that experience of growing up! When did you first hear about the BSU? And what did you think about this special experiment?

OK, I think I knew that the Special Unit existed even before I personally started working in prisons. I heard about it while I was a student and certainly by the time I'd been a Master's student, I knew something of it. Jimmy Boyle was certainly a public figure during that period and a number of people that I spent time with at that time were extremely interested in what he was doing; and I read *A Sense of Freedom* not long after that. It was hard to be moving in that world without knowing who Jimmy Boyle was at that point, at least in part, should we say.

It's very different from today, actually.

Yeah. Absolutely, if you give students those books to read now, or any of the other books that people in the Special Unit produced, there is a sense of discovery but this is usually not something they have thought of or heard of previously. But also, at the time what is sometimes also forgotten, not least by people who have particular interest in the Special Unit from the Scottish perspective, is that there was a small units strategy in England and Wales as well during the 1980s and 1990s. None of those units were arguably as radical as the Special Unit in certain senses, but some of them were doing quite interesting things. And part of the inception of the project that Will and I worked on with Tony Bottoms came from something called the 'Research and Advisory Group on the Long-term Prison System', of which Tony Bottoms and Roy King were the academic members. They had produced a report in, I think 1987, that was all about models of control and order in long-term English prisons. So, there was quite an active interest in it; in finding out what the available ideas and practices were that might be applied or adapted or rejected when they started thinking about both regimes in long-term prisons generally, but also in this kind of special units subsystem that then existed. That's why Alison Liebling and I have to this day an uncompleted proposal to revisit that whole question on a whole of UK or comparative basis rather than simply focusing on the Special Unit as the one-off entity that we sometimes think of it as being.

Can you reflect on how the press presented the Special Unit? Also, how were the smaller units in England and Wales different from the Special Unit?

Well, the English units were less well-known and, in a way, less notorious. However, this is actually quite a... somebody needs to do a PhD about this in itself. The small units that existed in England and Wales during the late 1980s, when I was involved, were preceded by something much more contentious, which were called the 'Control Units' at Wakefield. The Wakefield Control Units were much more comparable to the so-called cages in Inverness and the unit at Perth that turned out to be so contentious in the history of Scottish prisons. Those places provided a really important counterpoint to the Special Unit. One has to bear in mind that the creation of the Special Unit didn't immediately lead to the closure of those things in the Scottish context. In the end The Cages lasted almost as long as the Special Unit itself. However, the Control Units in Wakefield were closed down because of various cases that were brought at the time. There was always a sense during the 1980s and 1990s that the prison system of England and Wales, and the prison system in Scotland, were on the hunt for something that would make a difference, that would alleviate a problem that was endemic within the long-term prison systems as being forever on the brink of potential major disorder. And then, of course, on a number of occasions that disorder occurred in explosive forms both in England throughout the long-term prisons really, and certainly throughout the 'dispersal' prisons, and in Scotland at Barlinnie and at Peterhead in particular.

You mentioned the Inverness cages. So, these kind of stopping points remained open?

I believe that The Cages were last used in 1991, and formally closed in 1994. They became contentious, but partly through the sort of publicity that surrounded Boyle and his story. And then the fact that there was an alternative approach that was being piloted at the Special Unit that made it unthinkable that one could manage without them. But on the other hand, there were segregation units throughout the Scottish Prison System, most notoriously, Peterhead, which did remain in being throughout the entire history of the Special Unit. They were never discontinued just because something more interesting and progressive existed. And there are prisoners in Scotland in very long-term segregation as we speak, of course.

When did you start your fieldwork? Was it in the summer of 1992?

Well, the first time I went to the Special Unit, we were still finishing off our English project, and if you read, re-read should we say, *Prisons and the Problem of Order,* in the final chapter there's a table which sets out what we call a speculative model of forms of social order in prison. In that model, the Special Unit is one end of a spectrum. And at the other end, there are the various forms of very closed, very controlled, as we might now say, *locked down* kinds of environments, as most notoriously in that period at Marion Penitentiary in

Illinois, but also as at Inverness or Wakefield. We were working with the idea of a spectrum of possible states of institutional ordering of which the Special Unit was always a part. The first time we visited was very briefly, but that would have been in about 1990 while we were writing up the book.

What was that visit like? Do you remember your first time walking into the BSU?

Yeah, I do, yeah. I do remember because I remember a particular encounter with one Special Unit prisoner, the classic Glaswegian wee hard man, I guess you might say. He kind of walked up to me when we first went in, he looked at me and said, you might say sceptically, something about, 'Oh, so you're from Cambridge.' I said, 'That's right. That's where we've come from.' He looked me up and down dismissively and said, 'I'm from another planet, pal.' I didn't forget it and it was certainly quite impactful.

So that was the first time that you went and then when you went to do the piece of work, the report you were writing. What was that experience going back?

It was very challenging… I had spent quite a lot of time doing recent prisons field work by that time. I got quite used to being in and around certain kinds of prison environments. I had been used to being away from home doing it, so those things I was familiar with.

But the Special Unit was always a bit more kind of immersive. You know people nowadays have difficulty I think grasping the physical reality of it. It was so deeply within the confines of Barlinnie Prison that you went across the sterile area and then you turned to your right and went through this other little gateway into the world of the Special Unit, which was the old women's wing. And it was tiny. It was cramped. It wasn't purpose built. It was cramped internally. It did have a small garden. It was surrounded by rather high walls, beyond which there was just more prison. So, you felt right, deep, deep inside something. And it took a while getting in and out for visitors and for me, which is a long-winded way of saying once you were in, you didn't kind of go out during the rest of the day very much. I would stay in for the entire day.

I would arrive kind of early in the day and I would just stay there, and unlike in most prison settings where, you know, you come to a certain point in the afternoon and everybody's behind their door, that never happened in the Special Unit. So, I would just stay and I was on this short but intense period of field work in Glasgow where I knew very few other people, so I tended to spend the evening there too. I was only in the Special Unit for about six weeks. But during the time that I was there, I was there from, you know, 9 or 9:30 am until 8 or 9 at night, 12 hours a day. And that meant I was eating with people there, either with the staff or the prisoners or both. And I was just spending my whole time there. Which also meant that because people were allowed to have visitors in their cells, the conversations that I had with people, I did do formal interviews that I recorded and transcribed, but they were the culmination of just hours upon hours of conversations with those individuals. So, by the time I conducted the interviews with the six or seven out of the, I think there were eight prisoners who were there at the time, I felt I knew them quite well.

So, a lot of those conversations weren't recorded?

There were hundreds of hours of conversations that weren't recorded.

You were getting to know people, and they were getting to know you. You talk about the hot seat, like being in the hot seat.

The whole thing felt like the hot seat in some respects. The hot seat is just the name given to the position occupied by the visitor at a Special Unit's Tuesday meeting. It wasn't just me. If people wanted access or they wanted to do something in the unit, and there might be many things that they wanted, then they needed co-operation and agreement from the prisoners and staff—the Special Unit community. They might want to make a film or they might want to come and make another TV documentary. Or, they wanted to do this or that; they had to undergo this kind of process.

I was working on a report commissioned by the SPS to evaluate the Special Unit and Shotts Unit. I was co-working with Alison Liebling, who was in the Shotts Unit, and we were being supervised by Keith Bottomley, who was the principal investigator on the project, and we were the two contracted researchers, each delegated to one of those two places. Access in both cases meant agreement on the part of the staff and prisoners, whereas on the whole in my experience up to that point, access meant agreement by the Governor of the prison, whether or not you could get anybody to talk to you, but you formally 'had access' from the Prison Service and the delegated authority of the Governor of the prison. In this case, access was an agreement between the members of the Special Unit community, meaning both staff and prisoners.

When you arrived in the early 1990s, how was art used in the unit, if at all at that point, because this is over two decades after its inception?

One of the first things that some of the prisoners invited me to do was to play five-a-side with them. Um, which was certainly an experience. The Special Unit had its own slots in the gym so the Special Unit prisoners didn't mingle with anyone else. We played five-a-side there and I got bashed up a bit [laughs]. And it was all kind of interesting. And one of the prisoners said something along the lines of the five-a-side's fun and we love the Special Unit, but we're not into all that arty farty stuff! We like talking to Peter Whatmore (he was the unit psychiatrist, and he was a bit of a sort of guru figure for some of these guys). They would nominate a number of things, especially access to their families and other visitors as being kind of great things about the unit. But at that point in time, they mostly didn't say much about the arts.

And I think it was true, actually, that there wasn't so much of that happening there any more by 1992. I think there were a couple of people who were writing, in some sense, autobiographical work or who were talking to historians, biographers, or filmmakers in some shape or form, because there was still quite an active cultural interest in the unit. There were one or two people who were making art. There was one person in particular who was extremely interested in ceramics. But the other people there, their pastimes, their external hobbies were keeping pigeons or gardening rather than creative arts as such.

Even so the people in the unit very much described themselves to me, two or three cases in particular, that they were working *on themselves* as they saw it. They were trying very consciously to develop and craft a new sense of themselves in a different vision of their future and to signal a quite sharp distinction between their previous lives and the ones that they were hoping to live. And the talking to me, like talking to lots of other people who came in, the unit was part of that. But they weren't necessarily doing it through painting or sculpture or other artistic production.

That's interesting to think about because what the BSU is still remembered for, I think, in the forefront is that role of art.

Absolutely. I think it probably does belong to some of the... I wouldn't like to attempt a kind of periodisation of the unit's history off the top of my head. I think somebody probably needs to do that, mind you. I think that probably does belong more to the earlier phases of its existence, and that part of the way in which people, certainly elsewhere in the Scottish Prison Service, had become more sceptical about it. By the time I got there, some of those earlier aspirations seemed to have diminished. So, what was it doing now? There weren't these visible objects and artefacts that you could point to as saying, here's what the unit produces.

There were some charismatic individuals but not people who were associated with having written an award-winning autobiography or being feted by the Edinburgh or Glasgow artistic communities. At the same time, lots of people in the unit, let alone elsewhere in the SPS, were rather cynical about all of that and resented it. They thought that what had happened was that certain individuals had been adopted by people who saw them as somewhat kind of glamorous and a bit sexy—and they were quite glamorous and sexy people—and liked having them at their events and or kind of having been seen to be in some kind of association with them, and people were getting a little bit fed up with what they saw as being an exploitation. And I think there was something exploitative about some of it, frankly. But that's one of the reasons why some of those people themselves subsequently kind of walked away from the celebrity that they might otherwise have had. In fact, the second part of Hugh Collins's autobiography is called *Walking Away*, I think partly for that reason.

That's really interesting to think about. One of the things you also wrote about was the isolation and solidarities, and the idea that isolation can bring together those solidarities. During that immersive time that you were talking to the men in the BSU, what experiences of isolation and solidarities did you observe?

They did talk about that. People were certainly, you know, on the surface clearly much less isolated than what they would have been at other points in their prison careers because they were seeing and rebuilding their relations with their families and friends, and they were talking... I mean, one of the things that struck me about it strongly, and which I've tried to write about here and there, is that they wanted to talk about those things and those experiences and about themselves *a lot*. They had a lot of talking to do.

And that would include, because the relationships were different, talking to staff in a way that they would not have considered talking to prison officers anywhere else. But on the other hand, it would be easy to overplay the relationship between prisoners and staff in the Special Unit in that period. It wasn't as trusting and sharing as all that. I think there were boundaries. People chose whom they spoke to, and those conversations were still private. So, whether people felt isolated, I don't know, but one of the things that they all felt, to a greater or lesser extent, was something about privacy, I think. And they talked to me, or some of them did, but then I was only there for a strictly limited period of time. An intense one.

In your article, 'Out of the Digger', you say, 'probably my only greatest finding is that the only thing special about the special unit was the talk.'

Yeah, I still think that. Absolutely, I do. And you know, there are some other spaces where that happens. But it was somewhere where it happened a lot, and it was somewhere where it happened for a certain number of people who have been very much deprived of that opportunity until then and who had a lot of things to talk about.

I think their view, which I tried to convey, is that there would have been many reasons for people on a typical hall to be more guarded about some aspects of who they spoke to about what subjects, and where there would have been fewer opportunities to talk at some of those levels of reflectiveness, or depth or just length without making themselves vulnerable. A lot of the guys who happened to be there in that period, I think, were all feeling something to do with their incipient ageing and that, had they unburdened themselves in any of these ways in a standard prison environment, they would've been making themselves vulnerable in a way that they weren't prepared to do.

I think it was psychologically difficult for many people initially and perhaps ultimately if you didn't have the resources with which to respond to it. It could also be extremely tedious; you know how unstructured time can be both tedious and emotionally very challenging.

The last series of questions have to do with the report that you wrote in the aftermath of that. What were the main findings in the 1994 report?

I was trying to convey, because I was trying to be a proper researcher and to report what people had said to me rather than simply, if you like, my own inference; and what the people were saying to me was that the unit gave them the opportunity to step away from conflict, to step away from the previously ingrained identity as a gangster or a hard man, or a notorious convict in a small prison world like Scotland. It's not small enough, obviously. But the unit's smallness was something that was deeply precious to them, because otherwise they could not have seen, they had no way of envisaging another way of managing their lives in prison. They were all life sentence prisoners in this period and in different ways they were all looking for an opportunity to break with the past. That was the key thing about it. It didn't have a magic therapeutic wand, nor even the kind of specialness perhaps of the heyday of the artistic intensity. But it still constituted a kind of major punctuation mark in their prisoner experience, from which point they could begin so see themselves differently and to look at the world a bit differently. That may be why sometimes their ideas of the future could seem a little bit romantic and unrealistic.

One of the prisoners wanted to be released into the care of a religious order so that he would go from his rather monastic life in the Special Unit to living in an actual monastery, because that's what he could envisage as a form of a kind of peaceful life that wouldn't challenge him in the ways that had caused him so much trouble in the past. Another, perhaps more realistically, just wanted to spend his time with his family. I think they had a caravan somewhere in a caravan park on the coast and he just wanted to go there and be quiet, be near the sea, and all of those things. People had a very, in a way, limited and specific, not always realistic, idea of what life might be like.

But they kind formed those ideas, I think, partly in the Special Unit because they were different from carrying on being who they'd been previously. That was what it did for people looking to have some sort of break. The other main finding was that the SPS had produced a kind of stalemate with the prisoners.

Because the theory that made sense from the point of view of the institutional logic that prison systems think with was, okay, so if you've changed, then you have to go do a certain period of time in another prison to test that change and then become eligible for parole. Whereas the prisoners in the Special Unit all said, no, what we want is to be given our parole date from here and then move on. And it was a kind of an irreconcilable difference. The SPS wasn't prepared to compromise on the idea of the test and was very, very reluctant to release people directly from the Special Unit, whereas these guys, all of whom were more than ten years into a life sentence, most of them were already in the 40s or older at this time, not all, but most. One or two were way later in their lives and sentences and they couldn't stand the idea of going from that kind of quiet, somewhat retired life back to another prison. So, really, they had gone to the Special Unit and retired as big time prisoners and they couldn't face the idea of going back because there were younger, rougher, tougher people there. And the being tested was a test they couldn't pass and were actually quite fearful of and I thought that made every kind of sense to me. Some people contest this interpretation, I should say. But the prisoners concerned talked to me about it a great deal.

Also, tests are not always good indicators. In some way you would think the Special Unit would have been a kind of test?

It certainly was and people experienced it as such. The things that they said to me which are in that document have a lot to say about the ways in which they found that experience testing. But what their objection was to going, as they saw it, backwards to being tested to discover whether they were, in some sense, who they thought they'd got away from. It's an interesting idea, but do we apply this to other areas. The test of having, you know, stop drinking to be exposed to people drinking heavily. Is the test of having changed your diet to be given cake? I don't know.

Because we're like, here's this thing that you've worked so hard to not do and now the test is to put you into that situation. But it is ingrained in us, I think, and not without reason, that you don't take that person who's done such things in their life previously at their own evaluation, so some idea of a test must have seemed important to them. Can this resolution that this person made survive being tested? The question for me is, *which* test do you subject them to?

Exactly. Also, the test of going back into a traditional prison hall is not the same as the test of going into the community. You say in the article that you think the report may have possibly tipped a decision that was in balance or that had already been made. What do you think possibly tipped it?

I think there were many things, and the fact that there was always ambivalence about Special Units elsewhere in the SPS, including a certain amount of outright hostility to them, is part of the story. There's no getting away from that. The 'Nutcracker Suite' and all of that. Indeed, the fact that people are still talking about it at any level is somewhat extraordinary given that it's been 30 years without it. The SPS was certainly changing at the time, it was being led by a more forward-looking and hopeful, I guess, ambitious group; in a certain sense, a new generation of people. They actually, I think, saw the Special Unit as part of the previous story and their question was why did we need the Special Unit? Well, because, things were as they were at Peterhead, and because there were changes in Inverness and all of those reasons. So, their argument was, we can do without this now because we've moved on from that. They saw it as being part of that story, not part of the future.

And I can understand why they did, in a certain sense, they saw this progressive thing that was so kind of admired externally as being a bit actually much more ambivalently as part of the legacy of the conflictual and terrible story with Scottish prisons in the 1970s and 1980s and therefore that there was a sense in which there were some of the good things about it that could be reproduced elsewhere, that it didn't have a kind of magic that said, there can be only one, which is one of the very negative things about the 'specialness' of special units.

And that people who lauded it and admired it in a certain sense wanted to keep it just as it was in a way that became quite reactionary. And that's why I think there was a contradiction that kind of eventually couldn't be resolved from the point of view of the decision-makers in any other way than deciding that they could do without it.

If you can, take yourself back to the 1990s, after the unit was closed and the report was published. You wrote in 'Out of the Digger', that you didn't hear anything for a while from the SPS, and then you heard the unit was closing. How did that experience of conducting fieldwork in the BSU impact your future work in prisons?

Well, it probably contributed to the fact that although I've been involved in other prison projects and supervised a number of PhDs in prisons, I haven't done as much subsequent prison fieldwork as all that. It was quite hurtful, if I'm honest. It took me a long time to write that paper. I mean, it came out ten years later. I did do other things, and I was very involved in the other things that I was doing. But it's quite, you know, there was a certain divergence between, shall we say, the things that I did subsequently and what other friends, like Alison Liebling, did with her career, which is very much more prison focused than mine. I, at the very least, wanted a break from all that. I found it hard to accept the outcome or my association with it. I felt that the work that I'd done had been used by other people, but in ways that were not acceptable to me. And those involved using it in a certain sense not only for purposes that were other than the ones that I supported, but also in ways that seemed to me less than candid or open. So that was difficult, and disappointing, to me.

I know that other people, including people in SPS, have read that paper and feel some affinity with it. I found that affirmative, latterly. I know that some of them understand the nature of the problem, not just from my point of view, but the problem of the relationship between prisons research and the outcomes of that work. I think I developed a better feel, a more realistic feel over time, as to what those possible relationships could be so the fact that that one turned very sour, to me, didn't mean that the whole project was impossible. I think I've kind of come to terms with all of that relatively fruitfully and

I have relations with people in SPS that are important to me to this day. That's all fine. It wasn't so for a long time, though.

It's this idea that you can get burned by experiences of work and research the same way you can in a relationship?

Well, I guess that's true. I think as Bob Dylan says somewhere, 'either I'm too sensitive or else I'm getting soft' [both laugh]. I found it difficult to reconstruct exactly how I came to write it. I thought it was important that I hadn't been able to do it until that time. I guess it was something unfreezing in my own sense of what I was able to say about it, but also that I think that the mind is like a kind of compost heap in the sense that you know it takes time for stuff to become usable sometimes. Although there was a lot to be said that was difficult in that paper, I had come to a point where I felt it was possible to say something productive rather than just giving my own side of the story because I felt aggrieved in some way.

One of the things you wrote about in that article was the genius of what SPS did at the time was to have created a place beyond the terminus such as The Cages at Inverness or Peterhead. Does that exist in the SPS today? Has the SPS learned, if there is a legacy of these special units, is there something beyond the terminus?

I suspect not. The SPS, and perhaps other contemporary systems, have learned something about not driving people into corners to quite the extent that was happening in the 1970s and 1980s. And the SPS has a range of different options and places and institutions for people to go there and can be tried to give them another opportunity somewhere else in more conventional ways, that is, nevertheless wiser than it would have been in that period. And there isn't a Peterhead looming over the whole thing in the same sense as being, in itself, just an austere and inherently problematic place to be. Having said all that, I think there clearly are a number of people in that system who are in semi-permanent states of segregation for whom there are no obvious solutions, and that the system doesn't envisage solutions for them and most people have forgotten that there ever was a solution that might have been suitable for some of those people because the default position of prison systems when it comes to their most difficult prisoners is 'this is where it stops'. We might do our level best to be patient with that person. We have people who become very adept at conversing with them in certain kinds of circumstances, we kind of handle and contain them more or less humanely. But that's it. And I don't think there is an equivalent now at all.

The frustration that is felt, I guess by me, but not only by me, by other people who worked in the Special Unit, who were its leaders and practitioners over time and by people who experienced it as prisoners and who understood something about its impact in their life is that the legacy was so faint and, in some ways deliberately so. It was put aside in some sense for an extended period of time. So yes, I think the traces of the Special Unit have become quite hard to see now in Scotland.

Thank you. Is there anything you've thought of that I've not asked you about?

You asked me something about the media coverage earlier. There was a lot of hostility. There was also pride. So, one of the interesting things about the place of the Special Unit in Scottish contemporary history is this ambivalence, I think that, you know, on the one hand there was this sense that once upon a time, in that moment Scotland did something that was ahead of what, more or less, anybody else was doing. It was bold. Daring. And in some ways, you know, unlocked a problem. A small and niche problem in a certain sense, but a serious problem, and in a way that nothing else would have done. And that it had the imagination and the boldness to do that thing.

But at the same time, it was also widely detested, including by quite a number of influential people elsewhere within the SPS. And partly on grounds of fairness that I can also understand and relate to other prisoners. To people who just did their sentences and went home. To ordinary prisoners and prison officers and their experiences and their families and their being much more numerous. It's always the case within subsystems of education systems or prison systems or hospital systems, that the most difficult people get the most resources.

It also meant that those people we're also getting transferred closer to home. For most of them, Glasgow was home. They were getting to see their families all day long. They were getting stuff other people never got. It was difficult for those people to then translate that into saying, this reveals some very significant defects in the rest of the prison system that needs to be addressed. Instead, they tended to say the Special Unit is an anomaly that can't be tolerated.

Which is interesting and I think related to what you would have written about in terms of it being labelled an experiment. However, it was never replicated.

Never replicated and never evaluated, until it was too late. That was where that paper came from. Because my sense was that by the time I went there to offer the evaluation, it was already too late.

I remember, as a student, reading about the BSU and thinking how unusual that the SPS, instead of doubling down, did something different. There is still relatively little written about the unit. It's sporadic and it doesn't seem to be embraced by the SPS as part of what they chose to do and how they chose to work, and I wonder if that's connected to the lack of legacy?

Yeah, I think, in a way, it's a consequence of the lack of legacy. It's a circular thing. Certain people felt that the unit in being closed down had to be repudiated. It meant that they couldn't build a legacy on it. There are only so many things you can say about failed relationships. Either it was always bad or it went wrong, but either way it wound up being bad. Legacy is problematic. The legacy was problematic for the system of which it had been a part, but on many levels, in terms of both the ways in which it couldn't be integrated either by the reactionaries who always hated it or by the progressive managerialists who couldn't assimilate it. From that point, the legacy isn't strong enough to be the thing on which to build foundations of something new. That's exactly why we need to look at it again now.

PART III

LEGACIES AND LESSONS

CHAPTER 14

The Genesis and Legacy of the BSU

Andrew Coyle

Backstory: Peterhead, Scotland's Convict Prison

Any account of the creation of the Barlinnie Special Unit should necessarily begin in the former Peterhead Prison on the Northeast coast of Scotland. The violence which was endemic inside that prison in the late 1960s and early 1970s, and which spread to what became in effect its segregation annexe within Inverness Prison 100 miles to the east of Peterhead, led directly to the opening of the BSU in 1973. A generation later the removal of the high security prisoners from Peterhead in the early 1990s led, at least indirectly, to the closure of the BSU in 1995.

From its opening in 1888 Peterhead was of symbolic pre-eminence in the Scottish Prison System: it was the country's only convict prison, a grim and depressing fortress set on Salthouse headland jutting into the North Sea, holding men who had been sentenced to imprisonment with hard labour. Each day the convicts were conveyed over two miles on a private railway to the quarry at Boddam where they extracted granite for the construction of a new harbour of refuge just below the prison, supervised by warders armed with rifles and cutlasses. In 1949 the court sentences of penal servitude and imprisonment with hard labour were abolished but men serving long prison sentences continued to be sent to Peterhead and worked in the quarry until it closed in 1957.

By the late 1960s the description 'long-term prisoner' in Scotland was applied to anyone serving a sentence of over 18 months, that is, who was eligible for early release on parole. Those serving a first prison sentence were held in Edinburgh

Prison; those who had served a previous sentence but who were assessed as being likely to conform to the prison regime were held in Perth Prison; while those who were assessed as being unlikely to conform, as well as some who had an especially high profile or who were thought to be particularly dangerous or to be a high escape risk, were sent to Peterhead Prison.

Throughout the 20th century the majority of the Peterhead staff were recruited from the local Buchan area. Their cultural roots were far removed from those of the prisoners, most of whom came from the central belt of Scotland, predominantly from the Glasgow area. For the prisoners, the relatively remote location and the harsh climate added to the brutal rigours of the regime and there was a sense of isolation which eventually became alienation. There was also a symbiotic relationship between Peterhead and the rest of the Scottish Prison Service (SPS): staff in other prisons regarded Peterhead as being 'different', the end of the line; while Peterhead staff themselves felt that their role in taking prisoners who could not be managed in other prisons was not sufficiently acknowledged by colleagues elsewhere.

From the 1950s onwards Peterhead was increasingly characterised by what were described as 'acts of violence, subversion and increasing tension.' The SPS responded initially by constructing a special segregation unit within Peterhead and, in 1966, by converting part of the small local prison at Inverness into what was in practical terms a segregation unit for men who could not be managed in the Peterhead segregation unit. Inside each small cell prisoners were confined to an area behind a grille which stretched from floor to ceiling. Far from reducing tension, extended use of what became known as 'The Cages' in Inverness led to what an official report described as 'a vicious circle of violence and retribution which appeared unending' and which culminated in 1972 in a bloody disturbance in which several prisoners and staff were seriously injured. It was clear that an alternative to the 'iron fist' response was required.[1]

---

1. For a more detailed history of the longstanding problems in Peterhead Prison and the Scottish Government's responses over decades see Coyle, A (1991), *Inside: Rethinking Scotland's Prisons*. Edinburgh: Scottish Child.

The Establishment of the Barlinnie Special Unit

In 1971 the Government appointed a working party to 'consider what arrangements should be made for the treatment of certain inmates likely to be detained in custody for very long periods or with propensities for violence towards staff.' The working party started from the premise that the problem which had to be resolved lay not within Peterhead as an institution but with the reaction of a small number of individual prisoners: 'The problem of prison violence is very much a personal one, specific to the individual who is violent.' It concluded that the Prison Service should create 'a special unit for investigation and treatment of prisoners who are violent or potentially so.' It went on to caution that this unit should be 'not so attractive that inmates will behave badly so that they may be sent to the special unit.' It concluded, 'What we recommend can, at this stage, be regarded as solely experimental. We can give no guarantee of success but ... if it is successful it may indicate the way in which the penal system should be developed in future.'[2]

The working party recommended that this 'experimental special unit' should be set up in Perth Prison with a maximum of 20 places but it was subsequently concluded that the buildings there were unsuitable and instead attention turned to a small unit inside Barlinnie Prison which had previously held female prisoners on remand but at that point was lying empty. When the BSU opened in early 1973 with spaces for eight men the Government announced that its purpose would be 'to treat those inmates whose potential for violence stems from some degree of mental instability or whose length of sentence gives rise to difficulties in their being treated and contained within normal institutional regimes.'[3]

The undoubted success of the BSU in its early years was due to a group of individuals, including a far-sighted senior Scottish Office administrator (Alex Stephen who had chaired the 1971 working party), the first group of prisoners and key members of staff in the unit, ably supported throughout by specialist staff from the Douglas Inch Centre in Glasgow as well as by a committed group of art therapists, social workers and others from beyond the usual prison

2. Scottish Home and Health Department (1971), *Report of the Working Party on the Treatment of Certain Male Long Term Prisoners and Potentially Violent Prisoners*, Edinburgh: SHHD.
3. SHHD, Circular 73/1972. Edinburgh: SHHD.

environment. All of this came about despite the disadvantages of the cramped physical environment and its limited facilities.

The story of how the unit was set up and subsequently took shape, establishing a well-deserved international reputation for its innovative environment, particularly during the first decade of its existence, is told in fascinating detail in *The Special Unit Barlinnie Prison: Its Evolution Through Its Art* published by the Third Eye Centre in 1982 and is also covered in other chapters in the current volume. That same year the recently appointed first independent Chief Inspector of Prisons carried out a one day inspection of the unit. His subsequent report had little to say about the creative activities of the men other than that they were 'determined by the personal interest of each individual in a variety of occupational activities' but it reported positively on the 'personal relationships which are established between staff and inmates and their relatives.'[4]

Response to Unrest in Scottish Prisons in the 1980s

The latter half of the 1980s was a traumatic period in Scottish prisons, with an outbreak of serious violence in Edinburgh Prison in October 1986, followed over the next 18 months by dramatic and highly publicised riots in Peterhead, Barlinnie, Glenochil and Shotts prisons.[5] A single thread, which ran through all of these disruptions, stretched back to Peterhead. The main protagonists in the Edinburgh riot were Peterhead prisoners who had been transferred to Edinburgh Prison for what were known as annual 'accumulated visits' with their families and the root of their grievance was the harsh treatment which they were receiving in Peterhead. Several of the prisoners who later took three officers hostage in Barlinnie and paraded them on the roof of a hall in the full glare of the national media had recently been in Peterhead and the focus of their complaints was the Barlinnie Governor, who had previously been in charge at Peterhead. Two of the major riots occurred in Peterhead itself, with the second one being brought to an end by the intervention of an SAS army unit.

4. HM Inspectorate of Prisons for Scotland (1982), Report on HM Special Unit Barlinnie.
5. The SPS immediate operational response to these incidents is described in Coyle, A (2002), Prison Governor in R Flin and K Arbuthnot, *Incident Command: Tales From the Hot Seat*, Aldershot: Ashgate Publishing: 176–197.

In contrast to the conclusion of the 1971 working party that the 'problem of prison violence is ... specific to the individual who is violent,' there was a greater awareness in the late 1980s of the need for a root and branch review of the entire long-term prison system in Scotland. The SPS produced a series of policy papers, culminating in 1990 with *Opportunity and Responsibility: Developing New Approaches to the Management of the Long-term Prison System in Scotland*, which laid out a comprehensive set of arrangements for the future management of all long-term prisoners.[6] There were two main principles underlying the new strategy. The first was the need to be proactive in ensuring that the vast majority of men serving long sentences could serve their time positively in what was known as the 'mainstream' system and that this should be done by recognising 'the mutual responsibilities of the prisoner and the prison authorities.' The second was a determination to minimise and eventually to eliminate the use of solitary confinement for the small group of prisoners who could not be held in general accommodation. This was to be done by creating a number of small units which would 'provide a range of additional opportunities geared to the personal development of these men within a small supportive environment.'

In implementing the first element of this plan the new Shotts Prison was to become the main high security establishment for men serving long sentences, while Peterhead was in future to hold mainly prisoners who were required to be protected for their own safety. This was in effect a belated official acknowledgement of the underlying problems in Scotland's former convict prison. (Whether it should then have been converted for use as a 'protection' prison, as had also happened to the former English convict prison in Dartmoor, is a subject for discussion elsewhere.) The *Opportunity and Responsibility* document also confirmed that the two main small units in Scotland were to be the existing BSU and a new unit with 12 places within the enlarged Shotts Prison.

The Final Years of the BSU

The location of the unit within Barlinnie Prison in 1973 had happened for entirely pragmatic reasons—it was the only place available at the time. Its

6. Scottish Prison Service (1990), *Opportunity and Responsibility: Developing New Approaches to the Management of the Long Term Prison System in Scotland*, Edinburgh: HMSO.

facilities were very basic and it stood between the reception area and the kitchen of the main prison, both of which were quite insufficient for the needs of the large number of prisoners they served on a daily basis, and there had been a longstanding plan to demolish these buildings to create space for the reception area and the kitchen to be rebuilt to appropriate standards. As part of what is described above, the design plans for the new high security prison at Shotts included a custom built small unit, originally meant to replace what had initially been intended to be the temporary arrangement in Barlinnie. In the event, the opening of the new prison at Shotts was delayed until 1987 and its small unit opened three years later.

By that time, a number of other factors were in play. Firstly, the high water mark of the first decade or so of the BSU's existence as a vibrant community was little in evidence. In an interview in *The Scotsman* newspaper in 1986, Ken Murray, a key influence in the early years of the unit's existence, expressed his 'much disillusioned view' that by that point 'the commitment to making the unit work was markedly less evident with both staff and inmates.'[7] He went on, 'It strikes me that nobody wants anything stimulating to happen anymore. That's the last thing they want. They want a quiet life and no fuss.' An external observer who had wide experience of working creatively in prisons in a number of countries wrote to the current author following a visit to the unit in the early 1990s to express disappointment that what she had found 'didn't appear to reflect anything of its generally accepted reputation ... To be frank, the atmosphere felt moribund and there was little evidence of the innovative energy the unit built its reputation on.'[8] In his final inspection report on the unit in 1993 HM Chief Inspector of Prisons concluded that it had become 'slightly fossilised, a victim of its own impressive mythology and thus apparently unable to move forward.'[9]

Another important factor was the changed relationship between the unit and the rest of the SPS. At the end of the 1980s the BSU had no direct contribution to make to the resolution of the new generation of violence, most of which was once again related to conditions and circumstances in Peterhead. Following the decision in 1990 that Peterhead should lose its role as Scotland's

7. *The Scotsman*, 6 August 1986. Interview with Ruth Wishart.
8. Personal communication with the author.
9. HM Inspectorate of Prisons for Scotland (1993), Report on HM Special Unit Barlinnie.

main high security prison, most of its prisoners were transferred to Shotts Prison and eight of them who had been held in virtual solitary confinement in Peterhead were the first entrants to the new Shotts Unit. At that juncture there were no places available in the Barlinnie unit for any of these troubled and troubling young men.

Writing in 1992 the immediate past Director of the SPS, Peter McKinlay, expressed a revealing opinion: 'The BSU was and is ahead of its time. It should continue to flourish and help prisoners who found no other hope in the system. But I believe its impact—and that of other similarly inspired units—will always be relatively limited in relation to the problems of the SPS.'[10] Within a year or so there had been a radical change of personnel at senior levels in the Scottish Office and the SPS. Many of the new officials shared, and may even have inspired, the conclusion of the Chief Inspector of Prisons that the unit had become 'a victim of its own impressive mythology'; the BSU was not part of their vision for the future of the Prison Service. It would appear that Scottish Ministers were in two minds. In response to the Chief Inspector's report and a separate independent report which had been commissioned by the SPS[11] the Secretary of State commented, 'I agree that closure of the Barlinnie Special Unit is not desirable'; but at the same time he announced that a special working party would be set up 'to consider the role and purpose of the BSU and make recommendations.'[12] The working party reported in October 1994 and its conclusion was stark: 'The BSU should be closed ...'[13] However, the working party was at pains to emphasise 'that it is simply the physical facility which it is recommending for closure and not the concept or ethos of small units.'

In January 1995 the last occupants of the unit were transferred to other Scottish prisons and approaching 22 years after it had opened the BSU stood empty.

10. McKinlay, P (1992), Good Staff-Prisoner Relations Key to Success of Scotland's Supermax, *Journal of the National Prison Project,* Vol. 7, No. 4, Fall 1992: 22–25.
11. Scottish Prison Service Occasional Paper 7/1994: An Evaluation of Barlinnie and Shotts Units, Bottomley K, Liebling, A and Sparks R. Commenting on the BSU, the authors of this report concluded that they did not regard closure of the unit as a serious option, but went on to note that 'the Unit's unsatisfactory interfaces with the mainstream system' was a most pressing issue.
12. Scottish Government (1993), Response to HMI Report 1993.
13. Scottish Prison Service (1994), Report of Working Party into the Future of Barlinnie Special Unit.

The Legacy of the BSU

As the 50th anniversary of the opening of the unit came and went it became possible to identify several key lessons from the manner in which it operated, some of which have been learned by the Prison Service and some of which, unfortunately, have not.

Humanity in prisons

The key to any stable and humane prison lies in the nature of the relationships between the people involved, particularly staff and prisoners, and this above all was the foundation of the success of the BSU. Jimmy Boyle, among others, has identified this in his writing: 'What made the Unit unlike any other place was the way staff and prisoners were allowed and encouraged to sit down and talk together. This was the single most important factor of the Unit.' At its most basic, this implied a recognition of each person's common humanity and a mutual respect for each other; this was a lesson for all prisons which remains as crucial today as it did in 1972.

Self-expression, choice and responsibility

Traditionally the broad parameters of prison life are determined by rules and regulations which are imposed from above and there is little opportunity for individualism or self-expression. Another of the key features of the BSU was the freedom it provided for men to determine within very broad parameters how they spent their days. The central feature of this 'non-routine' was the power (and the responsibility) to choose. In the words of the late Joyce Laing: 'What was different about the Special Unit was that we gave people the atmosphere and the privacy and the respect to express themselves in whatever form they were able to. It was that expression that was important, not the quality or sale-ability of their work.'[14]

Contact with family and friends

An important consequence of imprisonment is the restriction which it places on a prisoner's contact with his or her family and circle of friends. This is an

---

14. *The Scotsman*, 6 August 1986. Interview with Ruth Wishart.

indirect punishment for the prisoners but also for all other family members, particularly partners and children. The arrangements for frequent and extended visits from families and friends helped the men in the BSU to develop new relationships and to renew or strengthen old ones in a positive manner. The location of the unit was an important factor in this respect: the vast majority of the men were from the Glasgow area, which enabled families and friends to visit regularly, often spending the whole day in the unit.

The size of the BSU

Most prisons are large impersonal institutions, many of them overcrowded, often with a high rate of turnover and with limited facilities. Individual expression is difficult and likely to be discouraged; anonymity is often a tool of personal survival. The opposite was the case in the BSU. With such small numbers there was no hiding place, either for prisoners or staff. Some found this environment too challenging or threatening and a small number of both prisoners and staff chose to leave the unit to return to more traditional environments. However, the majority thrived and expressed themselves positively in a manner which would have been impossible elsewhere.

A Final Word

Prison systems are frequently reluctant to learn the lessons of their successes and to apply positive experiences more widely. For example, Grendon Underwood Prison in England is often hailed as an example of the successful treatment of men serving long sentences who have had difficulties in other penal settings.[15] Yet over 60 years after it opened Grendon is still regarded as unique and its lessons have never been applied more widely. Though there has been limited use of small units within one or two prisons in England (such as the Wormwood Scrubs Annex mentioned in *Chapter 1* and by the private sector at Dovegate Prison which has a large therapeutic unit built on its own variant of the Grendon

15. See Genders, E and Player, E (1995), *Grendon: A Study of a Therapeutic Prison.* Oxford: Clarendon Press.

model).[16] The same criticism can be levelled against the SPS with respect to the BSU. Within limits the SPS can claim to have delivered on the first part of its 1990 agenda, to improve the general treatment of prisoners serving very long sentences; but it quickly ignored the second part, the provision of special facilities to meet the needs of a few individuals. In November 1999, some five years after the closure of the BSU, the SPS announced the closure of a number of its smaller low security prisons, the incorporation of the Shotts Unit into the main Shotts Prison and the 'mothballing' of the other small units.

The closure of all small units in the SPS has meant that for the last 20 years a handful of prisoners who cannot be held in general accommodation for whatever reason have been held for extended periods in what amounts to solitary confinement, transferred regularly between prisons from one segregation unit to another. This practice was severely criticised in 2015 by the UK Supreme Court[17] and also several times by the European Committee for the Prevention of Torture and Inhuman or Degrading Treatment or Punishment (CPT). Following its visit to Scotland in October 2019 this committee expressed concern at the use of long-term segregation for several prisoners, citing the case of one man who had been held in these conditions in multiple prisons 'more or less continually for *ten* [emphasis added] years.'[18] The CPT recommended that the Scottish authorities should 'seriously consider the establishment of smaller therapeutic units for the small number of prisoners concerned.' In its response the UK Government asserted that 'Removal from association is only used sparingly by the Scottish Prison Service and for the minimum time necessary.'[19] It did not respond to the CPT recommendation about the need for smaller therapeutic units. In addition, in July 2023 a report by HM Inspectorate of Prisons for Scotland found conclusive evidence that the SPS continues to use

16. See Cullen, E and Mackenzie, J (2011), *Dovegate: A Therapeutic Community in a Private Prison and Developments in Therapeutic Work with Personality Disordered Offenders,* Hook: Waterside Press.
17. UKSC 2015/58, *Shahid v Scottish Ministers.*
18. Council of Europe (2020), Report to the UK Government on the Visit to the UK carried out by the European Committee for the Prevention of Torture and Inhuman or Degrading Treatment or Punishment (CPT) from 14 to 18 October 2019, CPT/Inf (2020) 28.
19. Council of Europe (2020),Response of the UK Government to the Report of the European Committee for the Prevention of Torture and Inhuman or Degrading Treatment or Punishment (CPT) on its Visit to the UK from 14 to 18 October 2019, CPT/Inf (2020) 29.

long-term segregation and that its current use is neither 'sparing' nor 'for the minimum time necessary'.[20]

Sadly, it would appear that the legacy of the Barlinnie Special Unit has been erased from the institutional memory of the Scottish Government and the Scottish Prison Service.

---

20. HM Inspectorate of Prisons for Scotland (2023), A Thematic Review of Segregation in Scottish Prisons, Edinburgh: HMIPS.

CHAPTER 15

The Scottish Press and the Special Unit

Brian Wilson

The Scottish media played a critical, pernicious role in the life and death of the Barlinnie Special Unit (BSU). Throughout its existence, there was a concentration on its prisoners and their activities which bordered on the obsessive. Not all the publicity was negative if one knew where to look. The great weight of popular coverage regarded the Special Unit, at best, as an aberration to be treated with suspicion and, at worst, a challenge to the deep-rooted assumption that prisons should be places of retribution rather than rehabilitation.

In the current era of vastly reduced press sales and influence, it is difficult to comprehend the scale of Scottish newspaper circulations in the 1970s or the power their word commanded. When the Special Unit opened, the *Daily Record* was selling 700,000 copies a day in a population of little more than five million. Its arch-rival, the *Scottish Daily Express*, was still selling 550,000. By the mid-1970s, the new kid on the block—the *Sun*—was challenging the *Record* with sales of 350,000, even in the absence of the full Scottish edition that would later overtake it. The *Record's* stablemate, the *Sunday Mail*, and the more austere *Sunday Post*, both sold over one million copies each week—truly astonishing rates of penetration which politicians crossed at their peril.

It was a fiercely competitive environment and the popular dailies all had crime correspondents, deeply immersed in Glasgow's gangster culture. The reputation moulded by *No Mean City*, the book about Glasgow gangsterism in the 1930s, still hung over the city and was assumed to reflect a public appetite for a regular diet of coverage for the gory side of city life and the hard men who inhabited it. Rehabilitation did not figure prominently in public discourse.

The names of the men who became the first prisoners in the Special Unit, and particularly that of Jimmy Boyle, were already well-known to readers of the popular Scottish press. In fairness to the press, the degree of violence and criminality involved in these individuals' previous careers could scarcely have gone unreported or understated. In the climate of the early 1970s, if legislation had been required to underpin a 'soft' approach to the treatment of long-term violent offenders, it would have been faced down by the howls of newspaper outrage about 'kid glove' treatment of prisoners. Only the extremity of circumstances in Porterfield Prison (Inverness) allied to the fortuitous coincide of humane, visionary individuals in key roles at a particular moment allowed it to materialise.

The announcement of the BSU's creation had not attracted great attention — or outrage — probably because its purpose was, as described in *The Scotsman*, merely to provide 'specialist treatment' which sounded more psychiatric than anything more subversive. This gave the unit breathing space to develop its actual character and it was not until 16 months after it opened that the authorities were ready to lift the lid when it was agreed, with the approval of the Special Unit community, to invite the press in to see for themselves.

Martin Dowle later wrote, 'The Special Unit at Barlinnie Prison had its best press on 25 July, 1974. How can you be sure? Simple. That was the first — and last — day that the unit was opened to the Press.' The logic is plain: open a place up and let people look at it occasionally over a period of time and the result will be understanding and generally compassionate writing. Close it up and seal it off from the world, and innuendo, rumour and the uncertain world of permanent leaks will become the order of the day. And so, it proved to be.

In *A Sense of Freedom* Jimmy Boyle recalled the utter novelty of that ground-breaking day. He wrote: 'They came in just like other visitors ... For the first time in British history the press had been allowed to sit down in a prison with staff, Prisons Department people and prisoners and have a straight talk.' The coverage which followed, he recalled, 'supported us tremendously.' There was some enlightened commentary in the Scottish press and no negativity.

At that stage, the fact that hitherto dangerous criminals had lived for 16 months without incident within prison walls created limited potential for public or media offence. Stuart McCartney of the *Scottish Daily Express* wrote about Jimmy Boyle: 'You listen when he tells you that the only currency among these five men is honesty—amongst themselves but more importantly towards their prison officers... In the past 18 months this man whom I once considered totally beyond redemption has found faith, hope and charity.' In the *Glasgow Herald*, Jim Hewitson wrote: 'The visit to the "murderers' block" has turned out to be a rather surprising, almost baffling, encounter with a bunch of "nice guys".'

This coverage heightened interest in the Special Unit and widened the audience, which was always going to be high risk. The press invitation was probably designed, in part at least, as a softening-up exercise on public opinion in advance of greater privileges being extended to prisoners. In that respect, its success was short-lived. The triggers for a rapid volte face were a proposed *World in Action* programme for ITV and an outing by Jimmy Boyle, by then emerging as a sculptor of great potential, to the Edinburgh Festival just a few weeks after the press visit. Newspapers which had given at least a qualified welcome to the unit's work were caught up in an auction of outrage about what the Scottish Police Federation's spokesman described as 'glorification' of 'murderers walking the streets.' The tone had been set for the negativity that followed.

A significant political event, called a General Election, had occurred in the interim. One of the key figures in bringing the Special Unit into existence had been the Scottish Office Minister, Alick Buchanan-Smith, a liberal, patrician Tory, who had subsequently visited the unit and pledged continuing support for its work. In February 1974, Labour came to office with Willie Ross as Secretary of State and Harry Ewing the junior minister responsible for prisons. Neither shared a natural empathy for prison reform and certainly not as a priority in a period of political uncertainty. There was a second General Election in October 1974 by which time the Special Unit was securing far too many headlines for political comfort. The barrage of publicity which accompanied Jimmy Boyle's Edinburgh excursion was not the kind of problem that a government fighting for survival welcomed. By that point, the unit had entered the realms of controversy and most of the Scottish press was in full cry.

It was not only the Government that had changed but also the Opposition. The Shadow Secretary of State for Scotland, Teddy Taylor, was a right-wing populist who was only too happy to provide the quotes which made the headlines and increased the political pressure on nervous Ministers. Every setback for the unit was turned into an opportunity by its critics. In response to the attack by Duncan Bathgate on a fellow prisoner in 1976, Taylor wrote in his *Express* column: 'I am horrified to learn that knives are readily accessible to prisoners with records of extreme violence within the Special Unit. I have always been unhappy about this particular unit and the philosophy behind it.'

The bleaker events in the unit's history, in particular the death of Larry Winters, continued to feed the appetite for sensationalism and hostility in which the *Daily Record* took a prominent role. Following a Fatal Accident Inquiry into the death, at the conclusion of which the Sheriff called for a review of the unit's operations, allegations emerged about drug-taking as well as access to drink and sex. The *Record* opined: 'The public must be told whether the allegations are true; if true, what steps are being taken to enforce liberal, but realistic, discipline in the unit? Otherwise, a bold experiment will blow up in the face of those who want it to succeed.' Liberal commentators pleaded that Winters had been a victim of the old regime rather than a product of the new one, but these were small voices in the storm of indignation.

Bruce Millan, whose instincts were more naturally empathetic than those of his predecessor, had become Secretary of State for Scotland in April 1976, but found himself confronted with this constant stream of negative stories about the Special Unit. The one that appeared to push him over the edge towards a review of its workings was publication of *A Sense of Freedom* which had been written by Jimmy Boyle 'under the strict understanding it would not be taken out of prison.' Teddy Taylor had promptly demanded an inquiry and expressed astonishment that a prisoner should be allowed to criticise the prison system. *The Scotsman* reported Millan's response on 7 August 1977: 'My inquiries have not been conclusive but suggest that the material was taken out surreptitiously by a visitor to the unit and thereafter ... made available to a publisher.' A fundamental review of staffing ratios and 'replacing staff who had been in the unit for a long period' was announced. It was really the beginning of the end for the Special Unit.

As *The Times* Scottish correspondent, Ronald Faux, wrote at that point: 'The lobby condemning the experiment to find a new way of handling long-term, difficult prisoners has grown increasingly vocal. To them the Special Unit has become an enfant terrible of the Scottish Prison System ... According to the reformers, it is the spectacular failures that reach the headlines. What the unit has achieved for the Prison Service, for the men concerned and for their families is more often overlooked.' But who read *The Times*?

Another cause célèbre which greatly excited the Scottish press was the romance and then marriage of Jimmy Boyle and Sara Trevelyan in 1980. Like so much else that led to negative press stories about events inside and outside the unit, details of the wedding ceremony were the subject of leaks from within police or prison services. Instead of being held in Glasgow, the ceremony was moved to the village of Balfron. Instead of being a private affair, it was turned into a media circus with photographers climbing drainpipes in an effort to get a picture of the Registrar performing the ceremony. I recall writing about it and quoting the Registrar saying how pleasant the couple were but that the press were 'such a scruffy lot.' It was calling them 'scruffy' that really caused offence!

In retrospect, it would be difficult to dispute that most of the stories which appeared about the Special Unit were of legitimate public interest. The whole concept was so different from what was normally expected and accepted about prisons that it was bound to attract press coverage, as were the individual episodes with which it was peppered over more than a decade. However, it was the negative tone of that coverage and the search for fault—fuelled by leaks—which cumulatively made it politically dangerous. Such sympathetic press as existed was marginalised by hostile and indignant coverage which assumed that readers were on its side, though that was never really put to the test.

In the end, the Special Unit became just too much political trouble and was encouraged to fade away. The initial intention of its redemptive philosophy permeating the whole of the Scottish Prison System was overtaken by the rearguard action to defend the unit itself in the face of media and political negativity. It is a history that also explains why nothing remotely similar has been attempted in the intervening decades. Who would take that chance? Jimmy Boyle wrote in 2016, 'No lessons have been learned. If anything, things have got worse. The prison system seems to be a lost cause. No-one cares.'

The Scottish press did not kill off the Special Unit. Ultimately, that could only be a political decision. What it did, however, was to create an environment in which that became much more likely in the absence of any strong counter-pressure, which nobody since has summoned the courage to revive.

CHAPTER 16

Remembering Jimmy Boyle, Misremembering The Barlinnie Special Unit

Mike Nellis

Introduction

Jimmy Boyle is indeed Scotland's most well-known reformed ex-offender, and in certain quarters of the Scottish media it was a public identity he was never allowed to transcend, although the 'reformed' part of his image has been relentlessly and cynically maligned. Initially, in the years after his release from prison in 1982, Boyle deliberately capitalised on this identity because it enabled him to speak critically on matters of crime, punishment and social justice with an authority that few others could have mustered—and to promote and celebrate the place and the people who had made his reform possible. For 30 years, from the 1970s to the start of the new century, Boyle's story and the story of the Barlinnie Special Unit (BSU) were seamlessly entwined in Scottish media and the wider Scottish popular imagination, although as time passed less attention was paid to the innovative character of the unit, and more to a distorted characterisation of Boyle himself.

There were always two parallel versions of the Boyle/Special Unit story. One version saw Boyle as the unit's supreme vindication, the living proof that its creative, dialogical approach worked to unleash the latent talents and change the behaviour of once-violent men, and was something to be emulated. The other side saw the activities Boyle was permitted to pursue inside (and even more so outside!) the unit, the new 'artistic' company he kept, the recognition his sculpture and writing achieved and the lifestyle he took up afterwards as proof, rather, *of all that was wrong* with its indulgent, 'liberal' approach to rehabilitation. A man as violent and fearful as Boyle had once been — convicted of murder despite his not guilty plea — should never have been given such privileges, as this constituency perceived the opportunities that the unit was giving him.

Over time, this latter narrative has become the dominant one. Significantly, it became suffused with innuendo that the apparent change in Boyle's outlook and demeanor was disingenuous: as a jaded prison governor told me decades later, 'Jimmy Boyle wasn't reformed by the system, he beat the system.' After years of strenuous violence in the harder prisons of Scotland, this argument goes, Boyle weighed up the perks available in the Special Unit and simply seized on the chance to be top dog in it, as he had always done, in whatever setting he had found himself. While technically he became an 'ex-offender', no longer involved in gangland criminality, he was never — so the word spread — as 'reformed' in character as he affected to be, and the gullible liberal professionals who bestowed 'conspicuous forgiveness' (Brown, 2014: 28) on Boyle were simply being fooled. Jeremy Isaacs, the head of Channel 4 television, who was later to produce the film of *A Sense of Freedom*, recognised the deeper cultural roots of such vindictive attitudes:

> 'The Scottish tabloids treated Boyle as a giant of crime and for the most part were theologically, Calvinistically, unforgiving; he was bad, and could never change; predestination marked us all, for life. The Special Unit's attempt to treat violent prisoners as human beings capable of reform was doomed, therefore, to failure. People like Boyle, given responsibilities and "encouraged to grow"? Nonsense; we were being conned.' (Isaacs, 2006: 257)

Jimmy Boyle had actually acquired criminal notoriety before he ever set foot in the Special Unit at the age of 29, in 1973, as many young criminals had done in post-war Glasgow, courtesy of their own bad behaviour, malign 'police sources' and their tame journalists, and sensationalised news reporting in the Scottish press. His reputation as a gangland enforcer and the several failed attempts to convict him of murder in the 1960s had ensured strong police animosity and outraged media attention towards the 'baby-faced' villain. His assaults on prison officers in HMPs Peterhead and Inverness in the early 1970s earned him 'worst of the worst' status in the penal system: the officers' assaults on him got less coverage. The vituperative press comment received by the BSU was not exactly new: it simply followed a pattern of reporting on prisons and prisoners in Scotland set in the 1945–1964 period, when 'readers of the *Sunday Post* were alternatively reassured to see enemies of society behind bars and scandalised at the privileges they were alleged to enjoy' (Harvie, 1998: 81). This reporting mostly played into the sentiments and prejudices of the respectable Scottish working-class, and the lower middle-class, who were the main readership of these papers. Historian Sydney Checkland (1981) had rightly noted that working-class Glaswegians felt negligible sympathy towards protection racketeers who taxed and intimidated their communities and businesses. Trade union leader Jimmy Reid (1981) shared these views, although it would be mistaken to give the impression that tentative forgiveness was never forthcoming if people showed signs of changing. Sometimes it was: working-class activist and founder of the Craigmillar Festival Society in Edinburgh, Helen Crummy (1991: 226–7), for example, took Boyle at face value when, after she visited the Special Unit, he offered to design a huge concrete play structure for children on her estate, as an early step towards giving something back.

Nonetheless, the kind of standardised notoriety Boyle acquired as a typical-if-proficient proto 'hard man' in the Glasgow underworld was immeasurably surpassed by the fame bestowed on him during and after his time in the Special Unit. After 1977, he became something new: a published writer with a criminal past who was championed by artists and progressive penal reformers. After his release from a mainstream prison in 1982 (two years after transferring from the Special Unit), be became a man who could articulate his own social concerns in the broadsheet press, and seemingly had a new class affiliation. He became and remained, quite literally, a celebrity on the Scottish cultural scene at least until the end of the century, although in several respects — and for those who despised what he had accomplished and represented this was a particularly galling aggravation — there were elements of legend about his evolving story.

Thus, he spectacularly transcended his class and neighbourhood background, defied his nominal destiny as a hard man from the Gorbals, suffered in, but survived, a brutal prison regime, thrived in a better one, discovered talents as a sculptor he never knew he had, found acceptance among people he would never otherwise have met and married an attractive and resourceful woman — Sara

Trevelyan—a junior hospital doctor who had come as a curious visitor to the Special Unit, and of whom he rightly said (in the dedication to a later book) 'in giving so much of herself [she] helped me make it' (Boyle, 1984). He and Sara then undertook supportive and campaigning work together that would not have been feasible for him alone, setting up the Gateway Exchange in Edinburgh to work with people who use drugs, experience homelessness, and those with HIV. They co-established the unofficial Independent Enquiry into the Use of Violence at HMP Peterhead in 1986 (Scraton, Sim and Skidmore, 1991). Last but not least, Boyle travelled internationally to sculpt, made considerable money, and sometimes drove around provocatively in a donated blue Rolls Royce (Isaacs, 2006: 268).

No other modern Scottish life—no other reformed ex-offender's life, for that matter—had had a trajectory like Jimmy Boyle's. The likely social destiny of a person who, between the ages of 12 and 38, counting his time in juvenile institutions, had spent only 12 and a half months in freedom, and five and a half years of his overall time in custody in solitary, was never promising. From the 1930s onwards, earlier generations of criminal hard men in Glasgow had done time and eventually stopped offending, but they never left their class of origin. Some became 'good family men' and even club leaders. A handful fought their way up to become the city's 'crimelords' (Davies, 2013). Some sank into alcoholic stupor, some were murdered by rivals. Boyle's desistance from violence, the seriousness of his commitment to art, his articulacy, his change of lifestyle, and the influence he acquired in penal debate, was quite different—and spectacular in comparison.

The sheer distinctiveness of Boyle's life story—the incarcerations of his childhood and youth and the campaigning activities of his adulthood—guaranteed that he remained newsworthy. What is notable however is that over time this trajectory came to be seen by others, if never by him, as something incidental to what had occurred in the BSU, the place where it actually took shape, without which it would not have happened. The means and processes by which a violent man might give up violence—arguably the lesson that most needed to be learned—got written out of the media narrative. While his original memoir and diary, and the subsequent flow of newspaper articles ensured that Boyle never entirely lost ownership of his story, aspects and versions of it have been continually retold or touched on by others in serious journalism, less serious 'true crime' publications, three movies, a play and a French documentary. No other reformed ex-offender in Britain acquired such a diverse cultural presence as Jimmy Boyle. This chapter examines these various representations, and addresses the media-driven erasure of the Special Unit from Boyle's story.

Reformed Ex-Offenders and Celebrity Criminals

Most western countries have periodically produced ex-offenders who temporarily become serious commentators on penal reform after writing memoirs in prison, or shortly after release. Several have had popular movies made about their lives, but public interest in each one is invariably short-lived because most opt for lower profile, normal lives and because, after a while, another one supersedes them in the literary or media spotlight. Some, to the chagrin of their liberal champions and the glee of their detractors, fall from grace and reoffend (Nellis, 2012). In Scotland, and indeed in Britain more generally, Jimmy Boyle's fame as a reformed ex-offender lasted almost 40 years, much longer than is usual for such writers, and even now, it has not faded much, although he has lived outside Scotland since 2002, and speaks less frequently on penal matters.

Alongside his artistic activities inside and outside the unit, Boyle's memoir *A Sense of Freedom,* whose provenance is covered by Rupert Wolfe Murray in *Chapter 4* of this volume (see also Boyle, 1984:28), was the initial basis of his fame and authority as a penal commentator. Uniquely for a British prison biography, *A Sense of Freedom* has been almost continuously in print since 1977, originally with Canongate and Pan MacMillan, later with Lomond Press (1995), most recently with Ebury Press in 2016. At different points in time, this paperback could be found in Scottish bookshops shelved under true crime, biography, or even Scottish literature (Wilkes, 2006). Twenty eight years after its publication the Scottish Arts Council/Scottish Book Trust (2005), with the richest of literary heritages to draw on, listed *A Sense of Freedom* in its 100 Best Scottish Books, perhaps the only prisoner autobiography ever to gain such an accolade.

Boyle's second book *The Pain of Confinement* (1984)—in diary format, revealing much more detail about his life in the Special Unit than his first—was also published by Canongate and later (in a combined volume with *A Sense of Freedom*) by Lomond Press. It added considerably—and convincingly—to Boyle's stature as a reformed man. His third book, *Hero of the Underworld* (2000) was a startling phantasmagoric novel which drew on his own experiences of confinement and leaving prison, as well as those of people attending the Gateway Exchange (Shaikh, 1999). It dwelt as much on psychiatric as penal issues, and may have alluded to abuse that Boyle himself suffered in juvenile institutions, about which he had not written directly before. For his ever-present detractors, however, it did not need to be *about* him—it was simply enough that it was *by* him, and East Kilbride pensioners were mobilised to boycott a reading and book signing of *Hero* (Logan, 1999; Brown, 2014). Later the same year he did a reading at the Edinburgh International Book Festival, but because the official publicity referred to him (unhelpfully) as having been 'imprisoned for something he did not do,' a leading Conservative MSP demanded its withdrawal, because Boyle's murder conviction still stood (BBC News Online, 27 August 1999). Serpent's Tail, the small English publisher specialising in risk-taking literature served Boyle well with *Hero*; whilst never exactly famous, it acquired literary cachet, and remains a collectible item online.

Boyle's memoir and diary, the 'media circus' surrounding his marriage to Sara in 1980, his artistic success and his release into a celebrity lifestyle two years later, guaranteed that others would want to have a say about him. He was famously disparaged in the memoirs of unsympathetic politicians and police officers (Taylor, 2008; Mclaughlin, 2012). Serious crime journalists like Robert Jeffrey (2002; 2009) wrote respectfully of him and the unit, but Scotland's long-established 'true crime' publishing industry never ceased from applying its own formulaic terms to him, focusing on early bad deeds at the expense of later law-abidingness, and celebrating notoriety. Up to the end of the century, at least, Boyle retained his own voice and had allies in the media who took him seriously, but it became progressively more difficult to avoid disparaging 'true crime' framings of his story. Nonetheless, over time, in a small but useful counter-trend, Boyle earned significant footnotes in serious studies of modern Scottish history, including *Chamber's Scottish Biographical Dictionary* (Goring, 1992:47) and *The Illustrated Encyclopedia of Scotland* (Macleod, 2004) and he entered Scottish folk memory.

If the tabloid press remained mostly hostile to Boyle, the broadsheet press did much to foster a more positive image of him, and he appreciated the platform it gave him. Boyle was first given celebrity interview treatment by conservative journalist Lynn Barber (1985) in the *Sunday Express* and liberal lawyer-novelist John Mortimer in the *Sunday Times*. Mortimer (1986:17), in particular, was not wholly convinced by Boyle's deterministic, sociological account of his own violent behaviour but conceded that by availing himself of opportunities in the Special Unit he had redeemed himself: 'Jimmy Boyle's story does show what a creative penal system might do for the whole of our society in reforming criminals.' This core point was then somewhat lost in Mortimer's (1986: 17) revelling in the opulent décor in the 'Victorian House in Edinburgh' where Boyle lived after his release. Subsequent obsession with Boyle's domestic ambience all too often eclipsed the more significant lessons that travelled in him, and slowly muted any messages about the Special Unit's significance. BBC News Online (27 August 1999) reported on his '12 room house in Edinburgh's new town,' his second home in France and 'a recent newspaper story (which) put him sixth on the list of desirable people to meet at an Edinburgh dinner party.' This never meant that serious broadsheet pieces about him and the unit ceased appearing—crime journalist Duncan Campbell's (1999) was exemplary—but it was a reminder of the ease with which what truly mattered about him could be lost sight of.

The serious work in which Boyle and Sara Trevelyan were involved generally had a lower profile. Whilst running the Gateway Exchange in Edinburgh, they also financed Calton Athletic for a year (1991–1992), a Glasgow drug rehabilitation project based on football, which had been set up in 1985 by David Bryce (1949–2011), ex-gang member and a man who struggled with addiction, a veteran of the same penal institutions as Boyle, though they never met each other until after their release. Bryce (2005) is heartfelt: 'I can't ever thank Jimmy Boyle enough for the support and encouragement he gave us and the opportunity to open our first premises.' Bryce's story was ghosted by a journalist who elevated it above 'true crime', and also praised in a foreword by Irvine Welsh (2005:97), by that point a bright star in the Edinburgh literary firmament because of his 1993 novel *Trainspotting*, an acerbic celebration of youth, drugs and criminality in Leith.

Not all Boyle's former acquaintances spoke well of him. Whilst appreciative of his support and example in the unit, at least in some respects, Hugh Collins' own memoir paints a generally unflattering portrait of Boyle, the reasons for which would be complicated to disentangle. Similarly, Sebastian Horsley

(1962–2010), the bohemian son of a Quaker businessman who had strongly supported the Special Unit, who was an initially admiring associate of Boyle for ten years, a fellow director of the Gateway Exchange and former business partner (importing champagne) turned against him. He says he had once 'been excited at the idea of having a modern day Rimbaud and Verlaine-type relationship' with him, but became dismissive and cynical: 'Jimmy didn't want friends. He wanted disciples. And he hadn't changed—his manipulation was simply violence with gloves on' (Horsley, 2007:173).

That some people found Boyle's drive and determination abrasive and self-centred is undeniable, but the view of him as ungenerous and insincere was not shared by his professional associates. Jeremy Issacs, acquainted with him for nearly 20 years, expressed a more common view:

> 'I saw for myself the good he did, and everyone knew of. After years of it, though, he reckoned he had paid his debt to society, and began to enjoy himself...I find him one of the most remarkable men I know. His courage and strength give strength to others. The anger in him has burned out, the endurance and the charm remain.' (Isaacs, 2006:268)

Jimmy Boyle and Sara Trevelyan separated in 2000, and Boyle moved to Cap d'Antibes on the Cote d'Azur, and later to Marrakech. He indicated to *Scotland on Sunday* that this was likely a permanent move because in Scotland he was forever 'judged on my past rather than my present and future' (quoted in Gardner, 2002). He enjoyed a level of personal anonymity (and appreciation as a serious artist) in France that had eluded him in Scotland, and felt that this benefitted his and Sara's children, who were otherwise exposed to constant media reminders of who he had once been. But Boyle remained newsworthy, even abroad. Art teacher-journalist Fiona Jardine (2009) wrote this of him:

> 'His transformation from lawless gangland enforcer to well-heeled and well-behaved sculptor is something of a civic and national proverb. We see the city in the man, we see the social and political value of art in its redemptive powers to integrate the disenfranchised individual with the powers of his own expression, in uniting the divided self, and more than this we see evidence of an economic miracle. These days—with notable contempora-

neity—Boyle appears in newspaper interviews as a multimillionaire property developer, doing up riads in Marrakech, while current cultural policy promotes the arts as almost failsafe engines for recession-proof growth, making him something of a poster boy for the benefits of exploiting "creative skills".' (Jardine, 2009: 19)

This is technically accurate, but it absolutely loses sight of what made Boyle interesting and important in the first place: that he was a once violent man who changed for the better in a therapeutic community designed by progressive penal administrators and staffed by decent and talented people—and that his trajectory in life could so easily have been otherwise had this unit not existed. His transformation, for all its flamboyance, had seemingly been rendered mundane by 2009, something that anyone could have done, if they just got lucky, as he obviously had. On this telling, his success was nothing special, and Jardine was simply reflecting the pervasive absence of curiosity on anyone's part at that point as to how it had ever come about—how it had been enabled to happen—and whether that was still pertinent now. Furthermore, adding insult to injury, Jardine judged Boyle's artwork 'outmoded', good enough as art therapy but no longer in accord with the principles being taught in art schools.

The continuing interest in him, she concluded, 'has more to do with his notoriety than his significance as an artist,' oblivious, it seems, to the fact that this notoriety had been artificially sustained by media preferences and 'true crime' protocols, and their symbiosis with political constituencies who simply wished Boyle ill. Fifty years on from his criminal heyday in the 1960s any claim that a man as reformed as Boyle obviously was could—or should—still be reduced to his 'notoriety' was, from a penal reform standpoint, deeply depressing. While it was timely of Ebury Press to reissue *A Sense of Freedom* in 2016, so that Boyle's own voice—and a new afterword—could be heard directly again, his oft-made weary observation that certain Scottish media would never let him be more than his violent past was still being vindicated in 2009.

It also says something about lapses in cultural memory by 2009 that a younger journalist like Fiona Jardine seems not to have grasped that interest in Boyle, and in the Special Unit itself, had almost *always* been framed in terms of deeper, art-positive cultural moments in Scotland and, indeed, had helped to create some of them. The most obvious of these was the way in which the experimental arts community around Richard Demarco and Joseph Beuys took Boyle up and championed the work of the unit, which — the case can be made — were vital to its initial political survival. A more mundane rendering of the same impulse was a laudatory account of the Special Unit in a book celebrating the city's famous and long-running TV police drama, *Taggart*, published on the eve of Glasgow becoming European City of Culture in 1990 (McManus and Chandler, 1989: 144–48). Mark McManus, its prestigious star, was a working-class actor who had himself been a sometime visitor to, and occasional theatrical performer in, the Special Unit. It did the unit no harm to have a fictional (if not real-life) police officer taking municipal pride in it, and to have a gruff, personable actor affably calling its residents 'the guys', whilst regretting that despite its success it was embroiled in a 'fight to stay in existence, and the immediate future is unpromising' (ibid, 146). Other ways in which various artistic media narrated the story of Boyle and/or the Special Unit warrant more detailed attention. Nationally and internationally, making theatre, film and documentary out of reformed ex-offenders' lives, often adapted from their memoirs and autobiographies, is far from new. More so than any other example of such men, Jimmy Boyle's story has been appropriated and reworked in all these formats — and most recently a novel — although rarely in ways that preserved or celebrated what mattered about him.

Representing Jimmy Boyle

The Hard Man (1977)

Tom McGrath (1940–2009) was a Glasgow-born poet and jazz musician, immersed in the counter-culture of the 1960s (he was a co-founder of the *International Times*), and, in 1973, founder and inaugural director of the Third Eye Centre–'a shrine to the avant-garde' (Fisher, 2009) on Glasgow's Sauchiehall Street. Third Eye exhibited some of the Special Unit's early sculptures and, at the point when McGrath was turning to playwriting, he and Boyle got to know each other. He approached Boyle about writing it — the police hassled him, saying he was being gullible, that Boyle was an evil manipulator (Boyle, 1984: 105) but the result of their collaboration was a fearsome piece of political theatre whose first performances the police actually sought to boycott.

It was first produced at the Edinburgh Traverse Theatre in May 1977, later at the Edinburgh Festival and still later that year at the Institute of Contemporary Arts (ICA) in London (with Peter Kelly playing the renamed Boyle character, Johnny Byrne). It was intended from the start to be an intervention in contemporary debates about poverty, violence, The Cages and the Special Unit—a special showing of *The Hard Man* was arranged for councillors and judges in July 1977 (Boyle, 1984: 144), although to what immediate effect is not clear. The play covers Boyle's/Byrne's childhood and adolescence, his eager, inexorable absorbtion into low-level protection rackets, his equally inexorable brutalisation in prison and his dawning insight that prison functions to flush away society's waste products, people like himself. Byrne is both participant and narrator, telling the story in flashback from prison, explaining his politicisation. He contrasts his unreflective immersion in the violent culture of Gorbals tenements with both an emerging awareness of why his life is like it is and of the freedom needed to change. 'The animal is thinking,' Byrne self-deprecatingly tells a sheriff. 'He's beginning tae figure it out' (Boyle and McGrath, 1977:51). The film ends with Byrne in The Cages at Inverness Prison smearing his body and face with excrement—more visceral to see on stage than to read in *A Sense of Freedom*—in order to hold baton-wielding warders at bay. The last spoken line is, 'This is my version of my story' (McGath and Boyle, 1977:70) and no-one who watched could have doubted that in Scotland the telling of it was overdue.

Tom McGrath was a very talented playwright, who crafted Boyle's story into very powerful theatre, using stories and incidents that Boyle told him about when he visited the Special Unit. Quite apart from its raw topicality, *The Hard Man* was noted for its experimental techniques—choreographed violence accentuated by percussive music—and was quickly dubbed 'one of the most controversial plays of the decade' (Stevenson, 1987:159). It came to be regarded as one of the six best Scottish plays of the 1970s (Findlay, 2001) and entered the repertory. A youth theatre performed it in Stromness in 2003. Students from The Royal Scottish Academy of Music and Drama did a rehearsed reading of the play at the Citizens Theatre in Glasgow, as part of a season of Gorbals plays in May 2006. It was performed by East Kilbride Repertory Company in June 2007. McGrath consolidated his reputation with many more acclaimed plays and remained central to avant-garde arts in Scotland over a 30 year period, actively involved in promoting political theatre. All his obituaries recalled *The*

Hard Man as a significant achievement. It was revived, with Boyle's support and approval, at the King's Theatre in Edinburgh (and briefly toured) in 2011. Despite a period-piece feel it still presented as 'pummelling and bleak—this testament to the spirit of survival still carries a grim force' (Fisher, 2011). In 2017 it returned to the Traverse Theatre as part of the Edinburgh International Film Festival, as a script-reading rather than a fully staged play, giving Byrne's role to acclaimed actor Kate Dickie, all of which showcased the undimmed power of McGrath's dialogue (Leadbeater, 2017).

A Sense of Freedom—The Film (1981)

Glaswegian-born TV producer Jeremy Isaacs bought the rights to the book *A Sense of Freedom* in 1979 and approached Scottish Television (STV) to film it. Not all its managers were keen, but Director Bill Brown pushed it through. Greenock-born scriptwriter Peter MacDougal and Edinburgh-born director John MacKenzie were signed up. Although not Isaac's first choice (he had wanted Bill Paterson) an upcoming Scottish actor, David Hayman, was picked to play Boyle. The Labour-led Glasgow City Council, however, was hostile from the start, anticipating that it would glorify a man who had already been glorified too much and be bad for Glasgow's image (Boyle, 1985: 222; Jeffrey, 2001: 53). Isaacs sums up:

> 'Glasgow, or some of it, was up in arm's over our film on "Scotland's hardest man", as they persisted in calling him. We needed room to film in. Glasgow's councillors repudiated the short lease we had negotiated on premises they owned. Scottish Television successfully injuncted the council to compel performance. *The Daily Record*, a lively leftish tabloid, had it in for us, the news editor daily urging his reporters to find evidence of shock or horror at our presence and intentions. After days of headlines—"Residents Outrage at Murder Movie" sort of thing—the *Record* finally gave way gracefully. Eight days into filming, on an inside page the demure crosshead appeared: "Quiet day on Boyle film".' (Isaacs, 1989: 23)

Unsurprisingly, the Scottish Prison Service (SPS) would not allow filming on its premises, so Kilmainham Gaol Museum, in Dublin (frequently used as a set in prison movies), was used for the interiors of all three prisons depicted — Peterhead, Inverness and Barlinnie. The film itself showed nothing of the Special Unit; rather McDougal's visceral script reprised *The Hard Man*, concentrating on 'action on the streets, endurance in prison', only ending with Boyle's arrival at Barlinnie and 'his dawning realisation that a new beginning was possible' (Isaacs, 2006: 258). Rather lamely, Isaacs describes it as 'foreshadowing but not delineating his growth and rehabilitation' (Isaacs, 1989:23), adding later that the 'complex relationships' in the unit 'deserved, in truth, another film entirely' (Isaacs, 2006: 258; Boyle, 1985: 262) noting that prison officials were unhappy that the film ended where it did, without showing something of his subsequent rehabilitation, and in retrospect, in terms of the debate it engendered — or didn't engender — this was a misjudgment.

Ideally, *A Sense of Freedom* should have begun in the Special Unit's yard, with Boyle/Hayman working on a sculpture, with the main story then told in flashback. As it was, despite McDougal's commendable intention to depict and expose the unjust brutalisation of a man in the modern Scottish Prison System, and to celebrate his resistance, the film over time served to fix in aspic the image of what Boyle had been, not the more interesting issue of what he had become. That is not to detract from such brilliance as the film contained. The closing shot — a freeze frame of Boyle, arriving in the unit for the first time, using a blade given to him by an officer to break the string on the parcel of property he has brought with him (as described in the book) — is as powerful and apt an ending as could have been imagined.

Scottish Television (STV) presented *A Sense of Freedom* as posing the question what should be done about Scotland's violent hard men. On the night after it was screened a lengthy live discussion of the issues it raised was televised, where the work and philosophy of the Special Unit was fully acknowledged and Ken Murray memorably went head-to-head with the hostile leader of the Scottish Prison Officers' Association. Both film and discussion drew large audiences, leading Isaacs (2006:266) to write 'I would put penal reform high on the list of subjects to which television should return, year on year.'

Star David Hayman won great acclaim, and has subsequently had a stellar career as a TV, film and theatre actor, and director. He has remained conspicuously interested in penal issues, starring in a four-part BBC prison drama *Underbelly* (1992) and using his income to finance his political and campaigning activities, including his Spirit Aid charity, which has organized filmmaking with young prisoners in HMP Polmont. Significantly, soon after starring in *A Sense of Freedom,* Hayman directed the movie of *Silent Scream* (1989), about another prisoner in the Special Unit, although again, without making the unit the focus.

Silent Scream (1989)

Silent Scream was scripted by Bill Beech, one of the early artist-visitors to the unit who had been particularly close to Larry Winters, whose story the film tells, using the same title as the posthumously published book of Winters' (1979) poems. Winters was one of the original prisoners transferred to the Special Unit—and the only prisoner ever to die there, of an overdose aged 34, in 1977. The film received £1m funding from Channel 4 and The British Film Institute, but none, despite requests, from any specific Glasgow agency. Journalist Robert Jeffrey was later to lament the persistence of attitudes from the days of *No Mean City* (a serious, 1935 novel which had famously dramatised the connections between poverty and gang violence in Glasgow, which the city council did its best to discredit).

Winters had murdered a barman in Soho, London in 1963, and had been sentenced to life imprisonment, which he mostly served in Scotland, his home country. The film opens in the unit and dwells on Winters' efforts to deal with trauma and the effects of addiction to medication that the prison authorities had originally prescribed to alleviate his depression. It is mostly told in flashback, concentrating on Winters' childhood and family, his life in Glasgow and Carbisdale (in the Highlands), touching on his brief time in the Parachute Regiment. He is shown making a visit home from the unit, accompanied by guards, his first time outside a prison in 13 years. *Silent Scream* was not focused on the unit as such, but it raised searching questions both about what made a man become violent, and how such behaviour might be dealt with. Winters was centre stage in it, played by Iain Glenn in a widely acclaimed performance. Both Jimmy Boyle and Ken Murray were represented, although not as major characters. HMP Barlinnie graciously permitted some exterior filming, but the Special Unit's yard was recreated in a studio some miles away.

The film won a Silver Bear award at the Berlin Film Festival, and a Scottish best actor Bafta for Iain Glenn. In 1999, Richard Mowe, curator of film at the National Museum of Scotland, listed it as one of his top 20 Scottish films. Its reputation as an art movie endures, and while it has never quite been a touchstone in its own right in debate about the unit, it was the basis of a Howard League Scotland event in 2023, which commemorated the 50th anniversary of the Special Unit's opening, with Bill Beech in attendance.

The Debt Collector (1999)

The Debt Collector movie was written and directed by playwright Anthony Neilson, funded by Film4 and the newly established (1997) Glasgow Film Council. Although it fits tidily within the familiar sub-genre of 'released prisoner movies', it tells a story that would have had neither currency, interest nor fascination had not Jimmy Boyle's life story provided the initial template for it. Nicky Dryden, a former enforcer for a Glasgow loan shark, who had specialised in intimidating debtors by assaulting their relatives, has served 18 years in prison. He is now an acclaimed sculptor, married to an attractive woman journalist and living amongst affluent friends in Edinburgh. So far, so Boyle-like. It then personalised the animosity and resentment that Scottish police officers seemed to have towards Boyle, condensed into the fictional character of Gary Keltie, the officer who had secured his original conviction, who systematically harasses Dryden into using violence again. This time he kills, although more-or-less in self-defence.

The film ends with Dryden broken and humiliated, acquitted of murder, but physically disabled, spurned by his former middle-class friends, his marriage ruined. Billy Connolly played Dryden — brilliantly, as it happened — but the film was ill-disguised wish fulfilment for those critics of Boyle who had felt cheated by the absence of a real-life fall from grace. In the character of Keltie (played by Ken Stott), it exaggerated the lengths to which unforgiving Glasgow police actually went to undermine Boyle, but this could have been explored in better ways. Although mostly set in Edinburgh, *The Debt Collector* was mainly filmed in Glasgow as a condition of funding — something of a riposte given the city council's refusal to co-operate with the making of *A Sense of Freedom* and *Silent Scream.*

The Debt Collector won an International Film Critics Award in 1999. Cynically, Neilson claimed that his film was merely probing the myth of the Scottish 'hard man'–but it was the idea of reform and redemption, the possibility of change for the better, that it was actually shredding. It played on the idea that while Boyle had admitted some of the bad things he had done, he had not admitted them all, and was thus still deceiving his admirers. Boyle had been contacted for advice by Film4 before production—but he was understandably unhappy with the result, not least because the controversy surrounding the film predictably led the tabloids to resurrect his 'dark past' all over again (Logan, 1999).

La Rage et le Reve Condamnes (The Anger and Dreams of the Condemned) (2001)

In Britain, both the BBC and ITV (*World in Action*) made short but illuminating documentaries about the BSU between October 1974 and April 1975 in which Boyle, among others, had been interviewed. They served a local 'current affairs' agenda, but no major British documentary about the unit was ever made. However, In 2001 French documentary maker Jean-Pierre Krief made the 67-minute *La Rage et le Reve Condamnes* about the use of creative arts in the rehabilitation of prisoners, which stands as one of the best ever films on the subject. It was inspired by Krief's reading of *A Sense of Freedom,* and then meeting Boyle in Cap d'Antibes after he had moved there. Scenes in French prisons are intercut with sections of a lengthy interview with Boyle, talking about his experience in Scottish prisons. Kreif, a respected filmmaker from KS Visions used Boyle as the living proof of the therapeutic value of art in prison, and as a counterpoint to a French prisoner who has his art materials confiscated. Short, impressive interviews with Ken Murray and Joyce Laing were also used, which ensured they were given their due place in Boyle's story. 'In France,' according to Krief, where the film was a great success, 'no one has a bad word to say about [Boyle], he's not thought of as being a bad man. He has paid his debt to society and we can learn from his life' (quoted in Seenan, 2002).

La Rage et le Reve Condamnes was widely shown in European art cinemas—but not in Scotland—and won an award in the FIFA Montreal 2002 awards. Boyle himself had felt that a French filmmaker would tell his story less ambivalently than a Scots filmmaker, and judging by the way *Scotland on Sunday* (Gardner, 2002) reported the making of the film he was right. The article itself was informative about the film and quoted extensively from Krief and other sources, but it inevitably concluded with the standard potted history of Boyle's earlier life (just as Seenan's 2001 *Guardian* review did), and solicited a standard condemnatory quote, in this instance from Bill Aitken, the then deputy Justice Minister in the Conservative Party, who 'was not impressed with Boyle's Gallic makeover':

> 'I'm sure that Mr Boyle is much more comfortable with the image of being a Scottish rebel, but unfortunately the families of his victims might not be comfortable with it. One is dead and the other, a prison officer, had his eye gouged out. Mr Boyle is extremely fortunate that the legal system has showed him a degree of indulgence he did not deserve. If he is happy with the apparent attitude of the French towards his appalling and abhorrent acts of violence then perhaps it is better that he stays there. It would certainly be Scotland's gain.' (quoted in Gardner, 2002)

In the course of getting hold of a copy of *La Rage et le Reve Condamnes* some years later—for a private showing in Scotland—I corresponded with Jean-Pierre Krief. It fell to me to tell him that Ken Murray had died, in 2007. His response was deeply memorable: 'Ken Murray was a high quality man. One of those whose behaviour erases the lowness of several others' (personal communication by email, 19 September 2009). Quite so.

The Blade Artist (2016)

Irvine Welsh (b1958) achieved overnight fame with his 1993 novel *Trainspotting* in which four dissolute friends, Renton, Sick Boy, Spud and the illiterate, psychopathic brawler Francis 'Franco' Begbie create mayhem and misery in Leith. Subsequent novels, including a sequel and a prequel to *Trainspotting*, consolidated his reputation as a man who spoke of what he knew about life on a peripheral housing scheme, as did an acclaimed film (and its sequel) of *Trainspotting* in 1996 and 2017. Robert Carlyle, the edgiest of Scottish actors (who had debuted years before as a prison officer in *Silent Scream*) memorably caught Begbie's manic sadism in both films. In 2016, Welsh extended the novel sequence with *The Blade Artist*, a solo update on Begbie, who had avoided the drunk-in-the-gutter fate that sensible Renton had once expected for him. Respectable Jim Francis—as Begbie is now known—lives and works as a high-paid sculptor of grotesque shapes in California. Married to Melanie, an attractive art therapist whom he had met during his last, life-changing prison sentence (where his artistic abilities were discovered), and now with two young daughters, he is ostensibly a reformed ex-offender himself. The novel's plot turns on Begbie returning home to Edinburgh after hearing that his estranged son Sean, one of two boys from an earlier 'common law' relationship, has been murdered.

Boyle's own son James who suffered drug addiction from just such a relationship, had indeed been murdered in 1994. But Begbie here is much less of a changed man than even Nicky Dryden in *The Debt Collector.* Despite a patina of sophistication, and some political patter, he remains the Begbie of old, still a 'blade artist', as well as a successful sculptor. Unbeknownst to his new family, even in California he still indulges a taste for violence on people he deems deserve it. Back in Edinburgh's gangland, he tortures and kills his way to the tragic, twisted truth about his son's violent death. Few critics were wholly convinced by Begbie' surprise transformation, and most recognised Welsh's shameless appropriation of Jimmy Boyle's life experience, but without ever denying the novel's literary verve or insights into gangland milieu.

The Blade Artist was seemingly Welsh's bid to write in the Jekyll and Hyde tradition, exploring the supposed co-existence of good and evil in the temperaments of some Scottish men. Nonetheless, for such an astute observer of masculinity and criminality—and one whose Foreword (Welsh, 2016) to the Ebury edition of *A Sense of Freedom* showed just how well he understood the real Boyle's achievement and significance—it was mortifying that he opted not to explore in fiction the tortuous processes of desistance from violent behaviour, because if any modern Scottish writer had the literary ability to do that, it is probably him. Instead Welsh offered his readers more of what they liked, and more of what generally sells, in dark crime fiction—gore: as *The Scotsman's* reviewer said 'the narrative plays on a reader response that at once wants Begbie's rehabilitation to work, and yearns for him to go radge' (McGill, 2016), which he does.

Welsh's commanding accomplishments now straddle books, film and television, so it was not particularly surprising to learn in 2021 that *The Blade Artist* was in development as a six-part tv series, with Robert Carlyle set to reprise his career-defining role as Begbie. If this proves as popular as anticipated, it does not bode well for any completely honest telling of Boyle's story: it may be the *coup de grace.* Upto now it has mostly been writers and film-makers hostile to Boyle who have obliterated the truth of what, with the help of others, he did to change his outlook and set his life on a new course in the BSU. For Welsh to do it in 2016 from a position of ostensible friendship with, and apparent respect for, Boyle is to my mind questionable and serves the ever more precarious memory of the unit badly, in keeping with the 'Boyle-never-really-changed' lobby. Some comfort might be taken from the fact that *The Blade Artist* is being adapted by Jenni Fagan, a younger Scottish poet and novelist who I believe has greater sensitivity to redemption stories, but the optics of conflating Begbie and Boyle is never going to work to the latter's advantage.

Conclusion

The erasure of the BSU from Scottish cultural life does not reflect well on the country's penal politics, or its media. The SPS learned some lessons about treating prisoners with civility from the unit, but after its closure in 1994, there was negligible likelihood of its more radical elements being emulated elsewhere in the prison system. Officialdom was actually ambivalent about its success in reducing violent behaviour, and was not keen that it be remembered. Nonetheless, the unit had made an impact on liberal opinion and had no shortage of public defenders, but far more hostile opinion was always mobilised against it, more effectively, in more diverse media, to the point of overkill — and erasure.

Liberal opinion often missed a trick, yielding ground that should not have been given. It was an unfortunate misstep that the film of *A Sense of Freedom*, well-intentioned and important as it was at the time, said nothing about the unit. While there was always a personal element in the conservative media attacks on Jimmy Boyle there was also a sense in which they were proxy criticisms of the unit itself, a prison that was not a proper prison, and ought not to exist. What better way to discredit the unit than to discredit the man who had most obviously proved its worth, on its own terms? Although more recent attacks on Boyle have been self-propelling and unmoored from any lingering anxiety that the unit could 'come back', the skewed reasoning in them still constitutes to be an obstacle to progressive penal practice because it insists that bad men never change and that it is never worth the effort creating opportunities for them to do so.

A case in point. In 2014, Allan Brown, former *Sunday Times* journalist and a one-time Journalist of the Year, included Boyle in a 'scurrilous' book on *50*

People Who Screwed Up Scotland, keeping company, among others, with Robbie Burns, Sean Connery and Alec Salmon. Some entries were tongue-in-cheek but the one on Boyle seems little short of character assasination, offered up in the name of ordinary Scottish people who had every right to see Boyle, even after all this time, as nothing more than a 'confirmed scumball' (Brown, 2014: 26). That was ten years ago, but the demolitions do not end. Even as Boyle approached his 80th year, with half a lifetime of law-abiding achievement behind him, a recent series on past 'crime stories' in the *Glasgow Times* (a local daily newspaper) distilled him down mainly yet again to his mid-twentieth century criminal identity, complete with a mugshot of his 'baby faced' former self, police reminiscences of his 'odious' character and judicial denunciations of him as 'a dangerous menace to society' (Silvester, 2023). Jimmy Boyle deserves better. To focus so heavily on his long past offending instead of the successful, law-abiding man he has been most of his adult life, is questionable and emphasises all too clearly what I say about how sections of the media have 'misremembered' Boyle rather than his (and the BSU's) unquestionable achievements.

Could the narrative ever have been different? Boyle devoted the concluding 40 pages of *A Sense of Freedom* and almost the whole of *The Pain of Confinement* to his experience of the Special Unit. Numerous other articles and memoirs explained how it worked. It was not a mystery, to those who were interested. In the Afterword of the Ebury edition of *A Sense of Freedom* Boyle summed up the experience, as far as one paragraph ever could:

> '*Although they got some things wrong, the one thing they got* absolutely right, even though we initially hated it, was the insistence that we all sit down in a community and talk things through. In those early days, there would be walls of silence, and frequently some prisoners, and indeed staff, would walk out of these meetings. The thought of sitting down and talking to the enemy was anathema. The chasm of distrust between us was vast. *It was however, the acorn that was to create the oak.*' (Boyle, 2016: 300 emphasis added)

It ought not to have been impossible at any point in the unit's life or immediate aftermath to have dramatised and celebrated these processes, and the life of the unit more generally, in a film. *Silent Scream* touched on them, but they needed a stronger cultural marker, a touchstone movie that was as accurate and compelling about the Special Unit as *A Sense of Freedom* had been about The Cages, something that might have impressed itself on the Scottish imagination. In view of the indelible imprint that Jimmy Boyle has made on Scottish culture it is not impossible that his story will continue being retold, and one would like to think it would finally be told honestly and accurately, giving the unit its due and necessary place. More likely perhaps is a documentary—maybe a drama documentary—which could take some of its cues from *La Rage et le Reve Condamnes,* which to date is the best cinematic testimony we have of Boyle's, and the Special Unit's accomplishments.

References

Barber, L (1985), Jimmy Boyle: Is There Life after Life?, *Sunday Express,* 27 October 1985.

Boyle J (1977), *A Sense of Freedom*, London: Pan.

Boyle J (2005), The Gentle Giant. Community Arts Newtown Reading Room.

Bryce D (2005), *Alive and Kicking: A Story of Crime, Addiction and Redemption in Glasgow's Gangland,* Edinburgh: Mainstream Publishing.

Campbell D (1999), Hand Over Fist, *The Guardian,* 23 January 1999.

Carrell C and Laing J (eds) (1982), *The Special Unit Barlinnie Prison: Its Evolution Through Its Art,* Third Eye.

Checkland S G (1981), *The Upas Tree: Glasgow 1875–1975 ... and after 1975–1980,* Glasgow: Glasgow University Press (2nd edition).

Collins H (1997), *Autobiography of a Murderer*, London: MacMillan.

Crummy H (1991), *Let The People Sing: The Sttory of Craigmillar*. Privately published.

Ferris P and McKay R (2001), *The Ferris Conspiracy,* Edinburgh: Mainstream Publishing.

Findlay B (ed) (2001), *Scots Plays of the Seventies: An Anthology,* Newbattle: Scottish Cultural Press.

Fisher M (2009), Obituary: Tom McGrath, *The Guardian,* 1 May 2009.

Fisher M (2011), The Hard Man—Review, *The Guardian*, 4 April 2011.

Gardner C (2002), 'Rebel' Boyle Finds raison d'etre, *Scotland on Sunday.*

Goring R (ed) (1992), *Chamber's Scottish Biographical Dictionary*, Edinburgh: Chambers.

Harvie C (1998), *No Gods and Precious Few Heroes: Twentieth Century Scotland,* Edinburgh: Edinburgh University Press.

Horsley S (2007), *Dandy in the Underworld,* London: Sceptre.

Isaacs J (1989), *Storm Over 4: A Personal Account,* London: Weidenfield and Nicholson.

Isaacs J (2006), *Look Me in the Eye: A Life in Television,* London: Little Brown.

Jardine F (2009), Michael Stone: Invoking the ghosts of Gulliver, in the programme for the Bik Van der Pol exhibition 'It isn't what it used to be and will never be again', The Centre for Contemporary Art, Glasgow 10 October to 21 November 2009.

Jeffrey R (2002), *Glasgow's Hard Men: True Crime from the Files of The Herald, Evening Times and Sunday Herald,* Edinburgh: Black and White Publishing.

Jeffrey R (2009), *The Barlinnie Story,* Edinburgh: Black and White Publishing.

Leadbeater R (2017), The fearless Scots actor stepping into the role of Glasgow hard man, *The Herald,* 28 May 2017.

Logan B (1999), Are you Looking at Me?, *The Guardian,* 18 June 1999.

Macleod I (2004), *The Illustrated Encyclopaedia of Scotland,* Edinburgh: Lomond.

Malzahn M (1987), The Industrial Novel. In Craig C (ed), *The History of Scottish Literature Volume 4: Twentieth Century,* Aberdeen: Aberdeen University Press.

Margolis J (1994), *The Big Yin: The Life and Times of Billy Connolly,* London: Orion.

McGill H (2016), Book Review: *The Blade Artist* by Irvine Welsh, *The Scotsman,* 2 April 2016.

McGrath T and Boyle J (1977), *The Hard Man,* Edinburgh: Canongate.

Mclaughlin B (2012), *Crimestopper: Fighting Crime on Scotland's Streets,* Edinburgh: Black and White Publishing.

McManus M and Chandler G (1989), *Taggart's Glasgow,* Oxford: Lennard Publishing.

Mortimer J (1986), Boyle's Law—Jimmy Boyle. In *Character Parts: Collected Interviews from* The Sunday Times< Harmondsworth: Penguin.

Nellis M (2012), Prose and Cons: Autobiographical Writing by British Prisoners. In Cheliotis L K (ed), *The Arts of Imprisonment: Control, Resistance and Empowerment,* Farnham: Ashgate.

Reid J (1981), Like the Birdman of Alcatraz Without the Birds, *Glasgow Herald,* 21 February 1981 (collected in *As I Please: The Collected Journalism of Jimmy Reid,* Edinburgh: Mainstream Publishing).

Scottish Arts Council/Scottish Book Trust (2005), *100 Best Scottish Books,* Edinburgh: The List Ltd.

Scraton P, Sim J and Skidmore P (1991), *Prisons Under Protest,* Milton Keynes: Open University Press.

Seenan G (2002), Glasgow Hard Man is French Film Hero, *The Guardian,* 18 November 2002.

Shaikh T (1999), Book Review: *Hero of the Underworld, New Statesman,* 26 February 1999.

Stevenson R (1987), *Scottish Drama 1950–1980.* In Craig C (ed), *The History of Scottish Literature Volume 4: Twentieth Century,* Aberdeen: Aberdeen University Press.

Silvester N (2023), Glasgow Crime Stories: The History and Life of Jimmy Boyle, *Glasgow Times,* 16 January 2023.

Taylor E M (2008), *Teddy Boy Blue,* London: Kennedy & Boyd.

Winters L (1979), *The Silent Scream,* Edinburgh: Polygon Books.

CHAPTER 17

How the Unit is being Archived and Commemorated by Glasgow Life Museums

Claire Coia

Project Curator Billy presenting at the exhibition launch of 'Barlinnie Special Unit—A Way Out of a Dark Time' in Kelvingrove Art Gallery and Museum, 2017. © CSG CIC Glasgow Museums Collection.

With a focus on the value of community-led research, this chapter looks at the exhibition 'Barlinnie Special Unit—A Way Out of a Dark Time' (2016–2017) curated by prisoners in HMP Barlinnie, the conversations it generated, and how the art and archives are continuing to inspire new research and resources. Tracing the histories of the Barlinnie Special Unit (BSU) and investigating its legacy, this project became a platform for rekindling dormant conversations, stimulating new debate on penal reform, and reuniting people who had passed through the BSU's doors as prisoners, staff or visitors.

An Invitation for Trouble

The BSU was a highly flammable cocktail, comprising Scotland's most dangerous prisoners and liberal thinkers in the fields of criminology, psychiatry, art therapy and sociology. To some, it was an exploratory step in penal reform, requiring a dismantling of prison hierarchies and the building of community. Others saw it as pandering to violent individuals who refused to accept their just punishment and conform to the system. In any case, it was certainly a unique solution to a unique problem. These 'troublesome' prisoners who were disrupting the system, causing harm to prison officers and peers alike, were given unprecedented opportunities for personal growth, supported by a small but influential community of movers and shakers in the field of criminal justice. Given that these individuals represented 0.2 per cent of the prison population, it was not only a divided society who had misgivings about this radical experiment: mainstream prisoners and prison staff were frustrated at this 'special treatment' for a highly select group of suspect individuals. Adding to this volatile concoction was the fact that, unlike the mainstream prison with its impermeable walls of silence, the Special Unit was open to visitors—including politicians, the media and artists. The experiment was under the spotlight, and the prisoners were rarely out of the tabloids. Admired and abhorred in almost equal measure, the Special Unit still never fails to elicit an opinion.

> 'I wouldn't bring in artwork by Jimmy Boyle. The prisoners have strong feelings about the Special Unit': HMP Barlinnie Learning Centre staff member, 2014.

> 'The Barlinnie Special Unit? You need to speak to Willie McGurk! He was a prison officer in the Special Unit and he'll tell you everything!...I'll go get him!': Prison Officer at HMP Barlinnie, 2014.

From the anticipation of trouble to the anticipation of a lively discussion, these comments reflect a divided opinion amongst prison staff; a division that is reflected in the public as well. That the BSU is still controversial 50 years after its inception, and long after its closure, indicates a strong emotional response towards the perceived 'glorification' of former criminals, and perceptions of what prison should be.

The BSU Collection at Glasgow Life Museums

In 2012, Glasgow Life Museums received a small but important collection of artworks created in the BSU. This was part of a larger donation by Scotland's first art therapist Joyce Laing. Her pioneering work in the field of mental health helped patients and prisoners to express themselves, and this collection comprises over 1,000 works of art which she collected from hospitals and prison spaces, as well as gifts from people whom she had befriended or supported during periods of mental ill health or imprisonment throughout Scotland. A generous gift from Professor David Donnison (British academic and social scientist) in 2010 had included a small but impressive selection of artworks from the unit, and Glasgow Life Museums had previously purchased two small sculptures direct from the BSU in the 1980s. Lacking context, these artworks were scattered in the museum storage, but the objects' stories and the role that the arts played within the BSU were brought back to life with Joyce Laing's donation.

Knowing very little about these artworks, what better way to find out about them than to create a dedicated research project with prisoners in Barlinnie itself? Trusted by the Scottish Prison Service (SPS) based on a decade of partnership work, I was permitted to bring objects from the BSU to generate conversations, despite advice that it could provoke trouble. When the project gained momentum, the community partners, especially those concerned with the welfare of prisoners, were warned repeatedly against potentially glorifying the men of the BSU by having a public exhibition, and of the tabloid backlash that would ensue. Most new conversations about the unit began with 'What you've got to remember is that…,' followed with a caution not to get lost in arty ideas about a highly troubling experiment. The assumption was often made that as a curator, my agenda was to celebrate the collection. Glasgow Life Museums is in fact full of troubling art, artists and historical artefacts collected over centuries—and full of troubling absences. Many people do not see their worlds represented in galleries, or they find themselves misrepresented. Museums are not neutral, and never have been, since historic collections tend to serve the already privileged.

> 'We do not associate prisons with art. We do not associate them with creativity. If we think about them at all, it is when our attention is drawn to them by newspaper, radio or television reports of escapes, violence or noxious descriptions of insanitary conditions in those huge Victorian buildings. They are shrouded with fear and a sense of mystery. Not the mystery that lies at the heart of creativity, but the mystery of danger and evil, which lies on the latitude of destructiveness.
>
> Art we associate with the peace and quiet of galleries. Sometimes they are large, elegant and imposing, carrying the authority of the state, which has spent public money on acquiring the paintings and sculptures they house. Sometimes, equally overwhelming, they are small private temples into which the average citizen is afraid to wander. In both settings they convey a sense that art is for a special group; a priesthood who know something the rest of us don't know': Kay Carmichael.[1]

1. Kay Carmichael (1925–2009) was a weekly visitor to the BSU in her capacity as a social scientist, policy advisor and influential Scottish activist. Extract from her personal writing courtesy of her husband Professor David Donnison (1926–2018).

Today, museums work to address issues and redress inequalities and create more inclusive spaces. How we do this, and *who* we do this with, is no small undertaking.

Researching Collections with Experts by Experience

A prisoner I once worked with compared himself to a museum object. '1982.106 is the number on the rock I am holding,' he said. 'It is a museum catalogue number. I know like me, it is not free to go where it wants to go.' Although housed in a state-of-the-art storage facility, many of the objects in Glasgow's collection are numbered and accounted for, kept in locked cabinets, physically cared for but not always in plain sight. Glasgow Life Museums cares for over 1.4 million objects but for reasons of space, less than two per cent can be displayed in our museums at any one time. Glasgow Museums Resource Centre (GMRC), on the South side of the city, is a world-class museum storage facility, with 17 climate-controlled 'pods' which are home to over 98 per cent of our collection. GMRC is a busy hub, with over 100 staff members caring for this vast collection and making it accessible to the public in open storage. The facility is accessible on a variety of levels, from the provision of quiet research rooms to tours and extensive public programmes. Not everyone, however, is able or willing to visit museums in person.

The Open Museum is the dedicated outreach branch of Glasgow Life Museums. The team is based at GMRC, but the Open Museum is not bound by museums walls. We take the collections out of storage and into the heart of Glasgow's communities, to people who can't, won't, or don't engage with museum venues. Together we work to provide access to the collections and create meaningful partnership projects with a wide range of people who are traditionally excluded from museums due to social, cultural, economic and/or physical barriers. We take objects out beyond the walls of the museum for people to engage with on their own terms and turf, from loud and lively community groups to people who are often rendered invisible by society. My specialist remit within this dynamic team is working with people in spaces of confinement, such as hospitals and prisons. Together we explore, research and exhibit collections kept in storage.

Institutions such as museums, learning establishments and prisons are power laden. The widely held assumption is that *we* teach, *they* learn. This implies a hierarchy of who holds power and knowledge, and who the beneficiaries are. Curators may be gatekeepers, but they are not always the experts, and museum staff do not have the time and resources to research every object in their care. Some objects become divorced from their stories and forgotten in storage, their histories becoming buried over time. Breaking down hierarchies and working *with* experts by experience, however, can lead to meaningful projects and an exchange of knowledge which benefits both community and museum.

The BSU — 'A Way Out of a Dark Time'

The purpose of this project was to create a relevant and contemporary context for these historical objects from the BSU. We wanted to draw on people's insights and lived experiences of the carceral environment to interpret the collection. This process involved taking the collection beyond the confines of the museum walls and back into the same space where the art had been created. Working in partnership, Glasgow Life Museums, New College Lanarkshire, the SPS, the University of Glasgow, and the Citizens Theatre provided the training and resources that the students would need to develop their research and curate an exhibition. The students carried out archival research, wrote the interpretation, developed radio production skills, and hosted discussions and interviews with the people who had originally been involved with the BSU. Delving into the forgotten histories of the unit and generating new first-hand accounts, the students brought the museum objects — and the story of the BSU — back to life. Through investigating the past, this project created a platform for exploring current criminal justice themes, the role of the arts in the criminal justice sector, reigniting conversations and bringing together a wide range of people including academics, museum and criminal justice professionals, artists, prison staff, prisoners, returned citizens, third sector organizations, and the general public.

Sharing Power

A few weeks into the project, I was asked by the group's tutor, 'When are you going to start *teaching* them about the Special Unit?' It was an understandable question on their part. The students were confused, apprehensive, and didn't grasp what was expected of them; they are used to a structured learning environment and refer to the education classes as 'school'. I had tailored exercises to harness competing energies in the room to create a democratic and safe space for everyone—from tutors to troublemakers, the confident and opinionated, the bored and the restless, to the shy and self-doubting. Staff were actively brought into the conversations, seating was shuffled. We talked about the unit, but also had side conversations about life in general over cups of tea. So far, they had learned how to handle museum objects, how artefacts are cared for in museums, how to research archives and the basics of museum interpretation. But with the exhibition date looming, when would I start teaching them about the BSU? I repeated: 'I'm not here to teach you. This is *your* exhibition, *your* research.' The first step had been to upskill the students in basic curatorial practice, share power and establish rapport. With this in place, the research could start. Identifying the key messages for the exhibition, choosing the objects, and writing text came later.

Despite being known as 'the longest experiment in penal history' the unit was never fully evaluated. The students read the autobiographies of former BSU inmates, the few academic papers written, and consulted the archives, but huge parts of the story were missing, leaving it largely open to speculation. The students and staff began to compile a long list of questions. I brought people who had lived experience of the unit to Barlinnie for them to interview. Armed with resources combined with curatorial skills, the actual research and interpretation of the artworks could begin, and the pace picked up. Every single person was committed to making the project happen. The Scottish Studies tutor, 'Barbed Wireless' radio station lecturer, and Communications Hub team devoted hours of extra time with the students; staff from New College Lanarkshire, and the SPS worked together with the Open Museum team to navigate the complicated logistics of making the project work, and the students took work back to their cells, initiated the creation of additional resources, and undertook extra classwork to make sure the project was completed on time. The partnership, shaky at first, had become unshakable.

Revisiting Barlinnie

Entering the reception area, I take Joyce Laing, David Donnison (husband of the late Kay Carmichael, a lead social worker and regular visitor to the BSU) and Larry Butler (an artist and visitor to the BSU) through the staff entrance. Like going through airport security, we take off our coats, shoes and bags and place them on trays to be X-rayed. Our mobile phones are put in lockers. A friendly prison officer uses a metal detector to scan our bodies. We wait for the Learning Centre staff to collect us. It's a busy day. The tutor greets us, and we begin the process of journeying through the locked gates to reach the Learning Centre. 'It wasn't like this when I worked here,' says Laing with slight exasperation at the wait. 'You just walked into the Special Unit. This [reception area] wasn't here. It's all changed.' Our guests receive a warm welcome from the students, cups of tea are made ('We got you nice teabags—don't drink the prison stuff, it's rotten!') and we settle in for a group discussion, each student asking questions that we have so far been unable to answer from our small pile of available evidence. This is where the real learning begins. Other guests have been invited for the upcoming sessions, including psychotherapist Sara Trevelyan, who married Jimmy Boyle in the unit. Conversations begin about how to interview Sara—'What can we ask her?' 'Is this question too personal?' Individual guest interviews are conducted and broadcast by Barbed Wireless and the research snowballs as people come forward with their contacts and ideas:

> 'We're interviewing Johnnyboy Steele for our next [radio station] broadcast—he was an ex-inmate of the unit—he wrote a book. He's got loads of great stories': Prisoner.

> 'Claire, you're going to be happy with this! A couple of colleagues used to work in the unit, we'd asked but they didn't want to get involved in the unit stuff. Now they're up for it!': Prison officer.

'Have you read the evaluation of the unit written by Richard Sparks[2] which closed the unit down? I can get a copy from the Mitchell Library.[3] He would be a good one to interview': Scottish Studies tutor.

The project spanned January 2016 to November 2017 over two phases: the initial period of research, curation, and an exhibition at HMP Barlinnie which then led to an exhibition in Kelvingrove Art Gallery and Museum, Glasgow, supported by a strong public programme of events. The exhibitions at HMP Barlinnie and Kelvingrove were a resounding success. The students had interpreted the artworks in such a way as to provoke questions rather than controversy, opening a public arena for discussion. They devised tours, presentations, and a panel debate. Over half the prison population visited the exhibition at Barlinnie—unheard of for an arts-based project.

Project Curator James presenting at the exhibition launch of 'Barlinnie Special Unit—A Way Out of a Dark Time' in HMP Barlinnie, 2016. © CSG CIC Glasgow Museums Collection.

2. Barlinnie Special Unit and Shotts Unit: An Assessment. Issue 7, 1994, *Scottish Prison Service Occasional Papers*, A Keith Bottomley, Alison Liebling, Richard Sparks, Scottish Prison Service.
3. A large public reference library in the centre of Glasgow, which houses the City Archives.

The students achieved a total of 20 Scottish Qualifications Authority (SQA) qualifications through the research and interpretation of the collection for display. Many of the participants continued to support the public exhibition at Kelvingrove after their release, taking part in talks, tours and events, and presenting at the exhibition's high-profile public seminar. 'Barlinnie Special Unit—A Way Out of a Dark Time' further led to the creation of a radio programme by Barbed Wireless, a short film which was later shown at Tramway, Glasgow, as part of the Koestler exhibition;[4] numerous press articles, television features on BBC Scotland and Scottish Television (STV) News; as well as articles in *Museums Journal, STIR* and *Inside Time*. The project won a prestigious Koestler award. The students at Barlinnie took full ownership of this project, gave it wings and watched it fly to unimagined heights.

From Controversy to Conversation

The unique environment of the BSU was most certainly of its time and if simply commemorated as a historical event, strong opinions will be elicited but never developed beyond the Marmite 'love it or hate it' response. Celebrating the artworks without careful consideration of the complex themes and emotions that they provoke would create a singular, simplified and stagnant reflection of the past—a radical experiment never to be repeated—of little relevance to people whose lives are touched by the criminal justice system today. Without due care, an exhibition of BSU art could invalidate people's experiences of crime and create a highly triggering space. If we acknowledge the unit as 'troubling', however, a new space for dialogue is created: a space not only to explore our responses towards the BSU but also to consider the nature of crime and the steps we can take to create safer communities. In 'staying with the trouble'[5] a space is created where we can question our taken for granted beliefs about prison and what prison is for.

4. Narrative: A Koestler Arts Exhibition for Scotland, Tramway, Glasgow, 10 November to 22 December 2017. Koestler Arts is a UK prison arts charity.
5. Philo, C and Parr, H (2019), Staying With the Trouble of Institutions, *Area*, 51, 2: 241–48.

'The BSU was a successful experiment for a select number of prisoners but there was little on offer for the majority. A huge shift has happened today in terms of education and therapeutic services. Today every prisoner can access the prison learning centre to sign up for a wide variety of classes and courses. Counselling and addiction services are also available. Why then is Barlinnie still a revolving door? More can be done. The BSU showed how prison could be; it was a place of hope for those who had none. The BSU should not be remembered as a shameful secret, but a successful experiment and not to lie at the bottom of a box. Maybe it's time to stop the machine and service the parts': 'Barlinnie Special Unit—A Way Out of a Dark Time' exhibition text.[6]

Going Forward

Enthusiasm for the project was infectious. Information about it spread by word of mouth, and people were generous in sharing their connections and leads, helping to bring together people who had lived, visited or worked in the Special Unit for the first time in decades. The exhibition and public programme generated new audiences, and exciting links were made between people and organizations, catalysing new and unexpected conversations. Different voices and resources were brought to light, hinting at hidden potential and larger stories. Bill Beech was invited to the seminar by Sara Trevelyan, which led to an exciting addition to our public programme: a screening of the 1990 film *Silent Scream* about BSU inmate Larry Winters, starring Iain Glenn and Robert Carlyle, written by Bill Beech and directed by David Hayman. Bill introduced the film, presenting a selection of photographs, artwork, and video footage from his extensive personal archives. These archives and artwork became publicly accessible during his 2019 exhibition and public programme at the University of Hull, 'I Am The Coyote', also featuring an impressive display of Richard Demarco's archives, and artwork created in response by students in HMP Humber's Graft Studio. Artworks were loaned for this exhibition from artists including Caroline Tisdall, JoAnn Baker and Jimmy Boyle, shining light

6. Extract from the 'Barlinnie Special Unit—A Way Out of a Dark Time' exhibition text written by current prisoners in HMP Barlinnie.

on art that had not been seen in public for decades. More material continues to surface: hundreds of hours of video footage of the unit taken by previous inmates Johnnyboy Steele and TC Campbell have emerged. Further archival material has since been donated from Joyce Laing's collection to Glasgow Life Museums and is currently being processed for public access. There is still much to be discovered and new research is underway. At Glasgow Life Museums we are currently developing plans to utilise the art and archives of the BSU to create new resources in partnership with people who have lived experience of the criminal justice system. Sparked by objects in a museum storeroom, the legacy of this project lives on in the hearts and minds of people as the conversation continues.

CHAPTER 18

How the Unit is Being Archived and Commemorated by the Coyote Fund Archives

Bill Beech and Jane Whitaker

The process of establishing the archive began informally in 1974 through our interest in teaching and learning. It began formally with material from the various collaborative projects mounted by prisoners and visitors during Richard Demarco's Edinburgh Arts programmes, and subsequently the first exhibition of the work of Jimmy Boyle and Larry Winters outside Scotland. Notable amongst these in the holding is *You Can Film Them But You Can't Show Their Faces* in the burgeoning form of video art and shown at the Serpentine Gallery's *The Video Show* in London in 1975. The initial phase supporting exhibitions and conferences continued up to 1982 including providing material for the exhibition and book *The Special Unit Barlinnie Prison: Its Evolution Through Its Art* at the Third Eye Centre in Glasgow. Further material was then added in the development of the illustrated script leading to making of the 1989 feature film *Silent Scream.*

Throughout the period, the work of prisoners and their collaborations continued challenging social conscience, behavioural and cultural norms against a background of institutional censorship. No matter the ordinariness or extraordinariness of the experience, the emphasis was placed on the experience itself, in which prisoners and visitors gave an emphasis to what Joseph Beuys described as 'Social Sculpture'. The value of the archive is in the quality of evidence that was generated, the high quality analogue photographic prints, negatives and 35 mm slides, of everyday events. There is also an extensive collection of daily National Newspaper Clippings, 1973 to 1982, the complete collection of

The Key, the unit magazine, exhibition catalogues, video (now transferred to exhibition quality digital format), letters, documentation, reports and papers, leaflets, significant art works in terms of sculpture, illustrations, fine art prints and drawings.

In the build-up to the Hull University UK City of Culture exhibition in October 2019, the fragile nature of the collection was acknowledged and steps taken to further digitise elements to conserve and make them available for wider public access. Importantly at this stage, the process of restoration and conservation was extended alongside Professor Caroline Tisdall's esteemed Coyote Archive collection of fine art prints, selected publications, exhibition materials and writings relating to Joseph Beuys and Professor Tisdall's direct involvement with, and work of, the Special Unit. It also included the rediscovery and inclusion of extraordinary unseen photographs by the American photographer JoAnn Baker based on a reconnection 45 years after JoAnn made her first and only visits to the unit in 1974.

The aim of the archive to commemorate the BSU exhibitions led to the 2019 exhibition 'I Am The Coyote', followed on the highly successful 2016 Glasgow Museum exhibition 'A Way Out of a Dark Time' with examples of 'the social function of art' and how the Special Unit exemplified the way the arts can help build creative solutions to support the disadvantaged or disaffected within our society.

Importantly in 1974, the iconography that emerged out of the need to communicate and overcome issues of institutional censorship sent the Special Unit message via the work of the prisoners over the walls into the public domain. The preservation and display of the material from this time is now intended to encourage a resurgence of interest in the unit's relevance to the challenges faced in prisons today. In doing this, the material also casts new light on a period of the work of Joseph Beuys that has largely been ignored. The structure of the 2019 exhibition 'I Am The Coyote' covered two phases. The first phase, produced as a by-product of the art action staged inside and outside the prison for the Edinburgh Festivals of 1974 and 1975 onwards. The second phase in 2018 centred on work produced as an outcome of research undertaken by existing prisoners and staff in the HMP Humber Graft Studio. This was based on the prisoners asking, 'Am I the coyote?' and the contemporary significance of lessons that could be taken from the transformative implications of the mentoring, teaching and learning that took place in the Special Unit.

Sally Coates (2016) suggests, 'There should be no restriction on the use of education funding to support the creative arts, personal and social development opportunities, and family or relationship courses. These can be used to engage prisoners in education and support them to make progress against their personal learning plan.' The aim of the 'I Am The Coyote' exhibition was and is that the creative process embodied in the collaborative framework that produced the art works, and the participatory experience evidenced, would help define formal and informal approaches to learning and teaching. A photograph from the exhibition showing HM Prison Humber learners announcing their workshop appears in *Chapter 3*.

The idea of engagement with teaching and learning is here based on a continuing appetite for dialogue extended by the preservation of the unique elements of the work of the unit. 'I Am The Coyote', therefore, took Beuys' proclamation, 'New Beginnings are In the Offering' and the significance of the creative access further, facilitating the scope for research beyond the work simply shown in the Brynmor Jones Gallery. Access was provided to additional selected material from the archives held by Demarco, Tisdall and Beech and Whitaker in the form of new recorded interviews, with Boyle and Tisdall. Reports, letters, scripts, etc. were made available to be accessed by appointment in the Brynmor Jones Library special collection during the exhibition. Related events included 'In Conversation with Richard Demarco and Andrew Marr: Can Art Help—the Political Divide in Britain?'; film screenings of *A Sense of Freedom* and *Silent Scream*; a Drawing Workshop with the Graft Studio and a series of three Friday Night Debates examining the issues raised by the exhibition.

The Coyote Fund Archive continues to promote exhibitions and research that supports the understanding of the legacy of the Special Unit.

Reference

Coates, S (2016), Unlocking Potential: A Review of Education in Prison. Ministry of Justice: https://assets.publishing.service.gov.uk/media/5a7f537eed915d74e33f5bf5/education-review-report.pdf (accessed 29 February 2024).

CHAPTER 19

Graft Studio — A Community in HMP Humber's Art Department

Graeme Brooks

An Artist Goes to Prison

In the Spring of 1999, Charlotte Hosker, who was the progressive and innovative Head of Art at HM Prison Everthrope, which later was to become HMP Humber, had seen an exhibition of my paintings at a local art gallery and contacted me about a part-time teaching role in the prison. This sparked my interest and intrigue immediately, as I suddenly recalled distant memories of a former tutor's passionate enthusiasm on art in prisons, which I had been too young at the time to grasp. I was a Foundation Art Student at Hull School of Art in 1982 and was great friends with another student, Emma Beech. Emma's father, Bill Beech, happened to be the Head of Fine Arts. Bill was, and is, gregarious, generous and hospitable, often inviting me out for meals. An entertaining raconteur, he was always enthusing about Joseph Beuys and the Special Unit at Barlinnie Prison. He talked about the idea of art as rehabilitation, all of which I knew little about and did not really care about at the time. However, I would humour him by trying to listen and perhaps learn something, which must have planted a deep seed somewhere in me.

Prior to my first prison visit to Everthorpe, I had received official guidance about dress code, security and expectations, so when I turned up and walked into Charlotte Hosker's surprisingly, large, dynamic and industrious workshop, I was shocked at how familiar everything appeared. I felt immediately at home, everyone looked like me with a utilitarian shaven head and facial stubble, replicating a family reunion experience. Suddenly, the noise of activity fell silent, everyone turned and focused on me with quizzical expressions and puzzlement, probably thinking I was dressed up to get married in the chapel or I had come to say goodbye and had bought a cheap suit from Argos with my discharge grant. My grandad was an aspirational and successful housebuilder and, whether working laying bricks or relaxing at home, always wore a tie proudly. My father was a shipping accountant who was never seen at work without his matching suit and one of his obligatory 1970s nylon kipper ties. So, now feeling conspicuous and uncomfortable, I asked Charlotte if I could put my jacket somewhere, and she pointed me to a small staffroom where I quickly removed the tie, unbuttoned my collar, rolled my sleeves up and returned to the studio ready for work, all within 20 seconds, akin to Mr Bean.

The lads' reaction to my sudden reappearance from behind the door was totally transformed with one quickly and comedically shouting over, 'Hey mate, you've just missed your pretentious twin brother!' They had immediately nailed me, seeing straight through me and we all began laughing and never stopped. This was a valuable and crucial lesson in first impressions, rapport and communication and the tie never went back on for 21 years. By removing those 'pretentious' barriers and openly admitting my error, I was immediately accepted and warmly received as we began a synergic journey and relationship together, which would transform my life and the lives of many others.

Interestingly, a few years later when my now close colleague and collaborator, Lisa Smith, initially came to look round one lunch time, Charlotte opened a door and I was the first male Lisa saw inside the prison and she often recalls thinking, 'Whoa, he looks a bit dodgy.' Then Charlotte introduced me as a fellow art tutor, but I am not sure if Lisa's opinion has ever altered. The truth is I am one of them, a testosterone fuelled fragile man, with reactive tendencies, issues and insecurities who has let people down. I have not always made the right decisions under pressure and I don't always learn from my mistakes, all of which made me an effective teacher and learner in this sector. We are all only one bad decision away from losing our liberty, but one good decision away to beginning to free ourselves.

Creating Graft Studio

Around the year 2000, the Art Department were invited to show their work inside the prison's chapel and a group of students and staff sat discussing ideas for the title of the forthcoming exhibition. They suggested 'Graft', which at first, I was naïvely uncertain of the title, yet the more I thought about it, the more I liked it and the powerful term has stuck for more than 20 years. 'Graft' is prison slang for committing crime to raise funds. In the wider society, the term is used for hard work or being active. The dictionary explains 'graft' as splicing of one plant to onto another to aid regeneration, or surgical 'skin graft' to cover a wound, repairing the damage of serious illness or trauma.

All these connotations describe exactly the ethos of the teaching team and the rehabilitative needs and aspirations of the students. That moment was the catalyst for our transformative development and we all began to think bigger, broader and deeper. The Graft Studio and team ethos was born. We now had a collective name, spirit and manifesto to which we all felt compelled to nurture, uphold and belong. Whilst Charlotte was already instrumental in the annual Koestler Prison Art Exhibitions, what started as a small show in a prison chapel, soon became a non-stop series of many hundreds of exhibitions inside and critically outside the prison walls in a plethora of high-profile galleries and community institutions. The Graft team were always working towards something and often on many large projects simultaneously, we were determined to impact, communicate and interact with the outside world and 'art world' simultaneously. As practising artists, the teaching team would often show their work alongside the students which dismantled the traditional hierarchy and promoted an inclusive team ethos of 'learners' working and showing together.

One colleague, Darren Rodgers, was pivotal to Graft and the National Art Provision. A Fine Art graduate in a photography studio, he was enrolled about a year after my appointment. We worked closely together establishing the Graft progressive formula and our manifesto. We both talked about the Graft Studio as an ongoing 'work of art', always in a state of 'flux' to reflect its learners' needs and requirements. Hence this perception as an experimental 'Social Sculpture', Happening or Performance enabled us to deliver a diverse and exciting syllabus of trial and error like shaping a natural slab of clay, enhancing and developing certain vital successful elements and removing those parts which were less effective. Whilst we created an environment for free and safe expression and rehabilitation, it was the diverse students working together who made the exhilarating Social Sculpture so very successful.

We adopted an adventurous intrinsic 'Punk' experimental approach to make things happen quickly and maintained and infused a high level of energy, activity and vibrancy within the workshop to encourage genuine positive mindfulness, self-confidence and an ambience of 'escapism' without any of us leaving the room in the centre of a security citadel. Thus all the students desperately wanted to be part of it, they recognised we were an alternative workshop where it was possible to break rules of art and enjoy and celebrate diversity without negative judgement. We simply liked making new adventurous stuff individually or in groups then showing it inside and to the world outside to give something back to the communities to aid the students own healing and guilt. We instilled and proved that personal and group creativity, personal development and giving back induces and provides a similar enhanced buzz to drugs and criminal activity.

Students are not told what to do, they are asked what they would like to do, to achieve, learn, improve or change? We attempt to stimulate a dormant curiosity and enlightened understanding of others by sharing and exchanging ideas, in an environment where being different is not an issue, but an opportunity to experience first-hand diversity. Graft has an open and loose interpretation of what 'Art' should be. Every day we encourage some kind of live, group interactive presentation by staff or students, which could be discussion, poetry, song, music, dance, comedy, film, technical demonstration, challenge, game or quiz. We attract, welcome and invite many diverse visitors, partners and customers from the outside world who, where possible are encouraged to share their specialisms, roles, concerns and feedback with the Graft team for knowledge, understanding, progression and development. We have no minimum qualification for entry, so anyone can join regardless of previous experience or aptitude. We welcome those 'hard to reach' learners who have exhausted their involvement in other areas, classrooms or workshops due to personal challenges or disruptive behaviour. We can usually offer them a vehicle, platform or medium to manage their conditions, raising their confidence and self-esteem dramatically.

Graft Studio Exhibitions

Graft has a continuous rolling vocational programme of exhibitions, some within the prison and others local or national, so we are continually working towards a project, a commission, public event or taking a show down. Late in 2012, the Graft team won a bid to represent Britain in Jeremy Deller's 'English Magic' Venice Biennale, along with HMP Parc from Wales and HMP Shotts in Scotland. We had an already established group of Military Veterans and Civilian Students who were encouraged to make work as a reaction to the Iraq War during a series or interactive workshops with erudite guidance from Jeremy. All those who took part in the project found the experience liberating and healing, yet few realised the power they were contributing to the national 'aftermath narrative'. Jeremy invited some released students to travel to Venice to witness the show first-hand which was truly transformative. Later the exhibition returned to the William Morris Gallery in Walthamstow and then elements were shown at the British Council, and in Bristol.

Prior to the Venice opening Jeremy contacted me to explain that the press had covered the preview and tipped me off that *The Guardian* were publishing extensive reviews in their Saturday edition. I bought 30 copies, enough for everyone. That following Monday was one of the most emotional experiences during my career, as we witnessed a group of invisible, silent locked away students in a Yorkshire prison scrutinising their work over the full colour centre pages whilst in astonishment, disbelief and tears. One student remarked, 'I can't wait to show my Mum on visits, I've been in the papers loads of times, but never for anything *good*!' It resonated so strongly when another explained that no-one had previously listened to him, yet here using the language of art, he was communicating from Venice his experiences, opinions and views with hundreds of thousands of people simultaneously in the outside world. His body was locked away and thoughts disregarded, yet he found an 'early release' medium to free his mind and voice for the world to see and hear.

In 2019, inspired by the work of Richard Demarco, Joseph Beuys and other artists affiliated with the Barlinnie Special Unit (BSU), we mounted the exhibition 'I Am The Coyote' at The University of Hull. Beuys work is esoteric, so we used role play in order for the men in the Graft Studio to absorb and understand his art. Whilst planning and preparing our work for the 'Coyote' show we had a new, adventurous learner enrol with the Graft Studio; when he walked through the door, I could not believe my eyes and our good fortune. He looked exactly like Joseph Beuys with the exception of being six-foot-five! I already had the hat, but sourcing a fishing waistcoat was challenging. Still, when he was eventually in costume, we were all rolling about with hysterical laughter, closely comparing him to the historic images in books. We recreated and documented 'How to explain pictures to a Dead Hare' and some of the classic period shots of Beuys with the Coyote, and with Richard Demarco, who I stood in for, plus images of 'our Beuys' making a cardboard 'Fat Chair'.

The lads were now hooked and intrigued, so I set a team competition to see who could make the best Beuys costumes from prison newspapers plus the best Coyote costume from a roll of fake brown fur we had stashed in stock. Then we set the rules where each coyote had to travel the length of the studio on a wheely board to 'fetch' three classic Beuys' items (hat, jacket and shaman's stick) from the other side of the studio and return to Beuys in the shortest possible time for a reward of a small bag of coffee. The coffee was shared amongst the group by the winners which indicated their team spirit, pack mentality, empathy and loyalty. We documented the entire process and the images formed part of our contribution to the 'Coyote' exhibition. This crazy 'Performance/Action' allowed us to discuss and embed complex concepts about the Human/Coyote respect/evolving relationship and American history plus discuss the theory of Pavlov's Dog and Graft rewards, stimulating salivation for a taste of the tutor's coffee. No other vehicle or medium could have taught so much in such a short amount of time.

One week, later Richard Demarco and his team came to spend a few days with us and visited the Graft Studio and gave an astonishing, captivating and emotional speech which left the men in floods of tears. Following this we couldn't help maximising the rich potential by getting 'our Beuys' dressed up in his garb and re-enacting a classic series of images of our 'too tall' fake Beuys with the real 'larger than life' Richard Demarco! Richard's involvement from the original coyote to our contemporary version over 45 years later was a tribute to his longevity, passion and pivotal dedication to the subject.

The 'I Am The Coyote' exhibition was the perfect summary to my 21 year career in offender learning, allowing me to return to my own neglected full-time art practice. My departure enabled the Graft team to restructure and refresh to combat the new challenges of the Covid-19 outbreak and an essential studio relocation. The students needed the creative art cognitive 'flow state' more than ever to manage their personal mental health and distract from fears and concerns for their families outside. I have always needed help, and the lads humbled, enriched and inspired me continuously. The dedicated and diverse teaching team made all of our aspirations not just possible but incredibly successful. Eighteen years ago, we needed to recruit a cover member of staff and we fortuitously employed a Goldsmiths' graduate called Lisa Smith who immediately recognised and appreciated the potential of the unique environment and learners. I collaborated closely with Lisa on all of the hundreds of exhibitions and projects, she covered my basic IT skills, shared my dedication and social conscience, plus she made every day an absolute joy. I know the future of 'Graft' is in safe and secure hands. This future must be preceded by a shared understanding of what is needed to support people leaving custody. As part of the *I Am The Coyote* catalogue we outlined the need to have contact lists for support agencies that aid people in finding shelter, food and support. These 'Graft Survival Guides' can be produced and updated by ex-prisoners to share content, advice, tips and strategies. At Graft, we share a collective belief and knowledge that art is a powerful transformative tool, but we also need to provide people with information and support upon release from custody.

Final Thoughts

The Graft Studio remains the antithesis and antidote to isolation, where all are invited to regain or rediscover their uncontaminated identity, positive behavioural traits, passions, personal potential and taste the power of freedom, choice, teamwork, purpose, hope and thus recovery. As 30 men celebrate their individuality collectively a curiosity, enlightened understanding and natural empathy evolves and extreme views are quickly exposed as toxic and inappropriate. The studio is a melting pot of the male human condition. The large brutalist studio walls are totally obliterated and radically transformed by inspirational, diverse and continually updated murals covering every inch of available space, reflecting the current members, to which all are invited to contribute. When new starters arrive at the door they quickly realise they are stepping into a totally new and different environment, and we are always aware that they have chosen a new direction, experience and alternate experimental journey. We never tire of witnessing the dramatic relaxation of body language, facial features and guard as the environment and potential early freedom of spirit pervades their bodies and minds. During my 21 years of service we have positively impacted and enhanced probably over a thousand inspirational students, plus employed 15 fine art graduates as staff, who have all added their own colour, energy and design to the rich and revolutionary tapestry of Graft.

Whilst the BSU and Graft Studio share high profile kudos within the prison sector, they should no longer be perceived as *special*, unique, radical niche, experimental or esoteric. Following the Covid-19 pandemic, we have all experienced a taste of lockdown isolation, restriction of free movement and lack of stimulation and communication, with many turning to new creative therapeutic pursuits to manage and maintain our mental health. Thus, following a world of undeniable evidence, art intervention support courses must become 'standard', ubiquitous and essential within all prisons and secure establishments if we are serious about rehabilitation and reducing offending.[1]

1. Graeme Brooks' 2019 photograph of 'I Am The Coyote' taken at the Graft Studio appears in *Chapter 3*.

CHAPTER 20

Arts in Prisons: Research, Tensions and Prospects

Kirstin Anderson

Introduction

Writer Rachel Kushner said in response to her book *The Mars Room* at the Edinburgh International Book Festival in 2018 that 'Art can allow someone to ask questions about what is justice.' Since the days of the Barlinnie Special Unit (BSU), the use of the arts in prison settings has led many to reflect on the concept of justice and the impact of imprisonment. Arts practice in prisons, in Scotland and internationally, has grown substantially as demonstrated by numerous third sector organizations that aim to support people in custody through arts programming, universities that engage students in studying and preparing to practice in carceral settings and an expanding research field that cuts across subject areas in the arts, social work and criminology.

Key moments of growth of arts practice in Scottish prisons include the innovative largescale project Inspiring Change, which involved seven national arts organizations working collaboratively in five Scottish prisons over one year (Anderson et al, 2011), to the current practice of third sector organizations, such as Vox Liminis, engaging communities to think about imprisonment more widely through the arts rather than through the traditional prism of 'fixing' the prisoner (Urie et al, 2019). For some scholars, there is a shift in direction in considering the arts as a form of resistance against the prison system itself (Fleetwood, 2020). Despite this growing interest in the use of arts in prisons, far more than there was in the days of the BSU, the work continues to be fragmented in Scotland due to lack of consistent funding, difficulty in accessing prisons and lack of public understanding and support. In this chapter, I discuss how arts in prisons practice and research has developed since the closing of the BSU in 1994, the tensions in this practice and research that result in a constant dance of forward and backward steps that stall progress and, after 50 years since the opening of the BSU, the future prospects for the arts in Scottish prisons.

A Piano in a Cell

It struck me immediately; the photo, two inches by one inch of a man sitting at an upright piano, his hands in playing position. A piano in a prison cell (Carrell and Laing, 1982: 118). The presence of instruments and materials to create art in prison is not new, but a piano in a prison cell is unusual and most likely would not be sanctioned in a prison today. However, this is a photo of a man in a cell in the BSU. It is important to note that the role of the arts in the BSU, suggested by Ludovic Kennedy (1982:4) were 'not acclaim for the art, but therapy for the artist.' Art therapy is a distinct practice, one that often gets muddled into discussions of arts in prisons and how the work is 'therapeutic' or 'calming'. There have been instances of arts therapy in Scottish prisons since the closing of the BSU, mostly in the form of short-term projects, but reflections on this work, at least in the academic context, are few and the practice is not well-documented.

Joyce Laing (1984) wrote eloquently on the challenges of establishing the arts in a therapeutic way in prisons; the messiness of the practice in environments where the work gets lost amidst the numerous rules and regulations of the institution. She also clearly articulates how we might consider art education and art therapy as 'points on a continuum, both being complementary to the other' (ibid: 119). Laing proposes that the arts are used by people who are imprisoned to express themselves, that whether based in educational or therapeutic contexts, 'the arts are communication' (ibid). What do imprisoned people communicate through art? And, perhaps more importantly, how does research in this area shape what we hear, see and feel about the experience of incarcerated people?

Research

Although inconsistently documented, prison governors have supported artists and organizations to come in and lead projects in Scottish prisons for decades. It is difficult to articulate the scale and diversity of practice of arts provision in Scottish prisons as the routes into the prison are varied and the practice, and projects, are not consistently documented or reviewed. Some individuals teach arts education classes in visual arts, drama and music in prison Learning Centres as part of the contracted education provision. Before education was contracted outside of the Prison Service, self-selected officers might teach guitar to some men in the hall, the chaplain might lead the singing of hymns in the chapel and art rooms exist in most prisons in various forms. I know of a volunteer musician who led a choir with a group of men in HMP Glenochil for years simply because the Governor supported the project. Another example, the Citizens Theatre, based in Glasgow, has worked in prisons for decades and now works with communities impacted by imprisonment as well. The practice of the arts in prisons has been there all along; research, however, is still catching up.

Unlike in other parts of the UK (Hughes, 2004) and in some American states, Scotland does not yet have a body of research that documents and examines arts in prisons in a historical context.[1] Research and evaluations of projects led by artists and third sector organizations are growing in this area. In a survey conducted in 2008 on music provision in Scottish prisons, Anderson (2011) found that eight out of 15 prisons offered music provision, sometimes within an education context but not always. All 15 prisons had offered music provision in the past or had planned provision. A range of musical activities were included in this practice including composing music, learning how to read music, and playing instruments. The study notes that the provision was not documented anywhere on the Scottish Prisons Service (SPS) or contracted colleges websites.

In 2010, there was support and funding secured for a large-scale arts pilot in Scottish prisons. Inspiring Change involved seven national arts organizations working with Learning Centre staff in five prisons in a range of art forms including music, drama and many types of visual arts.[2] The final report of the

1. The author is currently undertaking research on this topic.
2. The Inspiring Change project is beyond the scope of this work. Please see the final report by Anderson, et al (2011) in the References at the end of this chapter for more information.

year long project found that the sessions were valued by participants because of the high level of professionalism of the artists and practitioners leading the projects, opportunities for participants to work towards a performance or exhibition of their work and sharing their experiences through art with their families and communities (Anderson et al, 2011). Inspiring Change was unique in many ways, but one important element was its scale. In addition to the numbers of organizations, artists and prison staff that participated in the arts projects, Inspiring Change involved over 230 people in custody, including young people, women and people serving short- and long-term sentences. This was certainly one of its most unique features as previous projects, including the BSU, worked with small groups of prisoners. Because of its scale, Inspiring Change engaged the Prison Service in a way that previous projects had not; as an entity. The result of this is that the time in which the project took place, and for some time after its completion, felt like a door had been opened to welcome the arts in Scottish prisons. Funding opportunities increased for arts practitioners to develop projects, the SPS were more welcoming to arts practitioners and a group of artists started the Scottish Prison Arts Network (now Justice and Arts Scotland) to support people working in the sector.

STIR, an arts magazine created in 2012, received funding from the Big Lottery and Creative Scotland. New College Lanarkshire set up the project in HMP Shotts; the magazine features art, poetry and other creative writing; every issue is put together by an editorial team of men in prison. Thorpe (2015) wrote an artist's guide, in partnership with the SPS, to working in Scottish prisons. Sections in the guide included Working with the SPS, Project Planning and Sharing Work. In 2019, Glass Performance launched Polmont Youth Theatre in HM Young Offender Institution Polmont, the first registered youth theatre in a Scottish prison. These are just some of the highlights of work and practice that took place in the last decade; there are many more projects, small and large, which were led by arts organizations and independent artists that are not mentioned here due to space. During the early days of the Covid-19 pandemic, Scottish prisons, like the outside world, went into lockdown. Arts organizations developed creativity packs to go into prisons and, once lockdown restrictions began to ease, alternative programming for the safe delivery of arts practice in prisons and in the community. Still, this work is piecemeal and inconsistently documented.

Tensions

There are several tensions within the arts and justice sector, as may be expected due to the different priorities of the organizations and professionals that work in this area. I would like to highlight three of these tensions, first, the issue of accessibility, second, how prison services shape the art made by people in custody and research of arts practice and thirdly, the contribution that arts research makes towards society's continued use of imprisonment.

First, the issue of accessibility is not new to arts practitioners and researchers in this area. Prisons are historically closed institutions and, despite a century of prison reformers' work in the UK, it is not until relatively recently that the general public has knowledge of some of the inner life of prisons beyond sensational news stories or films. Understandably, a prison service has processes of entry in place and security measures that are intended to monitor what goes in, and what goes out, of a prison. This, of course, is not new. The preface to *The Special Unit Barlinnie Prison: Its Evolution Through Its Art* (Carrell and Laing, 1982) discusses the challenges in working with the Scottish Office through the then Prisons Department (as the service was known before its current organizational form as an Executive Agency of the Scottish Government in 1993). While attempts have been made by the SPS to streamline access for artists and practitioners to one central contact after the completing of the Inspiring Change project, this in fact limited the amount of access for artists and made it more difficult for organizations to work in prisons.

Secondly, there is a tension present in how prison services potentially shape the art made by people in custody and how research of arts practice is undertaken. Little is known about how artwork created in Scottish prisons is censored, by the Prison Service or self-censored by prisoners. Reviewing the art pieces created by the men in the BSU, compared with the artwork presented in issues of *STIR* or submitted to the Koestler Awards for Arts in Criminal Justice, shows a stark difference, for example, in how the human body, sexual desire and the pain inflicted by punishment is presented. With this shaping of the art itself comes the potential of shaping the research on arts in prisons. For many years, artists and arts organizations working in this field have found themselves in a dilemma; showing to funders that arts practice in prisons is connected to reducing reoffending rates. While there is research to show that engagement with the arts may contribute to secondary desistance, the adoption of a non-offending identity, for many years arts organizations have been expected to show that their projects can help towards a person not reoffending once they leave custody. This is, of course, extremely difficult to establish as most arts projects do not follow people once they have left custody and, even for those that do, there are many factors that can contribute and influence whether someone reoffends again (e.g. housing, substance abuse, mental health and relationships).

Thirdly, there is a tension in the contribution that arts research makes towards a society's continued use of imprisonment. More artists and practitioners are aware and knowledgeable of the impact of imprisonment and their contribution, whether intended or not, to sustaining that system. Can arts organizations and practitioners work in prisons, and with prisons systems, to provide opportunities to create and sustain art making practices without contributing to the harms of the prison? A number of arts organizations that work in this sector have expanded their remit to include work in the community, and not focus solely on practice in prisons. Research has shown the grasp of the prison extends beyond the prison walls, it is worth considering the impact of a growing arts and justice sector on sustaining that grip and questioning if there are other ways artists can work with communities impacted by imprisonment.

Prospects

If artists choose to continue working in prisons, access, funding and committed support from the SPS and the Scottish Government is key to the sustainability of the arts in Scottish prisons. Without these three elements not only is the delivery of the arts sporadic in prisons, but programmes also lack the consistency to develop and grow. Access, funding and committed support from the SPS and the Scottish Government is key if there are to be more than just pockets of practice in Scottish prisons.

We must think critically about how research on the arts in prison shapes the practice. The men in the BSU had unstructured time to develop their art. They created multiple sculptures and poems over time, shared them with the community (both in prison and outside of prison) and developed a practice. The current structure of arts provision in Scottish prisons does not provide the same opportunities. Despite this, people in custody continue to make art. They continue to share it with their loved ones in visits, to participate in programmes the prison allows to run and submit to the Koestler Trust for some recognition. But the practice is in constant flux and will continue to be unless committed support from the SPS and the Scottish Government is established, and access and funding is made more accessible for artists and practitioners.

Art will remain in as long as humans are kept confined in them. Artists and practitioners will continue to try and work with people impacted by the justice system, and researchers will continue to document and evaluate. I propose we do not wait another 50 years to revisit the question about the value of the arts in prison, there is plenty of evidence and experience to suggest that they are of value to prisoners, artists and communities. Perhaps, as Kushner suggests, we can go even further and use the arts to ask deeper questions about what justice is for people in Scotland and beyond.

References

Anderson, K (2011), *Music Education and Experience in Scottish Prisons*. Unpublished PhD thesis, University of Edinburgh.

Anderson, K, Colvin, S, McNeill, F, Nellis, M, Overy, K, Sparks, R and Tett, L (2011), Inspiring Change: Final Project Report of the Evaluation Team: http://www.artsevidence.org.uk/media/uploads/evaluation-downloads/mc-inspiring-change-april-2011.pdf (accessed April 2018).

Carrell, C and Laing, J (eds) (1982), *The Special Unit Barlinnie Prison: Its Evolution Through Its Art,* Glasgow: Third Eye Centre.

Fleetwood, N (2020), *Marking Time: Art in the Age of Mass Incarceration*, Cambridge: Harvard University Press.

Hughes, J (2004), 'Doing the Arts Justice. A Review of Research, Literature, Practice and Theory', Unit for Arts and Offenders/Centre for Applied Theatre Research.

Laing, J (1984), 'Art Therapy in Prisons'. In T Dalley (ed), *Art as Therapy: An Introduction to the Use of Art as a Therapeutic Technique*, New York: Routledge: 115–128.

Thorpe, J (2015), *Working in Scottish Prisons: An Artist's Guise*: https://www.creativescotland.com/__data/assets/pdf_file/0005/33836/Artists-Guide-Working-in-Scottish-Prisons.pdf (accessed April 2018).

Urie, A, McNeill, F, Cathcart Frödén, L, Collinson Scott, J, Crockett Thomas, P, Escobar, O, Macleod, S and McKerracher, G (2019), Reintegration, Hospitality and Hostility: Song-writing and Song-sharing, *Criminal Justice Journal of Extreme Anthropology*, 3(1): 77–101.

Conclusion

Kirstin Anderson and Claire Coia

During its existence, the Barlinnie Special Unit (BSU) was met with both empathetic support and condemnation, depending on whom you spoke to, and this response remains today. Unless recounted in prisoners' autobiographies, which is how, for many, the unit is lodged in the public's imagination, many of its stories remain ephemeral and fragmented, as fading memories and anecdotes exchanged in passing. However, the traces of the Special Unit are found in scattered collections of art, binders of newspaper clippings and personal archives, which is one reason why this book is in your hands just now.

HMP Barlinnie has a notorious reputation in Scotland, and the philosophy of the Special Unit stood in stark contrast to the prison, a place of regimental discipline. As discussed by David Cooke in *Chapter 12*, 'Evaluating Violence Reduction in the Unit', the therapeutic community of the BSU resulted in a reduction of violent incidents, however, the methods used in the Special Unit were often seen as controversial, and it was difficult to ignore the press presentation that the unit enabled dangerous individuals to 'beat the system'. Up until that time, the unit was led and looked after by its small community of prisoners, staff, visitors and advocates in the community. As Mike Nellis highlights in *Chapter 16*, 'Remembering Jimmy Boyle, Misremembering The Barlinnie Special Unit', the Special Unit was constantly in the press and the threat of closure was present for years before it was closed in 1994 without protest or fanfare; this could explain why the Prison Service has not learned from the mistakes of the Special Unit, as well as its success.

We propose, however, that this is not the end of the BSU story. While this book does include perspectives not heard before, there is still much to explore about the experiences people had in the Special Unit, especially the last decade of the unit's operation. We need a better understanding of the complexities of the therapeutic community experienced by prison staff and prisoners in the Special Unit. We lack the stories of men for whom it was not a solace, who requested to be transferred out of the unit because the therapeutic community required full participation, which can be challenging and exhausting, especially after imprisonment in traditional regimes. It was not possible to just 'keep your head down' and get through your sentence in the Special Unit, and there were many who found the approach difficult.

There are a number of lessons to take away from the preceding chapters. Firstly, these chapters urge us to consider the use of small units throughout the Scottish Prison Service, the BSU being only one of them in Scottish penal history. As Andrew Coyle discusses in *Chapter 14*, 'The Genesis and Legacy of the BSU', the European Committee for the Prevention of Torture and Inhuman or Degrading Treatment or Punishment (CPT) reported after their visit to Scottish Prisons in October 2019 that the Scottish authorities 'should seriously consider the establishment of smaller therapeutic units.' This has not happened. The most recent version we have of small units in Scotland are two Community Custody Units (CCUs) for women; the Lilias Centre in Glasgow, which can house 24 individuals, and the Bella Centre in Dundee, which can house 16 individuals. Neither of these are therapeutic units and most women in the SPS will serve their sentence in HMP Inverness, a facility that is designed to house up to 103 individuals. There are no small units of any kind for young men or women, nor adult men; the largest population in Scottish prisons.

A thread that runs throughout the chapters, experienced by prison staff and prisoners, is the important role of talking, and prisoners having the ability to express their thoughts, feelings and concerns to each other and to prison staff. It is difficult to express how different the relationship between prison staff and prisoners was in the Prison Service in the 1970s; the notion of talking to each other and making decisions collectively in the way used in the Special Unit was new territory for the SPS.

One key aspect of a therapeutic community is the collective and yet, we would be remiss to not mention the number of times individual people came up as necessary to the spirit of the Special Unit. We remember with fondness Ken Murray and Joyce Laing throughout these chapters; both innovators and champions of the Special Unit. Their foresight, persistence and care was the dynamic influence that led the unit in its infant years. Many artists visited the Special Unit over the years, one of the most important being the esteemed contemporary German artist Joseph Beuys. His dedication to the unit was deeply intertwined with his regard for the men inside the BSU as artists. In terms of former prisoners, many associate the Special Unit with Jimmy Boyle. One of the first prisoners in the unit, he produced numerous sculptures, published memoirs and a play about his experience of imprisonment. Many people came to know about the Special Unit through his book, *A Sense of Freedom*. In later years, others may have encountered the BSU through the artwork or autobiographies of Hugh Collins, Johnny Steele, Larry Winters and TC Campbell. Of course, there are many men who, while incarcerated in the Special Unit, developed greatly from the community. We do not yet know their stories.

This collection has brought together perspectives of academics, artists, prison officers and prisoners; all of whom hold the memory of the BSU in different ways. For some, perhaps prison reformers and many artists, the Special Unit can be seen as a beacon of imagination and success. From this perspective, the unit was a reminder of how a prison service can choose to take a different approach in treating people detained in custody. For others, such an approach is no longer enough. Scottish prisons are still, very much, prisons and many people incarcerated in them still face, albeit in different ways from 50 years ago when the Special Unit opened, degrading and debilitating consequences of confinement.

The Victorian buildings of HMP Barlinnie, including the small building where the Special Unit was housed, are set to be replaced with HMP Glasgow in 2026, the largest prison Scotland has ever built. The design and ethos of this new prison is perhaps the furthest away from the design and ethos of the BSU. The building of HMP Glasgow is a reminder to us that not understanding the significance of the BSU, its strengths and weaknesses, has resulted in lessons unlearned and an unquestioning allegiance to the use of imprisonment in Scotland, and the ever-expanding growth of the prison population. We hope this book can re-open dialogue about the BSU and that it will inspire further research and study of this unique time in Scottish penal history.

Select Bibliography

Bird, J (2017), Spatial Autonomy and Desistance in Penal Settings. Case Study: The Barlinnie Special Unit (1973–1994). In Hart E, van Ginneken E (eds), *New Perspectives on Desistance,* London: Palgrave Macmillan.

Boyle, J (1977), *A Sense of Freedom*, London: Pan Books.

Boyle, J (1984), *The Pain of Confinement*, London: Pan Books.

Collins, H (1997), *Autobiography of a Murderer*, London: Macmillan.

Cooke, D J (1989), Containing Violent Prisoners: An Analysis of the Barlinnie Special Unit, *British Journal of Criminology*, Issue 29.

Cooke, D J (1991), Violence in Prisons: The Influence of Regime Factors, *Howard Journal of Crime and Justice,* Issue 30.

Cooke, D J (1997), The Barlinnie Special Unit: The Rise and Fall of a Therapeutic Experiment. In Cullen, E, Jones, L and Woodward, R (eds), *Therapeutic Communities for Offenders,* London: Wiley.

Coyle, A (1987), The Scottish Experience with Small Units. In Bottoms A E and Light R (eds), *Problems of Long-Term Imprisonment,* Aldershot: Gower.

Coyle, A (1991), *Inside: Rethinking Scotland's Prisons*, Edinburgh: Scottish Child.

Gibson, R (1987), Return to Barlinnie Special Unit, *Prison Service Journal,* Issue 65.

Jeffrey, R (2009), *The Barlinnie Story: Riots, Death, Retribution and Redemption in Scotland's Infamous Prison*, Edinburgh: Black and White Publishing.

Nellis, M (2010), Creative Arts and the Cultural Politics of Penal Reform: The Early Years of the Barlinnie Special Unit, 1973–1981, *Journal of Scottish Criminal Justice Studies,* Issue 20.

Steele, J (2002), *The Bird that Never Flew*, Edinburgh: Mainstream Publishing.

Stephen, I (1988), The Barlinnie Special Unit: A Penal Experiment. In Backett S, McNeill J and Yellowlees A, *Imprisonment Today: Current Issues in the Prison Debate,* London: Macmillan.

Whatmore, P (1987), *Barlinnie Special Unit: An Insider's View* in Bottoms A E and Light R, (eds), *Problems of Long-Term Imprisonment,* Aldershot: Gower.

Wilson, D and Brookes, M, A Failed Success: The Barlinnie Special Unit, *International Journal of Prison Health,* August 2020, Emerald Publishing.

Index

A

B

H

R

T

Y

C EFT

BOOK THREE

By David Green

HELL IN HAVEN CITY
AN URBAN FANTASY

EERIE RIVER PUBLISHING
www. EerieRiverPublishing.com

Eerie River Publishing
www.EerieRiverPublishing.com
Hamilton, Ontario Canada

Paperback ISBN: 978-1-998112-20-3
Digital ISBN: 978-1-998112-19-7

Edited by Shona Kinsella
Cover design by Grady Earls

Book Formatting by Michelle River of Eerie River Publishing

ALSO BY DAVID GREEN

Hell In Haven City Series

The Darkness In The Pines: A Hell In Haven Prequel Novella

Devil Walks in Blood: Special Edition Books One and Two

Empire of Ruin Series

Before the Shadow

In Solitude's Shadow

Path of War

Beyond Sundered Seas

At Eternity's Gates

Never miss a new release!
Follow David on his Facebook page and
sign up for his newsletter.

www.facebook.com/groups/davidgreensreaderverseofmadness

‘To all the found families, wherever they may be.’

"In the middle of the journey of our life I found myself within a dark woods where the straight way was lost."

- Dante Alighieri, Inferno

CHAPTER ONE

18th DECEMBER, 2024
HAVEN WOODS

I have nice days every now and then. Sometimes, I wake up in the morning, take it easy, grab a cup of coffee and let the world pass me by for a spell. Yeah, some days are like that. Then there's the others. The days that make me wonder which Hellspawn my parents pissed off beyond belief on the day I came kicking and screaming into the world, all red-faced and angry. Screaming bloody murder at anyone who'd listen. Days when every goddamned creature in Hell decides, seemingly at once, that my continued existence is an affront they just can't abide, no matter how much they'd really like to. They appear in force, human, demon, ghost, and creature alike, together as one, and make it their absolute mission to make me regret the day I was born.

Today, bloody and bruised, alone in a god-forsaken, freezing forest in the middle of nowhere, a week before Christmas, the signal on my cell all but non-existent, and a warren of fae warriors, sent by Lilith herself, with murder and revenge on their collective minds, is one of those days.

Let's add it to the fucking list.

Name's Nick Holleran, by the way. Haven City's one and only Paranormal Investigator. I'm the guy who died, shocked to the core at finding my soul rising up to a Heaven I didn't believe in, only to be dragged back down to my meat suit as the docs patched me up. Then I found out Hell's real too, and all us humans have been living in it since, Jesus, I don't know, right after the dinosaurs? Never did ask, not even the time I came face-to-face with Lucifer himself, seeing as life leaked out of me at the time – again – I didn't get to every question I had. Nice fella, by the way.

Maybe Jesus would know. I'll make sure to ask him if we ever cross paths.

Look, my mind kinda rambles when I'm panicked. Or nervous. Or up shit's creek without a you know what. Right now, I'm all three. Well, in the quest for complete accuracy, I'm leaning against a tree, sweat and blood pouring off me, holding my breath, one hand clamped over my nose, so I don't fog the cold December air, and trying not to squeal when I pull the tiny darts these fae bastards have unleashed at me. They might be the size of my pinky finger, but man are they sharp, and these maniacs have hit me with at least twenty of them.

It's funny. Fae, even though they're about the size of my hand middle finger to wrist, pack a punch.

Now, you might say I had it coming, and you might be correct, but only if you've never had a run in with a fae before. I have. In fact, I need their, ahem, materials to create a powerful arcane weapon called an Expunger. A weapon that's pretty much a last resort, but a last resort I seem to fall back on way too often, and I'm all out. Hell's been active of late. Too active, though it isn't a surprise. Folk keep telling me a storm's coming, and I can smell it myself but it ain't hit yet. Sometimes I gotta bear in mind that entities like Lucifer and the Nephilim have existed for millennia, and what's soon for them might be a couple hundred years for a guy like me. But shit's going down at a faster rate than ever before, and more weirdness finds itself in my path than ever before, hence the need for more Expungers.

Understandably, Lilith, Queen of the Fae herself, takes exception to me harvesting her flock for their wings, and swore to make me pay, and just me; even though there are countless other humans who've sent fae to Lucifer-knows-where when they expire.

And guess what?

Today's that day. Glory fucking Hallelujah.

The angry flapping of wings causes me to forget about the tiny spears skewering my hide. Pressing against the tree's trunk, I sink lower, coiled like a snake. A serpent who skipped dinner, with crampy calf muscles and blood loss. Just need to hide, let them pass, and I'll head out in the other direction, all quiet like. Find my Mustang on the forest's outskirts and floor it until Haven's garish lights welcome me home. Maybe I'll keep going till I hit Portland, just for safety's sake. Not a bad idea, but not one I'm ever likely to do. One, I got history in the big city I'd rather forget and two, I got people in my life right here.

So, I'll sneak out. That's all I need to do. Simple.

"I smell Holleran," comes a hiss, and I hold my breath even harder, making my lungs burn. "He came this way!"

The...flock?...of fae hover above the path a little ways beneath me. See, I had the bright idea of getting above them, and yes, despite what people might say, I do have great ideas every now and then. An old buddy of mine, Harry, who usually got the supplies needed for Expungers and the like, told me fae never look up. 'Cos fae fly, they reckon they're above everything that matters. As someone often accused of arrogance, game recognized game, and I took advantage of it.

Don't seem to remember these bastards giving Harry such a hard time, now I think about it. Sadly, I seem to have a negative effect on people *and* creatures.

Peering down, darkness tugs at the corner of my eye and, despite knowing what I'll see when I glance to the side and really not wanting to, I go and do it, don't I?

In the shadows, the darkness billowing out from him like a ragged black cloak caught in the wind, is Charon.

Think of Death from the *Seventh Seal*, *Death Takes A Holiday*, or, Hell, *Bill And Ted's Bogus Journey* but make him look like Clint Eastwood in your mind's eye and dress him all in black, even down to the Stetson. While you're at it, instead of the scythe, give him the biggest sword that anyone this side of a Nephilim can carry, and when you meet his eyes, you see the memory of every soul that ever graced Hell, and a complete lack of empathy for them.

That's Charon. He's the Ferryman, Osiris, Hades, Hel, Ah Puch, and any other mythological figure of death personified. It's all him, and he's jonesing for me to bite the bullet. Jonesing *bad.*

See, I shoulda died a couple of times. Getting away with it the first time pissed Charon off well enough. And he met me soon after I recognized the earth for the Hell it is, to explain exactly that. But the second time? I got lucky. Lucifer himself intervened. Waltzing into a trap in the Wheeler basement meant I executed the one built for old Morningstar himself, and, after a selfless act from yours truly, the devil decided he'd walked through enough blood for one night and healed me for services rendered.

Reckon I don't get any more of those 'Get Out Of Death Free' cards.

Charon's followed me ever since. Says he can't see my destiny, and he doesn't like that. Not one little bit. So, he keeps tabs on me, and when I see him in times like this, I get the impression he doesn't only *think* I might die, he *wants* me to so he can balance his universal and eternal ledger of dead souls.

"Fateless. Perhaps this is the night," he hisses, voice carrying over the wind like air escaping from a hundred stone covers cracked open.

Fateless. That's what he calls me. I wanna tell him to shut the fuck up, but I know well that when Charon wants to speak to someone, only their ears will hear it. He visits everyone at their time of death, when their essence stays in Hell, and no one remembers him, or what he says.

Except for one time.

For a long while, I didn't understand Charon's purpose in Hell. He didn't take anyone, well, anywhere. Folk died, and if they didn't go up to Heaven, then they stayed here unless they faded into the Lord knows where. One of Hell's many mysteries, and fuck me if there aren't many. But Charon… A few months ago, I worked a case, and wound up in a confrontation with a Devil Worshiper with delusions of grandeur. Shit went down, as shit usually does, and the sonofabitch wound up dead. Charon watched, no doubt hoping I'd slip up, but a weird thing happened. We occupied the same space, just for a moment, and I heard what he said when the Devil Worshiper asked if Lucifer had come for him at last.

'No. I am much more than that. Come. The Seal awaits you.'

See, the ghosts that don't ascend and don't stick around in Hell *do* go somewhere, after all. They don't just fade away. Charon takes them to the Seal.

A little while later, I asked Charon about it. After he overcame his shock that I heard him growl those words, saying it wasn't possible, he told me maybe I'd see it one day. That maybe he'd take me there. Since then, I've searched long and hard for it, and come up with nada save for talk of the biblical seven seals. Charon's is *the* Seal.

"Will you not speak with me, Fateless?" Charon hisses again, the shadows so dark any of the fae searching the forest below would spot the black smoke as soon as they look up.

I glare at him in response. If he's wanting me to say something to blow my hiding space, I'm saying squat. I didn't almost die yesterday, you know?

"Spread out!" comes a shriek from below, and Charon's black eyes glitter in the darkness. "Find Holleran. The Queen says he must pay!"

Lower, Nick, lower. Just keep your head down. It's nice and dark. They won't see you. Just stay still, don't rise to Charon's bait, the sonofabitch, and it'll all be…

The vibration buzzing from my jeans pocket almost makes me jump from the spot, and the sound of *Hey* by The Pixies, ironic, echoing through the forest nearly causes my heart to force itself straight through my goddamned chest.

Mental note: next time you're stealthing your way through a forest with a…Pack?… of fae on your tail, at least put your cell on silent, Nick.

"He's above us!"

I don't know why, but when I spring to my feet, the multiple wounds screaming at me as I open my legs up to a sprint, I pull my cell out and take a look at who decided on the worst possible moment in my recent history to call me. It's Rosa. My girlfriend. One of the two people in my life I can't do without.

I *did* tell her I'd die for her when I was a little, er, merry recently. This isn't exactly what I had in mind.

I switch the cell to 'off' and move, ignoring Charon's grin as I tear past him, and duck as spears come flying my way.

For a wild moment, I think about turning my cell back on and seeing what in the Hell Rosa wanted, but now's not the best time for checking in with the sweetheart, you know?

"Why does this always happen to me?" I snarl, branches smacking me in the face, head, and shoulders as I push my way through the goddamn trees that, all of a sudden, appear more plentiful than they did before, like Lillith herself has glamoured the forest and instructed the ground to grow more trees pronto.

Maybe she has.

"It is because the universe demands your death, Holleran." Charon's voice, like two tombstones rubbing against each other for whatever reason tombstones might rub against one another, drifts through the foliage. "Be seeing you."

Fuck you, Charon, you boney sonofabitch.

Look, even as I think it, I know it's not my best insult, but I ain't ever been chased by fae before and my brain's occupied by the small matter of staying alive.

I throw a glance over my shoulder, and it's a bad idea. Not only does a jolt of pure panic surge from my gut and into my chest, I stumble, and my feet catch against a twig or whatever the Hell's in my path, and, soon enough, all I'm seeing is the world blur as I'm rolling head over heels down an unfairly rough and uneven slope.

The wounds I already got complain. The bumps, fresh cuts, scrapes and bangs I'm earning scream, and, behind me, the fae wail their guttural cry, sensing the end of old Nick Holleran. I'm sure Charon's still watching, too.

I slam into a trunk, my head ringing like a gong, but I haven't got time to feel sorry for myself. Groaning, I half-stumble, half-scramble into a lurching run, and fumble inside my long black jacket, which, torn and shredded from catching against every branch I've hurtled past, really isn't suitable for a chase through a forest at any point of the year, never mind winter. But inside it… Well, I ain't completely defenseless.

As my fingers wrap around the grip of my Ruger-57, a sliver of extra strength pumps through my legs and pushes the pain away from my injuries and burning lungs, and I turn, arm extended, and aim at the nearest fae I see, and squeeze the trigger.

The bullet, soaked in holy water, cuts through the air after the muzzle bangs, and slams into one of the little monsters chasing me, leaving a shower of purple blood, wings and spears flying through the air as the corpse drops.

Ruger-57 one, little fucking spears, zero.

Except they sting like… Not even gonna finish that thought, but I do squeeze off another shot.

This one sails wide, but it's bought me a little space, though it doesn't do me much good. I've no idea where I am, what direction the Mustang is, or how in God's name I'm gonna get there. What I wouldn't give for a bunch of Fomorians right now. Fae hate 'em. Hate 'em! They'd go up against each other and leave me alone, but that isn't gonna happen. Not only do Fomorians live in water most of the time, they're only in Ireland, and Haven Woods, Oregon is a long fucking way from there.

The ground evens out, and I stumble again, not expecting it, but I keep myself from falling by throwing my hand out and using a tree to steady myself, firing off another round without looking as I sprint into a clearing. Screams of pain followed by howls of fury tells me it's a direct hit, and maybe killed one of the fuckers, too.

If I get away from this, I'm gonna come back and get the wings, because a) I'm a stupid bastard who clearly has danger avoidance issues, and b) snagging fae wings is obviously a pastime that's getting harder every day, and I won't just find 'em lying about anywhere.

For some reason, probably from the lack of oxygen to the brain from all this running, I snigger, but the laugh explodes from my lungs as I collide with what feels like a brick wall.

In a forest.

Falling backward, my ass meets the dirt, and I glance around, shaking my head to see what I hit, but don't see anything except for fae emerging from the trees, wings a fluttering, jagged teeth bared in delight, one of them chewing on a stick of… Is that celery? Ugh, just when I thought these little shits couldn't get any worse. Celery! Behind them, Charon waits, sword in hand. Eager as Christmas, which, to be frank, is only seven days away and fuck me if I wasn't looking forward to it this year. Diana had big plans, and I had them for Rosa, too.

Jesus Christ. Diana… As the fae close the circle, I can only think of her. The second of my two. The eternal child, dead in the 1960s, a prisoner to her past and mostly frozen in my office for years, staring at the walls. I helped her a few months ago, when she sprung Awareness, and, in truth, she helped me back, and I've looked after her since. What's she gonna do without me? Rosa doesn't see the world like I can, and they can't talk to one another.

Why do I do so many stupid things? I'm forty-two years old, for Christ's sake! When am I gonna get some sense?

As light blinds me from right ahead of where I'm looking, the answer hits me like an eighteen-wheeler.

Never.

From the light, a being emerges, and her magic's what I went and ran into. Lilith, Queen of the Fae, and an ethereal being who swore to see me dead years ago. Tonight, she's gonna get her wish.

CHAPTER TWO

WHAT KEEPS HELL TICKING OVER

Now, whereas your regular fae kinda look like demented pixies, what with their mottled purple and blue flesh, razor-sharp teeth, and crimson, staring eyes, Lilith is exactly what you'd picture when reading or hearing the words '*ethereal, otherworldly creature*'.

Just a hand's width under six feet tall, the searing light surrounding the Queen of the Fae comes from within her pale skin making her black eyes and raven hair shimmer all the darker. She wears the luminosity like a cloak—seriously, I've laid eyes on her more than once and I'm none the wiser whether she's buck-ass naked under that glamor—and those rosebud, blood-red lips curling into a cruel, triumphant smile have got my name on them.

One thing about Lilith. Not that she needs it, but she puts funny thoughts into the minds of humans if you haven't noticed my rhetoric about her. Many a person's fallen into her thrall, and all she usually needs to do is crook her perfectly manicured finger.

"Ah, Lilith," I mutter, doing my damned best to stare into those midnight pools of hers instead of getting blinded by the fucking light, and give her my best lop-sided grin. The one that makes me look all boyish and disarming. "Long time no see. What brings you out on a night like this?"

When faced with certain death, make a joke. That's what I always say. Look, it's got me this far. Somehow.

"Nick Holleran," Lilith purrs, voice like poured honey made

by astonishingly pissed off bees. "I have never appreciated your sense of humor."

I point at myself, confused, like I'm Han Solo facing Princess Leia, and as I do, I realize that along with getting myself some sense, I really should have grown up at some point over the years. Well, isn't gonna happen now, so what's the point in worrying about it?

"Look, Lilith, it's not like your fae are innocents, is it?" I snap, tired of acting all nice all of a sudden. A patch of darkness catches the corner of my eye, but I ignore it. I'll only find Charon grinning at me, what little breath's left in his chest baited, as he waits for the killing blow. "Fair's fair. I've harvested some of your kind, you do the same with plenty of mine."

"Harvested?" Lilith snarls, those perfect red lips curling a little more. I give my head a shake and drop my gaze a little. It's damned hard to resist her, and she ain't even trying. "Harvested."

I glance around, avoiding Charon, since his toothy smile's still fresh in my mind from a second ago, and take in all the fae hovering around the clearing, wings fluttering, fangs on display, eating fucking celery, racking my brain for a way outta this mess. Not got enough bullets to shoot my way out, and the cold realization of impending death crawls out of my gut and into my chest. I've tried to ignore it, to push it back down, to tell my jokes, but this is it.

A while ago, I didn't care if I died again or not. Now, with Rosa and Diana in my life, with my genuine, real-life friend Ruby down at the Styx, and the nagging questions about Hell gnawing at me, I don't wanna go. Sure, chances are I'll come straight back to Hell, revenge is a sin and I've committed it even if I thought I did the right thing, but there's no guarantee I'll be Aware, is there? And Rosa won't see me. Won't know I'm there. Plus, there's the Seal, and the place Charon takes some special folk he selects. Reckon he's just waiting to steal me away as soon as my skin's shed, and I ain't signing up for that shit. No, sir.

So, I can buy myself a little more time until an opportunity presents itself. *If* one does, but I'm fresh out of other options.

"Poor choice of words," I say, spreading my hands, the Ruger heavy in my grip. Raising an eyebrow at it, I tuck it into my holster, and grin. "Let's say we come to some kind of agreement, Lilith? You *know* I need Expungers, and there isn't any other way to make 'em, and those Expungers keep Hell safe from all kinds of fucked up things. You know there's a Dagon cult in Haven now? A fucking Dagon cult. You think your kind's gonna be safe when the creatures of R'lyeh come knocking 'cos those dumb bastards are gonna stir them up? Expungers, Lilith. They're a last resort, but sometimes it's the only ticket in town."

Shit. My fear's added so much passion to my voice I think she might go for it. *I* would. From under my brows, I peer at Lilith. The clearing's quiet except for the fluttering of wings and the crunch of goddamned celery as her creatures wait for their queen's decision, and she's doing nothing but peering down at me, head tilted to one side.

Then she smiles.

Before I know it, she flows forward, closing the distance between us in less than a millisecond, and lifts my chin with a long finger, forcing me to stare into her deep obsidian eyes. Electricity jolts from her fingertips and through my body. Breath catches in my chest and all I can do is stare as my hairs stand on end. Folk would kill to gaze into those eyes, and have done plenty of times over the centuries. Would climb into space and jam the moon on a stick if she asked for it. If she so much as whispered, legions would fall at her feet and march on her enemies. No, she wouldn't even need to ask. To be around her, to peer into her eyes, to have her skin pressed against mine is command enough.

Then she blinks, and I do too, and from some place in the back of mind, the real me breaks the surface and gasps for air and whispers a name.

Rosa.

Nah, I'm not falling for Lilith. This Queen of Fae. This creature who's killed more humans than any mad dictator since she first crept out of the dark corners of Hell. She doesn't control me, and she won't. Lilith can devour me, can shred the flesh from my bones or torture me for decades if that's what her corrupt little heart wants, but her charms won't work on me. I won't let 'em. As the devil himself said, I got one life left, and now I've better things to live for.

Our eyes meet again, and I show her my teeth, the smile not-so lopsided or boyish now. "So, what do you say? We calling a truce?"

Lilith smirks, and that smile ain't so pretty anymore.

"Your words make sense, Nick Holleran, and it is true a certain balance exists in Hell and across reality. The wings of my children are needed else all manner of foul demons and wicked creatures would run amok. Ones that would no doubt hunt my kind into extinction, and it is true that I allowed your friend Harry to take what he needed without giving him much in the way of trouble, respectful as he was in his dealings with me, and how he showed remorse." She pauses, and my heart gives a giant, relieved thump. Wind stirs, messing with the leaves on the forest floor and causing my trench coat to flutter. For a moment, I reckon it's all coming up Holleran, but then she shows me *her* teeth, and those black pits for eyes turn feral. "However, you make a grand mistake. Why do you think I care about the problems of Haven? You think we cling to these woods, that my domain extends only where you can see it? No. Let your Dagon cult stir what they will, it does not affect my fae. And even still… I just do not like you, Nick Holleran. You are not the only safeguard against reality's scum, and, in the grand scheme of things, no one will miss you."

Fuck.

Holding her eyes, my hand drops to the Ruger's grip. I ain't going down without a fight. Might not kill her, but at least I'll leave my mark, a wound or two to remember me by.

Those fingers on my chin spread, and they dig into my jaw, clenching it tight as Lilith's otherworldly beauty twists, spasms, morphs into the true horror lurking beneath, the pale skin searing red, mottled and angry, the perfect, flat white teeth elongating into fangs, and the light like Heaven surrounding her collapsing on itself as darkness spreads from its core. I expect the stench of decay to fill my nostrils, but something sweet does instead. Weird, huh?

Well, this is fucking it. Charon, you bastard, I hope you're happy. Take me to this Seal of yours, at least reveal it to me for my goddamn troubles.

Lilith's jaw widens like the Alien Queen itself, and I pull the Ruger clear, jam the business end into her ribs, and squeeze the trigger.

The blast sounds like a thunderclap, and wind slams into the back of me as screams filled with dismay emerge from the rolling rumble of the Ruger's muzzle, and I fire again. But it isn't so loud this time. Frowning, pulling my stare from Lilith's, I glance down at the smoke rising between us.

Did I do that?

The screams of fear aren't coming from her, she barely looks like she's noticed the two pieces of lead slamming into her gut, even though violet blood oozes out of her. They're coming from her children, and there's another cry. A louder one. A furious one.

The thunder roars again, and the wind crashing into me knocks me forward into Lilith, the Ruger firing once more as my fingers fumble, and the Queen of the Fae lets go of me.

"What is this?" she hisses as I drop to the floor, multiple tiny wounds screaming at me, and my calf muscles threatening to cramp up for good measure. "What is she?"

She?

Lilith throws her now-clawed hands up in front of her face, and I spin, shielding my own eyes. A sun's appeared in the forest clearing. A fucking sun.

Now, it probably isn't that, but I'm damned if it isn't as bright, and the scream coming from it... Squeezing my eyes tight, I cover my ears and grit my teeth against the pain in my head as little fae bastards disintegrate around me, wailing their death throes before non-existence cuts them off like the sound never tore from their lips.

Claws dig into my shoulders, and fetid, hot breath spreads against my cheek.

"I will get you, Nick Holleran," Lilith snarls, her voice almost swallowed by the cacophony. "Mark my words, human! Your days are numbered! My children aren't my only weapons! *Bíodh do pheacaí mar dheireadh agat!*"

Now her scream adds itself into the mix, and low and behold I'm shouting too, huddled on the floor, wind whipping around me, ears covered but filled with anger, fear, and the pounding of my frantic heart as I'm sure, no, certain, the earth beneath me is about to split open and send me plummeting down to some unknown, fiery, hateful layer of Hell for all the sins I've ever committed—but not before my cranium pops first. It just can't take the pressure and, with my feet kicking against the dirt, wave after wave of hurt lancing through my skull, I kinda hope it does and takes the easy way out. My fingernails dig into my scalp, my throat burns but then, a clear, undeniable fact unfurls in my mind. I'm about to die. There's no second chances, no talking my way out of it. This. Is. It.

The air pops, and I can only hear my own screams.

Am I dead? Do my screams follow me? Wait. I died before and it sure didn't feel like this. Taking my hands away from my ears, I open my eyes, squinting at the shining light before me, frowning as it fades, and a small, grayish figure emerges from it.

"Diana?"

Still dressed in the 1960s-style frock she died in, all washed out in that specter way, decades-old blood caked and crusted on her dark cheeks, my ward, the eyeless ghost girl who haunted my office for years before finally talking to me and tasking me with finding her killer, stands before me, mouth open and angry, short arms outstretched and, if she had eyes, I know she'd be glaring.

"You didn't answer your cell, Nick!"

"My cell?" I sound stupid when I mumble the words. Like they mean nothing to me, like I almost don't understand them or what Diana said, and I'm just repeating them because it sounds like I should. Like I should say *something.* "Answer my cell?"

See. I did it again.

Diana lowers her hands and some of the tightness leaves her face, a long-suffering condescension, one teenagers of any decade excel in using, taking its place instead.

"Yes, that plastic device you're always staring at. Rosa called you, and you never answered. Thought you might need my help."

"Wait, Rosa's here?" I struggle to my feet, scanning the clearing. Lilith's gone, but bits of fae litter the place. Lots of wings, actually, but, for once, I could barely care less. All my muscles shiver at once. More like a spasm.

"We followed you when you said you didn't need our help. Nick, you really needed our help."

"No shit," I mutter, rubbing the back of my neck then wincing. Don't curse in front of the kid, Nick, you goddamned idiot! Huh, no swearing in front of the kid who just obliterated a swarm, a pack. A fucking menace. Whatever you wanna call 'em. A forest full of fae. Dead fae. If Lilith hated me before... "Thanks."

If she could roll her eyes, I reckon she would.

"You need to stop leaving us behind, Nick. We're not children."

I point at her. "Rosa might not be, but you are, and, if you've not forgotten, you're dead."

"So?"

Teenagers!

"So, being dead doesn't mean you're safe in Hell. You know that! Look, you've poured through Harry and Maeve's books. It isn't always safe for the dead. For anybody."

Diana glances around at the fae bits and shrugs. "Seems pretty safe to me, and that doesn't explain why you keep leaving Rosa behind, does it?"

Squeezing the bridge of my nose, I shake my head. "Look,

let's just get out of here, okay? We'll talk about this when we get home."

I glance around at the massacre surrounding me. Shit, we'll talk about a lot.

"Follow me," Diana smiles. "You were heading in the completely wrong way from your car, by the way. Another few minutes and you'd have fallen into a stream."

Bending over as she walks away, I collect a few handfuls of fae wings. It's what I came here for after all, and I went through a ton of trouble to let them go to waste. Plus, Lilith said she'd still get me, so I won't be coming back here any time soon. Her children aren't her only weapons? And what was that she screamed? What language? Sighing, I try to quash the coldness rising from the pits of my stomach. I got much larger and more immediate worries.

How the fuck did Diana do that? How? I follow her, the forest now silent except for the crunching my boots are doing on the fallen leaves and bits of fae, the moonlight shining its silver light down on us.

How? A discussion for another time. She's too pissed at me to have me talk about her new-found superpowers, and a gut instinct tells me I'm about to face the music from the most important people in my life. Well, sure is a night to remember.

CHAPTER THREE

TROUBLE IN PARADISE

Rosa didn't say a word to me after I traipsed out of the forest, shuffling behind Diana with my hands thrust into the pockets of my trench coat, trying to ignore the flashes of pain and the crusting blood making my clothes stick to my skin. Our eyes met, and I could see the anger mingling with relief, but she just hopped into her car, Diana sliding in beside her in the front, and tore off into the night.

Not sure now's the right time to mention that I might have gotten away unscathed if she hadn't called my cell. Probably never the right time, truth be told. The pregnant 'might' would be used like a bludgeon.

Sighing—seem to do that a lot these days—I climbed into the Mustang and fumbled for the pack of cigarettes in my breast pocket that aren't there anymore. Gave up the smokes just after the kid became Aware due to her constant disapproval. I'm still sitting there, wearing grooves into the steering wheel instead. Ten and two, just like I was taught. Truth be told, those fae fuckers would have caught me well before Diana showed up if I hadn't quit the smokes. Now I can breathe a little better when I'm running, but a slow, long drag on a death stick wouldn't go amiss right now. The hot, rancid sweet plumes flushing down my throat and into my chest, that second when I'd close my eyes, savor the rich foulness, then let it out in an easy—

"Ah, give it a rest, Nick!"

My fist thumps the horn, letting out a sudden, indignant blast and I scratch at the nicotine patch on my bicep. One of many covering my skin, let me tell you that, and I'm gonna have to add more after tonight.

Fuck me.

Letting out another sigh, one that feels almost as good as lighting up a cigarette and taking that first drag but, of course, not quite, I stick the key in the ignition and smile as the engine purrs, and *Da Vinci* by Weezer splurts into life. Rosa told me I needed to broaden my musical horizons, and I argued that a band whose first album came out in 1994 but are still producing work, are just that. A little bit of a cheat. I liked them anyway; they just haven't been in my rotation for a while.

She didn't agree but seemed satisfied at not having to listen to the same few bands playing on repeat whenever she's around me. Progress, right? Compromise. The concepts all solid relationships are built on.

Whistling to the tune, I let the Mustang crawl over the shoddy mud trail, driving on auto-pilot as Diana's fae-busting entrance plays again in my mind. Kid's always been special. No denying that. She's an empath, and had that ability when she lived, too. Not common, and I'd never seen it present in a ghost, but I've found little information since detailing her potential. Whatever she could do while alive, her power only increased in death since she became Aware. In Hell, that's when a ghost stuck in a loop stops repeating the same sequence and starts…living…again. That wasn't the end of her bag of tricks, though. No sir, it wasn't. Soon after, and I mean within a matter of days, Diana could open doors, pick up cups, use the fucking TV remote, and slam a Devil Worshiper weighing at least two-hundred and eighty pounds into a brick wall and pin him there. Since then, she's added to her talents, as tonight has proven.

But this? She had Lilith scared. Made her run. Lilith. Queen of the fucking fae!

Up ahead, in the far distance, red rear lights streak in the darkness. Rosa's probably giving me a lashing, Diana listening to her, unable to respond to one another—Rosa can't *See* so I often act as a supernatural translator when the kid doesn't leave rudimentary notes or signs for her to read—but no doubt in full agreement and I can't blame them. Harry used to come out here alone, but I'm not Harry as Lilith made perfectly clear, and I got plenty of enemies in Hell. Reckless of me, but I'm just trying to keep Rosa and Diana safe. Though, as they always remind me, they don't need me to do that for them. Another lesson I gotta learn, right? Life in Hell sure is hard even before demons get added to the mix.

First things first. Information on Diana, and intuition tells me asking the kid about it is a terrible idea, and, contrary to popular belief, I try to avoid those if I can help it.

"Cell? Call Ruby," I bark, pulling the Mustang onto asphalt and off the dirt trail.

Ringing replaces Weezer's meaty guitar riffs, and I drum in time with it, a habit I picked up from back in the day.

"Nick!" Ruby replies, voice a little staticy from the poor coverage out in Haven's sticks. "You know I'm working, don't you? I'm not at your beck and call whenever you expect it!"

"Well, you could have ignored me," I reply, grinning. "Guess you can't resist, eh?"

"That, or it's a really quiet night in Hell for once. What's up?"

Ruby runs a place called The Styx, a two-level bar nestled in the heart of Haven City, one floor populated by the goths who spend their time mumbling while listening to the most awful trash music ever created, though I do try to catch The Tomb Of Nick Cage whenever they're in town. The goths aren't aware but would be fucking thrilled to know they're sitting on top of a basement full of ghosts, demons, skinwalkers, ghouls, Nephilim and whoever else swings by Ruby's to blow off a little steam. It's like the vibe of the place draws 'em near. The living who're in the know descend into the lower level too, and it's a fantastic place for information. What Ruby doesn't hear isn't worth knowing, and she's always on the lookout for those in need, living, dead, or otherwise.

She's a friend, and in all honesty, I owe her more than she does me, and she's spent over sixty years aware of Hell, though you'd never guess her age by looking at her. Not by a long shot, bucko.

"Look, I came across a..." Static tearing through the speakers makes me wince. "Ruby?"

"...What? Nick! You cut out for a second..." More static, like a fucking chainsaw.

Up ahead, a long way ahead on the straight dark asphalt, Rosa's red rear lights flicker, and the static turns from a chainsaw into a jet engine. Weakness washes over me, and I sag onto the steering wheel, mouth so dry my tongue's stuck to the roof of it. Shaking my head, I clear my throat, blinking hard so I don't drop off.

"Ruby?" I shout, glancing out at the black night. "Can you hear—"

The static cuts off, like it never existed. Strength returns, and saliva rushes into my mouth like water through a broken dam.

"Nick! Jesus, where are you driving through, Area 51?"

"No, but I wouldn't mind checking it out one day, heard lotsa great things about the place." Wisecracks come as easy as sucking in air, now I don't feel like sliding from my seat and under the steering wheel. "Can you hear me now?"

"Like crystal," Ruby replies, faint chatter from the Styx echoing behind her. It isn't all that quiet. She's a sweetheart. "You said you came across something?"

"Yeah, a ghost with powers I haven't seen before."

Ruby laughs. "Can't you get Diana to look it up in that old library of yours? You could make a killing charging people to come use that place, you know."

Harry left me his place when he ascended into Heaven, with his wife Maeve, already an Aware ghost for decades, following him. Eventually. It's a homey place, three bedrooms, a kitchen, two restrooms, a couple of studies and a couple of centuries of hard-earned knowledge of all things Heaven and Hell. Harry came from a long line of Truthers, normal folk who understand the truth of the world, and Maeve died when they were all too young. They stuck together, the nature of her death meaning Harry could see her, and they kept charting their acquired information, meeting me along the way. It isn't a complete index, no way, but it's good enough, and me, Diana and Rosa add to it when we can.

But, with just that one off-hand comment, Ruby's got right to the heart of the matter.

"Ah, I mean, yeah, I would do that, Rubes." Why do I always rub the back of my goddamn neck when I'm uncomfortable? "Thing is. The, ah, the ghost is—"

"Diana." Ruby's voice takes on a hard edge. She's protective like that. "What happened?"

The sigh I let out sounds like my tires losing air. "It's like this..."

"Shit, she blew Lilith away?"

I brought Ruby up to speed, her listening in silence while I rambled to my little heart's content, and left out the parts where Rosa and Diana are both pissed at me. Mainly because they're both right and I don't need to hear Ruby telling me the same goddamn thing.

"She didn't kill her, at least I don't think so," I mutter, easing my foot on the Mustang's gas as I enter the city. "Made her run, though, screaming something in some language I don't know, and I reckon Lilith ain't scared of many."

"Be with you in a minute!" Ruby calls, then sighs. "I can get you more fae wings for the time being for Expungers. I'll get them made for you, too, it's not safe for you to go looking for them at the moment."

"Gee, I appreciate the sentiment, Rubes, but Expunger's aren't at the top of my list of priorities at the moment. What about Diana? You ever heard of a ghost doing something like that?"

The kid does lots of unusual stuff. The way she can communicate with Rosa when I'm not around just being one of them. But her act in the forest? Ruby's silence when I told my tale spoke volumes.

"In a minute, I said!" Ruby roars, and that isn't like her. Firm, yes. Aggressive, maybe. Outright shouting? Nah. Like I said, she's protective of Diana, we all are, but Ruby takes everyone under her wing. "Nick, I can't talk now, even if I didn't have a group of pucks looking for whisky. You know how they are when they wanna drink. Swing by tomorrow, yeah?"

I nod, a little deflated, but I get it. The problem will keep for one night. "Sure thing, Rubes. Talk to you tomorrow."

Music replaces the background sound of the Styx but for once I ain't listening as I gaze outta my windscreen, taking in Haven with only half of my brain, driving on autopilot, snaking through traffic, stopping at lights, seeing the living and the dead go about their business in the driving, Oregon rain. A pack of skinwalkers in their animal form chase down a sidewalk, howling in joy at their urban exercise, Aware ghosts watching bemused, the Unaware, well, not interested. It's oddly comforting, even though it's cold out there. Not freezing enough to put a halt to the downpour just yet but I reckon it's about to turn. Frost dusted the asphalt a little while ago, but the rain's melting it away for now.

Honestly, I thought my life and me had come to some kind of understanding. Was it perfect? Hell no. How can it be when, well, you know. But I had Rosa and Diana, got my fair share of cases, the local PD and me worked together from time to time, and, for once, I hadn't tried to run at the first syllable of commitment. Weird shit happens all the time in Hell, and I make plenty of mistakes, but tonight's sunk rocks in my gut.

I'd been keeping Rosa and Diana at arm's length for a while about my work. Not the nature and details of it, I promised Rosa I'd quit doing that, but I'd been lone-wolfing them more than I should, and it was always gonna come to a head. That, I could deal with. I'd present my case, apologize, come to a compromise all nice like. Combining that with the girl wonder and the Queen of the Fae's vendetta against me increasing to eternal levels kicks matters up a notch, make no mistake.

I pull into the drive of Norris Street – it's in a quiet part of Haven with relatively little dead, but I did go toe-to-claw with a couple of Amarok on this street not too long ago, proving there isn't now safe port of call in Hell no matter how much I want one – and let the engine die as I rest my forehead on the steering wheel. Fuck me, I'm hurting. I'm tired, but I gotta face the music.

Wish it could be tomorrow, though.

Opening the door, I swing my legs out, one by one, groaning when stiff and punctured muscles protest against my using them. Did I mention I'm not as young as I used to be? I'm not. Now I'm at the age where my goddamn right knee aches from letting it lie against a goddamn mattress all night instead of thanking me for the rest I've given it.

Glancing around, I check for Charon, and let a sigh of relief rattle out from between my lips. At least he doesn't think Rosa or Diana's gonna kill me tonight, but, look, I can't really rule that out, can I?

Patting my pockets and making sure I've got the fae wings, the almost translucent shitty bits of Hell-pixie that got me in this mess in the first place, I hobble toward the door, my arm doing this weird half-raising and falling thing like it doesn't know if I should ring the doorbell to my own home, or if I should march right in there, but fate intervenes.

The door swings open, causing the holly wreath sitting on it to swing, and Rosa's standing there, dark eyes blazing, beautiful face tight with anger but then she takes me in, and some of that fury ebbs away. Some.

"Jesus, Nick, you look like shit now I'm seeing you properly."

"Nice to see you, too," I reply, cracking a little wise. Everyone loves a little wise.

Rosa's finger jabbing into my face tells me that, right now, she doesn't appreciate a little wise.

"Don't think that you coming home cut to shreds means I'm not pissed at you, Nick!" She grabs my hand, and I'm wise enough to swallow the squeal of pain when her fingers press against one of my wounds, and she pulls me inside. "I thought you'd learned after last time?"

"Last time?" I mutter, the analytical part of my brain taking in the new holiday decorations Rosa's put up since this morning, but my thoughts are coming slower than normal. Lady loves the holidays, and so does Diana. "What last time?"

"Exactly!" Rosa snaps, steering me into the main study, the one with the majority of the books, and pushing me into the armchair like I'm made out of paper and string. Diana's sitting in another one, reading a book. For a moment, her head tilts back and her pits meet my eyes, and she sticks her tongue out. The radio's on, spitting out the evening news, and if the two most important people in my life weren't fit to tear me limb from limb. I'd say it was pretty idyllic in Casa de Holleran. "There's been so many last times with you it's hard to keep track!"

I wipe a hand across my forehead, and my fingers come away sweaty. On a bitter cold night like this?

Snow starts falling outside the window. Maybe I'll take Diana for a snowball fight in the morning, like I always wanted my old man to do with me. Maybe—

"Nick? Are you even listening to me?" I blink and focus on Rosa. Can't tell her I was drifting off, so I nod, searching my memory banks for an appropriate response.

"You talking about when I went looking for the Wild Hunt?" I ask Rosa as she turns away and rummages through a drawer. "'Cos that was just a hunch, nothing more, and I didn't want to bother you two. Didn't know I'd damn well find 'em, did I?"

I pull at my tee shirt. Sweaty. Why's it so goddamn hot in here?

"The Wild Hunt," Rosa snarls, glancing at me, then bites her lip. "Is it about the time I went looking for the Wild Hunt, he says."

"Nick?" Diana pipes up. I glance at her, and the room dances when I do. "Tell Rosa you're poisoned, and you need Doe Elixir immediately."

The book she's reading's called '*Of Fae and the Unseen*'. Immediately? She doesn't sound all that excited about it. Poisoned. Of course. Fae sons of bitches!

Explains that weird static before, the weakness, too, funny vision, the heat and wandering thoughts. Goddamn it.

"Rosa? Diana says I'm poisoned, and I need Doe Elixir immediately."

She glances into the corner our little ghost girl's reading in, and smiles. "Thanks, Di." Then she turns to me and scowls. "I know that already, and, lucky for Mister Go-It-Alone, I have just what he needs."

I press a hand to my chest and lean into the chair, feeling really fucking awful, truth be told.

"My hero."

She thrusts a small vial at me, a label with Harry's handwriting scrawled across it. "Drink this. Now."

When my fingers reach out for it, I reckon I'm gonna grab it just fine, but my senses have other plans. The vial splits into two, matching the number of Rosas and Dianas, and my clumsy hand knocks the actual antidote into midair.

Dandy.

"Hope you've...got more..." I slur as it tumbles in slow motion, my tongue thick and heavy like a salted slug left in the baking sun and, to be honest, I'm not sure I even say the words out loud.

I fall backwards into my chair as the Doe Elixir drops, a blaring warning alarm sounding in my mind, telling me I'm in trouble but I'm just too cooked to care, when Diana appears before me in less than a blink of an eye, the antidote floating, caught by her powers.

"This is the only one we've got, Nick," she says, each syllable cracking like thunder, the room around her losing its color until it's washed out like her but dark around the edges. "You'll die before we can make up any more."

Die. I'll die. Dying's bad, Nick. We got work to do. A life to live.

Nodding, I struggle to sit forward, and my arm shoots out again, like a punch-drunk boxer attempting a valiant final stand after one Hell of a pummeling from Ali himself. The vial bobs out of the way, and a firm weight settles on my chest pushing me back into the chair.

"Murghtpft—" I say, but it comes out as an indignant, muffled squawk. My jaw's forced open and clamped that way as the vial's shoved into my mouth and the foulest fucking liquid I've ever tasted hits my tongue.

I try to cough it out, to splutter, but my head's forced back. My waving hands are slammed to the armrests, and Diana's eyeless face fills my vision, the thudding of my heart beats and overpowers any other noise.

"Thought you'd be better at taking your medicine, Nick." Her voice cuts through the pounding like it's the only sound that exists. She shakes her head. "Adults."

Flames lick the insides of my throat. Fucking flames. Wincing, I strain against the chair, powerless against Diana as she holds me there, as the Doe Elixir slides into my stomach. How much of this am I drinking? The vial was tiny. Tiny! My jaw snaps shut.

"Swallow," Diana commands.

Wincing, it's all I can do.

I fall forward, and Rosa rushes to stop my face from smashing into the carpet.

"Jesus, Diana!" I gasp, glancing around, vision showing me just one of everything again. She's in the corner again, book in hand. "What the Hell was that?"

"You were dying, Nick," she says, explaining it to me like I'm five. "There wasn't time for you to make a face and spit your medicine out."

I meet Rosa's eyes. The anger that swam there just minutes ago's gone. Concern, that's there. Damn right, it is. The room's colors returned to normal, and my tongue's under control again. Not sure that's a good thing with my mouth, to be honest.

"Look, I can't argue with that, kid," I say, shaking my head and settling back into my chair, "but you can't just handle me like a ragdoll."

"Even if it means saving your life? That's twice I've done that tonight, by the way."

I hold my palms up. "Fine, you're right. Thank you, I mean it, kid. For both times, I appreciate it, and don't doubt I do. It's just been a night. Why don't you go watch some TV for a little while? Me and Rosa gotta talk for a bit."

Even without eyes, she stares at me like my sincere sorry isn't all that sincere. Apologizing doesn't always come easy to me. Especially after being manhandled by a teenage ghost with superpowers.

She bounces up to her feet, never one to turn down a chance at catching up on her programmes. Having not watched a single show in almost sixty years meant she's got one Hell of a 'to be watched' pile.

"Just nod, say you're sorry and you'll do better, Nick," she says, giving me a too-sweet smile like she didn't obliterate a...murder?... of fae and handle me like a newborn lamb tonight. "Much better. You can make it up to me later."

Mischief! A mischief of fae. Fuck me, that's an understatement.

I watch her leave, the voices on the radio filling the study's silence then meet Rosa's eyes when Diana disappears around the corner.

"What the Hell was that?" she whispers, dark skin a little paler than usual.

I blow out my cheeks. "Puberty?"

Rosa hit me on the shoulder. "Bastard."

"Hey, I'm in recovery here," I mutter, rubbing the area of impact. She packs a punch, the years of Aikido more than paying off. "It's been a night."

"Sorry. Are you feeling better?"

I glance around, and things don't spin. Counting that as a win.

"A little."

"Good." Rosa nods, and a spark of anger ignites in her eyes again. "What were you *thinking*, Nick? Or not thinking? I thought we'd been through this fifty times? A hundred! You can't keep doing this!"

"I know, I know." A hint of static crackles over the radio. "I just—"

"Don't want to get anyone hurt," Rosa growls, expression dangerous, "but that isn't your decision to make for other people, and what about yourself? Going alone, into a den of fae who've sworn to kill you, which, by the way, is frankly ludicrous in so many ways. I expected better from you."

"Ah, don't tell me. You're not angry, you're just disappointed."

Me and my big mouth. That little flame of anger turns into a bonfire.

"Nick." Rosa breathes out. My name almost curls in the air like smoke. I itch one of the nicotine patches. "I *am* angry *and* disappointed. This isn't the time for jokes, you almost died!"

It's always the time for jokes. Thankfully, I have the sense to think the retort instead of saying it, else Rosa might actually kill me.

"Look—"

"Don't give me, 'look', Nick. With you, a wisecrack or an excuse always follows." Rosa bites her lip and leans forward, and, as I'm reminded most times when I look at her, I realize how goddamned lucky I am she puts up with a schmuck like me. "I appreciate how open you've been with me since the Clancy case a few months back. Jesus, a few months back. Feels like years! I told you this wouldn't work between us if you kept me at arm's length from your work Hell, and you listened. But letting me act like the Oracle from Batman isn't going to cut it. I am *not* your secretary, Nick, and I'm a big girl. I can look after myself, and I won't have you telling me I can't, which is what you're doing every time you go it alone."

I sigh. Do it a lot living with two women who have a ton more sense than I do, and I sense this isn't the best time to bring up the time she went chasing after a Devil Worshiper alone. We all make mistakes, but Rosa learns from hers. Gotta give her that.

"Reckon Diana feels the same way," I mutter instead. "But you should have seen her tonight, and I don't mean her Florence Nightingale on steroids act."

Rosa leans back in her chair. "Tell me about it."

Static interrupts the radio again, an angry blast, and the weakness washes over me once more but it ain't just me who stares that way. Rosa does too, frowning.

"You can hear that?"

"The static?" she asks, turning her frown on me. "Sure."

"Was it doing that before I got here?" I ask, pointing.

"No," Rosa replies slowly, meeting my eyes. "Why?"

"Probably nothing. Kept happening for a while when I spoke to Ruby on the way over." Even though she's just given me a lashing about not being square with her, my mouth clamps up when I'm about to tell her about the weakness. Old habits die hard, right? "Other things, too. Didn't look like a storm coming in. Snow, yes, but not a storm."

"Other things?" Rosa asks, a dangerous look in her eyes. "We *just* spoke about this."

I lean forward, completely serious. "Rosa, are you a mind reader?"

It would explain a lot.

She thumps me again as more static erupts from the radio, then lets out a cry as the light bulbs and holiday decorations flicker. Getting to my feet, hand on my Ruger, I approach the study's door, peering out into the corridor as the white noise builds.

"Diana?" I shout over it, peering over in the den's way. "You okay, kid?"

"TV's busted," she shouts, voice sulky. "What's going on?"

House and car alarms drift in through the brick and mortar from outside. Glancing over my shoulder, I nod at Rosa. No time like the present to show off the new and improved Nick Holleran.

"Stay right behind me," I say, wincing as the static throbs. "Diana, come here!"

She's by my side in a flash, neck craning as she takes in the flickering lights.

"I'm not doing this," she says, turning her eyeless sockets on me.

"Didn't say you were. Can you feel anything?"

It's a neat trick of hers, being an empath. She's like a warning signal for Hell, able to sense emotions from a ways off. Saved my hide more than once, and you better believe the kid reminds me of each and every one on a daily basis.

"No," she replies, frowning. "Nothing at all. Not even from you or Rosa."

"Crap," I mutter.

"What's she saying?" Rosa shouts so I can hear her over the white noise. "I don't feel so good."

The lights are flickering like an experiment gone wrong in some funky 1950s Holiday themed sci-fi flick, and that weakness hits me again like a wave.

"She's saying this isn't..." As soon as I shout my reply, the static cuts off, and the normal radio chatter resumes like nothing's happened at all, and the bulbs lighting the house get back to working like they should. "Normal."

Glancing at them, I wave my Ruger toward the front door and head for it, taking time with my steps. Alarms are still sounding outside after all, even though the static's gone. Rosa and Diana follow, floorboards creaking beneath us.

Reaching the front door, I ease it open, and the cacophony of car and house alarms greet me. Other folk are outside, some with weapons like me—God bless America—others shouting questions across the drives, all looking as confused as anyone else, their holiday decorations bright and proud.

Aside from that, the night seems normal. Snow's falling harder than a trickle, it's cold like it should be for mid-December, and the weakness in my limbs is gone.

"Hey, Hudson!" I shout over at my neighbor who's standing outside in his jocks with a shotgun in his hands. "See anything?"

"Naw," he yells back, the red and blue lights shimmering on his gleaming tighty-whities. I wanna shield Diana's pits, but she isn't looking that way. Thankfully. Hudson ain't leaving much to the imagination. "TV started playing up, and my lights were on the fritz."

"Same here, buddy," I reply, turning to Diana. "Anything?"

"Everything's as it should be, I feel all their feelings. Anxious, worried, annoyed," she replies, shaking her head. "Not like before. For the first time since I can remember, I couldn't sense a thing, Nick. Not a thing."

I glance at Rosa, then smile down at the kid.

"Why don't you get back to the TV. Hell's a little funky sometimes, right?"

Nodding, Diana turns and heads into the house, but I peer outside, eyes narrowed, looking for anything. Even Charon, the sonofabitch.

"You believe that's all it was? Hell being its usual funky self?" Rosa asks, breath fogging the air.

"No." I meet her eyes, and my hand takes hers. "Something weird's going on, and I got a feeling it'll find us before too long.

Always fucking does."

Rosa gives a glum nod but squeezes my hand before heading inside. I wait peering into the corners where the holiday lights don't reach, and that's where I see him.

Charon. Staring back at me. Grinning.

"Was that you?" I whisper, and even though he's at least fifty yards from me, I know he hears it.

He shakes his head, grin growing wider.

I take a step back and close the door. He can get his kicks some other time, I'm not playing whatever game he's playing.

CHAPTER FOUR

COMING TO AN AGREEMENT

Lying on my bed, pillows propped beneath my head, I'm struck with a good news, bad news situation. Might as well start with the pleasant stuff, right? It's been an hour, and we haven't suffered a repeat of the static attack. I checked the whole house over, upstairs, down, and in the basement without finding a reason for it. Nothing in the backyard, too. So, a freak occurrence, one of many on a daily basis in Hell?

Normally, I'd say yes, if it happened to be a one-off. But it ain't. Same shit happened on the way home, a resounding crescendo to Diana's forest performance.

So, I'm being followed by some kind of creature I haven't come across before? That's a maybe, and part of the 'good news'. If whatever the thing is that's causing this static is coming for me, it's had its chance. Twice. So, it's either after me, and it's wary, or it isn't after me, and I'm just in the vicinity.

But fuck me, right? I gotta go looking either way. It's my job even if no one's paying. At least I gotta find out what this thing is before events go the way they usually do in Hell, and that way is south. Always goddamned south.

Hey, good news. Good news first, Nick. From what I can tell, no one's been hurt. I scanned the news channels for a while, and they haven't reported anything out of the ordinary for a cold Wednesday night in Haven City.

That's where the good news ends.

Bad news… Where to begin? Diana's behavior, and yeah, I'm well aware I'm sounding like a pouty parent right now, is a major goddamn concern. Kid's always been tough and smart, she had to be with her upbringing, but combining those traits with her growing powers? I'm grateful she saved my ass, more than grateful, but the way she handled me like a snappy dog at a vet puts a sack of stones in my gut. What if she just decides that's the way it's gonna be from now on? There's only a few ways to put a stop to a ghost's controlling methods, and, honestly, none of them are routes I wanna drive down. And that's taking for granted she's a normal specter.

Then there's the Lilith problem. It'll rear its head again. Ruby says she'll keep me stocked up on Expungers, but I can't always rely on someone else, can I? I did that with Harry and Maeve, and didn't learn as much about Hell as I thought I did. A sigh heaves its way outta my chest and into my throat and out into the world as I reach for a book on my bedside table. They made this for me, Harry and Maeve, and thrust it into my hands not long after we met, though it took my stubborn ass far too long to delve into its pages. Glad I did, saved me from more than one sorry situation.

Well, they didn't make it just for me, not really. It's their notebook, an almanac, all first-hand notes of their own dealings with Hell, filled with advice that goes against the expected Truther grain, and other asides. They even used it to communicate with one another, little notes here and there from Harry to Maeve, reminders of stories to tell her…

I wonder if me and Rosa will do the same? Harry trusted Maeve. Nah, that's the wrong notion. I trust Rosa, I just don't trust Hell with Rosa. But Harry did, even though a final death for his wife could have meant kaput. Game over. And, just to add a little more bad news to the pile, the static interrupted the discussion Rosa wanted to have with me, and it's hanging over me like the sword of Damocles.

Flicking through the book, I find the page with Lilith, the

sketch of the Hell Queen capturing her pretty well. There's plenty on her origin, detailing the Tuatha dé Danann and so on, but my attention is captured by Harry's spider-like scrawl at the bottom of the page.

'Always bring plenty of iron if you think you are going to meet one of the fae. Line your clothes with it so they can smell its stink from a few miles away, and maybe learn a little Irish.'

Iron. So that's his secret. The winged bastards hate the stuff, I knew that. But filling my pockets and clothes with it is information I should have absorbed well before my sojourn into the Haven Woods.

"Ah, shit," I groan as I shift my weight and about twenty or so puncture wounds scream at me. Still haven't seen to them, venom aside. "It's been a night."

"Yeah, it has." Rosa's standing in the bedroom doorway, a tray filled with band-aids, salves and a great steaming cup of joe on it. "Are you ready for some more? It isn't over yet."

"Wonderful," I mutter, putting the notebook aside. Diana calls it *'Holleran's Handbook to Hell'*, and I kinda like the sound of that. I've added my bits to it too in the last few months, but I can do more. Do better. In everything. "Bring it on."

"Oh, I can leave." Rosa raises her eyebrows, half-turning away with her precious tray. "You can help yourself, big guy."

"Ah, no, sorry," I say, wincing as I reach out for her then collapsing against the pillows. "Reckon I deserve a little more setting straight, huh?"

"What you need is some time off, Nick." Rosa crosses the room, the scowl on her face pretty damned cute if I'm being honest. It always is. Not that I'd tell her that. *'Hey, Rosa, come and show me that scowl of yours, it really does it for me.'* Not only would it make me sound like a freak, it'd really bring on the thunder. "It's the holidays, can't you just take a week? Would it kill you?"

"It might!" My exasperation cracks a smile as I shuffle up on the bed so she can sit down. I take the coffee and gulp it down. Mighty fine cup of joe. "Look Rosa, it's Hell. I don't know what's gonna happen one day from the next, and you saw what happened tonight with all the weird shit. You just can't account for any of that."

I wince as she dabs cleaning alcohol into the wounds on my arms.

"Take your shirt off," she mutters, completely focused on my punctures.

"Ah, usually I wouldn't say no, but reckon I'm not in any condition for that kind of business tonight."

"Wise guy." Rosa grins and kisses me, her lips lingering on mine for all too brief of a moment. "Take off your shirt so I can check you properly. Pants too."

"Yes, ma'am," I reply, groaning from the effort of lifting a piece of material over my head, and the weird lying down shuffling I'm doing to remove my jeans won't impress anyone. "Anything you say."

"Anything I say," Rosa mutters, sticking a band-aid on one cut and moving on to the next. I lean over to my table and grab a couple of fresh nicotine patches. "I just asked you to take some time off and you've given me excuses."

"They're not excuses!" I protest. "It's Hell, Rosa."

"Fine. I get that. But where are you going to go first thing in the morning?"

"The office."

"Exactly."

"It might be Hell, but I still have bills to pay. My office doesn't come free. Nothing does, right?"

Rosa sighs as she continues to work. "Shutting up shop until January 2nd wouldn't be the end of the world. When was the last time you spent some time at home?"

She presses her fingers against my chest, and I push my hand against them, holding them there, and meet her eyes.

"Rosa, I gotta help these people. My clients can come at any time, and who else is gonna help them?" I give her my trademark smile, and I hope it'll actually help me get what I want one of these days. "The cops? Butler and Gavin? Naw. There ain't no one else."

Rosa's finger jabbed under my nose is sign enough that my fucking smile has done nothing. Again.

"And that's the problem, Nick. This is the reason why I'm patching you up a week from Christmas Day. The reason why you look like you need at least three weeks on the couch."

"Hey!" I rub at my jaw. I don't really look that bad, do I?

"Nick," Rosa warns, sticking another band-aid in place. "You think you can help everyone. *Everyone.* Even me and Diana, but who's going to help you? Who are you going to *let* help you? The Lord above knows we've tried time and time again for you to stop being so stubborn and let us do it, but you pull shit like tonight and go off alone, humanity's last safeguard against the worst of Hell!"

"You know, you've really got a way with words." Look, I know it's a mistake as soon as the words leave my mouth, but sometimes I just can't help myself. Reckon it's some form of sadomasochism. "Poetic, really. Must be all that working in the library, huh?"

See? I just added a couple more for good measure.

Rosa presses the next band-aid down with more force than is reasonable, reminding me her strength comes from teaching Aikido, and my sudden intake of air and wincing doesn't relieve it.

"Don't get smart with me, Nick," Rosa snarls, getting real close to my face, noses almost touching. Don't get smart? Might as well ask me to grow another arm while I'm sleeping. "You keep going like this and you're going to get yourself killed. You might wind up in Hell still, but who are you going to help then?"

"What do you want me to say?" I bite back, more than a little heat in my voice. "That you're right? 'Cos you are, I know that. You can look after yourself a damn sight better than I can. I know that too."

"Then what's the problem, Nick? Seriously?"

I let my head drop and give it a shake. *I don't want to lose you. Or Diana.* But I can't say that either, can I? Because I'm stubborn, and because it isn't fair. Rosa *is* right. I'm going out into Hell alone most of the time, putting myself in harm's way, and they might lose *me*. That's how life works. But I gotta say something. Give her an iota of my reasoning. She deserves that at least.

"Alright," I say, lifting up my hands. A show of peace and time to come clean. Time to stop being a stubborn ass. "Alright. I'm taking your own choices away from you. That's something a dick would do, and, for all my failings, I do try to only be half of a dick at the best of times." I raise a hand again as Rosa's mouth opens, no doubt about to tell me to quit it with the jokes. "It's just... At the cabin with Marvin Clancy? When he called me, told me he had you. I never wanted to have that fear again, Rosa. So, I let you in on my cases, like you asked, told you about every aspect of my life, like you wanted. But I kept you from harm's way, because when that sonofabitch purred down my cell, when he gloated. When I saw you tied to that chair?" I shake my head. "I can't let it happen again."

She lays her palm against my cheek, and I look up, meet those deep brown eyes. Easy ones to fall into and willingly drown in for eternity, eyes deeper than any fae queen's.

"Nick, there's only so much one person can do. You understand that, don't you?"

"Yeah," I whisper, pressing her hand against my cheek more. "Sorry."

"Don't give me 'sorry'. Don't give me words." Rosa grins. "Give me action."

The lop-sided grin forms on my face once more. "Told you I'm not in the shape for that."

Laughing, Rosa kisses me again, her body a comforting weight against my chest, then pulls away.

"Maybe I'll make do with cuddles for tonight, huh, big guy?"

"Well, I hate to disappoint," I murmur, kissing her neck as I toss the notebook aside. "You done patching me up?"

"You'll live," Rosa breathes, hands in my hair.

"The kid?"

"Reading in the study."

Her teeth nip at my collar bone, sending electricity buzzing through my body. Much better than fucking static.

"Ah, you shut the door already," I whisper, fiddling with the small buttons at the front of her shirt. "Excellent forward planning."

"Nick?" Rosa says, pulling away from me and moving the tray onto the floor.

"Yeah?"

"Switch the lights out, stop talking, and kiss me, will you? And don't almost die again. I mean it."

"Yes, ma'am," I say, following her orders. How could I say no to any of that?

The vibrating of my cellphone wakes me up, even though I'm not ready for it yet. Room's still dark, and will be till at least 9am, but Rosa was right about more than one thing last night. I need some rest even with the weird static attacks that need investigating.

"Switch it off," Rosa grumbles, head nuzzling my chest.

"Reckon I'll ignore it and it'll go away, like that rash I had that time."

"Jesus, Nick, way to spoil the mood."

"Sorry."

But the vibrating doesn't stop. Groaning, I reach out and pull it from its charger, the caller ID fuzzy from the sleep still holding court in my eyes.

"Holleran?" I croak, then cough. Then sneeze. Why not clear my throat for good measure? So I do.

"Catch you at a bad time, Holleran?" sneers the voice of Henry Butler, one half of one of Hell's biggest pains in my ass.

His partner Lori Gavin's the other, and they're both major obstacles in my quest for an easy working relationship with the local PD, and a simpler existence. Even after I threw 'em a bone a while back and snagged them the culprit of a decades-old cold case, which gave them major kudos, and a front-page story on the Haven Chronicles, they shake me down at any opportunity. What's more, they sully the good name Holleran, and tell anyone who'll listen I'm a phony, a crank, and probably much worse.

My standing with the rest of the PD *has* improved, even beyond the one or two contacts I got there but long story short, either one of these bozos calling me at the crack of, well, not dawn, as the sun's not even up yet, is bad news.

"Never a bad time to talk to you, pal," I croak, running my hand through Rosa's hair. "How's the wife?"

See I can play nice.

"Fuck you, Holleran, I'm not in the mood for your sarcasm." Well, at least I tried. Just can't catch a break sometimes. "You left for your office yet?"

I swallow the *'does it sound like I've left for my office'* that's teetering on the tip of my tongue.

"Not yet." Then the question, the enquiry of my whereabouts, belatedly raises my hackles. "Why?"

"Me and Detective Gavin just so happen to be in your area."

Shit. Wait, why's my stomach flipping? I haven't done anything wrong! Frantically, I search my memory just in case, and it agrees with me. Being chased through the Haven Woods is relatively low profile for me.

"Yeah?"

"Yeah. Real close, in fact. And we're with a known associate of yours."

Fuck. Now my stomach's in knots, and Rosa lifts her head from my chest, peering up at me. Sitting up, I give my head a shake. Someone I know is in trouble?

"Know a lot of people, Butler," I reply, trying my damned best to keep any panic or anger from my voice. "You'll have to be more specific."

"Gladly. I seem to recall, back in your snoop days, you used to do a bit of work for," he pauses, and chuckles, "people in Haven without the best of reputations. Shit sticks on shit, huh?"

"Had bills to pay, Butler, and my taste for greenbacks and where they came from wasn't fussy back then."

"I'll bet. You did work for Russell Greaney, right? The Irish Don, I hear they call him."

My blood runs cold. "Might have."

"Now, I know when you ended up with three bullets in your chest, you told the PD it was a simple mugging gone south. Wrong place, wrong time and all that." Butler's voice has got that smug tone to it, the one that always makes me wanna sink my knuckles into his mouth. I flick the cell on to speaker. "But we all know the truth. You were working for Greaney that night, weren't you? Tailing Dean Wheeler."

Rosa gives her head a shake, eyes hard.

"Am I gonna need a lawyer, Detective Butler?"

A pause.

"Nothing like that, Holleran, we're all friends here, and, like I said, we're in the area. Working a case. You know Russell Greaney's son?"

"Can't say I do."

His name's Kieran Greaney and, yeah, I actually do. Seen him about, and he's the one who delivered my *'gifts'* for not ratting on his old man after my first run-in with Wheeler, including the ten thousand dollar check I still ain't cashed.

"Did you know he lives near you? You must have. Everyone knows his reputation, right?" Butler laughs again, a sound like a fucking weasel with a mouth full of trash. "Sorry, I should say 'did'. I'm staring at his corpse and let me tell you, it's got us baffled. Some of the cops here, the coroner too, mentioned *your* name, saying it looked like something you'd deal with, and you know what, Holleran?"

"What?" I breathe, staring at Rosa.

"It got me and Detective Gavin thinking. Maybe you *would* know a little about this, seeing as you work in the *occult.*" That fucking laugh again. "Plus, you're local, and it might just be me and Detective Gavin here, but we think you might hold a grudge. Kieran Greaney isn't the first mobster you've got previous with who's turned up dead."

'*Don't. Get. Smart.*' Rosa mouths, just when a retort worked its way onto my tongue. I swallow the fucker.

"Mobsters die all the time, Butler," I say instead, trying to make my voice all breezy. "It's kinda jotted down as a known risk in the job description."

"Ho, fucking ho, Holleran." Funny, people used to call me that back in High School, but Henry Butler isn't laughing with me. "Not like this, guy. Not like this. So, am I having to send a squad car around to pick you up, or are you coming of your own volition?"

"Look, Butler," I snarl, a little tired of his shit. Rosa cradles her head in both hands. "You want my consultation, you can pay my going rates. Unless I'm under arrest, I ain't doing squat. I don't know anything about this. I haven't even laid eyes on Kieran fucking Greaney in years, and I never wanted to. Plus, I was here all night. I got an alibi."

"From your girlfriend, Holleran? You know that won't hold up."

"Not just her, and don't you dare call her a liar," I snap. "My next-door neighbor, Hudson. Spoke to him last night."

"That's Zack Hudson, right?"

"Right."

"So that's your story, huh? You're sticking with it."

"It isn't a fucking story, pal."

Rosa's shaking her head now.

Henry Butler lets out a slow, wheezing laugh. "Well now. Detective Gavin and me? You might not think too much of us, and the feeling is completely mutual, but we're good at our jobs. We arrived here in the early hours, back when you were all tucked up and cozy. We asked around. Heard about some weirdness in the area. Flickering electricity, static noises, all that kind of thing.

Then we saw the corpse. Zack Hudson's known to us, so Detective Gavin gave him a call, as we know he lives next door to you. You know what he said?"

"What?" I grate, squeezing the cell with so much force it might snap.

"He said you weren't there all night, Holleran. Our friend told us you took a trip out somewhere, and you weren't looking too hot when you returned home. So, I'll ask again, smart ass, you want me to send a squad car over, or are you going to willingly assist Detective Gavin and I in our investigation?"

Rosa meets my eyes, and she nods like she's encouraging a two-year-old to open their mouth and take their medicine.

"I'll be right over. Ping me the address so I know where I'm heading." I hang up, sick of Butler's voice already.

God knows I'm telling the truth. I know Greaney lives in the area, but I don't know where. I didn't plan on saying it, but that little nugget might turn into gold if Butler and Gavin try to arrest my ass.

"What are you going to do, Nick?" Rosa asks, sitting up and pulling the duvet tight around her. Course, that leaves me shivering.

"Not much choice, is there?" Shaking my head, I swing my legs outta bed. "Guess that means no week off before Christmas, huh?"

"I don't mean, 'what are you going to do' as in, 'are you going?' Of course you're going." Rosa reaches out and takes my hand, stroking the back of it with her fingers. "I mean, are you going to give them all a bunch of shit like usual?"

She grins, and I can't help but laugh.

"And here's me thinking you were worried."

"I am! But so long as you mind your manners, big ask I know, you'll be fine," Rosa replies. "I give you permission not to bring me along on this case, because I'm off today, and I don't feel like getting out of bed just yet."

"Yes, ma'am." I set about searching for my clothes, not seeing the point in getting dressed in fresh ones for Butler and Gavin's sake. Looking down, I sigh. Forgot I'm covered in band-aids and nicotine patches. "Gonna bring the kid, though."

"You think something Hellish is going down?" Rosa asks, stifling a yawn.

"Maybe." The t-shirt going over my head muffles my voice a little. "They're saying this body doesn't look normal, and that static shit spread to wherever Greaney's joint is. Could be connected, so I reckon backup is needed. Maybe she turned something up in one of those books last night."

Crossing to the bed, I lean down. Man, Rosa's lips taste good, even first thing in the morning. For a moment, I stagger, my body tempted just to climb back into bed, but my mind takes over. It isn't good practice to piss off the local PD. Well, any more than I usually do.

"Nick?" Rosa calls as I'm leaving.

"Yeah?"

"Behave."

I flash her my lopsided grin. "Hey, it's me."

Sometimes I *am* like Han Solo.

"Ugh!" Rosa groans, her shout forcing its way through the closing door. "That's what I'm worried about!"

"Kid?" I yell. "Come here."

"What?" Diana shouts, her voice coming from the front study. "I'm reading, Nick!"

What I wouldn't give to get some appreciation around here. I'm just trying my best to be a good boyfriend and a fine role model to Diana, but no one's written the handbook on easy domestic living while raising your ghost kid. Yet.

I stick my head into the study. Kid's sat in my chair—it's her favorite—and there's a whole stack of books teetering in a pile next to her.

"Been reading all night?"

"And I still am."

I swear if I roll my eyes anymore around Diana, I'll end up

looking like her one of these days.

"It's morning, and we might have a case. You coming or not?"

She peers up from the pages—have I mentioned, beyond Hell being what it is, how weird it is to see a ghost with no eyes *reading a book*—and gives me the sweetest smile you ever did see on a little girl's face.

"How nice of you to ask!" She sticks out her tongue. "Like you're going to even think about leaving me behind anymore, Nick."

Jeez Louise.

There's even better news than a particularly snappy teenager from the 1960s in my immediate future. A blanket of snow's settled on Haven and with it, frost.

"Guess I'll get the car warmed up," I mutter, grabbing the windscreen scraper from the dresser.

One of those nights just rolled over into one of those days. Welcome to the life of Nick Holleran, Haven City's one and only Paranormal Detective.

Jesus Christ it's cold!

CHAPTER FIVE

BIG TROUBLE AT THE LITTLE SEVEN ELEVEN
19th DECEMBER, 2024

Smiling as the heat pumps out of the Mustang and right into my face, I follow the GPS instructions and take a right. Turns out Kieran Greaney lives a little too close for comfort, though the same state is plenty chafing. Honestly, I coulda walked the distance, but Butler only sent me the address with the message "wise-ass" when I'd scraped the last of snow from the car's windscreen, and I wasn't not driving after all that effort.

"That hat suits you." Diana's next to me, book in her hands, peering from page to page as I let the Mustang crawl through the yet-to-be gritted streets. Accidents happen with haste and all that. "You should wear it more often."

I take a glance in the rear-view mirror. Rosa bought it for me on my birthday one year. It's a little wooly for my tastes, but the warmth it provides is better than nothing. I even threw on a sweater under my trench coat. Cold be damned, but it must be acknowledged. Sometimes I think about moving someplace warmer, but the idea of all year-round heat just makes Hell feel somehow more hellish. Occasional snow and lots of drizzle takes the edge off.

"You find anything about the static?" I ask, keeping two hands on the wheel as the tires slip.

"Not much," Diana answers, frowning down at the tome. "A

lot of these are old, Nick. Ancient. From when there wasn't any electricity; so there could be a ton of creatures in Hell that have the same effect. Did Harry and Maeve stop collecting knowledge?"

"They wrote most of theirs down in the notebook, but I couldn't see anything in that either before I turned in for the night. Except for things I should have already known about fae and the like."

"Before you got distracted, you mean."

I raise a warning finger. "That's adult business, you hear?" Change the subject, Nick. "Most of the books they have are ancient because, well, Hell's been around a long ass time, and there isn't much new. So Truthers stopped writing books."

"That's stupid."

"Why?"

"Because of this situation we're in, Nick." Diana sighs. "These creatures might have been around a long time, but technology hasn't. We didn't expect WiFi to keep the Wild Hunt in place so they couldn't jump realities, did we?"

"Don't remind me," I mutter, wiping a hand across my face and scratching at the stubble on my cheek. "Try to forget I ever met them."

"To stop collecting knowledge just because you think you know all there is to know is pretty dumb." Diana peers at me, the eyebrows above her eyeless pits raising. "Sounds exactly like something you would do."

"Look, it's too early to start bickering with a teenager; even I know I'll never win that battle." Washed-out specters do their thing on the sidewalks. Wonder if some of 'em even know they're up to their knees in snow. Sometimes I reckon the Unaware are poor sonsofbitches but other times, I reckon not knowing is a blessing. Not that I'd ever like to end up that way. "What about the weakness?"

"Weakness?"

"Ah, shi—" I change the curse into a clearing of the throat. "Yeah, I didn't mention that."

"Keeping secrets still, Nick?"

"Just other matters got in the way," I reply blandly. "When the static hit, my muscles turned to water. Like I just wanted to lay down and sleep. Or die. And what about the effect it had on you? The emptiness. Anything about that?"

Diana makes an angry sound in the back of her throat. "Well, if you'd told me about the weakness last night, I'd have looked out for it." Her eyebrows form a frown. "I can't remember reading anything about it, though, or the feeling I had."

That's the other thing. How to prod the conversation on to her and what she did. Not just how she manhandled me like I was an Imperial Officer on the Death Star, and she was Darth fucking Vader, but what she did to the fae. What she did to Lilith.

Jeez, is this what being a parent's all about? Difficult conversations with moody kids that nobody wants to have but you if you don't bring it up, who's gonna? Almost makes me look at my folks in a different light. Almost. Their problems didn't begin with tricky chats we'd all rather do without, though. Didn't end there, either.

I shudder as that night in the backyard floods back to me. The look on my parents' faces, the shovels in their hands. The step I took toward the hole in the dirt, even though my mind pleading with me, told me to run away. The pure anger in my mom's eyes. The slackness in my old man's.

'*You shouldn't be here, Nicky,*' she hissed, knuckles white as she grabbed the shovel. '*You're always turning up where you're not wanted.*'

"I might not have been able to feel anything when the static blared last night," Diana says, her voice pulling me from my memories and fuck me if I'm not glad for it. "But I can feel plenty right now. What's bothering you? And don't say 'nothing'. I *hate* it when you say nothing."

Greaney's place isn't too far away, but still distant enough to make me have to answer her. Well, I *did* have to bring it up sometime, and I'm talking about her, not my parents. That night

I'm taking to my grave and keeping quiet even when I reappear in Hell.

Turning to Diana a little, one eye still on the icy road, I steel myself. "What happened with you last night, kid?"

"You were about to spill the only antidote we had, and you would have died if I didn't step in." Diana's fingers tap against the book. She does that sometimes when she's uncomfortable. "What was I supposed to do?"

"Look, I get that, I do, and I know I wouldn't be breathing if it weren't for you, but the way you grabbed me? You can't do that to people, Diana."

"Even if it means saving them?"

"I'm not gonna get all Uncle Ben on you and talk about great power and great responsibility and all that, but—"

"Who's Uncle Ben?"

I blink. "You haven't watched Spiderman yet?"

"It's on my list," Diana replies, folding her arms across her chest.

"Spiderman's still on the list? You said you were gonna watch it!"

"I'll get to it! There's a lot I need to catch up on. What's this Uncle Ben got to do with anything?"

Sighing, I pull over into a Seven Eleven's parking lot. Coffee sounds good right about now, but I gotta deal with this first. Leaving the Mustang running—did I mention the temperature would freeze Lucifer's nutsack?—I favor Diana with my most patient of patient smiles. The one I reserve for clients who don't know what the Hell they're talking about. I use it more often than I'd like.

"Look, kid, you can do plenty of cool stuff, there's no doubt about that, and those things you can do, they're getting stronger. What you did with those fae? You had Lilith scared!"

A small smile breaks out on her lips. "I did, didn't I?"

"Yeah." I reach out and take her hand. Ice runs through me, but it's worth it just to make Diana feel a little more alive. She told me once contact's the thing she misses most about being alive, and I'd be an even bigger schmuck for not doing what I can. "You had *Lilith* scared. Queen of the damned fae. Think about that." Diana frowns and gives a slow nod. "I don't know what you can do, kid, and neither do you. I ain't saying stop, don't even want you to. Want you to *think*. Want you to use that awesome brain of yours to figure out just what you are, 'cos kid? You aren't just some ghost hanging around in Hell. You never have been. You and Rosa are right, I'm not gonna try to keep you away from my work all of the time, but I want you prepared, okay? Do you understand me?"

She nods and grips my hand. "I scared you last night, didn't I, Nick? When I overpowered you."

I give her my smile. "Don't worry about that, kiddo."

"I'm sorry."

"Look, we're all learning here. Me, you, Rosa. Got a lot to figure out, but we'll do it." I shake my head and open the car door. "Still can't believe you haven't watched Spiderman, though. What's wrong with you?"

Getting out the Mustang, I let the door close and give Diana one last look. She's smiling down at the book, the lucky recipient of a Nick Holleran dad talk. A pretty damned good one if I do say so myself. With a spring in my step, I head towards the store, almost slipping on the ice when that spring in my heels gets too jaunty for anyone's good, and take a more measured approach.

Before coming to a full stop.

Ducking behind a dumpster, I stick my back flat against the side of the Seven Eleven and prick up my ears. A little further down from me, talking in the side street, looking more than a little worse for wear, are Suraz and Absin. Haven's resident Nephilim.

Their gold and black armor's missing plates in places, and covered in black ichor, and so is their obsidian skin, and the golden blades strapped to their backs, swords easily the size of your average human male.

Suraz, I see from time to time, especially after he took a special interest in my ass around the time of the Clancy case. For a while, he tried to hide it and stalked me from afar all around Haven, but now he makes his presence known. He's got no fucking choice, frankly, 'cos it's like being hit by a freight train any time he turns his focus on me.

Absin, I don't know personally, and see her seldom. Here's something I do know about her, and the reason I haven't just marched up to them and said 'howdy'; she's taken an interest in the infamous Seal.

Now, I've read my Dante. I know all about the seven layers and the seven seals and yadda, yadda, yadda. From what I can gather, there sure are multiple levels to Hell, ones I ain't had the pleasure of laying my eyes on yet, and fuck me if I plan to. There may well be seven seals, but this is *the* Seal, and I'm mighty interested in it. Especially because Charon's involved in it, and he's promised to show it to me. Didn't sound like the kind of vow I'd like him to hold up his end on either.

So, that's why I'm lurking behind this stinking dumpster, in the freezing fucking cold, because you'll never know what I might hear. Look, I'm a PI. Eavesdropping comes with the territory. If someone's got a secret, don't stand at the side of a Seven Eleven talking about it, right?

Right.

"...I have to get back, Suraz." Absin's got a voice like a running river. It's all calm on the surface, but it's got some power behind it. Enough to sweep a rooted boulder out to sea. "This was a diversion I did not need."

"The Seal will hold for some time yet," Suraz replies, all gravely and monotone. You know the type. He's the Nephilim version of Jon fucking Snow. "And this '*diversion*' was anything but unnecessary."

Breath catches in my chest. The Seal. Bingo.

"What has happened to you, Suraz? A score of Galla escaping to the upper layer should not trouble you. A mere century ago you would have not even thought about asking for help."

Armor clinks, and I fight the urge to peer around the side of the dumpster. Listen, Nick. Just listen.

"It is not just the Galla, Absin. If you were not so enthralled by the damned Seal, you would see what is happening up here!"

"The Seal throbs, Suraz. Heaves." Absin's almost purring. I know obsession when I hear it. "Perhaps if you came to me, you would understand, too. Perhaps if you had not lost yourself in your vices, you would see the bigger picture."

I jolt as the wall I'm leaning against trembles and, despite myself, I peer around the dumpster. Suraz's meaty hand is wrapped around Absin's throat, and he's slammed her against the Seven Eleven's wall. Folk inside probably think they've felt a tremor or the like. Suraz is baring his teeth, snarling almost, while Absin follows suit.

Reason whispers in the back of my mind. It tells me to get the Hell out of there before two Nephilim throw down.

I tell reason to fuck off, even though it makes a very good point.

"Listen to me, Absin, and listen to me well, for I tire of your obsession with that place!" Suraz snarls. Humans would melt before his fury if they'd have survived the broken neck from the hand around the throat and the snapped spine from the slamming into the wall. "Galla are the *least* of our concerns in Hell. The *least*. The gathering storm is about to break. The lower levels are swarming with demons, and as more pierce the surface innocents will die before their time, all across the globe. Walls throughout this very city have Enochian writings scrawled across them, and the Dagon cult on the eastern coast spreads its influence. A Church of Marid has appeared in New York, and another opens in London. Then there are the creatures, Absin! Amarok, fae, golems, vampires and more *pour* from below and everywhere, and each time I face them, the question throbs in my mind. Where have you been when I have fought them alone?"

I frown. Below and everywhere?

"At the Seal."

"At the Seal," Suraz sneers, and I'm second guessing my decision not to slip off for my cup of joe, truth be told. "The human Holleran faced down the Wild Hunt not so long ago, stumbling on them by accident. He almost died. Again."

Bullshit. I gave as good as I got. Honest. And, what's more—

A husky, melodious, completely unexpected sound brings my thoughts to a screeching halt. The noise causes my stomach to flip right on over, and over again a second time for good measure. Absin's laughing. *Laughing!*

"What is so funny?" Suraz snarls, asking the question for both of us.

"I would be careful about mentioning Holleran if I were you, Suraz."

"Why?"

The overly dramatic pause causes sweat to bead on my forehead despite the chill.

"Because he is hiding behind that dumpster over there. Your love of human substances has clearly dulled your instincts."

Fuck me.

Before I've even had the chance to check any of the shadows for Charon's toothy grin, the dumpster I'm hiding behind gets ripped from where it's stood collecting filth and garbage for God knows how long and goes flying further on down the alley, spilling its contents as it spins, crashes and scrapes to a stop.

Suraz stands in its place, Absin picking herself up from the ground, a grin on her face, and my friendly neighborhood Nephilim's shoulders are heaving with the lungfuls of breath he's expelling, fogging up the space between us with each huff. His golden eyes are burning as he glares at me, but I stare at the dirty ground right in front of his feet. It's tough going to withstand the focus of a Nephilim at the best of times, even after a tete-a-tete with Lucifer himself, and this really isn't the best of fucking times. Suraz's fury hits me like a storm hit ocean crashing into a particularly bothersome cliffside.

"I'm not cleaning any of that shit up."

The words just tumble out of my mouth. Did I ever mention

I ramble and quip when I'm nervous? Because I do. Even when I know, for certain, me talking in general is the completely wrong thing to do.

"Holleran," Suraz hisses, the weight of his fury pressing down on me. Part of me, a huge goddamn part, actually, begs me to shuffle on backward, but my stubborn side flat out says no. Stupid stubborn side. "How *dare* you eavesdrop on us?"

And with being stubborn comes indignation.

"Hey," I snap, pointing at him like I'm Harrison Ford again but still not quite meeting his eyes, "you're one to fucking talk, Suraz. Haven't you been stalking me since the night I met your boss?"

If I wasn't staring at his chin, I might not have seen it. Suraz goes to say something, then clamps his jaw shut, before opening it again. What the Hell was he going to say? Something about Lucifer?

"Be that as it may," he says instead, "your presence is not welcome here. Leave us. Now."

"Wait one moment." Absin draws up alongside him, and, right now, this alley's feeling mighty cramped. The Nephilim are both well over seven-foot-tall, and almost half as wide each. It's like standing in front of two golden-armor-clad U-Polar double door freezer units. Ones that carry swords the size of small ponies. "I would like to speak with you, Nick Holleran, and discover what Suraz finds so fascinating about you. Do you supply him with, what do you humans call it, heroin, perhaps? He does love it so."

If a hole would ever form beneath my feet and swallow me up, God, please, make it this moment. Please. If you're listening, and you don't despise my ass, just do it for me? The heat rising from my cheeks is enough to melt the ice and snow smothering Haven, and that isn't anything compared to the sheer molten anger pouring out of Suraz.

Closing his eyes, thank Christ, his obsidian, stony face twitches, spasms, and breath hisses out of him, like a punctured tire filled with venom instead of air, and he spins, hand reaching over his shoulder to the hilt poking over his shoulder.

"What's the Seal?" I blurt out. Really, I fucking scream it. If these two would have gone at it earlier, the dumpster might—*might*—have offered me some level of protection, but now?

If these two Nephilim throw down, I'll be making a one-way trip right back to Hell, but at least I'd lose a ton of weight. My distraction works. Suraz blinks, gazes sidelong at me, his hand still in the air, fingers flexing, then lets it fall to his side. His rage made him forget I stood there, and seeing as he's tracked my every movement for months, that's saying something.

"The Seal is not something that concerns you, Nick Holleran," he grates, turning back to me, though his gaze is still fixed on Absin. "It does not concern anyone save for those it concerns."

The Nephilim stare at each other, eyes glinting like nuggets of gold in a snow and garbage filled alley. It doesn't concern anyone save for those it concerns? What?

"Is that a riddle? Look, it's one of the weirdest things I've ever heard in my life, and I've heard, and seen, plenty of weird shit in my time, particularly in the last five years." At some point during my rambling, I realize the Nephilim—Nephili?—are both turning their burning regard my way, but it sure as shit doesn't stop me. "Now, I've heard a bit about this Seal in the last few months, and as my old ma used to say, my curiosity would get me in trouble every now and then, but once I hear something a few times, and come across a couple of...Nephilus?...arguing about it, you can say my interest is mighty piqued. So, spare me the riddles and the 'it isn't for you', and tell me what the Hell it is."

No sooner do I let loose the last word, does Absin flow forward, lifting me from my feet and letting them dangle, her hand gripping my jaw like a vice, and her full focus slams into me. Ever took a plane ride? You know that sensation when the craft speeds up then lifts from the ground when the G-Force nudges you? It's like that, times a thousand. This is what astronauts must feel every time they blast off into space, but at least they've got their fancy suits and comfortable chairs to sit in. I'm being held in the air by my jaw and nothing else.

I wanna look away, but I can't. Wanna close my eyes, but my lids won't do what I'm telling them to. Absin's sheer will commands me to stare back at her as she rummages through my mind, my soul. My skin crawls as those thick fingers of hers peel back layer after layer of my being, my history. Hopes and fears. None of it interests her. Not much, anyway. She blasts by Rosa without a pause, shrugs at most of the cases I've worked.

Pressure builds right behind my forehead. A headache without the pain but it fills my skull with wool, pushing the bone against my skin. Feels like it's gonna pop.

My encounter with Lucifer grabs her for a moment, as does everything Diana in general, and she lingers on her longer than on her boss. She pilfers moments with my parents, my childhood, moving without rhyme or reason, studying my later years, times at The Styx with Ruby, and then she finds it. My fears. The things I bury.

Charon. His particular interest in my death. What he wants. How could I not fear it, even if I don't want to admit it to myself? I do, and now Absin knows, too.

'*Oh, my, Nick Holleran, he has taken an interest in you, has he not? The Fateless. Yes, that would concern a creature like him.*' Absin's voice explodes in my mind, but I can't answer her. I can't do shit. I'm a ship caught in a whirlpool, hoping for the best. '*You heard the words he spoke to this Marvin Clancy of yours, and he spoke of The Seal. Yes, Charon* would *know all about it. Most interesting indeed.*'

The building pressure disappears, and my feet crash into concrete as Absin lets me go, the surprise of it causing me to slam face-first onto the ground, the stench of dirty snow and ice filling my nose.

A finger reaches under my chin and pulls my face upright, and I'm staring into Absin's face again. Beautiful but terrible and without any of the sadness Suraz's holds. This time, and fuck me if

I'm not thankful, she doesn't blast me with all of her focus.

"You are not special, Nick Holleran, no matter what Charon thinks. You are just an equation he has not solved yet." Absin cocks her head to the side as if puzzled by my mere existence. "Remarkable entities surround you, nonetheless. This girl, Diana. Your *parents*. Suraz. Lucifer himself. Charon. Yes, I return to him at the last. The Keeper of Death is unknowable, emotionless. Alien. He has existed since before time, and will be the one who ends it, they say. What links you to him? I see why the Seal burns into your mind, and it is the *only* reason I have the smallest sliver of interest in you. The Seal dominates my thoughts too, and I must return to it."

Straightening, she lets my head drop, not caring if my nose smashes into the ground or not.

It does, and it fucking hurts.

Rubbing at it, blood warming my hands, I scramble to my knees. "What is it? Tell me!"

Absin glances at the frowning Suraz, who's looking as deflated as a balloon that's been left tied to a radiator since the fourth of July, and shrugs.

"It is death, Nick Holleran, and it comes for us all." She shrugs. "Stay away from it if you wish to continue in this plane of existence for as long as you can."

She stalks away, somehow lithe despite her size, leaving me alone with Suraz. I shuffle up against the wall, searching my pockets for tissue and finding nada. Guess the cuff of my coat's gonna have to do.

"I would heed her words," Suraz tells me as I mop up my bloody nose. "The Seal is not meant for mortals, Nick Holleran."

"And heroin isn't for Nephilim, for Christ's sake, Suraz!" I snap, tired of being treated like crap all morning. "I heard what you were talking about before that, too. You're struggling to function. That's what Absin says. What's the matter with you?"

His face tightens with anger but, right now, I don't give a shit if he pummels me into the ground. I ain't *important*. Just the people I surround myself with are, right? Well, let's see if I'm important enough for Suraz to give a shit about what I say.

He takes a step toward me, and I steel myself for it, but goddamn it if I don't look him in the eyes when I do, pressure be damned.

The anger evaporates when he meets my glare, and he sighs instead. Kneeling, he produces a strip of linen out of...well, either he's a magician or he's torn it off from whatever robe he's wearing under all the pieces of his plate mail, and he hands it to me. For a moment, my stubborn ass refuses, but the blood staining what's now my favorite coat changes my mind.

"We Nephilim are born in pain, Nick Holleran. We are the spawn of angels and demons, and both view us with nothing but scorn. All except Lucifer. Just as he did with your kind, when everyone else thought you all *unimportant*." His choice of word isn't lost on me. Also, another factoid. Nephilim are the children of angels and demons? Fuck me. Some family get together. "Some of my kind carry deep anger. Some despair, others sadness and grief. I have all of those, such is my lot, but we all share something. A longing for Heaven. We have seen perfection, Nick Holleran, it was, and still is, our home and its absence leaves a hole in our souls. Absin fills it with obsessing over the Seal, others like Caon and Sitir rule over their own levels of Hell. We are immortal, exiled, and we must find some purpose. I fight, Nick Holleran, and I do my Lord's bidding, but it is not always enough for me, so I turned to other distractions." He drops his stare and whispers, almost to himself, "Even that was not enough."

Look, I appreciate his candidness, but that's not the whole story. I know when someone's keeping a secret, Nephilim or not.

He blinks, and turns back to me, and gets to his feet. "Absin may not see your importance, Nick Holleran, but Lucifer does, and that is important to me. But let me give you some advice."

Pulling the tissue away from my nose, I check if the flow's stemmed yet. Kinda.

"Shoot. I'm all about unsolicited advice."

"Do not listen in on my conversations again." He glances toward the parking lot. "He is all yours, little one."

My jaw drops. Diana's standing in the alley way's entrance, and, at Suraz's word, she flows forward, peering at me.

"Are you okay, Nick?" she asks. "I felt the jumble of emotions and came looking, but Suraz wouldn't let me come forward while she was still here. That other one."

"Absin," I mutter, struggling to my feet and staring off after the disappearing Suraz. A junkie Nephilim, the son of an angel and a demon. Think I've heard it all. "I'm fine. If you can call getting threatened by the cops and treated like a ragdoll by a Nephilim before nine o'clock in the morning fine. Hell of a start to the day, eh?"

If I was in better spirits, I might laugh at my own joke. Diana takes my hand, and I turn her way. Heh. Spirits.

"You see why this one-man show act has to end?" she asks, peering up at me, eyebrows drawn down over her pits.

"Jeez, I was just getting coffee!" Shaking my head, I lurch toward the Seven Eleven. "Wait in the car, I think I can handle the rest on my own."

Diana, even eyeless, gives me a dubious look. I can handle it if there isn't some creature lurking inside who I've managed to piss off or hates my guts, that is. Rubbing at my nose, I grimace at my reflection in the mirror. Disheveled and bloody. Sure getting tired of being tossed about the place, that's for sure.

Another thing's certain. The Nephili's—yeah, let's go with that—warning about the Seal isn't gonna put me off. Don't reckon I'll figure it all out today, or even tomorrow, maybe not even next year but, one day, I will.

That's a promise.

"Better be a good cup of coffee after all that," I mutter, glaring at the automatic doors like my life's and all its issues are their fault. "That's all I'm saying."

CHAPTER SIX

CRUSTY, GRAY, AND LIFELESS

Sitting in the car outside of Greaney's joint, I sip at my coffee and wince when the cheap, too-bitter liquid rushes down my throat. I can almost hear Rosa's words as I take another reluctant gulp.

'Nick, if you want good coffee, don't go to that Seven Eleven. How many times have I got to tell you?'

A smile breaks out across my face. One more time might do it. Might.

"You should think about Rosa more often," Diana murmurs, still engrossed in her book. "I like it when you feel nice inside your heart. Makes a change, you know?"

"Yeah, I like it, too." Sighing, I take another gulp. At least it's warm. "You ready to go inside?"

"I didn't come along for the ride, Nick."

Goddamn teenagers.

"Right. How about a little less sass?" I reply, opening the door. Cold air blasts me in the face, sets my nose to aching again. Cleaned myself up in the Seven Eleven's restroom. Couldn't turn up to a murder scene all bloody and beaten, could I? Well, I could, and I have, but not today. Not with Gavin and Butler sniffin' at my ass, thinking I might be involved, and they've got a witness saying I came home looking not all that hot. "Tell me anything you can when we're in there, okay? Anything."

“Sure thing, Nick.” Diana flows outta the open car door, gazing around. “All feels as you would expect. There’s a lot of tension. A lot of boredom, too.”

“Yeah, that’s a murder scene, alright. You get used to anything. Look at me, talking to a teenage ghost like you’re my best friend.”

“Oh, we’re much more than best friends, aren’t we?” Diana looks up at me, a small smile on her lips. “I’m your savior.”

Shaking my head, I cross the road, taking in the details. Area’s nice, much swankier than mine though it ain’t too far away and is pretty reputable too, as far as Haven goes. Most of the houses on the row are in the mansion class, what with their own walls, security gates, CCTV and, giving a cursory glance, personal guards. The house right across from Greaney’s has one standing behind the gate, peering out at the commotion. Cop cars fill most of the available spaces, and there’s plenty of official looking folk passing this way and that. Most staring down at the screens of their cells, others staring into space with their arms folded tightly across their chests.

A sensation itches in the back of my mind. Gazing around, I frown, trying to figure it out. My instincts prod at me, pointing something out, something missing, but I just can’t grasp it. Maybe if I stay outside long enough…

Changing my mind, I catch Diana’s pits and nod at the joint across the road and jog over. I’m not certain what I’m walking into in Greaney’s, and I’ve found out through plenty of suffering and mistakes to get the lay of the land before walking into what might be an ambush.

“Hey, buddy,” I call, flashing the security guard what I hope’s a genuine smile. “Some morning, huh?”

Guy reminds me of one of the Hemsworth actors, the little one who nobody loses their minds over. L… I wanna say L, something. I’ll ask Rosa. Thor, I know, but the other two just merge into one in my mind, apart from the height difference. Anyway, dude looks like him. Stoic and small.

"Yeah, you can say that," he drawls, and fuck me if he isn't an Aussie. Is it him? Weirder things happen every day in Hell. "I haven't seen so much action around here in years."

"You know what's happening? That's Kieran Greaney's place, right?"

Little H, as I will forever call him, eyeballs me then raises one of his brows. "I think you know that already, seeing as you're here. Let me guess, you're from the Haven Chronicles."

"Guilty," I say, raising my hands, the steam rising from my piping hot coffee. "That obvious?"

"Let's just say I've dealt with reporters before, and I know the song and dance."

He holds his hand out flat through the gate's bars, palm up. Nodding, I pull a twenty from my pocket, and slap it down. Little H doesn't even look at it. Sighing, I pull out another twenty and add it to the pile.

Little H curls his fingers around the notes and takes his hand away. Tribute accepted.

"So, whadda ya know?" I ask, taking a step nearer. Diana's still staring across the way, brow furrowed.

Little H gives a conspiratorial glance left and right, before taking a step closer himself. "They say Kieran Greaney bought it."

"Jesus Christ, you think?" I breathe, shaking my head. "I ain't paying forty dollars for that! When did it happen? Tell me that at least?"

"Hard to say." Little H shrugs and clams up, his hand extending through the bars again. No wonder Chris is the popular one.

Biting my lip, I pull out another twenty and grab his hand when I place it on his palm. "No more, okay? That's sixty. Talk."

"Like I said, it's hard to say," he replies, folding the note away. "Medics arrived before sunrise, about six o'clock. Twenty minutes later the cops started piling in. Son of who he is, there's a lot of interest. You're the first from the press, though. Guess you'll get the exclusive, huh?"

"Guess so," I mutter, glancing over my shoulder. "You were here all night?"

"Yeah, that's my shift. Clocking off in an hour."

I meet his eyes. "See anything? Anyone going in or out?"

Little H shrugs. "Can't say I was paying all that much attention. Neighborhood is quiet enough, so I was watching a movie."

The Avengers? Just imagine that. Should I ask… No. No. I can't. Can I?

"And nothing weird happened?" I press instead, all professional like. "Nothing stands out?"

Little H goes to roll his eyes, but then gives me a sharp glance instead. Stepping closer, cheeks almost pressed against the gate with his nose sticking through, he lowers his voice.

"Yeah, there was something, now you mention it." He frowns. "I kept getting blasts of static, just after ten. Probably a fair bit after, but I was engrossed. I've got that hyper focus, you know?"

"Sure." I wish he'd hyper focus on getting to the fucking point.

"Well, my screen went all wacky, not freezing like it usually does with bad internet. Staticy like in the old days. Kept getting louder, too, and my radio did the same. Lights flickering, all that crap. I got out of my booth, you know, to take a look around. You know what I saw?"

"What?" I breathe, and even Diana's looking our way.

"When the static blared its loudest, the security lights across the perimeter of Greaney's place didn't flicker one bit. Not one bit. Didn't really think about it till now, weird stuff happens in Haven, right?" Little H shrugs. "That worth your sixty?"

I glance at Diana. "Yeah, most helpful, my friend. What's your name?"

"Luke."

"Fuck off."

It just blurts out, I can't help it. That's Little H's name!

"What the fuck, man?"

"Sorry," I say, spreading my hands. "You just look exactly like someone with the same name. G'day."

Turning on my heel, I head away before Little H decides to scale his gates and give my ass a beating. Can't honestly blame him if he did, even if he did just pocket more than his hourly rate in less than five minutes.

"There's a weird feeling, Nick," Diana says as we cross the road. "I can feel emotions like normal, but when I focus on the house, I get nothing. Just like last night."

"You'd think the two were linked," I reply, winking at her as we head to the gates. A cop gives me a weird look. Can't say I'm not used to them. "Wish you were telepathic, kid. Means it wouldn't look like I'm talking to myself everywhere I go."

"That's the price you have to pay to bask in my glorious presence," she replies, smiling up at me.

"Were you always this annoying?" I mutter, trying to hide the smile. A cop at the open gate to Greaney's house is looking right at me.

"This is an active crime scene," she barks, obviously bored, her breath fogging in the cold morning air. "No press."

Why's everyone thinking I'm with the press all of a sudden? My pal Zia would love that.

"Name's Nick Holleran," I reply, favoring her with my lop-sided smile. Best to get off on the right foot and all that. "Officers Gavin and Butler are expecting me."

Her face turns from bored to an expression of utter disdain. "Oh, it's you. Go on ahead. Don't touch anything."

"Does everyone in Haven despise you, Nick?" Diana asks. As we traipse by, the cop speaks into her radio, no doubt telling my morning dates I'm here.

"Not everyone," I reply, taking in the scene. "Just most of the people I've met."

For once, there's no pithy remark from the kid. She probably senses I'm not actually joking. Anyway, Greaney's place is pretty idyllic, if you can ignore the towering walls stretching around the perimeter, cutting off the joint from the rest of Haven like these fuckers often do. I get wanting your own privacy, but these places look like their owners are trying to kid themselves that they don't live in a city, and that their neighbors have the exact same set up but, saying that, this place stands out. It ain't often I've come across a Japanese garden in Haven, and even I'm impressed, and I reckon flowers are to be enjoyed by other people.

Crossing over a little red wooden bridge and heading past a replica of a pretty authentic looking chashistu, I gotta wonder how much the landscaper charged for all this. Every now and then, I look at the ten thousand dollar check Kieran's old man signed for 'services rendered' after I didn't squeal about Dean Wheeler leaving three bits of hot lead in my chest, and the fact I only tailed him because old man Greaney hired me. I open the drawer I keep it in, take it out, turn it over in my hands, and wonder why the Hell the sonofabitch hasn't ever called me up and asked why I haven't cashed it yet.

Looking at this place, I know why. With the money this family has, they wouldn't notice ten thousand dollars still sitting in their account. It's a drop in the ocean.

The house matches the opulence of the gardens, and the same style runs through it. Everywhere I look I see Japanese influences, and I'm half expecting the staff working here to be dressed appropriately, but, thank fuck, they're not. That would have been just too much for me. I mean, admire another culture, a different way of life as much as you want, but…

"Jesus," I mutter as we walk through the open double doors.

You'd expect statues in a place like this, right? All these rich freaks have them. Even seen ones of the homeowners in my time, and self-portraits aplenty. What I ain't ever seen is a life-sized marble statue of the dead bastard I'm here because of, dressed in shining samurai armor as soon as I walk in through the goddamn door.

It's even holding a fucking sword.

"Well, we can rule one thing out," I say, studying the blade.

It's gleaming like the rest of the set up and if it's ever been used then I'm from Kyoto.

"What's that?" Diana murmurs, brows furrowed.

"Whatever killed Kieran Greaney took him by surprise, or he knew what, or who, the murderer was. If you've got a samurai sword in your foyer and someone's in your house looking for blood, you'd fucking use it." I glance around, footsteps echoing off the polished wooden floorboards from further in the house. "No signs of a struggle anywhere, either. Not on the front side of the house, anyway. Checked it over while we took a trip through Japan. All the windows and doors are intact, and I don't see any bullet holes or nothing in here, either. And if Greaney couldn't get to his sword in time, you can bet your bottom dollar he had a firearm close by."

Diana nods. "It's all fuzzy in here, Nick. The emotions... It's like they're dimmer than normal. I'm having a hard time feeling them."

"Interesting."

And by interesting, I mean shit. Unusual and interesting circumstances, while common in Hell, never bode particularly well for me.

"Holleran!" Henry Butler's bark comes from where the footsteps are growing louder. "You took your time getting here. It wasn't a fucking invitation!"

"Am I under arrest?" It's always a good deflection when dealing with the PD, that simple, beautiful question. Makes 'em squirm.

Turning, I wait for him and Lori Gavin to come to me. A small victory, but ultimately pointless as I gotta head back in their direction to look at the stiff. But still. Holleran one, asshole detectives zero.

"That remains to be seen." Lori Gavin gives me the old look up and down, eyebrows raised. That's the usual reply. "Stopped for coffee? Glad to see you're taking this seriously."

I shrug, then take a sip from my shitty coffee but savor it like it's made from Hell's most glorious beans.

"Didn't have time to make any when I woke up, and it's cold out. If I'm not under arrest, it sounds like I'm doing you both a favor by being here. Be lucky I ain't charging you by the hour for my expertise."

"Nick," Diana murmurs. "Are you trying to annoy them?"

Yes. Yes, I am.

Henry Butler snorts. "Expertise."

The usual disdain I get from him, but it doesn't look like his heart's all that into it.

"Well, you did ask me here, and you said you and your pals reckon this is in my ballpark." Eyeing the pair of them, I mentally climb down from my high horse. I've seen the look they're both wearing before. Butler and Gavin wear the expression of those who are questioning what they *know*. "Look, it's early, and I don't appreciate being accused of shit I haven't done. That's all. You wanted me here, now show me why."

Reckon that's just about as 'play nice' as I'm gonna get, and I tried. I really did.

Henry and Lori let their eyes meet for just a second, but being partners and all, they might as well have had a full-blown conversation. They've worked the beat a long time together.

"Like Detective Gavin says, no one is under arrest. Yet. We're not ruling anything out." I don't know if he's doing it on purpose, but his fingers brush the grip of his firearm on his hip. "But, yeah, we've never seen anything like this, and you can appreciate we've seen our share of dead bodies. And there's the weird shit. Waves of static, like someone used an EMP or something, only there's been no reports of blasts. Like I said, weird shit."

"And we've seen our fair share of mobsters dead, too. They all have shady pasts, right? Comes with the territory." Lori adds, meeting my eyes. There's something behind them, lurking just beyond the utter disdain. Something that looks a lot like shock or fear to me. "Follow us."

The detectives turn and head back the way they came, so

they don't see the grin of triumph I flash Diana's way. She just frowns up at me. Clearly, we don't have the same shorthand Butler and Gavin have yet, and she has no idea of my pyrrhic victory of forcing these bastards to take about ten extra steps.

They lead us down a corridor, still in the Japanese style, of course, and still without any signs of a struggle. It's pristine, like the cleaners just left. I pass by a photo of Kieran's old man and suppress the shudder. Russell Greaney. The Irish Don, indeed. At least he isn't here, and my involvement in this case is gonna begin and end here.

"Did his wife hear anything?" I ask as we walk, our footsteps making the only sounds. "Any of the help?"

"How do you know his wife was here, Holleran?" Henry asks, throwing me a frown over his shoulder.

"Assumed she'd live in her own home, that's all."

"Well—"

"No questions until after," Lori interrupts, and her partner falls silent.

I take a look at Diana so she can see my puzzlement, but she isn't looking my way. Her head's swiveling in all directions, and the kid's worry is etched into her face.

Great.

Maybe it's the static. It's a wrinkle, for sure. If the detectives are somehow, and finally, coming round to 'Hell on Earth is Real' they might have thoughts about pinning this on me. Lori did talk about mobsters and shady pasts...

Reckon my mug's about as worried as the kid's.

The detectives take a left, through an open door, and into what I'm thinking is Greaney's study. Room's packed with folk, some taking photos of the scene, some taking notes, and others just standing around without even trying to look busy. They're all blocking the body, anyway. I take it all in, studying the intact, closed windows, the organized desk, the clinically tidy room.

No signs of struggle. Not a single one.

"Everyone out," Henry barks, and he's looking everywhere

except on the carpeted floor. Lori's the same, practically eyeballing anyone who looks her way.

The photographers, notetakers and coroners file out, each taking a quick glance at me. I'm used to 'officials' sending funny looks my way, but this isn't that. Some of them are relieved.

"Now," Henry says, standing in front of me so the body's blocked. Someone threw a sheet over it before leaving the room anyway. Dramatic sonofabitch. "Why don't you take a look at your old pal Kieran Greaney and see if anything in your memory gets knocked loose."

"He's not my pal," I mutter as he steps aside. I kneel in front of the corpse, my fingertips itching as I reach out and grab the sheet. "I ain't ever—"

You ever had acid reflux? The one you just can't shift no matter how many antacids you swallow down? The type of acid reflux that keeps you awake at night and won't ever let you get comfortable? The one that burns your chest so it hurts, and each gulp of saliva like chowing down on vomit? The acid reflux that you swear is burning through your bones and making them soft?

As I pull the sheet aside, that sensation rushes up from my gut and into my throat, and it takes a mighty bit of willpower on my behalf to keep myself from puking all over Kieran Greaney. Or what used to be him.

A second ago, I was gonna say I haven't seen him, but I have. Course I have. I'm not his pal, and I haven't spoken with him in years, but I know him by sight. Like I said, he delivered his old man's care package to me all those years ago. About thirty-eight or thirty-nine, and a fitness freak, Kieran cut a figure of healthy masculinity, with his perfectly coiffed hair, shaped eyebrows, and designer stubble to add to the all-year tan he sported.

What's lying before me is crusty, gray and lifeless. Like Emperor Palpatine left out to dry in Death Valley.

Questions run through my mind as I take him in. He's wearing a silk robe with just a pair of slippers, like he just hopped out of a shower and threw something on, or had to grab something from his study. Maybe make a late-night phone call, but his skin...

Shaking my head, and mentally taking a hold of my stomach, I lean in closer. When I say crusty, I'm not joking. It's like all the moisture's been sucked out of the epidermis and the faintest of touches would crack it, turn it to dust. Same with the lips. His formerly jet-black hair's white, not gray, and his eyes!

Colorless.

He doesn't smell, either. Corpses usually do, especially ones that have been lying out for almost twelve hours. But the worst thing, the absolutely worst thing, is his face.

It's locked in a permanent expression of gut-wrenching terror.

The mouth's gaping, the eyes wide, the muscles tight and no doubt getting more taut with rigor mortis. It's like a bust, not too far away from the statue of him out front, but a thousand times more life-like.

I look away frowning, and I notice another thing. His index finger on his right hand's frozen in a point.

"I don't feel anything in this room, Nick," Diana whispers into my ear. There's no need for her to whisper, no one can hear her, but even I can sense the heavy weight crushing this room. It isn't right. "Not a thing. Not from you, not from them. It scares me."

I lean closer to the body again and make a small motion for Diana to come near.

"Check the whole house," I whisper, pretending to look into Kieran's eyes but really, I'm looking through them. I'll see that stare whenever I close my eyes for a long time. "See if he's here. Guy like him wouldn't go to Heaven."

Nodding, Diana flows away and I cough, and get to my feet. The detectives are staring at me. Lori with her arms crossed, Henry with his fingers brushing his firearm.

"Where'd you go last night, Holleran?" Lori asks.

I meet their eyes, one at a time, then throw a thumb over my shoulder. "You can't think I did that. You ever seen a stiff in this condition?"

"Like I said on the phone, *Nick*, this isn't the first mobster you're associated with who's ended up dead," Henry grates. "Remember Dean Wheeler *and* his wife?"

"I had nothing to do with either of those," I snap, lying. Had plenty to do with the latter, but Ruby cleaned it all up for me before the cops got involved. "Nothing."

"So you say," he snaps back. "But three we *know* you're connected with. Dead. All in unusual circumstances."

I fold my arms. "If you've got proof of my involvement, I'd love to fucking see it."

Henry opens his big mouth to give me a barrel full, but Lori holds a hand up. His jaw snaps shut.

"Look, Holleran, we're not idiots. We know this isn't normal. You're a PI, or were, anyway, before your new sideline, so I'm certain you scanned the place when you came in." She points at the desk, and the window behind it. "Nothing is out of place. Not a single thing. There are no broken panes of glass, no forced locks, no signs of a struggle, which leads us to two things." She takes a step toward me, her iron-like will on show. The movement brings Kieran Greaney's corpse into full view, and she doesn't bat an eyelid. "Either Greaney let someone in, someone he knew, or..."

I raise an eyebrow. "Or?"

"Remember Father Marvin Clancy?" Henry asks from behind his partner.

A frown etches into my flesh, confused at the sudden change in questioning. "How could I forget? Me handing him over to you gained you a front page spread. Probably a pay rise, too. I should take a cut."

Henry doesn't rise to the bait. "You know what he talks about? No, talking isn't the right word, Holleran. Babbles about."

"Enlighten me."

His fingers brush his sidearm again. Henry's itching to pull it. Itching.

"He rambles on about the day you took him in. When you visited him in his church." Henry nods and gives a half shrug.

"I'm glad the sick bastard got his and he's behind bars, and, at the time, I didn't particularly care how you figured out an almost sixty-year-old cold case. Father Clancy confessed, and I knew he was telling the truth."

Usually when these two pains in my ass shake me down, there's aggressive snark, threats. General boisterousness. Not today. Detectives Butler and Gavin stare at me with stony expressions and set jaws. I can tell when folk tell the truth too, most of the time, and whatever thoughts are running through these two goon's heads, they believe it.

"You still ain't telling me what our incarcerated priest rambles about, slick."

I fight the urge to take a look around to make sure Diana isn't listening. We don't really talk much about the man who murdered her.

"He talks about you, Holleran," Henry growls, and now there's a bit of the usual smoldering anger. "Says that you and some presence worked him over. That you talked this presence out of killing him and turning him into us. You know we don't believe your bullshit, you know we think you exploit wack jobs, but..."

"But." The word hisses through my lips.

Henry glances at the window. "The shit we're seeing out there at the moment. The unexplained deaths, the damage. Graffiti all over the place written in ancient, almost forgotten languages, the lab boys say. Now this, and all the reports of the weird static and flickering electricity last night, here. In this neighborhood. Made us think about what Father Clancy rambles about. About you and this presence."

Fuck me. A part of me is thrilled these two idiots are starting to see things my way, but they're onto a very particular path here. Their thought process unfurls in front of me, and I don't like it one bit.

"So that leads us to two working theories, like I said." Lori takes over, her chin tilted as she stares up at me. "You've got history with the Greaneys. With the Wheelers. Everyone knows it. Everyone. You took jobs for them back in the day, and the night you got…mugged…in that alley? No one will go on the record, but like my partner said on the phone, we know you worked a case for old man Greaney."

"So what? I've wanted revenge for over half a decade and picked my moment?" Why do I open my mouth sometimes? All sounds kinda reasonable when I say it out loud. I spread my hands. "Not that I did or anything."

Lori nods, a cold wry grin spreading across her face. "There's no damage. Greaney either knew who killed him and let him in, or you let this presence off the hook to do your dirty work for you because, as you said, this isn't normal, Holleran. Not by a long shot."

A lawyer sounds pretty hot right now. Not like any jury's gonna buy what these two are selling, anyway. Not the supernatural stuff. But the other theory? That I had a beef with the Greaneys and have been biding my time? Yeah, that might just stick.

"You might think we're reaching, Holleran, and I'm not sure if it's the atmosphere around Haven getting to us, but by the blood rushing out of your face I think we're hitting pretty close to home." Henry jabs a finger in my face. "I'm going to ask you Lori's question again, and I want an answer this time. No bullshit. Where did you go last night?"

Ah, shit, detectives, the Queen of the Fae sent her brood after me. Look, here are the wounds to prove it! Despite the winter chill, sweat pops on the back of my neck. Am I really gonna tell these bastards about my run in with Lilith and her creatures last night? Not the most cast iron of alibis, and even if they are starting to believe I'm not a crank, I'm not sure me spinning a tale about murderous pixies is gonna help my case.

"Went for a walk." Even when I say it, before I see their smug grins, I know how weak and wishy-washy my answer is. But that's all I got. "In the Haven Woods."

"The Haven Woods," Henry repeats. "You went for a walk. On Christmas week."

"Any witnesses, Holleran?" Lori demands, eyes shining like a cat surveying a bucket full of cream.

"No." I could say talk to Rosa, but all she can do is say what I said. Any cop worth their salt will call it second-hand info, any lawyer would scream hearsay. I could tell the devil I'm going to the store and go visit God instead, right? However, Henry's own words from this morning come back to me… "But I have a witness that I was home when the static hit."

"Your girlfriend, Holleran?" Henry snaps. "Weak."

"She's no liar." Now it's my turn to jab fingers. "We were at home when the radio lost reception. TV and lights flickering, too. But I wasn't talking about her. You can ask your pal Hudson. You know he saw me outside my house, but did he tell you he saw me *after* all that static, and I mean *right* after it happened. Seconds. Not minutes or hours. Now that I think about it, I heard a snatch of static before that on the drive back from the woods, about thirty minutes before the big one."

Victory is mine.

They might not believe Rosa, but they would when Hudson backs me up. I try not to smile, but I can't help it when Lori whispers into Henry's ear, and, when his eyes flick to mine, he deflates like a punctured tire.

"You got reports of static on the edge of the city, didn't you? The earlier one, but you didn't think I knew about that." Look, I'm a pretty good detective, okay? I can read a face. "See, this couldn't have been me."

"It doesn't prove anything, Holleran," Henry grates, cheeks turning a beetroot purple. "Nothing at all. You might have had eyes on you for the second bunch of static, but not the first."

I glance around. "Is this house on the outskirts of the Haven Woods? Plus, I was talking to someone on my cell when it happened. Ruby Masterson, she owns The Styx. Ask her, see what she says. Anyway, there's no proof the static and this murder are connected. Like you said, weird shit's happening in Haven all the time, and if the first wave of it hit the outer limits, it might just be a rolling blackout or something."

Folding my arms, I cock my head to the side, smiling as they whisper at one another again. Behind them, Diana appears and shakes her head. No sign of Kieran Greaney's ghost.

Another wrinkle. Sometimes, I love a wrinkle, depending on the circumstances of course, but not today.

"Look, I'll ask again," I say, interrupting the fierce conversation that sounds like a pair of put-out snakes hissing at one another. "Am I under arrest?"

Lori glares at me, then at her partner, then at the corpse, then back at me. "No."

"Then am I free to go?"

Henry looks like he's got a mouthful of lemons. "Yes."

I give a half bow. "Well, this has been just lovely. Because it's Christmas, I won't send you a bill for my time, though I'll offer you another helping of my expertise for free. Reckon something supernatural got him, but my plate's a little full at the moment so I won't be taking the case." I give 'em my best Han Solo grin, the one I *know* pisses people off. "Happy Holidays."

Sweeping past them, wind in my sails, I start training my mind to put all this shit behind me. Kieran Greaney was a piece of shit, and I won't shed any tears about it and like Henry said, there's been plenty of weird deaths in Haven lately, I can't investigate them all. Not like either of these bozos would pay me, and I got my bills. Sipping at my miraculously still-warm coffee, I flash Diana a smile, my spirits already improving. Like Rosa said, it's Christmas, and I need some time off. If the static happens again, I'll look into it in the new year. If it's targeting mobsters, I might wait until 2026.

"Holleran?" Lori's tone makes me stop in my tracks. It's that kind of tone, the type you can't walk away from even though you want to. "We'll be watching you, you hear? This isn't over."

I look over my shoulder and raise an eyebrow. "It is for me, sweetheart."

Now that makes me feel like a few million dollars.

Without another glance, I walk away, Diana with me, eyes forward, not caring to take in any more details. No way I'll ever come back to this place, and if I ever think about Kieran Greaney again it'll be too soon. A lifetime too soon.

"You know she's right, Nick. This isn't over." Diana's cold fingers tug at my hand as she takes a hold of it. "I'm scared."

I frown down at her, almost stopping, but there's still officials at the crime scene and some are looking my way.

"Why?" I whisper, frowning at the statue by the front door.

"Because there's no way a person with that dead man's past would get into Heaven, and his ghost isn't here. It should be, even if it's caught in a loop or Unaware."

We walk outside, and I take a quick scan before answering. "Maybe Charon took him to the Seal?"

"Maybe." The way she says it tells me the kid doesn't believe it. "But this emptiness around here, and during the static last night. It isn't normal, Nick, and I haven't ever felt anything like it, even when I was alive. This is going to happen again. I know it. You know it too, even though I sense that you're trying to fool yourself."

Passing through the gates, I head straight to the Mustang, nodding when Little H waves at me from across the way. Place is still crawling with all kinds, and it won't be long till the real press gets a hold of this story.

"Who can say what the future's gonna bring, huh?" Trying one more time to convince myself, even though I know she's right. Kid's always fucking right. Climbing inside the car, Diana slides in beside me. "It's Haven, Diana. These things happen."

"I hope so, Nick," she says, grabbing her book and opening it. "I really hope so."

Now who's trying to fool themselves? As I pull out into the road and the snow falls once more, the feeling she's right builds alongside the certainty that, somehow, I'm involved in all this.

I always am.

CHAPTER SEVEN

WHITE NOISE

Diana hasn't stopped talking at me since we pulled away from Greaney's joint, and, let me tell you something, that's a rarity coming from her, especially if there's a book nearby.

Or a TV. Kid loves her some TV. Guess it's a damn sight better than it used to be, right? With the one or two channels folk had to pick from. Too much choice these days, if you ask me. By the time I've trawled through all the options, it's time for bed.

Anyway. Diana.

"...And look at it this way," she says, peering up at me, eyebrows tight and drawn, washed out face the picture of teenage seriousness. Which is pretty fucking serious. "Is it right if you know there's a creature on the loose, one that's killed already, and you don't do anything about it? Morally, I mean. Its next victim would be on your hands, Nick, because there will be a next time. Killers don't just stop after their first murder, we both know that better than most."

"You know," I mutter, keenly missing the cigarettes again. At least me smoking them in the car would give Diana something else to yap at me about. "You'd have been wonderful in an Ethics classroom. Just wonderful."

"Well, if you don't go looking, I'm going to, Nick."

"No, you're not. That's just asking for trouble," I choke, chokingly. "Take it from me, I'm a master at that."

"I'd like to see you try and stop me. Or have you forgotten how I could throw you around like a laundry bag?"

I haven't forgotten. Truth be told, I didn't need the lecture or threats. My own mind wore me down before Greaney's joint disappeared from my rear view. But hey, I'm stubborn. Sue me.

"Alright, what do we know?" I ask, stuck in the mid-morning downtown traffic. Lots of folks attending to business in the city this close to Christmas, and the snow means the very worst drivers are out in force. Do they wait for this shit, and just take public transport every other day of the year? Anyway, it's taken me all of thirty minutes to stop sulking about Diana and Lori Gavin being on the money and accepting, verbally, that even if I don't want to, I'm involved in this. Or I'm involving myself in it regardless. "I know you don't have any idea about the manner of the creature, but what have we learned? What can we use?"

"It probably caused the static." Diana holds up one finger, then adds another to it. "Weakness in you, but we can ask Rosa about that, maybe it affected her. Did she say she felt anything?"

I frown. "No, and I think she woulda, right?"

"Right."

Diana unfolds a third finger as my lane starts chugging again. A ghost goes running right through the hood before hurtling through the air right beside my side window from some unseen impact. Poor bastard's reliving his death over and over. Unless he springs Awareness. A few months back, me and Diana checked out the site of her old tenement building, and she brought fleeting Awareness back to some sorry little kid who'd spent the past sixty years burning to a crisp. Wonder if she could do it for longer? Some of these souls deserve any kind of release.

"Something else we know," she says, holding up those three fingers. "It dampens what I can sense. We haven't come across anything like that so far, have we? Not Amarok, not Nephilim, skinwalkers, wendigo, fae, the Wild Hunt—"

"I get it." I switch lanes through impatience, though all it's going to do is let me trudge along with a slightly different view of all the vehicles surrounding me. "Another couple of items to the list; it started last night, it can move undetected, it frightens the crap out of its victims, which means it's so forceful that people who can't usually see this shit can, and it isn't Charon."

Diana frowns. "How do you know?"

"Because he watched from the shadows last night, after the static burst, but that doesn't rule out him taking Greaney to the Seal. He moves fast, right?" I shake my head. Fucking Charon. He could help me in a lot of ways, but he won't. Unless he thinks his help might kill me. "But... I asked if he'd done it, and he said no. He's many things, but he ain't a liar."

"So, we know quite a lot of things. Enough for a new entry in '*Holleran's Handbook To Hell*' at any rate." She gazes out of the window as the Haven city center skyline grows larger. "It takes souls, too."

"We *don't* know that," I snap. "Not for certain."

"Seems pretty certain to me, if Charon didn't take him, and he isn't in Hell. Nick, Greaney wasn't going to Heaven. That's what you said. So, his soul is gone. Taken."

Traffic's crunched to a halt again, brake lights illuminating the gray morning like holiday decorations as horns blare, making a ruckus but achieving squat. A light drizzle falls, the temperature just the wet side of freezing as I ponder her words. Kid sees matters with a clear head most of the time, and my gut tells me she's right again, but I can't discount Charon's involvement. I've seen the malnourished Clint Eastwood sonofabitch take a spirit away to the Seal, and there's a chance he did it with Kieran Greaney.

Is that what he does? Takes the baddest of the bad? Do their sins, their souls, carry more Juju than others, something that makes them stand out in a different way? Put it this way, if I was to book a flight to Berlin and visit the site of the goddamn Füherbunker, would I find Hitler haunting the place or did Charon steal that sonofabitch away, too?

If I ever go there, reckon I'll bring an Expunger just in case.

Saying that, Dean Wheeler did plenty worse than Kieran Greaney, and the ferryman left him in Hell, so what does that say?

Says I still don't know enough about this fucking place.

I run a hand over my face, fingernails digging into the skin a little. After almost six years of knowing the truth of the world, and all the knowledge I got at my fingertips, I still know jack shit. It's gotta change. It's gotta. All I'm doing is blundering around in the pitch darkness, somehow surviving, and last night's escapade proves itself as the perfect example.

"There's something else we should add to the list," I say, breaking the not altogether comfortable silence between me and Diana, as this new creatures' powers remind me of something. "Regular folks are noticing the increased Hellish activity of late, and I overheard Suraz. More and more Hellspawn are breaking onto the surface, he said. Emerging from the lower levels and *everywhere*. Not sure what that meant but whatever this is could be one of them, and Suraz might know exactly what that is."

"Then we find Suraz!" Diana beams, clapping her hands. Despite keeping her distance this morning, the two like one another. "Should be easy enough, he's always following you."

"He is," I mutter, gazing around, then it hits me. That missing feeling. The itch in the back of my mind that's been bugging me. It's him! Or, to be more accurate, the lack of him. "Except he isn't. When he's watching me, his focus falls on me like a weighted blanket, but it doesn't comfort me. Well, it didn't until today. Now I fu..., ahem. Now I miss it."

Diana glances at me, her smile slipping before she fixes it on her face once more. "I'm sure it's nothing. You said it yourself, he said he's got a lot on his plate, and he looked like he'd already been in a fight this morning."

"Yeah. You're probably right."

I thumb the music up a little, hoping Weezer's *Thank You and Goodnight* will help silence the sliver of doubt working its way up from my gut and swirling around my bullet wounds. Having Suraz following me all through Hell pissed me off, no doubt, but now he ain't? The Nephilim stuck to me like peanut butter on jelly without ever giving me any reason, and he saved my ass more than once. Him taking off and leaving me to my own devices should feel like a blessing.

It doesn't.

The sudden ringing of my cell, amplified by the Mustang's speakers, almost gives me a shitting heart attack. And I say 'shitting' for a very good reason.

"Nick? What's the matter with you?" Diana says over the noise. "You're a jumbled-up bag of nerves."

"You have no idea," I mutter. Examining the display, I smile a little, and answer my cell. "Well, well, well, Zia Bennett. If I weren't just thinking about you this morning!"

"Mr. Holleran!" comes the voice of the Haven Chronicle's most celebrated reporter. We met while I investigated the Whiskey Pete's case half a decade ago and we kept up a friendly working relationship since. Scratching backs, and all that. If the old crime flicks taught me anything, it's that it pays well for a PI to have a reporter friend, and the movies really didn't lie. Zia's fed me more information than The Beatles had number one hits. "What do I hear about you pretending to be press? Are you looking to change careers? Davey Teague's hiring, could put in a word for you."

I laugh, the tension in my shoulders evaporating. "Ah, no, don't think me and Davey would mix all too well, you know? Even though I did pull his favorite employee outta Whiskey Pete's unharmed. Now how would you know about me and my moonlighting as a member of Haven's press pack, huh?"

"Duh, have you met me? I'm Zia Bennett!"

Beside me, Diana's turned to her book again, a content smile on her face. Gotta remember, whatever I'm experiencing inside, she is, too.

"In my defense, I never claimed I was press. The dude assumed, and I didn't exactly disabuse him of that notion."

Zia laughs. "Well, why would you? If someone presumes,

play up to it, that's what I say. But it's a pain for me when the one guy who looks like he might say something tells me to buzz off because he's talked to the press already, and the person he described didn't pay all too well."

"Didn't pay? I gave him sixty dollars for scraps!" I shake my head. "So, you're looking for some information, Zia? They locked down Greaney's pad already?"

She sighs. "Yeah. Locked it up tight, Nick. No getting in. They won't even confirm he's dead."

There's the hint of a question in her voice. If she's been down there, and she has, she'd have seen the emergency vehicles. Other folk live in that house, Kieran's wife, the twenty-four hour a day, seven days a week staff, but she doesn't know for sure. I'll throw her a line. Why not?

"I saw his body. He is."

"You got inside?"

"Course I did, it's me."

"And?"

Diana's head spins to the side, like a dog who's heard the rustling of a food packet and as she does, a hint of static invades my line.

"Nick…pretend…bad…Come on!" Zia's voice swims in and out of reception. "…gotta…shitting…"

"I'll call you back!" I bark, flicking on my signals and cut sideways through the traffic, looking for somewhere to park. Anywhere.

"Nick, I can't feel anything." Diana's still staring out of the window, leaning forward so she's almost pressed against the pane. "It was there, all the emotions, all the life, and now… nothing! It's like a pocket of feeling just doesn't exist anymore!"

I find a spot and swing the Mustang into it, ignoring the honks of outrage at my wild maneuver and crappy parking. Can't remember if I hung up on Zia, or she ended the call, but pure static is pouring through the speakers now. Loud, hateful white noise from the depths of Hell itself, cutting into my brain, so insistent I wanna cover my ears and hide under the seat.

"Where?"

Diana points across the lines of traffic. We're on the edge of downtown, not too far from my old apartment, a pad I still own and I'm renting out because Rosa's smart like that. Her finger's aimed at an alleyway that runs behind the building. Can see my old window from where I'm sat. This ain't no goddamn coincidence.

"Over there." Kid's finger shakes as she moves it away from the spot, her voice wobbling as she explains. "The emotions come back a little on either side. Whatever this thing is, it's in there."

"Bout time I find out what it is then, eh?" I go to open the car door, then pause. "Now, kid, I'm not saying you can't come, but give me a minute or so, right?"

"Nick—"

"Don't 'Nick' me!" I snap, a little too harsh, truth be told. "Look, you can come along, but I wanna get a look at it first, and, like I said last night, just 'cos you're dead it doesn't make you safe, right? There's a good chance that thing took Kieran Greaney's soul, and I'm not letting that happen to you, got it?"

Wonder of wonders, Diana just nods. "I'll count to sixty."

"Make it a hundred," I mutter, pushing the car door open. "A slow one hundred."

"Nick!"

I slam the door shut, cutting off her protests.

I know what you're thinking. Nick Holleran doesn't learn the hard lessons that are dealt out to him. He had his ass beaten just over twelve hours ago and here he is, running head-first into danger, alone, the one-man show at it again.

Normally, you'd be right, but not this time. I meant what I said, and I heard what the wise souls surrounding me said, too. I can't do all this alone anymore, shouldn't have been doing it in the first place, but that doesn't mean I can drop others right into the middle of trouble because of it. Whatever this static-creating sonofabitch is, it might hurt Diana. It'll hurt me, too, if Kieran

Greaney's corpse is anything to go by, but I ain't planning on confronting it.

I wanna lay eyes on it. That's all. See what I'm dealing with, and if I can put it down right now, get the drop on it… that's a bonus and I'll take it. So that means, for the moment, leaving the kid behind. I hate to say this, but it's the truth. She's too unpredictable just now. Setting aside the danger I might put her in, she might well make matters worse by going all supernova again. Decision made, gonna have to leave with it till she can count to one hundred.

Right then, my brain decides to remind me I'm clean out of Expungers. Battenspurgers too. Fuck me. I ain't exactly prepared for a scrap with just my Ruger for company, but like I said, this is just a recon mission unless I get a chance I can't turn down.

Walking in front of the Mustang, I glance in. Diana's lips move as she's counting, and my hand falls to my Ruger's grip. At least I got that.

"Need to go through Harry and Maeve's books more thoroughly and see if there's any other weapons I can get my hands on," I mutter, eyeing the alley way and shuddering. Don't exactly have the greatest of histories with alley ways. "Some magical relic or something."

Huh, like magic exists. This is Hell, Nick, not Disneyland.

Suppose weirder shit happens down here every day, though.

I break out into a run, passing the Mustang's hood, weaving my way past the slow-moving traffic and to the other sidewalk, breath fogging the air a little. Rain's stopped and there's an icy bite to the air again. Pulling my trench coat a little tighter around my chest, I lean up against the wall of what used to be Behan's Wine and Dine, sadly now abandoned and shuttered, and peer around the corner.

Glancing over my shoulder, I reckon Diana's counted to twenty at the most. I suck on my teeth and run my tongue over them, sweat beading on my forehead and on the back of my neck despite the cold.

The alley way's a damned sight gloomier than it should be.

It isn't just whatever's lurking in there, it's what's behind me. Dean fucking Wheeler. Last time I went chasing down one of these things, he fired three pieces of lead into my chest. Practically killed me.

But he's dead, Nick. Dead and Expunged. No coming back from that.

Thirty. Gotta move.

Breathing in, and letting my fingers fall on top of the Ruger, the metal giving me a little courage, I pull it from its holster, grip it with both my hands. Nice and steady.

Once more into the breach we go.

My steps are heavy, even though I'm trying to walk light. It doesn't pay to go stomping after a thing you're looking to sneak up on. Fog flows in front of me when I breathe, like I'm vaping. My old apartment block is above me, and this alley leads right to the side street that links to the entryway to the underground parking lot. I might have glanced outta my window a hundred times and seen this alleyway and never gave it a second thought, and now I'm here. Without even thinking, I glance over my shoulder, half expecting to find the specter of Dean Wheeler following me, but it's just lines of traffic. Nothing more.

Ahead of me, a shape emerges from the gloom. A hunched, sloping figure, like it's in pain and it's sinking in on itself.

Forty.

I slow my steps, raising the Ruger. Whoever it is stands about my height, probably taller if it weren't so twisted, and a frown forms on my head as more details emerge. Colors, too. Its hair is a bright red, and the robe it wears is a mottled green and brown. The hem falls just above its bare ankles, the skin pale as chalk where the flesh isn't filthy from the crud-infested Haven streets. Its hunched shoulders rise and fall as it takes in breath, and the exhale fogs the air ahead of it.

Colors. Dirt. Breathing.

Those details rule this being a specter out. As do the whispers tickling my hearing. They're coming from ahead.

"...Feel him. Smell him all around me. Hungry, so hungry." The voice is faint, but the sound of it makes my back teeth ache. It's a guttural, strangled cat's mewling that sets my fillings to 'vibrate only'. "Ahead. To the side. Behind. But, up there, he was *there*. He might be still." The creature's head cocks to the side. Listening to a reply only it can hear. "But she hasn't sinned. I *can't*! Not her. No. Not yet. Must be stronger. Him, and those like him. Yes. Their sins are the sweetest of nectars and I can devour them... So hungry."

She?

Fifty.

Holding my breath, I train the Ruger's muzzle in the direction of the red-haired thing's cranium and take one more step forward.

The crack when my foot comes down against the glass on the alley way's ground echoes like a fucking firework let off at close quarters.

The thing spins, its eyes meeting mine, and, in that moment, I understand the fear etched into the face of Kieran Greaney's corpse, even though he should never be able to see this. The shock of burning red hair sits atop a face without form, a face without shape. Like it's a mockery of a human created by some creature who only read about facial features in a textbook. Its dark purple eyes are round like a true circle, set too far apart, and lack any pupil or whites. The nose doesn't have a bridge. Instead it's like a lone hill poking above a white surface, the nostrils misshapen black caverns peering out of it. Ears, pointed in all the wrong places, just from under its uneven, shaggy mane. Oversized, the tops almost adjacent to the top of its head, the lobes near its chin. It's a pasty white Picasso gone badly wrong. A hideous joke.

All that ain't the worst of it.

The creature's mouth hangs loose in a disconnected grin, its gray lips stuck to its face like lifeless slugs. Blackened sharp teeth reveal themselves in its maw.

I take all this in during the time it takes me to squeeze the Ruger's trigger, and the firing mechanism roars into action, the bullet aimed straight between those too-wide purple orbs.

The creature, hunched and twisted, shifts. I can't describe another term for it. The sonofabitch doesn't move, it doesn't roll. One second it's where I aimed for, the next it's closer to me and to my right, out of the way of the bullet's trajectory.

Sixty.

Then the weakness hits me.

Before, it felt like flu fatigue. The kind that makes you think slow and act even slower. The one that took the edge from your strength, but you could still walk to the restroom and take a leak even though your muscles felt like water.

This time, it's like they've turned to sludge and rubber.

The Ruger falls from my grip, my fingers no longer strong enough to hold onto it, and I drop to the ground after it, my back smashing against the concrete, my head cracking against the cement.

Dizziness hits me along with a warm, wet feeling, and the breath whooshes out of my lungs, but I can't lift my arms. I can't roll over. All I can do is watch as the monster shifts so it's lurking right above me, that slack grin aimed my way, those dead purple eyes meeting mine.

I blink, look away, and behind it, in the shadow, I see that boney Clint Eastwood-looking motherfucker Charon grin at me. If I had the strength to lift my Ruger, I'd send the last bullet I fire his way. Won't do shit, but at least he'd get the message. The Ferryman's alien eyes burn through the surrounding darkness, and I look away, back to the creature that's gonna end my life.

Seventy.

My thoughts jumble together, my brain struggling to make sense of my surroundings. The scent of strawberries fills my nose, and rushing water tickles the edges of my hearing as the sensation of a hook pulling from just behind my navel cuts through my core. The creature's maw opens wider, and there's too many pointed teeth in that ruination of a mouth. It lifts a finger, pointing it my way.

"Nick Holleran," it whispers, its voice jagged claws down a rough chalkboard. "*Bíodh do pheacaí mar dheireadh agat.*"

Wait. I've heard those words. Heard them before. Where...

Eighty.

A scream tears from my throat as the tugging at my navel explodes into burning pain. My back arches from the filthy alleyway ground and, I swear to God, I stare at my stomach expecting to see my spine explode out of it. My vision's red at the edges, the color of the creature's hair looming over me, another monster in an alleyway, but this time, there isn't no Heaven waiting for me. It's Charon and the Seal.

The creature cocks its head to the side once more, its wide grin getting slacker and a tortured half-giggle bubbles from its lips.

"There's no Charon for you, Nick Holleran," it wheezes. "There's only me..."

From the shadows, Charon charges forward, sword scraping across the ground, sparks flying in his wake. Then he lifts it, the blade overhead, and brings it crashing down, aimed at the creature. Charon. My fucking savior!

"Sin-Eater!" Charon's roar sets my head pounding. Makes my skull rattle. "The Fateless is *mine*!"

The creature—Sin Eater?—eyes still locked on mine, lifts a lazy hand Charon's way, like it's about to ward off a face-splitting blow from the Sword of Death but it really can't be bothered stopping it, it's too much effort, and death by body splitting would be much more convenient for everyone...

And the sonofabitch stops it in its tracks.

I'm not sure who's most surprised. Me or Charon. Him at some twisted, red-headed grinning freak absorbing the blow and stopping it like a grown adult would handle a toddler armed with a feather duster, or me, shocked at the pain and weakness leaving my body like it never existed, and at what's unraveling right before my eyes.

"You can't be. Already?" Charon hisses, eyes that hold the souls of billions wide in disbelief.

Sin-Eater shakes its head from side to side, its mockery of a grin a gash in reality revealing true Hell behind it.

"This one is spoken for, Dullahan. *Thosaigh an bás*!"

Shadows sweep in from the sides of the alley, and Sin-Eater twists its hand and pushes, sending Charon back into them. The sonofabitch straight up disappears. Just like that. Death himself. Death from every religion, every myth, each legend since stories began. Gone. Sent away. How?

Ninety.

"Sin is greater than death, Nick Holleran," the creature whispers. It can hear my goddamn thoughts. It's the only explanation. "Before death, there was sin." It giggles. "It'll exist afterward, too. Floating in the Great Divide when all that was created is no more."

The weakness slams into me again, but I wasn't just lying idly by and catching the show. My fingers danced their way over to the Ruger and when they curl around the grip, strength returns, flowing from my hand and into my shoulder, pushing the weakness away.

"Let's see how you feel about holy water infused bullets, motherfucker." Grinning, I aim the barrel right between Sin-Eater's eyes.

I squeeze, and the Ruger clicks. Out of bullets. No way. No fucking way!

"God damn it!" I scream and, in a fit of pure desperation, I throw the gun right at the bastard. It's all I can do. That one measly act of defiance.

One hundred.

The kid'll be leaving the car now, racing across the street, but it's too late. I just hope Sin-Eater wants nothing to do with Diana. I'm the one he wants, and my little eyeless ghost-girl must be the 'she'. Or maybe it's Rosa. Makes more sense, Charon called the kid a sinner, but maybe this new sheriff in town has a different view. But I need to stop this creep however I can.

My focus returns to the Ruger flying through the air, and as I desperately rack my head thinking of anything I can do, it slams into Sin-Eater's face. And it *screams.*

I huddle on the floor, covering my ears, squeezing my eyes shut against the torrent of noise filling my head. A thousand car alarms exploding at once batter my eardrums, try to pummel me senseless. I crack an eye open, needing to see. Needing to bring some kind of order to the cacophony of chaos assaulting me.

Steam rises from between Sin-Eater's fingers as it presses them against its ruined face. Still screaming, the lights in my old apartment block behind it flicker and those car alarms? They're real. Its scream of pain spreads like an EMP, distorting anything electrical in the vicinity.

Covering my ears, I scramble to my knees, looking for anything else to use. Maybe I can run?

"No!" Sin-Eater wails, pulling its hands away. A thick, Ruger shaped burn covers its face. Crimson against the snow. "Get away from me!"

Frowning, I try to stand, but ice floods my shoulder, and Sin-Eater shifts away, flickering and jerking like a monster from an old movie scene, away down the alley and outta sight.

"Are you okay, Nick?" Panic floods Diana's high-pitched voice. "Did it hurt you?"

I rub my temples, the echoes of the scream lingering, and give my head a shake. Pain eats away at me, and there's a warm wet at the back of my skull. Pressing my fingers there brings further agony, and my fingers come away bloody. Fucking great, but I've had worse. The Ruger's lying on the concrete, and I scramble over to take a look at it. Just as I thought, there's bullets left. Sin-Eater jammed it somehow.

"Yeah, I'm fine. I'll live." I turn back to her, grinning. "You'll never guess what—"

Tiny washed out palms come my way. A push. A frustrated

push, but it connects like a freight train.

First, there's the ice flooding through my body, from face to foot. Then pain like I've had a wisdom tooth removed without anesthetic. Next I'm flying backward, knocked clean off my feet, and more agony explodes from the back of my skull, again, as it slams into the side of what used to be Behan's Wine and Dine.

"What the—" I manage, vision spinning, but then Diana's looming over me. And when I say looming, I fucking mean looming.

The kid's hovering in mid-air.

CHAPTER EIGHT

LESSONS GOTTA BE LEARNED ONE DAY...

Diana's a good foot off the ground, arms outstretched, her teeth showing as her lips curl back. Just when I thought things couldn't get any worse, my kid goes all fucking vengeance and fury.

Hell really has it out for ol' Nick Holleran.

"Diana." Despite the pain in my face, chest, and in the back of my head, I show her the palms of my hands. I should be angry. The kid just shoved me clean off my feet, but I haven't ever seen anything like this. Anything. "Hey. It's me. Nick. Come on, why don't you, ah, calm down and—"

"Don't tell me to calm down, Nick!" Diana's voice is deeper than before. Commanding. Pissed. "Don't you *dare* tell me to calm down. Not after this!"

"Hey, okay, you're in charge, kid. I won't tell you what to do." I push my back against the wall, straightening my torso out so I'm not all crumpled and beaten up, which I have been far too much for my liking this last eighteen hours. Less than eighteen hours, in fact. Fuck me. "Everything's okay. I promise."

"But it might not have been!" Diana thunders, and she pulls away from the ground a little more. "Rosa told you. *I* told you! Stop putting yourself in danger. Stop trying to protect us. And what do you do? *What do you do?*"

"I—"

"You ignore us! You ignore us, you tell us to wait, and you

almost get yourself killed *again*! You go into a dark alley to look at a creature you don't know with just a *gun*!" Diana's outstretched arms tremble. "Have you got a death wish, Nick? Is that it? Are me and Rosa not good enough for you?"

I get to my knees, edging a little closer to her. There's a light building up inside of her. A brightness. White like snow. Just like the blast that forced Lilith away last night. Flicking my eyes left and right, I see specters congregating in the alley, watching the commotion, Diana's screams and power no doubt drawing them here. They've come to view the show, but if she erupts like she did last night, it might be the last thing these poor bastards see in Hell. I can't risk that, no matter what it might do to me.

"Alright, I get it," I breathe, edging a little closer, shuffling on my knees. "I understand."

"No, you don't!" She screams, and the light gets that little bit brighter. "You say you do but you don't. If you understood, you wouldn't leave me alone when I can help. If you understood, you wouldn't keep putting yourself in these situations where you might die! Charon wants you, this other creature wants you. There's no coming back for you, Nick. There's no Heaven, there's no Hell. Not for you! Can't you see that?"

"Yeah, I can see that." She's staring down at me, but she isn't seeing. The kid's locked up in her anger, in her frustration. I get that, I've been there myself but right now, I've put the poor girl there. I've done this to her. Diana and Rosa's been trying to teach me, but I haven't been listening even if I've fooled myself into thinking I have. "One life left. Ain't that what Lucifer said? That's what I've got."

I shuffle a step closer, and she drops a touch. The light dims, just a touch. A blessed touch.

"Yes, and you haven't been living that way." A sob touches her words. "I-I-I...I can't—"

I'm in touching distance. Reaching out, I take her hands in mine, letting the chill seep into my forearms and into my biceps. Just let it spread. It's her, and I accept it.

"You can't *what*?" I ask, meeting those pits of hers, trying to imagine what she used to look like, but then I don't.

It isn't fair. This is who she is. Who she'll always be and I gotta understand that.

Diana stares down at our hands. "I already lost one family, Nick. Don't make me lose another, okay?"

I pull her into me, back to the ground, holding her against my chest, her icy essence spreading everywhere it touches. Shivers wrack my muscles. Goosebumps break out across my skin, and my teeth wanna chatter, but none of that matters. The tears stinging my eyes do. The thick sensation in my throat does.

"I'm sorry," I croak. "I didn't realize."

"You and Rosa are the only family I have left, Nick," Diana sobs against my chest, the white light gone, her voice back to its normal pitch. The ghosts drift away, show over. "Every time you go out alone, I think I'm never going to see you again. Every time. If you die, there's a chance you won't come back like I did. Charon. The Seal. Heaven. There's no guarantee."

I rest my jaw against the top of her head and let the moment drift. Huh, the smell of strawberries and the tinkling of water's gone, replaced by the usual alleyway stench of filth and crap. Back in Haven, the car alarms have stopped, and the slow churn of traffic fills the air once more.

"I won't leave you behind again," I say, nodding. "If that's how you feel, I won't."

She pulls away from me, bottom lip trembling. "Don't make promises you can't keep, Nick. I just want you to know, okay? My family died after me, I didn't get to say goodbye, but my dad went first and I didn't *want* to say goodbye, and I don't want to have that same thing with my new dad, okay? They were all taken away from me before I was ready, if I ever could be ready! I don't want to go through that again. Not with you."

Dad. Me. The kid's dad. Yeah, I look after her, but I never knew that's how she saw me... A part of me wants to tell her that's life, and we don't always get to say goodbye. Sometimes we gotta sit there and watch a loved one waste away. Other times we never know when Charon's gonna collect, even though he's stuck to me like a fly on shit. But this isn't the time nor the place. Kid's only been Aware a matter of months, and she's had to grieve for her family. Confront her murderer. Learn a new life in death, and I haven't exactly helped her.

"Okay, kid, okay. I'll do better." I get to my feet, her hand still in mine. "Let's say we head to the Styx instead of the office? Told Ruby I'd call by, and I could use a little patching up. Would you like that?"

She nods. "I would. Sorry for shoving you."

"No, you're not."

A small grin appears on her lips. "No, I'm not."

We head back to the Mustang, and I fish out my cell, sending Rosa a text asking her to meet us at the Styx. She can keep the kid occupied for a while, and I really could do with seeing her.

I gotta talk to Rubes, too. Not only about last night. Not only about the kid, and the static, the problems between the Nephilim and this Sin Eater, with its hankering for a taste of ol' Nick Holleran and its swatting away of Charon like he was a moth bothering a lightbulb.

I gotta find out if there's a different way. Mine isn't working all too well, and, like I said to Diana, I only got one life left.

Taking one last look around before I duck into the Mustang, I pause. Charon came looking for me, but Suraz didn't. He's usually always on my tail, I know he ain't been today, but I thought he might. For old time's sake.

Whatever's keeping him away from me won't be pleasant. Sighing, I get into the Mustang. A problem for another time. Got plenty on my plate already.

"I meant to grab you, that's all," Diana whispers, not looking my way.

"Huh?" I'm rubbing at the back of my head, and I reckon she noticed. "Oh, that."

"I just got so *angry*! All of a sudden. I was worried, and a little annoyed that you'd told me to count to a hundred, but not that furious." She shakes her head. "When the creature disappeared, all the emotions from around me, including yours, hit me like a wave. I thought I was going to explode."

No shit.

"Look, we'll figure it out. Okay, kid?" Damn, another wrinkle. She's turning into some kind of emotional hand grenade. "Don't worry about it."

She nods, frowning down at her book. I grip the steering wheel, staring at the slow-moving traffic. For a moment, I just sit there, heart hammering in my chest, the noise of the city merging into a cat's chorus in my ears, my brain unable to separate the sounds. A selfish part of me's glad Diana's so adamant about sticking by my side. She might keep Sin-Eater away, and I'm not sure what else can. Swallowing, I close my eyes, and flick the radio on, letting my tunes dampen the rest of the noise, giving me a moment's clarity. Just like I did when I was a kid, when it all got too much for me.

When's all this trouble gonna stop stacking up, huh? When I'm dead. And maybe not even then.

CHAPTER NINE

...BEFORE IT'S TOO LATE

It's early afternoon by the time we walk into the Styx. For a while, me and the kid just talked in the car. Well, she talked, and I listened, her admission about the sensory overload like the breaking of a dam. First, she spoke about her old man, and what it was like to lose him. She had to pick up a lot of slack at home then, which I knew about, but the kid never went into too much detail before. Then she moved on to the rest of her family.

"I knew when I became Aware and when you told me what year it was that my momma would have passed," she whispered, clutching her book to her chest. "But my sisters. I'd hoped to at least see them, Nick. I never got to say goodbye, or tell them what happened to me, and I never will."

Can't say I can comfort her. Telling her they're in Heaven won't do much for a lonely girl without a family. Least that's what I always figured. Never had the best of relationships with my folks, even before I stumbled on their sick little secret. It never bothered me when the reaper came to collect on them, and there's no doubt in my mind they got the end they fucking deserved. It isn't something I enjoy talking about, and there's no hope in Hell I'm gonna go into it with the kid. Not now. Not even Rosa knows. So I just listened. What else could I do?

After that, we just watched the traffic go by, the trickle of blood matting with my hair and crusting over, giving Rosa time to arrive at the Styx. I overheard Sin-Eater. It can smell where I've been, which means going to any of my regular haunts is gonna cause issues.

Unless I got Diana at my side.

Yeah, those pieces slid together pretty well for me without too much jiggling. Every time the static's hit, and the weakness washed over me, it went away because of Diana's presence. She sat in the car ahead with Rosa last night when the hints of static first began, she watched TV at home afterward when it exploded all around us. Both times, it went away, or turned its attention elsewhere. When Sin-Eater couldn't suck on my transgressions, it must have latched onto the biggest miscreant close-by. Kieran Greaney. It said it was hungry. Sin-Eater's gotta feed. If it can't suck on my soul, then... Well. Plenty of sinners in Hell.

In the alley, Diana must have been too far away. I stalled it when I hit it with my Ruger, but Diana forced it away when she arrived on the scene.

So, even if she didn't insist, the kid's staying by my side. Prudence trumps worry, right? Issue with that is, once Sin-Eater runs, Diana goes supernova. Wonderful.

I gotta talk it through with someone, and that's where Ruby and the Styx comes into play. I do my best thinking when I'm rubber ducking, throwing a load of crap at a wall until someone tells me to rein it in and take a look at what I've spewed a little closer.

Fuck me, right? I'm a collaborator after all.

The Styx is quiet, and that's when I like it best. Look, I'm a music lover—though, Tomb Of Nick Cage aside, the taste of bands on the upper level doesn't really appeal—but when business slows down, the chatting begins. Nothing like a little peace and quiet to talk some shop.

We head downstairs, nodding at the almost-mute bartender, Guz, whose face doesn't even twitch when I walk on by. Been coming here for just over five years, and I reckon he's said one word for every twelve months I've darkened his step. Music from the jukebox drifts through the door to the lower Styx, and I smile. Waylon Jennings.

Now, there's a ghost here who *insists* he sold his soul to the devil, Robert Johnson style. In fact, there's a spook who plays here on the regular who *says* he's the singer himself, but that's another story altogether. So, our soul-seller goes by the name of Hank Jones, a cowboy name if I ever heard one, and he looks the part. Walking in, he's in front of the jukebox right now, a wide stetson hat on top of a craggy gray face adorned with a heavy mustache. The denims and leathers Hank wears look genuine enough to me, as does his ankle-length duster, and he carries a pair of Smith and Wesson on his hips. Reckons he killed over thirteen men in the frontier days, including Billy the Kid, and that's what he sold his soul for; the title of the west's deadliest gunslinger.

Nice fella.

What he's doing in Haven, he hasn't ever said, and who killed him, he won't expand on. Hiding underneath his, admittedly fucking cool, brown leather duster is a gaping hole right above his heart. Looks like he got shot at point-blank range by a dude who wasn't looking to take any prisoners.

Guess deals with the devil have an expiry date.

Anyway, Rosa's sitting at a table near the jukebox, Ruby with her, and Hank's looking her way, crooning to ol' Waylon Jennings as he does, and he waves at me as I come in.

"Holleran!" he yells, sounding like an extra from the TV show Deadwood. "Long time no see, son. Your lady friend's swell company. Quiet, but perty on the eyes. Not that she can see or yammer at me, huh?"

The frown eating into her forehead disappears when she sees me, relief replacing it.

"Nick! Is everything okay? Is Diana okay? Oh, God, you look like crap."

Heading over, I give her a long, long kiss. Savor it. After the day I've had, I reckon I'm well within my rights to take my sweet time over it.

"Thanks. Diana's fine, she's right here," I murmur, finally pulling away. The kid's staring in the opposite direction and if her skin weren't all washed out, I'd say a little rouge has made its way onto her cheeks. "Been a morning. I'll let the kid bring you up to speed, I gotta talk with Rubes, okay?"

"Nick—"

"I'm not dodging or leaving you outta the loop," I say, indignant all of a sudden. I lower my voice to a hoarse whisper. "I just need her calming down, is all."

Rosa looks at me like I've forgotten how to speak English. "Nick, I can't hear Diana. Unless you're going to get her to slowly scrawl it all out for me."

"Oh." I rub the back of my neck, the dried blood thick under my fingers. "Oh, yeah. That."

Ruby clears her throat, and I catch the end of her eye roll she's sending Diana's way. "Sweetie," she says, smiling at the kid. "You've never been in the backroom, have you?"

"Your office?" Diana replies, frowning over at me. Guess she overheard. "No. Why?"

Ruby's smile widens. "I'll be honest with you, I think Nick wants to talk to me without you around, and I know that sucks, but he probably has his reasons."

"So he thinks," Diana mutters. Then she gazes at her shoes. "I kind of shoved him into a wall. Hard."

"You pushed him into a wall? Way to go Diana!" Ruby gasps and half laughs, pretending to be shocked. Rosa's jaw drops. "Plenty of people have wanted to do the same to him every day, sweetie," she says like I just clean stopped existing. "Don't worry about it."

"Hey," I mutter. Can't help it. "I'm standing right here!"

But everyone ignores me. The victim in this crime.

"I've got plenty of books back there." Ruby winks. "And a TV. Or you might want to go listen to the music upstairs?"

"No thanks, TV is fine." Diana's moving before the sentence ends, the door to the office behind the bar swinging open as she approaches and then closes behind her.

"Thanks," I say, taking a seat. Before I know it, my head's in my hands as the morning's full events hit me. "Not gonna lie, I got a lotta problems."

"And Diana is one of them." It isn't a question from Ruby. "Rosa was telling me about last night."

I glance at Rosa and smile. "It just got a lot worse. I don't even know where to fucking start. You already heard about the freight train act, anyway."

Shaking my head, I let a sigh ease out of me and think about where I need to pick up the tale, and it comes to me. It starts with the Nephilim while Rosa's brought Ruby up to speed on last night's activities. What a morning. And by Hell's standards, that's really saying something.

"First, do you have anything to clean the back of my head? A few Tylenol wouldn't go amiss, either..."

"Jesus, Nick." Rosa takes my hand and squeezes it, unaware of the gaggle of ghosts surrounding our table as I spilled my guts. A few came in while I did, fixed up on their own drinks of paintstripper and came on over. "Jesus."

Ruby listened to me without asking a single question. Barely looked away, either. Eye contact isn't my strong suit, so I spoke to the crowd. Multiple wet cloths on the back of my head came away bloody, but the throbs died. Good old American over-the-counter painkillers, what would we do without you?

"Sin-Eater," she finally says. "Can't say I ever heard of a creature going by that name."

The congregated ghosts shrug, faces worried but with nothing to say to help.

"Scram," I say, glancing at them all. "Unless any of you have anything to add?" They don't. Didn't think so. Rosa blinks, realization dawning, and she shivers. Turning back to Rosa, I shrug. "We might have heard of it. All manner of creatures have all kinds of names in Hell, right?"

"I guess."

"And like Diana said, we don't know the effect they have on modern tech if they ain't been around for a while." I offer her my infamous lop-sided grin. "Maybe if those freaks in the Cult of Dagon actually succeed in waking Cthulhu, all the microwave signals we have floating about the place might send him right off back to his eternal slumber."

"Wait, Cthulhu is *real*?" Rosa asks, jaw hanging open. "I mean, really *real*."

"Rosa, it's Hell. Everything's real." I hold up a finger. "Except werewolves. They don't exist, and I'm not sure why, but they don't. Or magic. I think."

But what do I know?

"Cthulhu..." she breathes. Starting to think this is all a little too much for her.

"Let's just go through this in case I missed anything." Raising a paw, I start checking off fingers. "Humanoid shape and form, affects electricity, radio and phone waves, has some kind of energy drain power, dampens the kid's empathy read, seems to sense where I've been, talks about sin a lot, can tell Charon to fuck off. Missing anything?"

"It doesn't like your Ruger, Nick." Rosa tilts her head to the side, then nods. "Well, not so much the bullets, it can stop those from firing, like you said, but the actual gun itself."

I pull it out of my holster, examining it. Faint scorch marks kiss the steel where it struck Sin-Eater.

"Another thing," Ruby says. "Seems like Diana keeps it away."

"Right." I nod. "Figured that part out already."

"And her keeping it away sent it elsewhere," Rosa mutters, shaking her head. "Anyone who's sinned."

Fucking Hell, huh? That's gonna be a real problem.

"Diana's right about Harry and Maeve's books, Nick," Ruby

says, tugging at her earlobe. "The knowledge they had is great, but we haven't exactly kept up on updating it all, neither did they, and it's spread across so many volumes. Much of what I know is transcribed from oral histories and the like. It isn't ideal for cross-referencing facts about creatures we're unsure of. I heard Suraz talking a few weeks back when he came in for a drink, warning Bob the Skinwalker about an influx of Hellspawn; creatures that haven't been seen in centuries are flooding into Haven and elsewhere. There's a ton we don't understand about this place."

I heard an idea I like, and I grab a hold of it.

"Cross-referencing. Like on a computer," I mutter, and a big ol' lightbulb appears over the top of my head. "Hey, Rosa, you work in the library! Couldn't you do that?"

The look she gives me makes the lightbulb pop.

"Oh, sure, let me just go and create a database of all the Truther's knowledge on Hell we have, and whatever Ruby has on it too, just like that." She rolls her eyes. "Should have it done in about two or three years. Does that work for you, honey?"

"Point taken," I say, rubbing the back of my neck. "It's not a bad idea, though..."

"No, it isn't." Ruby stares up at the ceiling. "And it's something we really should have done a long time ago."

"Maybe somebody has," Rosa says, biting her lip. "I don't mean to be critical, and I know I'm new on this scene, and I don't exactly understand much, but you and Nick can't be all there is, is there?"

I frown. "What do you mean?"

"I mean, I get that you're Haven's one-and-only Paranormal Investigator, and Ruby runs the Styx and knows plenty about Haven, but Hell isn't just Haven, is it?" Rosa shrugs. "And Haven's a pretty big place. Maybe there are others you don't know about. Harry and Maeve lived here, after all."

"In Haven? Think I'd have met them, right?" I laugh, but the smile on my lips fades when I glance at Ruby. She isn't exactly grinning. "What? There *are* others?"

Ruby folds her arms. "There might be one or two people I haven't introduced you to yet, Nick."

"What?" By the jukebox, ol' Hank scowls at me for shouting too loud and disturbing his tunes. But seriously? One or two people? "Who? Why?"

"Why? Because you don't exactly make good first impressions, that's why."

"She's not completely wrong," Rosa murmurs, and all I can do is laugh again.

It's one of those laughs. You know, the type filled with disbelief, a little bit of indignation, but a lot of understanding. If the last day's taught me anything, it's that I ain't winning any popularity contests. Their loss. I'm a great fucking guy!

"It isn't many people, Nick." Ruby's cheeks reflect the color of her name. At least she's a little ashamed. "The one I'm thinking of is a collector of relics and information. I don't know who it is, I've never met him, but I know how to get in touch with his people. The other... Well, we'll talk about them another time. They don't really like... people and they only get in touch with me when they need something."

"I don't like secrets, Ruby," I say with a petulant huff. "Well, that said, it's a start. Think you can arrange a meet and greet? Maybe this collector can help."

Ruby winces, which really doesn't help my hurting sense of justice.

"I'll see what I can do. You don't have the best of reputations, Nick."

"Really?" I deadpan. "Tell me more."

Ruby shrugs. "A lot of people think you're a little brash, smug, you don't play too well with others, and you attract the wrong kind of attention from people you shouldn't. I've heard the word 'schmuck' thrown around more than once."

This time I *do* make eye contact with her as I shake my head. "I wasn't being serious, Rubes."

The red in her cheeks deepens. "Oh."

"We can work on that," Rosa says, squeezing my hand again. "What about anyone else further afield?"

I glance down at her fingers wrapped around mine, and a lump forms in my throat. Here I was thinking all this might become too much for Rosa, and she's here, taking charge, making plans, and looking at ways to improve my admittedly flagging personal relations.

"I can make a few calls." Ruby sighs. "There's no denying I keep things local. With Harry and Maeve out of the picture that has to change. Now, getting back to Sin-Eater. You said it spoke in a language, Nick. Do you remember what it said? Just in the ballpark."

Drumming my fingers against the table, I shake my head. "No. I think I've heard the like of it before, but... No. Goddamn it."

A few cracks to the old noggin makes thoughts a little fuzzy.

"Never mind, we'll figure something out." Ruby gives me a weak smile. "We always do, right?"

"Eh. I'm still breathing, aren't I?"

The look the two women throw my way tells me I might not be for much longer.

Rosa clears her throat. "Putting aside Lilith, the cops up Nick's ass, the Nephilim in-fighting, and this Sin-Eater, what are we going to do about Diana?"

All three of us turn to stare at the office door. Wonder if the kid knows the discussion's now turned to her? She'd sense our emotions, alright. That's if Sin-Eater isn't around.

The thought makes me throw a glance over my shoulder. Place is still quiet enough, and there's always shadows but there isn't any Charon grinning at me from the gathering darkness for once. Could be my already weak popularity's taken a downturn, or Sin-Eater pushed the Ferryman a long, long way away. The pressing focus from Suraz hasn't returned yet, either. First time in a long time I wished either of those sons of bitches paid attention to me. I'd sure feel a damn sight safer.

"Figuring out exactly what Diana is and what she can do is a little more straightforward, I think." Ruby flashes a reassuring smile Rosa's way. "There are plenty of ghosts in Hell, and the search perimeters are narrower. Why don't you two leave the research to me on that front so she doesn't get suspicious? It can't be nice to have her family snooping around her."

Rosa doesn't so much as twitch when Ruby says the word 'family' and I gotta respect her for that. We ain't exactly what you'd call a normal set up.

"And the Collector," I say, rapping my knuckles on the table. "You'll get in touch? Tell them I wanna talk?"

"Sure, Nick." Ruby says 'sure' but the way her face looks when she's talking tells me she's anything but happy about it. "In the meantime, I suggest you two, and by two, I mean you Nick, treat Diana just the way she is?"

"And what's that?" I ask, folding my arms. Why's this pep talk aimed my way? Diana's the one who pushed me, for Christ's sake!

"Like a teenage girl who needs reassurance and love, but also a girl with a lot of power who can make a big difference."

Rosa lets go of my hand and gets to her feet. "Speaking of which, I'll go get her. I think it's time we went home for the night. Sin-Eater can't get us when Diana's around, can it? And you're definitely not going to the office now, Nick."

She stoops and plants a kiss on my cheek then heads behind the bar, my eyes having a hard time pulling away from her.

"Nick?" Ruby's voice disrupts my rapt attention.

"Yeah?"

"A little more advice for you, even if you don't want to hear it." She doesn't wait for me to say yes or no. "Let them help you. Both of them. I know Rosa isn't like us but if you keep trying to treat her like a delicate little flower then she won't stick around forever. You know that, don't you?"

I sigh. "I know. It's just that—"

"You want to keep them safe. I know that, and they do, too, but it isn't the 1950s. When you leave them behind, you're taking away their choice to act, you're telling them they're less capable than you, and no one wants to feel that way. No one of any sex or gender. You can keep them safe by working together, and they'll do the same for you."

The office door opens, and they come out, both smiling even though they can't interact. They're just happier in each other's presence, Diana no doubt finding comfort in Rosa's good soul. I was thinking about swinging by the office but after the day I've had, going home sounds swell.

"Don't forget this Collector," I say, getting to my feet. "Time's ticking, and if they can help, I need it right away. Just like you said. Help, right?"

"Sure, Nick, I'll do what I can."

Joining the others, Ruby waves our way as we head up the stairs and out into Haven. Sun's set, and the bright neon lights paint the snow-packed sidewalks. A blanket of the stuff's fallen since we arrived at the Styx.

"How'd you get here, anyway?" I ask Rosa, our footsteps crunching as they fall.

"Cab. Your text struck me as the serious type."

I grin. "You know me so well. Mustang's this way."

About two-hundred yards away, just where the car's parked, streetlights flicker. Store signs, too.

"Nick..." Diana breathes. "Oh, no. Not again. It's—"

Static interrupts street corner radios as I glance around, looking for any sign of the red-headed freak. Grabbing Rosa's hand, I point at the flickering illuminations.

"I know. Sin-Eater's here." I don't see it anywhere. "Keep moving. Let's put the theory of you being its Kryptonite to the test, huh?"

"And if it doesn't work?" Diana says.

"We improvise," I say, the supernova act fresh in my mind. "Another thing. Focus on your own feelings, not what you've lost, right? They're most important. Try and… I don't know, ground yourself or something."

Helpful, I know, but she nods, pits fixed on the snowy sidewalk.

Improvise. Even I don't like the sound of that, and I'm not exactly known for forward planning. We crunch forward, Diana's cold hand finding mine, my other clutching Rosa's. Around us, Aware specters pause, peering off at the funky shop signs. A few glance my way when they see me holding hands with one of their kind.

The streetlight above the Mustang turns solid, and a couple further down the sidewalk go on the fritz. Relief does a tap-dance in my guts.

"Come on, let's get to the car."

Pulling Rosa and Diana along, slipping a little in the ground-down snow, I pick up the pace, focused on the wave of flickering street lights and store signs we're forcing away. No, *we're* not pushing them back. The kid is.

Sliding to a halt next to the Mustang, I pull the door open for Rosa, almost shoving her inside, and rush over to my side, jumping in and starting the engine before I'm belted up.

Sin-Eater's gonna follow us, I know that. But it won't come near with Diana here. Pulling into traffic, I glance into my rear view, studying the kid as she peers out of the window, looking to catch a glimpse of Sin-Eater.

There's no way I'm leaving her behind now. My life depends on it. Not even deep down, I know that isn't fair. She's just a kid.

Kid or not, fair or not, it doesn't matter. This is Hell.

CHAPTER TEN

ANY CHANCE OF RESPITE? NOT A HOPE IN... DO I NEED TO SAY IT?

We don't say much on the way home. Rosa's got her head on my shoulder the entire way, kid's glued to her book in the backseat as the snow falls around us and all the Hellspawn milling around on the surface.

Despite it all, Hell's a pretty tranquil place at times. Makes me wonder what Heaven is like. I'll never see the place, so might as well daydream.

Christmas decorations shimmer as they hang from the sides of buildings, street signs, and trees, with all the yards and houses decked out in them, every neighbor and business trying to outdo the other. Ain't exactly the spirit of Christmas, but that went down the pan a long time ago, right? Decorations hang anywhere anyone can see, basically. It's that time of year. Reds, blues, greens, and whites. Wreaths sway in the gentle wind, and we pass at least three groups of carol singers congregating on street corners, complete with spectators of the living, dead, and otherwise variety.

Christmas. I looked forward to it this year. Me and Rosa planned to make it special for the kid, and I wanted to make it one to remember for them both. Staring outta my windshield though, watching all the Aware, Unaware, demons and Hellspawn pass on by, I'm struck with how stupid a notion that is. How can anything be *normal* in Hell even if it is kinda tranquil in this exact moment? Shit, I might go through Christmas week without so much as a sniff of trouble, only to have a pack of mannegishi stampeding right through my living room, and you can bet your bottom dollar they won't bring gifts. Or Mothman might come and land on my roof, pretending he's fucking Santa Claus.

Santa Claus. Huh? Is *he* real? It is Hell after all, and didn't I just tell Rosa everything except werewolves existed? Jesus, he's probably some kind of child-eating demon and maybe all these decorations are designed to keep the sonofabitch from attacking.

I mentally file that one away for another time.

"Happy thoughts, Nick," Diana murmurs from behind. "Happy thoughts."

I scowl for half a second, but let it slide away. She's right. Gotta think positive. Every job comes with its downsides, right? Firefighters don't go round worrying about fires that haven't happened yet, do they? This is the same when you boil right down to it. Well, kinda the same.

Well, not the same at all, but I'm gonna cling onto this sudden optimism with all my strength, goddammit!

"I got the turkey today," Rosa says, lifting her head from my shoulder, smiling as she gazes out of the window. "I thought it was a little rough, the city council closing the library for the holidays already, kids got to read and all that, but time off does come with its perks. Got you your present, too."

"Don't give me any hints," I say, grinning. "I'm a detective, I'll figure it out."

"A detective who has trouble deducing what's at the end of his nose most of the time." She laughs and plants a kiss on my cheek. "I'm so excited! You're going to love it!"

"Oh, so now you're upping the ante, huh?" I reply, glancing in my rear view. Diana's wearing a satisfied smile as she listens to us. "Telling me I'm gonna love mine, meaning I gotta pick really well when I decide on yours?"

Rosa does a fair job of letting out an indignant gasp, pretending she's all surprised. At least, I *think* she's pretending.

"You mean you haven't even decided on mine yet?"

I glance at her. Maybe she isn't pretending...

"I got a few ideas," I say, my voice a little shrill now I'm on the back foot. "Just wanna get it right, you know? This is our first official Christmas together. We always managed to miss it in the past."

"Managed to miss it? I always thought that was a ploy, so you never had to spend any money, you schmuck." Just when I'm convinced she *is* serious, Rosa winks, and kisses me on the cheek again. "I can't wait. *You're* going to do great. All I want is you and Diana at home, a few drinks, good food, a great movie, and an early night."

An early night, huh? Christmas does come but once a year, after all... Poor Christmas.

"Sounds wonderful. Any ideas for the movie?"

"Big Trouble in Little China."

I lean into my seat, shaking my head. "I love you."

"Don't make me say I know." Rosa smirks. "It's such a cliche."

"Right?" I say, slowing down as we turn into my avenue. "But I do love hearing you say it all the same."

She meets my eyes. "I know."

Ah, fuck. I really do love her, and I'm certain Diana the empath could back me up on that without any hesitation.

Rosa stretches and makes this little sound in the back of her throat when she does, a noise halfway between a growl and a purr. She's awfully cute when she does it.

"For a moment there, I almost forgot about all the nastiness and worry. Almost forgot we're literally living in Hell." She shudders then offers me a sad smile. "I could have had that ride last a lot longer. It's almost a shame we're—"

Christmas decorations and street lights going haywire cuts her off, and a sharp hiss from the backseat punctuates the background music in the Mustang turning to static. I pull the Mustang onto the sidewalk, scanning the street.

Sin-Eater's here.

"—home," she finishes, eyes as wide as saucers.

I spin in my chair, pointing at the kid.

"Focus on you and only you, remember? Don't panic because you can't feel anything, the emotions will return, okay? As soon as he's gone." Diana nods, and I turn back to Rosa. "We just stay together. Stay together, and Sin-Eater can't touch us."

"But he's going to go and kill someone else, Nick," Rosa whispers. "Unless we stop him. You said it was hungry, and you and Diana forcing it away has probably only made it worse."

Shit. When she's right, she's right, and Rosa isn't often wrong.

All the lights in the houses now are blinking on and off, and folk are pouring out into the street, some of them holding guns, others angry at their evening being interrupted by the lousy power company, or so they reckon. If only they knew the truth, they'd fucking hide and turn those weapons on themselves.

"Nick!" Ice seeps into my shoulder as the kid shouts down my ear, pointing through my window. "Look!"

All the house lights and decorations, even the ones outside mine, are on the fritz. All except my next-door neighbor's. Hudson's.

"Ah, crap," I mutter, hand falling to my Ruger. If I can't fire any bullets at Sin-Eater, I'll throw this at the bastard again.

"What is it?" Rosa asks, grabbing my arm as I reach for the door handle.

I nod at the solid beam of glorious lights from Hudson's joint. "Remember the security guard I told you about across from Greaney's?"

"Yeah?"

"Well, he said that when the static hit, all the lights in the neighborhood bugged out. All of them. Except the ones in Greaney's."

"Pretty big thing to leave out, Nick!" Rosa cries, opening her side.

"A lot's happened, can't expect me to remember every goddamn detail," I mutter, getting out of the Mustang. "Both of you, stay behind me but keep close. Let's go."

Keeping low, I hug the decorated hedges running down the sidewalk, keeping out of sight from any of the neighbors. Don't want anyone seeing me busting through Hudson's front door, especially if this goes south, and who am I kidding? Circumstances have an uncanny way of always going south where I'm concerned.

Thankfully no one's looking my way. They're all shouting back inside through their doors, asking for updates, staring up into the black night sky or yelling at their neighbors. Approaching my drive, I don't see Hudson standing in his, so I take a left, heading for the yard.

"Nick, where are you going?" Rosa hisses.

"Gonna climb over his fence. Don't wanna have to kick his front door in with folk outside."

"That... makes a lot of sense," she replies. Shocked.

The gate to the yard's open, and I hold it wide as Rosa rushes in with Diana flowing beside her. Nodding, I sprint over to the far side and pull myself over, scraping the inside of my thighs on the wood's edge. Rosa has no trouble, her Aikido training paying off in spades as she hoists herself over.

Diana just passes through it. Being a ghost has its perks. No stinging inner thighs for one.

Rubbing at my leg, I crouch, and pull my Ruger free. "Come on. Stay behind me."

"Won't Diana just force Sin-Eater away?" Rosa asks.

"That's the plan, but hopefully I can see some weakness first. We know very little about it, and we gotta learn what we can, when we can."

"What if the backdoor is locked?"

"What is this, twenty questions?" I breathe, shaking my head. "Now's not the time... But I'd rather break that one than the front, right?"

We edge forward, the silence pouring out of Hudson's is

ominous. I'm reminded of the old movie saying. '*It's quiet...*' I glance over at Diana.

"You alright, kid?"

"I can't feel anything from in there," she squeals. I'm getting good at reading her face, and she's on the verge of panic. "Nothing!"

"Don't try, okay?" I say, climbing the steps to the backdoor, hand stretching toward the handle. Please be unlocked, God. For once, make things easy for me. "Don't try. I know that's hard for you, but just do your best and forget about it. Your senses are gonna return real soon. I promise."

"Okay, Nick," she whispers. "I trust you."

Now that gets me right in the warm and fuzzies. Not many people have ever said those words to me, but I don't have time to bask in 'em. Gripping the handle and muttering another silent prayer and sending it the Big Guy's way, I ease it down.

No dice.

"Damn it," I mutter, glancing around, trying to spot any movement through the windows. Nothing there, either. "Only one thing for it."

Taking a deep breath, I study the glass panel above the door handle. Just a firm elbow to the glass. Sure, it's gonna make a noise, but it can't be helped now. Have to get in, have to pin down Sin-Eater before he can—

"Could just unlock it, Nick." I turn. A small piece of metal in Rosa's hand is glinting in the moonlight. A key.

"Where'd you get that?" I hiss.

Rosa rolls her eyes. "Under the flower-pot over there. Some detective you are, sweetheart."

Any other time, I'd laugh. Sweetheart!

Grinning, I take the key, slide it into the lock, send away my silent prayers, close my eyes and turn.

And the lock clicks, the satisfying sound hitting home better than the crack of a particularly stiff knuckle. The door's open. Holy Hallelujah!

I don't verbalize the sheer relief flooding through me, though. See, I need this to go all quiet if I wanna get the drop on this Hellspawn. Sin-Eater's gotta be stopped, and tonight's as good a time as any. Screw learning about the fucker if I can stop it dead right now. I'll just write a new entry into the handbook: '*Sin-Eater. Red haired and ugly. Speaks a funny language, eats souls of sinners, tells Charon to fuck off. Doesn't like a Ruger or Diana. X kills it.*' Job done.

What I'd do for an Expunger... Where bullets fail, an Expunger never does.

"Wait," Rosa hisses.

I raise an eyebrow, comically caught in mid-creeping motion like I'm in Looney Tunes. "What?"

"Do you have any idea on what might kill this thing yet?" she whispers. "If you have to?"

I scowl. "No."

"You could try salt," Diana murmurs. "Salt in shotguns."

I turn, a finger raised, and wag it.

"No, I told you, I ain't trying that again. Not after that poltergeist slammed me so hard into a wall, I almost lost five teeth," I hiss, my whisper fierce but thankfully quiet. "It might work for those damned brothers of yours, but it isn't rooted in reality, okay?"

Rosa frowns at me. "TV?"

I sigh. "TV. Ready?"

Static replaces the silence after the debate as we move inside the house. Pure, almost-deafening white noise pouring outta every electrical appliance capable of making a noise. Looking at the others, I wave my Ruger forward and head through the kitchen. House is the exact same layout as mine, messier though, and I move toward the hallway, inching forward. It just depends on what room Hudson is in, and if Sin-Eater's found—

Shit.

Didn't have to look hard. As we move outta the kitchen, Sin-Eater spins from where it's crouching over Hudson's prone body by the front door, and I stagger back, hit by a wave of weakness, fear and utter revulsion.

Those purple orbs it has glow through the angry red scar my gun left, shining above a ruined maw of a mouth, the jaw hanging lower than it should after it detached from my poor neighbor's goddamn face.

"Jesus, Nick!" Rosa screams, but I don't let the creature's effect stop me from doing what I gotta. Not this time.

A sliver of strength remains in my fingers, the ones I'm gripping my gun with. Focusing on it, the vitality spreads into my hand and up my arm, letting me lift the weapon. Aiming my Ruger, I squeeze the trigger.

Click.

Click, click. Click.

Fuck. What did I expect? I throw it instead. Sin-Eater stumbles this time instead of shifting, like it's lazy and slow after feeding. The weapon strikes it on the hip, and it screams. I drop to my knees, covering my ears as its wail tears at my ear drums, Rosa leaning on me, eyes squeezed shut, teeth gritted.

Then Diana shoots beyond us, screaming at the top of her lungs, coming to our rescue. I creak open an eye, expecting to see Sin-Eater flickering away with its tail between its legs, but it isn't. It's forced its way to its fucking feet.

Diana's a white ball of rage, Carrie on steroids, screaming up at the creature, but it's stepping forward, its loose jaw hanging. A giggle replaces its screams, high-pitched and deranged, making my blood twist.

It reaches up with both hands, feet planted, and grabs its jaw, pushing it back into place with a click.

"You are special girl. Very special," it simpers above Diana's screams. Despite the pain arrowing through my skull, I push Rosa behind me and struggle to stand, but I manage it. "But I am prepared for you this time."

Sin-Eater lashes out, its arm extending almost like a gnarly vine, and it strikes the kid in the chest, knocking her to the ground. The light inside her blinks out, and her screams turn to silence. Ah, fuck, no. But I got no time to do what my instincts are yelling at me, to go see if the kid's okay.

The creature's violet eyes turn to me.

"Alone at last," it whispers. Then it glances at Rosa. "Well, almost alone."

"You leave her the fuck alone," I growl, the weakness hitting me in waves, but I clutch onto some reserve of strength. I have to. "It's me you want."

Sin-Eater giggles again. "It is not me who wants you, human. I am but a tool, and a slave to another's will. For now." It points at me, fingernails black as coal. "But you are right, she means nothing to me, she is no sinner. But you..."

The creature flickers with the throb of a lightbulb, one moment it's in front of me and the next it's collided with me. Air rushes out of me as I crash to the floorboards, the too-heavy weight of the hunched, twig-thin Hellspawn bearing down on me, its face filling my vision. Rosa screams my name.

It leers at me. "Hellspawn? No. That is not my realm, human. I am more than that."

Weakness batters me, turning my muscles to slush. I bite down on my tongue, using the sharp pain to power my knee into Sin-Eater's soft and precious parts. It doesn't even blink, doesn't even grunt.

Movement in the corner of my eye. Rosa rushes forward and barrels into Sin-Eater, gun in her hands, knocking it sideways as she presses the Ruger into its body. I scramble up, weakness gone. Sin-Eater screams from the touch of the gun, and it lashes out, flicking Rosa aside like a rag doll. She slams into a door, the heavy thud echoing.

"Son of a fucking bitch!" I throw myself at it, the Ruger spinning away, forcing it to the ground.

It giggles. "Slave of one, more like!"

What?

I beat at it with my fist, pummeling its ribs, its chest, landing a few blows onto its scarred face, but it just laughs.

"Finished?"

Its black fingernails dig into my arms. Burning spreads through my limbs along with an onslaught of bone-deep weariness and nausea. It flips me over, pins me to the floor and straddles me, its violet eyes glowing, and stoops low over me so the tips of our noses almost touch.

The scent of strawberries and fresh grass fills my nostrils but I ain't just gonna lay here and die. Clenching my teeth, I throw my forehead into Sin-Eater's face. It squeals, it fucking felt that, and fiery liquid gushes onto me. Its bleeding, and its blood's purple, almost like its eyes.

But it doesn't let go. It doesn't budge. Sin-Eater's got me just where it wants me.

"You might have been important in the grand scheme of things, no matter what the Nephilim Absin told you," Sin Eater purrs, its high-pitched voice giddy, peering into my eyes. "But considering the larger plan does not mean anything to me."

Its lower jaw unhinges and that hook sinks behind my navel again, tugging, pulling. Fuck.

"*Get away from him!*" Diana's voice tears through the madness, and more follows.

Light. Searing bright light. I turn my head away, squeezing my eyes shut so it doesn't burn them from my sockets. Screams so loud I reckon blood's leaking from my ears. Another tug behind my navel, tearing pain at my stomach and then...

Nothing. Silence. No weight crushing me.

I crack one eye open. Light's returned to normal.

"Everyone okay?" I croak.

"Are you?" Rosa calls, and relief floods my chest.

"Nick, it's gone! I can feel it all again. I can feel..." Diana lets out a sob. "Oh, Nick. Oh, no."

Pushing myself to my feet, I know what I'm gonna find before I open my eyes. Hudson's corpse, withered, gray and twisted in fear like Greaney's.

"Don't look at it, kid," I say, steadying myself. Turning and holding out a hand, I pull Rosa up, too. "And you don't either."

"Nick…" Rosa's voice trembles. "I saw… I- I…"

"I know." I turn away from the corpse, I've seen all I need to, and pull her into my chest. "When a denizen of Hell reveals so much power, it can bleed over to folk like you. I wish you never had to see it."

"Is it dead?" Rosa asks, voice muffled.

"No. I don't think so." Even as I say it, I know I'm right. "Reckon the kid just forced it away is all."

She pulls away and peers into my eyes. "Is it all like that? Everything you see?"

"Some of it." There's no need to sugarcoat things. Not now. "Not much as bad as that, but some."

"How can you cope?"

I'm about to say, 'you'll get used to anything', but instinct stops me. That isn't exactly true. You can get numb to anything, sure, but that isn't what keeps me going.

"You help me cope. You and the kid."

I pull away, going to retrieve my Ruger. There's another scorch mark from where it struck Sin-Eater.

"You okay, kid?" I ask. "Thought it had us for a moment. Didn't think it could fight you back. At least now it knows you aren't a push over if it thinks it got you beat."

"There's a lot we don't know about Sin-Eater," she mutters, the light inside her gone again. "I'll survive, but we can't keep going on this way. What are we going to do next?"

I shrug. "Call the cops, I guess."

I glance outta the windows running down the sides of the front door. Neighborhood's returned to normal. Avoiding the corpse, I fish in my pocket for my cell, but Rosa's next to me, and she's got her hand on mine.

"Nick, you can't call the cops, and they're probably on their way over as soon as they received reports of the static hitting, anyway. Detectives Butler and Gavin suspect you, remember?" She glances at the gray corpse lying across the carpet, color drained from her face, but she's looking, and she isn't flinching away. "You have to go. Now."

"Go?" I shout, shaking my head. "I'm not going anywhere. There's no goddamn way I'm leaving you!"

"Nick, think!" She yells back, pressing her finger against her temple. "The cops are looking for blood, and they're going to pin this on you. Two people are dead; someone you have a bad history with, and your next-door neighbor. The same guy who spoke to the detectives about you just this morning. Nick, you have to go *now*."

The words are making sense. But leave? I glance at Diana. She's nodding. Two against one. I promised I'd stop trying to look after them all the time, but like this? Really?

"But Sin-Eater!" I protest. Not going down without a fight. "It just attacked you!"

"It's after you, it only went for me because I ran at it, and it can't get you with Diana around. I'll be fine." She grabs my hand and starts pulling me into the kitchen. "I'll wipe down the handles, tidy up, and leave. When the cops come calling, I'll say I met you in the Styx and you stayed there drinking. Go there, but get yourself cleaned up on the way over. Park the car where everyone can see it, and tell Ruby exactly what's happened. She'll cover for you."

I pause by the back door as she's cleaning down the handle I used with her coat. "Are you sure? Jesus, Hudson... If I'd just gone through the front."

"If we'd have gone through the front, people would have seen, and you wouldn't have an alibi."

"Ah, man, can we do this? Really?"

"Yes, we have to. I know you're not to blame for any of this, and it'll only get worse with you in a cell. Get out of here. Call me on your way over to the Styx. I won't answer. Leave a voicemail just saying you're checking in and you'll be home late. I'll text you back."

My jaw drops. "Who are you?"

"Your girlfriend." She gives me a quick kiss on the cheek. "Now get out of here and don't let anyone see you."

I'm about to say, '*I love you*', but Rosa doesn't give me the chance. She smiles, reaches up, and presses her palm against my face.

"I know," she says, reading my face like a magazine. "Now scram before they come busting through the front door!"

Seems like the smart thing to do, right? Nodding at Diana, we leave, keeping low even though, thinking about it, no one's gonna be looking this way. Despite the icy cold, despite my breath fogging the air, my blood's burning.

Sin-Eater, that sonofabitch. It's killing on my territory. Mobsters are one thing, my next-door neighbor? Sure, he ratted on me, but no, he didn't deserve that. The creature only takes sinners, correct, but in Hell that could mean anything. The kid here's a sinner because she stole a bit of money from her till at work so she could feed her family.

We move in silence, Diana using her special gifts to hide our tracks in the snow, the lights from the Christmas decorations back working as they should as I creep to the Mustang, listening out for the tell-tale signs of sirens. Reaching the car, I slide in, Diana beside me, and ease it into drive, lights off, and inch our way away from home. My stomach flips as I pass the joint. All the lights are on now, Rosa making herself at home. I should be with her. Not only because of Sin-Eater, but because of what she just saw.

I'm shaking my head before I even realize it. Fuck me, but what a woman. Hellspawn just revealed itself to her, pulling back the curtain of reality, and leaving a corpse in its wake, and Rosa's making plans to save my ass without skipping a beat.

"She'll be okay, Nick," Diana murmurs. "She's tough. Like me."

"Ain't no bad thing surrounding myself with tough ladies, is it?" I glance down at her. "You doing okay?"

"Yes. Focusing just on me helps a little, my emotions work just fine when Sin-Eater's around. Drilling into them means I don't notice what I'm missing too much." She frowns, noticing the road I'm taking. "Where are we going? Rosa told us to go to the Styx."

I wind a window down so I can hear sounds from the road better and turn the Mustang's heaters on full blast, the heat already fighting a losing battle against the chill.

"We are, but I can't take the quickest route, can I?"

Diana nods. "Because the cops might come in the other direction."

"Smart kid." I reach over and take her icy little hand, squeezing it. "Relax. We'll be there in no time. Completely unseen, I hope."

In the distance, in some other part of Haven, sirens wail, and I flick on the headlights, satisfied. At least something's gone right for once.

CHAPTER ELEVEN

WANTED MAN

I did as Rosa told me and found a prominent place to park the Mustang, smack bang in the middle of Main Street across from Meadow Park. Retrieving my woolen hat, and throwing the tissues I used to clean myself up with under the car seat, I wear it low as I enter the Styx, the collars of my trench coat high, hoping to God it hides my face. Well, God hasn't exactly been listening to me much lately, if ever. Maybe I should send my wishes Lucifer's way, at least we got a history.

Walking in, all too aware of the lack of focus from Suraz again, and the fact I don't see Charon grinning at me from the gathering shadows, I'm wishing I weren't as tall as I am, or I wasn't wearing a coat that stands out despite my love of it.

In my pocket, my cell vibrates just as I enter the joint, making my heart hammer a little harder. It's Rosa. I did as she asked and called her on the way over, but she didn't answer as planned.

'Sorry, missed your call. We had static again, and there are cops everywhere. Are you still at the Styx?'

Slouching a little, and avoiding eye contact with Guz, who's standing utterly nonplussed as ever behind the bar as, from the stage, the Tomb of Nick Cage's guitars crunch into life, I thumb a message back. At least folk are distracted.

'Yeah. More static? Fuck. Cops? Lemme guess, the chuckle twins up your ass? You want me to come home?'

Too much, or natural? For a detective, and someone who's good at smelling bull wherever I come across it, I can never judge myself. Probably should have thrown more shade at detectives Butler and Gavin.

"Um, Nick?" Diana shouts, grabbing my attention as we head down the stairs.

"Yeah?"

"Are you trying to stand out?"

I frown. "No. Why the hell would I do that?"

"Well, it's because you're wearing a wooly hat inside a building, a massive trench coat with the collar pulled up over your face, and you're walking like you're the hunchback of Notre Dame."

My cell buzzes again.

'*No, it's okay. Probably just looking into all this weirdness, it didn't last very long,*' Rosa's text reads. '*Don't be too late though, big guy.*'

Man, she's much more of a natural at this kind of thing than I am. Concerningly so.

Grumbling, I pull the hat from my head and shove it in my pocket and lower the collar. The lower bar's empty of the living except for Ruby, whose pink-haired head swivels my way as we walk in. Nothing but ghosts, and for that, I am eternally grateful. Less people to convince that I've been here all night. Lori and Henry aren't exactly gonna question ol' Hank, are they? Nope.

"Nick, back again!" Ruby calls. Couple of ghosts I don't recognise are sitting at the bar, cups of paintstripper sitting in front of them at the bar, an empty seat between them. "I thought you guys were having a quiet night? Where's Rosa?"

"At home," I reply, taking an empty seat in front of her. Diana gives a shy smile to the ghosts looking kindly in her direction. "And we've been here all night."

"Oh, Christ above." Ruby sighs and rolls her eyes. "If there's one person in the whole of Hell who could get themselves into trouble on the ride home from here, it's Nick Holleran. What did you do?"

"I didn't do anything, Rubes. Not this time." Glancing at my cell, expecting a call from the cops at any moment, I place it on the bar. "Look, I don't know how much time I've got, so listen up..."

And listen Ruby does.

"So that's it," I finish, glancing at the two ghosts I'm sitting in between. They were as rapt an audience as Ruby was. "We're hoping you could—"

"Lie to the cops," Ruby deadpans.

I wince. "Yeah."

My phone rattled a couple of times on the bar while I was talking, but I didn't check it yet. Texts could wait, and the phone call I expected from the cops didn't come. I reach for the cell, but I don't quite get there.

One of the ghosts clears his throat, a sound that always makes me re-examine my sanity. I mean, why does a ghost need to clear their throat, huh?

Anyway, one of the fellas clears his throat and it distracts me from grabbing my cell. He's dressed like an old railway worker, like one of the folks who used to shovel coal into the firebox, complete with the cool looking hat and dungarees.

"Sonny," he says, raising his paintstripper my way. "I can't speak for anyone else, and I've never heard of any creature like this Sin-Eater of yours, but if you need me to lie to the law, I will. You seem like a decent enough sort."

"Thanks, pal," I reply, taking a sip of the coffee Ruby made for me. "I appreciate it, but if the cops could talk to you, I'd have no problems, would I?"

"Well..." the fella replies, shrugging. "We could make 'em see."

I laugh. "What? Just kill Henry and Lori a little bit and

bring them back so they can see this wonderful world? Wouldn't that put me in their good books!"

Railroad man smirks and holds out his hand. "Name's Fred Rener."

"Pleasure," I say, taking his cold hand.

"When you've stopped bonding, Nick? Nice to see you making friends, and all, but is now the time?" Ruby shakes her head. "Jesus."

I suck on my teeth. "So, the cops..."

"You don't even need to ask," she plants her hands on her hips. "But remember, you—"

"Owe me," I finish. "I know. Plenty of times at this stage."

"And don't you forget it, wise guy." Ruby rounds the bar and heads for the stairs. "I'll let Guz know the story. Not the full one. Just you've been here all day."

"Can we trust him?" I ask, meeting her eyes.

"Nick, I've known him for thirty years. You don't even want to hear about the things he's seen. We can trust him."

Ruby heads up the stairs, and a lull takes a hold of the Styx lower and, not to say I'm often a huge fan of lulls, but this one is nice. It has, without a doubt, been one of those days and short of stopping Sin-Eater so the killings come to a halt, I ain't sure what to do. I've no idea *what* he is, never mind where he comes from and how to put an end to the freak. Sure, I've gleaned a few details, and I can drive it off, but all that does is put the fucker onto the scent of some other sinner. The creature's gotta eat.

Big question is, what have I done to get Sin-Eater on my tail? I'm a sinner, sure. Lucifer made that perfectly clear. I carried out the act of revenge, and that's a big no-no with the Big Guy upstairs, even though I was kinda tricked into it. Saying that, I reckon intent counts, and there was no doubt in my mind when I charged at Dean Wheeler, Expunger in hand.

But that can't be it, right? I'm Sin-Eater's numero uno. His number one guy. Like Jack Nicholson in *Batman '89* before he took a trip into a vat of acid but with less of the slightly weird rubbing of the shoulders and more soul-devouring horror.

'Cos that much is clear. No ghost sprouted outta Hudson's corpse, I didn't see any light appear in the sky calling the poor sonofabitch into Heaven—unlikely with his sinner status—and Charon didn't come swooping in to take him to the Seal.

Sin-Eater devoured his essence. Took it out of Hell, and that's that. Thought only an Expunger could do that but the fact's just another glaring hole in my Hellish knowledge.

Leaning back into my bar stool, I take another sip at coffee, half listening to the guy who claims he's Robert Johnson playing on the stage, letting the conversation from Diana and the ghosts trickle into my ear, trying to ignore the pounding bass and the stomp of feet echoing down on me from the floor above.

And then the door to the stairs swings open, and there, faces like a storm that wants to sweep me away, are Detectives Henry Butler and Lori Gavin.

My stomach does the Cha-Cha-Cha. I bet my phone rattling was Rosa warning me. Sloppy, Nick. Fucking sloppy. But hey, what could I do? Run and blow the alibi she's made for me? Hell no.

"Nick Holleran," Henry barks, taking a few steps forward and looking left and right. "Sitting in a dive alone when trouble's afoot. Fancy that."

I almost—*almost*—say I'm not alone. I'm so close to saying it, it really isn't funny. My mouth's open and my hand's raising itself to point all the dead surrounding me. Never mind jail, they'll take me to Haven City Sanitarium.

Ruby's standing behind the detectives, eyes wide, face tight, and my stomach stops flipping and sinks into my boots.

Did she get to Guz in time? Shit. Fuck me. Were they up there already, and Haven's most monosyllabic bartender told them I just arrived? Knowing my luck...

What can I say? I think about telling him I've been here all day, but if Guz ran his mouth already, then that's just a lie they can get me with. Fuck. Shit, shit, shit. Aw man, I know this is Hell, but someone is really pushing matters way too far now! What did I do to deserve all this punishment?

They're just staring at me. Everyone. Not just the detectives and Ruby. But Diana and Fred. The other unnamed ghost, and even Robert Johnson's stopped playing for Hank.

Say something that isn't fucking stupid, Nick!

"Well, I'm not alone now." There. That'll do. I ain't committed to anything. Just stating a fact. "You come for a drink? Styx doesn't quite seem like your speed, guys."

Great. I had to try and antagonize them, didn't I? At least I slipped into my natural demeanor.

Lori strides over to me, and she shivers slightly when she passes clean through poor ol' Fred, who's just sitting there with the thankfully empty paintstripper in front of him. Lori glances at it, nose wrinkling, then jabs a finger in my face.

"You've been here all day and you're drinking coffee, Holleran? Really? *Coffee*."

Oh, thank the Lord. Thank God. Praise be to all the fucking saints and angels. They don't know shit.

Still... they've got a point. Maybe coffee wasn't the best option for someone apparently day drinking during the silly season.

"Ruby's an old friend of mine," I say, meeting Lori's eyes. "Didn't want to get shitfaced while we caught up. She has to deal with enough drunks."

Lori grinds her teeth. Henry comes and leans on the other side of me, shivering when he sits in the seat the poor dead sonofabitch has already taken, who scoots out of his way, a hurt expression etched into his face. Ruby moves behind the bar.

"Are you really going to expect us to believe you've been here all day, Holleran?" Henry grates, his face real close to mine. So close the stench of the day's sweat fills my nostrils.

"Well, I wasn't here all day, was I?" I say, leaning back so I'm outta his way and I can breathe some of Hell's fresh air instead. "Paid a visit to the Greaney pad this morning in case you forgot."

"And you came straight here?" Lori snarls.

"Did a little bit of window shopping downtown first," I say, remembering everywhere the Mustang's been today save for the trip home. It seems like they don't know a thing about that. If Rosa was here, I'd ask her to marry me. Wait... What? Huh, doesn't really seem like a bad idea. Fuck, clear your head, Nick! I cough into my fist. "Then I came here. Like I said, Ruby's an old friend."

"And you've been here the entire time?" Henry asks again. "Alone?"

I shake my head and fix the most confused look I've got on my face. It's a pretty good one, to be fair. Rosa says I look a bit like Bill Clinton when he first wakes up when I do it. Not sure it's exactly a compliment now I think about it.

"No, my girlfriend Rosa came over for a while before going home. What's all this about?"

I glance at them, but they're looking at one another. Doing that '*partner's who've spent every day with one another*' thing they do so well.

Then Lori eyes my cell.

Ah, fuck.

She reaches for it, and Henry grabs me, slamming me against the bar, my cheek crashing against it.

"Mbhrfguer!" I shout, but I don't think they get the message.

"Hey!" Ruby snaps. "This is looking a lot like police brutality if you ask me."

"You'll stay out of this unless you want us to really delve into your books, you hear?" Lori snaps, glancing down at the cell. "What's the passcode, Holleran?"

"Go. Fuck. Yourself." I mutter when Henry grabs my hair and pulls me off the bar. "Oh, sorry, that's only three words, isn't it?"

Henry smashes my cheek against the bar again. Tangy iron fills my mouth. Diana's face enters my field of vision, and she's glowing.

Fuck.

"Look," I force out, pushing my head up, then spit out phlegmy blood. "Let's not do anything we all regret. Anything explosive, huh?"

I glance at Ruby when I say it, then direct my eyes Diana's way. She gives a start, her hands flying to her mouth.

"Hey, all Detective Gavin asked you for was your passcode, Holleran. You're the one being a wise guy."

"It's kinda my nature," I mutter, then try to nod. "Alright, I don't want any trouble, and I have nothing to hide." I flick my eyes Diana's way. "I'll just focus on myself. The code's six-five-eight-seven."

Really, I don't have much to hide in my cell. I just use it to call and text Rosa for the most part. Zia and Ruby every so often too, but I'm smart. I delete my texts. This shakedown isn't my first rodeo, hoss.

Lori punches in the code, then raises an eyebrow at me. "Seriously? You don't have much of an imagination, do you?"

Henry lets go of me, and I fix my trench and sit back into my chair, taking the tissue Ruby offers me, but she's only got eyes for the kid who's still glowing like a hand grenade ready to explode and doesn't even wipe my blood off the bar.

"Sweetheart, you wouldn't know where to begin with my imagination."

Henry claps me across the back of the head. "Show some respect."

My cell's screen illuminates Lori's face as she flicks through it, then she scowls.

"Story checks out," she mutters, tossing the cell at me. I fumble, but catch it. "It has the text to his girlfriend earlier today, he tried to call her, and he has messages back telling him about the static. She also sent him messages after we spoke to her, warning him we were on our way, but he didn't open them yet."

There you have it, kids. Not being glued to your cell pays off.

"Like me and Guz said," Ruby cuts in, "Holleran has been here all day."

"Sorry if we couldn't take your word for it." Lori looks anything but sorry. "But weren't you two sleeping together before Holleran hooked up with his new girlfriend?"

Ruby raises her chin. "I have plenty of fuck buddies, but I'm not a liar, officer."

Well, God bless her honesty. And, no, we weren't sleeping together, and never have, but Ruby convinced these clowns otherwise on a previous shakedown. Diana, a more normal shade of washed-out gray, flows behind the bar and takes her place beside Ruby who finally starts wiping at the countertop.

"If you've finished beating up on me and looking through my private shit without a warrant, can you tell me what all this is about?" I rub at my face. "Seeing as I'm a nice guy, I won't press charges."

Henry glances at Lori, who turns away, hands on hips.

"Your neighbor, Barney Hudson, is dead. Corpse is in the same shape as Kieran Greaney's. You can understand why we'd come looking for you."

I let my jaw hang open and shake my head, trying to look shocked.

"Hudson? Dead?" Then I let my anger take over. "And you thought I'd fucking done it? I told you this morning, this has got nothing to do with me! Fuck, is Rosa okay?"

"Your girlfriend is fine, Holleran," Lori says without turning around. "And you're off the hook."

"For now," Henry snarls in my ear. "This all smells a little too convenient to me, but we'll never make it stick, not with you having an alibi."

"That's because I've been here all day," I breathe, meeting the bastard's eyes.

"So you say, Holleran, so you say. But you'll slip up, and we'll be there. Believe us. We'll be there."

Henry strides away without another word, Lori already

heading up the stairs, and the door closes behind them.

"Fuck me." Relieved air rushes out of my lungs. "Jesus fucking Christ."

"If I wasn't dead already, I'd have thought I'd had another heart attack," Fred whispers, pressing his hand against his chest. "That was tense, sonny!"

"Thank you," I say, turning to Ruby. "You saved my ass."

"Nick, your girlfriend did. She's a smart girl." Sighing, she ruffles Diana's hair. "What now?"

"You mind if we stay here until morning? I know we're safe with Diana, but I don't really wanna put Rosa in harm's way if I don't have to." Then I grimace. "I know what you're both going to say about that. About me trying to protect people all the time."

"For once you're making sense. There's no point in leading this Sin-Eater on a trip through Haven, and the Styx has got protections of its own. If it's just fed, it might not be in too much of a rush to hunt for you again." Ruby nods. "I'll fix us up with a lot of coffee. It might be best to pore through some books while we're at it, too."

"Much obliged." I run a hand through my hair then rub at the stubble on my cheeks. "It knows every place I've been anyway. It's like a dog with my scent thick in its nose."

"And figuring out who set it loose might be the way to go, Nick." Ruby fixes me with a serious stare. "Diana can keep it at bay, it seems like your Ruger hurts it, but short of an Expunger..."

"That we don't have." I pull out my gun, turning it over in my hands, examining the scorch marks, my thoughts a little sluggish. To say it's been a day is a fucking understatement. "What is it about this thing it hates?"

"Well, what's it made out of?" Fred asks from beside me, peering down at it. "Mighty fine piece of kit."

"Well, it's alloy steel, right? Which is made up of iron." I frown up at Ruby. "Iron? Is that it?"

"Only one way to find out," Ruby replies. "Take a bunch of iron with you and throw it at the bastard, see if it stings."

I laugh. "Weird."

"What is?"

"Just that, last night, I was flicking through Harry and Maeve's old journal—"

"The *Holleran Handbook to Hell*," Diana interrupts.

I throw her a flat stare then nod. "Fine. The *Holleran Handbook to Hell* after my run-in with Lilith, and he wrote something similar. '*Always bring plenty of iron if you think you are going to meet one of the fae*'."

Diana's eyebrows draw down, but it's Ruby that speaks first.

"Fae. Is that it?"

"Naw," I shake my head. "Sin-Eater isn't fae. There's plenty of information on them, and they're nothing like what this is. It probably just shares some weaknesses, is all. You know, like how an Expunger will do for anything of Hell."

Ruby sighs. "You're probably right. Come on, it's a quiet night. I'll get you two set up in the office."

I get to my feet. "And I'll give Rosa a call first."

Ruby leads the kid away, and I head upstairs, nodding to Guz, and outside onto the snowy street, but no further than the doorway. I ain't stupid all of the time. There's a mighty powerful creature hunting me. If I could forget it, and the fact Henry and Lori's car's parked right across the road where they're staking me out, or the fact I don't feel Suraz watching me anymore, and, Hell, I don't even see Charon's toothy, humorless grin from the shadows across the way, I might enjoy the view. The traffic's died down, the snow's falling, and the Christmas decorations are lighting up Haven, making it all purty.

Shame I got a laundry list of worries, huh?

'*Nick? Are you okay?*' Rosa answers almost as soon as I punch dial.

"Yeah, I'm good. All thanks to you, huh? How's everything there?"

'*Still a lot of emergency vehicles, but they're starting to thin out. Did they come to you?*'

"Nothing I couldn't deal with." I pause. "I'm gonna stay here with the kid for the night, comb through Ruby's books, keep on at her about this Collector. Is that okay? Can't think of a safer place to work right now for a whole host of reasons, if you catch my drift."

'*Nick Holleran, asking for permission. Well I never! Of course, makes sense. I'll be okay.*'

"Don't be going anywhere, right?"

'*Nick... I'm not an idiot.*'

I refrain from mentioning the time she confronted a dangerous Devil Worshiper all on her lonesome.

"I'll see you tomorrow, Rosa. I love you."

'*Love you, too. Tell Diana the same.*'

Hanging up, I give the detectives a small wave before heading back inside. I got a lot of books to pound, and the night's still young.

CHAPTER TWELVE

WHEN THE PAST COMES TO BITE YOU
20th DECEMBER, 2024

I made an executive decision to leave the Mustang where it is. Look, it's early, and the thing's an icebox. Figuring I'm safe enough to jaunt through Meadow Park with Diana by my side, I swerved the idea of spending a good twenty minutes shivering as I get my car into a drivable condition.

Still, it's so cold I'm freezing my balls off either way.

"Do you feel it?" my breath streams out in front of me like Smaug the dragon when I talk to the kid, glancing down at her, memories of the last time we took a shortcut through here painfully clear in my head.

It's less foggy but, crucially, I don't have wendigo spirits, a pissed off Amarok, Charon, and a goddamned Devil Worshiper on my ass. I guess even bad situations like the one I'm currently in are relative.

"I can feel everything today, Nick," Diana replies, smiling. "It's wonderful."

"Didn't mean that, but good news all the same," I say, sticking my hands under my armpits to keep them warm. The maneuver doesn't really move the needle. "I meant the f... cold."

"You know I've heard people cuss before, don't you, Nick?" She turns her pits up on me. "I'm not some delicate little flower."

"Yeah, but there's such a thing as a good example and fine manners, you know?"

She laughs. Her chuckles always come from the belly and put a grin on my face. "No, I don't feel the cold. I don't have skin or blood, do I?"

"Fair point," I say, shrugging. "Just thought I'd ask. Leaving no stone unturned and all that."

We fall silent for a second, the snow crunching under my feet. The kid just kinda glides over it. She's frowning down at the white stuff, and I can tell she's gonna ask me something in... three... two...

"Did you find anything we can use before you fell asleep last night?"

Almost. Might have got the timing wrong, but my instinct proved me right. Another win for Nick Holleran. Getting mighty fine at this dad stuff.

"Ah, not much. It's just so goddamned hard to know where to look. We really have to get Rosa to make a database, or find someone with one already." We move outta the park and onto the sidewalk, the building my office is in across the street. "How about you?"

"Not a lot." She's still frowning, and I follow her stare.

The building doesn't just house my office, it's the place where that murdering sonofabitch Marvin Clancy Sr murdered her. We don't come by here much together, not after she spent sixty years there mute and staring into a corner until she sparked Awareness out of nowhere.

"You sure you're okay with heading in there, kid?" I ask, placing a hand on her shoulder.

A few early morning passers-by give me more than a couple of choice looks, standing as I am with my hand hovering chest high, talking to myself. If only they could see what I could on this sidewalk, Nick Holleran would be the last thing on their minds.

"I think so," she replies, nodding.

"It's just that Ruby said this Collector of hers will be in touch today, so I'm thinking the office is as good a place as any to set up shop." I give the sidewalk a quick scan and nudge in the direction of Henry and Lori's car pulling up near my office, too. Knew I'd find them here. Reckon they've stayed up all night waiting for me to leave the Styx, the dumb bastards. "And we might as well keep an eye on them, huh?"

Diana huffs out a heavy breath. "Okay, Nick. I can do this."

"Kid, reckon you could do anything."

She grips my hand in reply, literally pulling it out from under my armpit and, lo and behold, she makes it feel a little warmer. Not by much but it's a definite improvement and proof that even ghosts have more heat than a Haven winter. My other hand's jealous. Look, I'm a grown man and I really should own a pair of gloves, but I've always been better at looking out for other people than myself. Don't see that changing any time soon.

Walking up the steps to my building, I take one last glance over my shoulder at the detectives tailing me, and I gain a modicum of comfort from it. See, I'm used to all manner of folk keeping their eyes on me and the lack of it lately has got me into all kinds of trouble. Henry and Lori aren't gonna come to my rescue from anything Hellish, but it's something. At least if Sin-Eater strikes again they'll see I was inside my office the entire time and they'll crawl out of my ass a little.

One can fucking hope.

"I looked into Charon for a little while last night when searching for Sin-Eater didn't prove worthwhile," I say to Diana. Elevator's out, so we're taking the creaky, wooden stairs. Reckon talking about research might put her at ease, anyway. "Came across a couple of interesting facts."

"I'm sure you did," the kid replies, "but it's not exactly on mission, is it?"

"Well, I figured I'd look for anything that might have power over him, you know? Any manner of creature."

"And?"

"And nothing." Diana shakes her head, disappointed at my

news. "But I did find something."

She perks up a little. "You did say 'a couple of interesting facts'. I'm waiting."

I roll my eyes, but I can't be mad at her being tetchy. Kid's braver than me and she's always been pretty literal. If I say a couple, she expects two, right? Anway, I haven't ever been back to my family's joint in Portland, and I ain't ever been back to that alleyway, the one running between and behind *Kennedy's* and *Haven's Light*, two of the shittiest dive bars in Oregon. Reckon I'm not gonna any time soon, either.

"Well, fact one," I breathe, gazing up the stairs. Three more floors, Nick. Gonna have to make a New Year's resolution to get myself in better shape. "I found a passage saying Charon hasn't always existed."

"What do you mean?" Diana says, glancing up at me. "He's Death. That's always existed."

"Yeah, but so has birth. That came first. And, like Sin-Eater said, sin too. The scribblings I found didn't expand much on it. I typed it into my cell." I pull it out, smiling at the morning message from Rosa. I'll reply in a second, it's bad manners to keep anyone waiting, especially if you care about them. "It says: '*First is birth and with it Sin, followed by life with Death growing ever darker. But last is re-birth, and for Sin and Death the cycle continues until the end.*' Interesting, huh? Sin and death are capitalized, like they wrote about someone. Someone called Charon, right?"

"Could be. What was the other thing?"

"It talked about other realities. I think it meant the layers of Hell, but it called them 'planes of existence' and said you can reach them through portals. You think the Seal's one of them?"

We reach my floor, and I pause for a second, taking a breath, and pull out my keys.

"Oh, you and the Seal. I think the only people who will tell you about that aren't interested in sharing." Diana sets herself as I fumble with the key and lock, hands too cold to function. The kid sighs, then nods, and I hear the lock click. Unlocked, just like that. "What was the book you found this in, anyway?"

"An old one," I wink, grabbing the handle. "Called—"

The door opens, and my hand automatically drops to the Ruger on my hip, but I don't pull it. There's cops right outside the building on the street watching and listening, and, from the sonofabitch sitting in my chair, you can bet your bottom dollar there's other bastards staking them and my office out, too. Gun fire's only gonna bring a whole world of pain into my life. More fucking pain.

He sits there like he owns the place, chair positioned so Henry and Lori can't see him, but his minders sure can. Suited in an expensive-looking maroon suit, his gray beard perfectly cut and shaped to his jaw, his curly hair of the same color cut close to his skull. Even from here, those bright blue eyes of his shine across at me, hinting at knowledge only he knows, and he'll only share when he's good and ready. In his hand is the check I keep in my locked top drawer. The check for ten-thousand dollars written in my blood. I'm not surprised he's unlocked it, he did the same to the office door, too.

Sitting in my chair is Russell Greaney. The Irish Don, father to the deceased Kieran, and the man who gave me that check for services rendered, and one of the last people in Hell I ever wanted to see.

"There's so much grief pouring out of him, Nick, even though he doesn't look that way. It's almost crushing me!" Diana whispers, staring at him. She glances at me and frowns. "Wait. Do you know him?"

Yeah. I know him, alright.

The lines cut a little deeper into his face, and the dark rings surrounding those blue eyes speak of sleepless nights, but a grenade could explode next to Russell Greaney, and he'd give zero fucks about it.

"You know, Mr. Holleran, I often wondered when ye would cash this check." Greaney holds it up to the cold light streaming through the window between two fingers, his Irish brogue thick.

"What would push ye to do it? I know you've faced many a hard time since taking those three bullets, working for me no less, and ye have bills like anyone else. Never see anyone hammering down your door either, lad. Business is not exactly booming, is it?"

"Not gonna cash it." I step inside the office and close the door. "Don't need it."

"Yet ye keep it in your drawer, all safe and sound, eh? What, ye see it as blood money? All dirty and corrupt. Given to ye to keep your trap shut when the cops came asking. You take a principled stance against taking my money." A sly grin appears on his face. "Didn't stop ye from drinking the whiskey though, did it? And that's whiskey with an 'e', Irish style. The good stuff. Not your *whisky* missing the all important letter, sonny."

Diana's fixed beside the door, pits trained right on Greaney. If I didn't know better, I'd say the blood's drained from her face.

"Whisky's whisky," I say, doing my best to keep from reaching down for my Ruger. What I wouldn't give to sink a few in this fucker's chest, and what's a bit more revenge when you're already a sinner. "I had nothing to do with your son's death."

Greaney's face flickers, just a touch, but I see it. The mask of strength disappears for a second, and the grief the kid spoke of leers through. This sonofabitch might be many things, but at least he loved his son. I've known many fathers who didn't.

Greaney nods, glances out of the window as he flicks at his eye with his pinky finger, then turns back to me.

"I know that, but I know ye visited his house in the morning." He tosses his head toward the window. "Your friends down there suspect ye."

"They're not my friends."

"No, Mr. Holleran, ye are not really in the business of making friends." He points to one of the chairs in front of the desk. "Sit down."

"Not sitting opposite some sonofabitch sitting in my own fucking chair, Greaney," I snarl, my pact never to swear in front of the kid obliterated. Well, I'm not swearing at her, at least.

"Fine, stay standing. I admire balls in a man, Mr. Holleran, but watch what tone ye take with me." He takes another look at the check then puts it away in the drawer and slides it shut. "I have a business proposition for ye."

"I ain't working for you. Never again. Plus, I'm not in that line of business anymore."

Greaney smiles but those blue eyes of his aren't twinkling any more. "I'm not interested in your old line of work, Mr. Holleran. It is of the paranormal type I'm after."

A weird noise escapes my nose and throat at the same time. One's snorting, the other's choked laughter. Russell Greaney, the Irish fucking Don, wanting my services for *paranormal* purposes. Fuck me.

"Is this a joke?" I ask.

"My son is dead, Mr. Holleran. Is that funny to you?"

Just? Yes. Am I happy about it? Yes. Funny? Can't say it is.

"Be that as it may, hoss, I ain't working for you." I half reach for my pack of cigarettes then remember I quit. Huh, hadn't thought about that in a day, but I'd sure love a smoke right now. If only to settle these spiky nerves blowing about in my gut. "Paranormal or not."

"I can pay if ye take down whatever killed my boy. I saw the body, it wasn't natural or normal, and I know about the types of people ye normally take business from. Cranks, many say, but I don't agree. Maybe it's my roots; there's more magic in Ireland than anywhere else in the world, boyo."

Ah, so there it is. Can't accuse Russell Greaney of having a dull brain. No doubt he's seen all the police reports, saw my comments too, and after taking one look at his son's body put two and two together.

Still.

"Not interested in your money. The check in the drawer should attest to that."

Can't say I don't have my principles, no matter what Greaney thinks.

"If ye weren't interested in my money, Mr. Holleran, ye would have torn that check up and burned it a long time ago."

I meet those cold, killer blue eyes of his. "You misunderstand me, slick. I'm not interested in working for you, or anyone like you. My condolences about your son, but it's final."

Look, I know what you're thinking. I already know what killed Kieran Greaney, and I'm on its tail, kinda. Aiming to destroy it. Why not take the Irish Don's money?

Because that would be easy, and I swore never to do it again. It's not that working for him left me dead in a crummy alley way, or that my whole existence changed when Rosa held the blood inside of me, and stopped me from leaving. That was my *old* life. I worked for Russell and people like him plenty. Took their dollars and spent it without thinking twice. Thing is, it earned me a reputation. Henry and Lori? Part of the reason they hate my guts, a big reason, is because of the evil fuckers I did jobs for, and that reputation has stuck. I wanna be a better man, live a better life with my second one, and that's why I won't ever, *ever*, take the likes of Russell Greaney's green again.

Never.

The Irish Don sighs, then meets my eyes again, and I do my damndest not to look away as he's tapping his fingers on my desk. Eye contact and me don't mix at the best of times, and this prick could out-stare a painting.

"Ye know, I wasn't going to pay ye with money, Mr. Holleran." He shakes his head. "There are things much more useful than dollars in this life."

The frown furrows on my head before I realize I'm doing it. "What do you mean?"

His eyes flick to the doorway. Just for a moment. Wait... No. No. Goddamn it, no!

"Your lovely little friend over there is correct, Mr. Holleran. I am filled with grief, and there is nothing I wouldn't do to see my boy avenged." He stares right at Diana, and doesn't his face turn into the perfect image of a dapper, kindly old man smiling at his favourite granddaughter. "Come over here, dear. I won't bite ye."

There's been a few moments in my life where I've had what you could call an outer-body experience, and one of those was completely fucking literal, that being the day I died. Moments where time freezes and I kinda come out of my body, letting me survey everything surrounding me with a clear head despite the sheer enormity of what I'm seeing or hearing. That night back at my folk's house in their backyard was one. My death day another. The moment me and Charon shared a space and I heard his whispered words to Marvin Clancy.

And now.

Russell Greaney, the sonofabitch I've been avoiding for the last half decade, the bastard whose job I worked when I got set on this path I'm still walking, is aware of Hell. The Irish Don's not only aware of it, he can fucking *see*. Right now, with my past, present, and future colliding, I swim out of my body for a moment of peace and clarity before it all comes crashing into me. But the moment's over. The itching in my chest turns into a deep burn, and sucking in breath is like swallowing flames. Greaney's bright blue eyes twinkle and he smiles at me like a gray-bearded Frank Sinatra who doesn't care if everyone knows he's in deep with the mob.

Another factoid pops into my head, the analytical part never letting me down. Ruby said the Collector would meet me today.

"You're The Collector." My voice comes out as a croak and before I know it, I'm sitting in that goddamn chair, hand pressed to my chest, fingers in my other hand spasming as it fights to reach for my Ruger.

I could kill this hateful sonofabitch right now, but he'd just reappear, wouldn't he? Charon isn't around, and you can't count on him taking just anyone to the Seal. A dead but Aware Russell Greaney could cause a whole world of pain for me and mine, just like he could alive. Worse even, and I don't have any Expungers to put him down for good.

Greaney nods. "I thought it time we were properly introduced, Mr. Holleran. All the other business is my sideline, the work you know me for. Hell is what holds my focus, and it has since I was a small boy back in the old country. This is the real me, and I am The Collector you've been so interested in meeting. Surprised?"

"How long have you *Seen*?" I ask it automatically. It's like a courtesy between those who first meet and talk shop about Hell.

"Sixty-three years." He presses a hand against his chest. "My story is not so different from yours. My old daddy took me out on a hunt in Connemara. Chasing foxes and the like. They would never kill the healthy ones, the little buggers are wily enough to get away and quick too, but that was never the point with him and his fellows. They did it for companionship. Every now and then they would happen upon a sick fox and end its misery. On this day, my first hunt, they found one too weak to escape the horses. '*This is your turn, boy,*' he told me. Stern, he was. Always. A God-fearing man and handy with the belt. So I dismounted the horse we shared and approached the poor bugger, hands shaking as I held the shotgun. I had never killed before as I had just turned seven. I stood there, aiming down the barrel, the little fox panting on the ground, eyes closed like it knew what was coming and didn't want to look. But I couldn't fire. I could not pull the trigger. No, not me. Impatient, and more than a little disappointed, my old daddy jumped off his mount... and his ankle turned when he landed. A simple thing. A small twist of fate and nothing more. But his shotgun misfired as he fell, and the blast took me in the chest. It goes without saying that after I recuperated, my tales of ghosts, demons, fae, creatures, devils and demons did not go down well with him. A God-fearing man like him reacted as you'd expect."

Diana's approached him while he spoke, her fingers gripping the table's edge, taken in by the emotion he's keeping at bay but feeling. But Greaney only has eyes for me. Shot down by his old man. Christ above.

I sniff, and wipe at my nose, and remember who this sonofabitch is. The blood of thousands runs underneath Haven's streets, and Russell Greaney's responsible for oceans of it. "Nice story. If it was meant to make me feel sorry for you, it didn't work."

Greaney spreads his hands. "We're just trading war stories, are we not, lad? I know all about your Awakening, of course, and thought it appropriate to share mine as we begin our new venture together."

"What new venture? I ain't looking into your son's death."

"Ah, but ye already are." He leans back into *my* chair, legs outstretched, and grins. "I have kept an eye on ye, son, all these years. I've watched ye scratch around in Hell, blind, blundering this way and that, helping some but hindering yourself more often than not, and I've waited."

Fuck me, that cigarette would go down mighty fine right now. Whisky might not be the worst idea, even though it isn't even nine o'clock in the morning. With or without the 'e'.

"Waited for what?"

"For the right time." Greaney spreads his hands. "Due to our shared history, of course, I needed ye to be... open... to my assistance."

I raise an eyebrow. "And you think I am now?"

Greaney's kindly grandfather's smile turns into one a shark might wear. He holds up a finger. "I think you're being pursued by the police, and ye are the main suspect in the death of two people ye have ties to." A second finger joins the first. "Even though those simple minds are beginning to understand the world is not as they see it, they can't exactly put a demon of some kind at the top of their lists, and that demon is hunting ye." Greaney, the bastard, holds up a third finger. "Ye have come to the realization that your bullets, Expungers, Holy Water, and Battenspurers aren't enough in Hell, and ye are beginning to understand that all your dusty books only contain a fraction of the knowledge you need. Yes, Mr. Holleran, I'd say ye are plenty desperate."

I suck on my teeth with, for once, nothing to say. Nothing. He's right. I've been backed into a corner with nowhere to turn, and I'd banked on The Collector helping me out of it. What's the alternative? Keep forcing Sin-Eater away while he feeds on people around me? No way.

Pinching the bridge of my nose, I shake my head, then reach for a glass and the whisky on my desk. It's Happy Hour somewhere, right?

"Want one?" I ask, mostly out of habit. Hate drinking alone.

"It's a little early for me, son."

"Thought you Irish couldn't get enough of this shit?"

Greaney smiles, then nods, and I pour one out. "Ye should know about that, Mr. Holleran. Your father is from God's own country too, isn't he?"

I pause mid-pour. "You know about him?"

"Mr. Holleran, I know every little thing about ye and never suspect I don't. Now, keep pouring." I do, then he holds up a hand. "Done."

He takes his drink and closes his eyes when he sips at it and sighs.

"Not to your standards?" I ask, holding mine near my nose.

"Do you need to ask?" he replies, then turns to Diana. "And how are you finding Hell, dear, now you are Aware? I never saw you with Mr. Holleran before, so I'd say ye are new to it, yes?"

"Don't you fucking dare talk to her!" I slam the whisky onto the desk, making it rattle. Greaney doesn't even flinch. "You talk to me. She's off limits, you hear?"

"As ye wish." Greaney smiles at Diana, then turns back to me. "On to business, lad?"

I grab the whisky, take a sip, wince when it slides down my throat. Then take another for good measure.

"Sure, but I gotta know one thing first. Did Ruby know you're The Collector?"

Greaney tilts his head to the side. "Do you really think I'd go by the name of 'The Collector' if everyone knew who I was? I thought you were a detective, Mr. Holleran."

It's a good fucking point, but I'm not going to tell him that.

"So, you want me to kill the creature that did your son, and you say there's more to Hell than dollars, and I came to you wanting weapons. So you're looking to do a trade." I lean back into my chair. How's that for detecting? "What have you got?"

Russell Greaney drains his whisky then pours himself another without asking permission. Fucker does practically own Haven, reckon he's not used to asking. Then he grins at me.

"What do ye know about Excalibur, son?"

CHAPTER THIRTEEN

THE WORLDS ARE WEIRDER THAN YE THINK THEY ARE

Without warning, a laugh escapes my throat. Just one short bark of laughter. Then another. I glance at Diana, who's just staring transfixed by the crazy old bastard sitting in my chair, then I turn back his way again, rubbing at my forehead.

Then I laugh again. Every now and then, it's all anyone can do.

"What's so funny, Mr. Holleran?" Greaney asks, cocking his head to the side. "Did I say something to amuse ye?"

"Oh, no. No," I say, shaking my head and crossing my arms. "What do I know about Excalibur, you said. Take it you mean *the* Excalibur? The one belonging to King Arthur and his fucking Knights of the Round Table off in Camelot, right? Sure, I've seen the movies. Read some of the books. Pointy thing. Great at killing folk. Used to be in a fucking stone."

Greaney's blue eyes glitter in a dangerous way. He doesn't really have another way to look at a guy. "Ye mock me, son."

I lean forward, arms still crossed. "Oh, I'm sorry, hoss. *I'm* mocking *you.* Here I was, asking for help against some sonofabitch who's killed twice already, and you come to me, asking what I know about a fucking sword from a goddamned fairy tale. Jesus Christ, what a waste of everyone's fu—"

Greaney's palm hits the top of my desk with such force the whisky bottle topples over before rolling to a stop perilously close to the table's edge, the echoing sound cutting off my tirade. He holds my stare until I look away, like a dog who can't meet its cruel master's eyes for too long 'cos it knows who's in charge and what's coming his way if he continues to step outta line. Diana shifts beside me from one ghost foot to the other, and it's a wonder she isn't glowing and ready to explode.

"Mr. Holleran, I don't know why, but I expected better from ye, because even though your previous work erred on the sloppy side, ye always managed to get the job done. I thought ye may have brought such conviction over to your new role, but I see your knowledge is severely lacking." He leans forward, and bares his teeth in a humorless grin, showing off some crooked teeth at odds with his otherwise immaculate appearance. The jackal becomes the hyena. "In Hell, if ye have read about it, it exists, boyo."

"Except for werewolves," I mutter, still not able to meet his eyes. I stare at his bearded chin instead. "I know that."

"Ye may know it, boy, but ye don't understand it. *Everything* is real, and *everything* has some basis in fact. Now, did King Arthur and his pals ride around on gleaming steeds in the English countryside, aiming to spread chivalry and understanding in their wake? No, not at all. But, ye mark my words, they searched for the Holy Grail, and they fought demons, and their leader held Excalibur in his steel-gauntleted fist."

My fingers are itching to grab the whisky again, but I let them fiddle with the seams of my jeans instead. Everything is real. Everything has some basis in fact. Don't I always say that? Didn't I just say it yesterday? But this sonofabitch is right. I never really believed it. Just the things I saw with my own eyes. Arrogant, right? Guess you can't take the unbeliever out of the atheist, huh? Having Heaven and Hell revealed to me should have been lesson enough. An example that absolutely nothing's off the table as far as reality is concerned and that being so sure about anything until it walks down the sidewalk and says, '*hi, how's your morning going, slick?*' is a quick way to winding up with your back against the wall or rotting in a ditch.

I take a quick glance at Diana, then meet Greaney's eyes. I make sure I hold them, too.

"So, you're telling me magic's real, too?"

"Christ, boy, do ye try to make people hate ye, or are ye just plain dumb?"

I grin, can't help myself. "A little from column 'A'..."

Greaney rolls his eyes. "Smart arse. Yes, Mr. Holleran, magic is real, but it's rare. I've spent my life collecting relics and trying to understand this world we live in, but I don't get involved like ye do. I have a reputation to uphold and my... experiences... of talking frankly about Hell to those around me taught me to keep my mouth closed a long time ago."

"Alright," I say, pointing at the old man. "Magic's real. So's everything else—"

"Except for werewolves," Diana mutters in a tone that suggests she reckons she's completely lost her mind, like she can see and hear what's unfolding before her, but she plain just doesn't believe it. A little like me and Hell, I guess.

"Except werewolves," I agree, nodding at her. "And so's Excalibur. So that's it. You have it and you're giving it to me? A fucking sword to kill Sin-Eater? Can't say I'm not liking the sound of that." I look around, pretty goddamned excited all of a sudden. "So? Where is it?"

"Sin-Eater, aye. Ruby told my people all about the creature. Can't say I've heard the like of it, but it was all only second-hand information, you understand." Greaney takes a sip from his whisky. "Before we get onto what I've brought for ye, tell me what we're dealing with."

"We?" I ask, not even trying to take the heat from my voice. There's no 'me and Russell Greaney'. Not anymore. Shit. That was *before*. Before he revealed himself as The fucking Collector, keeper of relics and stacks of untold gnarly shit. This sonofabitch knows a fuck-ton more about Hell than I do.

Goddammit.

"Ye want my help or not, son?"

I raise my eyebrows. Even with this dude being who he is, I ain't gonna show him my belly so he can tickle it. He'd as soon as stick a knife in it if I didn't kick my leg in the right way. "Look, it seems to me like you want my help just as much as I need '*The Collector's*'. Sin-Eater ain't gonna avenge itself, is it?"

A shadow crosses Greaney's face. A spasm. This isn't a man who's argued with often, if at all, but he knows I'm right. This... transaction... is a two-way street. Quid pro quo.

"Noted." He steeples his fingers. "I have much knowledge. Ye might knock something loose. Try me."

I glance at Diana, who's finally looking my way after being transfixed by the blast from my past sitting in my chair. She shrugs. Kid isn't gonna argue.

"It's got red hair. Violet eyes—"

Greaney chops with his hand. Impatient. "I know what it looks like, Mr. Holleran. Ruby gave a full description, how it handled Charon, the weakness it spreads over ye. How iron seems to annoy it, how the little darling over there is able to drive it away even though it's fighting back. And I know that when ye force it to flee, it feeds on a soul elsewhere." He pauses, eyes glittering. "Tell me, how does that sit with ye? Knowing your only defense spells death to any other sinner around ye?"

"It reminds me you've gotta leave this place without the only protection we have against Sin-Eater, and your eyeball deep in sin." I flash him my teeth. "Reckon you gotta be careful, huh?"

The sonofabitch touched a nerve. He's right. Again. Every time we send Sin-Eater away, there's a good chance it'll kill someone else, and given that driving it away last time was harder than the first, one day Diana might not be enough. Letting my heart beat a little longer means some other poor bastard's soul gets devoured, and Sin-Eater doesn't leave much else behind after it sucks on what nourishes it.

Greaney returns my humorless smile, looking every inch the jackal warning another of its kind away from its den. "I want anything ye might have left out. No matter how small."

"Look, I told Ruby everything I knew. We spent the whole night researching it and came up with squat." I spread my hands. "It's not ideal, but I'm used to flying by the seat of my pants."

"Fighting alone and 'by the seat of your pants' in Hell is a sure way of losing your right to breathe, son," Greaney replies, shaking his head, disgusted. "I'm surprised ye have lasted this long."

The lop-sided grin forms without my say-so. Sometimes I just can't stop it. "I'm pretty hard to kill, hoss."

There it is. Hello snark, my old friend.

Greaney rolls his eyes and snorts. Diana shakes her head. One day, I'll find an audience who appreciates my genius. One day.

"If ye are finished, boy, we'll talk about Excalibur, since I'm not about to get anything else of note out of you about Sin-Eater." Greaney pauses, and I lean forward, hands on knees like some eager schoolboy at story time. "For starters, it's not a sword."

"Not a sword?" I ask, sinking back into my chair. Wait, why am I so crestfallen? I didn't even believe it existed a couple of minutes ago. "Right. Show it to me, then, whatever it is. Let's see if the juice is worth the squeeze."

A wry grin curves the side of the Irish Don's mouth as he raises an eyebrow. Maybe he does appreciate a decent turn of phrase, huh?

"It used to be a sword, but not any more." Greaney reaches into his jacket, and I tense, fully aware of the Ruger pressing against my hip, insurance in case he decides I ain't worth his time after all and opts to avenge his son. In a roundabout way, I can see that line of thinking. "It's something much more manageable than that."

He pulls his hand out, and I almost reach, but there's a black silk bag in the palm of his hand. Glancing at Diana, and favoring her with what I reckon is actually a genuine smile, he unties the bag and turns it upside down. Two chunky silver rings fall out and slam onto the desk with a thud.

I am an oversized Frodo. Greaney is the meanest Gandalf this side of Middle-Earth. Diana is my... Sam? She'd kill me if I said Gollum. Literally go supernova. She read the books when she lived, and when I told her there were movies, she flipped and demanded we—

Jesus, Nick, get a grip.

I lean forward, studying the rings. They're identical, right down to the symbols engraved into the outer side. The silver's bright, catching the gray daylight streaming in through the window. Fuck me, I just wanna touch 'em! Maybe *I'm* Gollum.

"This... is Excalibur," Greaney murmurs.

I look up to see him watching me. "There's two of them, slick."

His face spasms again. Why *do* I get my kicks from pissing psychos off? A psychiatrist would retire if I turned up on their couch. Just walk away. No amount of money could keep 'em trying to figure the mess that is Nick Holleran out. No Siree.

Greaney smooths the anger twisting his mouth, but it's still in his eyes. "One ring won't work without the other. Ye wear them on opposite fingers, push them together with the symbols matching, and the magic happens."

I grin at Diana. "Nice."

"From my findings, I'm told the blade was shattered in a battle between the so-called King Arthur and an Alpha-Demon." Greaney stares down at the rings like he's studying twin grandchildren for the first time. Besotted. Nothing he wouldn't do for them. They only have to gargle. "The survivors of the battle recovered shards of the blade and had them melted down. It cost me a pretty penny to get my hands on them, Mr. Holleran."

"Can I hold one?" I ask, reaching out before he can say no.

"That's why I brought it, boy."

I grab one and weigh it in my palm. Heavy and solid. Much heftier than it should be from its size.

"Wait, what's an Alpha-Demon?"

Greaney's jaw drops, almost comically so, and he stares at Diana first then turns his eyes to the ceiling. "Mother Mary of Jesus in Heaven above have mercy on me."

"Didn't have you down as the devout type, pal," I mutter, bouncing the ring, then slipping it onto my index finger. Nothing happens. Dunno what I expected. Shining light from the heavens, maybe? Invisibility? A full choral symphony? Maybe a blast of Wagner like in that 80s flick, Excalibur. Maybe something like that. Not just the admittedly heavy weight of the silver ring on my finger. "Kinda funky. What kind of magic are we talking about?"

Color me underwhelmed.

Greaney waves his hands. If I had to assign an emotion to his current visage, I'd say 'peeved'. 'Vexed', maybe. As much as I know he's the fucking Irish Don, a man responsible for more shady shit than Al Capone in his heyday, and an individual I'm predisposed into not liking, he's reminding me a lot of an elderly college tutor who can't quite believe or understand why he's been saddled with such a shitty student.

"Hold your horses, sonny. Ye really don't know what an Alpha-Demon is?" he asks.

I fold my arms, a single ring of Excalibur still on my finger. "No."

Greaney splutters, looking at me, then at Diana, like she might come to his rescue. Kid just shrugs. She has to put up with my shit on a daily basis.

"An Alpha-Demon is the equivalent of an angel." Greaney leans forward, gripping his whisky. "Hell's version of an angel."

"So, they work for Lucifer. So do the Nephilim." I shrug. "Honestly, the guy seems to have a bad rep, if you ask me. Nice fella."

Greaney frowns. "Ye have seen the Morningstar? Spoken with him?"

"Thought you knew everything about me, slick."

He glances over his shoulder out of the window, then fixes me with an ice-cold stare, pinning me to my seat like three bullets would. Or a sword for that matter. One that hasn't been melted down into jewelry.

"I know much, boy, but there are always some details that evade, much like this very situation with Sin-Eater. Mark my words well, Mr. Holleran. Ye may have survived an encounter with the Morningstar for whatever reasons he decided, but he is not some misunderstood individual. He has lived since near the beginning, and his mind is unknown to us. Lucifer is not evil as we would call it, but it can't be said he's good, either. He simply *is*." Greaney leans backward, takes a sip from his whisky and extends his neck to the side, cracking it. "The same goes for the Nephilim. Do they work for him? Who's to say, but the Alpha-Demons… They do not. Hope ye don't cross their paths without an attitude adjustment, boyo."

Christmas. The season of pep talks. Well, just so happens *I* know one or two things about Lucifer I reckon ol' Russell Greaney doesn't. Like how he and God are brothers. Don't wanna give the old man heart failure just yet, though. I'll keep that little nugget to myself.

"Excalibur?" I ask, pointing at the other ring with the finger. "You think it's enough to take down Sin-Eater?"

Greaney blinks, like he's just remembering where he is, then nods.

"There might be an element of trial and error involved, but I believe so."

"Great." Trial and error with a creature that devours souls on my ass. Fan-fucking-tastic.

"Study the symbols, son, many are self-explanatory. Flames, for example." He smiles. "I believe ye can work that one out for yourself."

I meet his eyes then look away, picking up the second ring and studying it. There's a cross, like the one they crucified Jesus on, a sword, three squiggly lines going vertical, and another set going horizontal. Greaney's right, the one I'm wearing has the same etched into it.

"So, I get to use Excalibur in exchange for stopping Sin-Eater?"

"Destroying Sin-Eater. I want it dead, Mr. Holleran, not just stopped." Darkness shines in his eyes. "Do ye understand me?"

I glance at the frowning Diana. She nods my way.

"Loud and clear, hoss. Now, is there anything else? If not, you can leave. Got a lot of work to do this close to Christmas."

"Speaking of Christmas," he says, reaching into his pocket again. "An early gift. Ruby told my people *everything*. She really is quite detailed."

He holds out an Expunger. Just the one, but it might make the world of difference in Hell.

"Thanks," I mutter, taking it off him and slipping it away. "Merry Christmas. I got nothing for you. You'll see yourself out?"

Greaney rises out of his seat, spry enough for an old timer, and fixes me with a withering stare.

"I'm not an idiot, boy." He points out of the window. "Like ye said, there's a creature out there feeding on sinners in your proximity, and ye and the girl being close are the only things that keep it away. The Lord knows my soul isn't pure. Ye can accompany me to the sidewalk, at least."

He walks away, not waiting to see if me and Diana follow him. She does right away, and I slink behind, pocketing the second ring, trailing behind them like a student being hauled into the principal's office. Mine and Greaney's footsteps echo on the stairs as we descend in silence, Diana in between us until we enter the foyer. Ol' Russell pauses at the door and turns.

"Now, I believe your friends from the local PD will be mighty interested in seeing me leave your office, Mr. Holleran, but that can't be helped. Tell them I was here to quiz ye about my boy. I will tell them the same when the chief contacts me to verify. Or I could get one of the lads to break your nose, but I don't think we need to resort to that. Those grunts out there aren't allowed to speak to me." He glances at Diana, then kneels in front of her, staring up into her blank face, even though I told him not to talk to her. Anger bubbles in my chest. "Ruby told my people everything, especially about ye. Tell me, girl, do ye feel anything out there?"

The kid stares over his shoulder like she's watching the traffic go by, then nods.

"It's out there. Waiting."

Greaney gets to his feet, smiling down at the kid before turning to me, the warmth smothered by ice.

"We'll be talking soon, son. Sin-Eater. Reminds me of a saying my old granny used to say when we were bould. *Bíodh do pheacaí mar dheireadh agat*. I was bould more than I'd like to admit." He sighs, then smiles down at Diana. "Merry Christmas, girl. Be seeing ye."

For me, the traffic outside moves slower than a snail's pace, and the sidewalk's as quiet as the fucking grave. Greaney moves away, but my hand moves on instinct, grabbing his shoulder and spinning him around. His anger doesn't really register with me, neither does the disgust twisting his features from my pawing at him. He snarls something, but I don't hear it.

"Those words." They come out like a slur. But I need to ask. "What do they mean?"

His eyes narrow, and focus obliterates his anger. "*Bíodh do pheacaí mar dheireadh agat*? You've heard it before. Ah, but your old man is of God's own country after all, maybe he said it, too. It means 'let your sins be your end'. My old granny was a wise girl, it seems."

"It's Irish?" I ask, my mind spinning. It's been right in front of me the entire time. The entire *fucking* time.

"Of course. Gaeilge. Did your daddy never teach you anything? Now take your hands off me."

Looking left and right, then waving toward the vehicle with Lori and Henry sitting in it—the sonofabitch—Greaney strides down the steps to his waiting car, but I'm barely paying attention. Diana paws at my hand, but I don't turn to look at her. Don't hear the words she's saying.

"Fae. Is that it?" Ruby had asked.

"Naw. Sin-Eater isn't fae. There's plenty of information on them, and they're nothing like what this is. It probably just shares some weaknesses, is all."

Goddamned arrogance on my part. The fae are rooted in Irish mythology. Dullahan, that's what Sin-Eater called Charon. The Irish mythological figure for death. It doesn't like iron. This all started right after Diana blew Lilith away. And those words in that language. *Bíodh do pheacaí mar dheireadh agat.* I had heard them said before, but not by my old man.

The Queen of the fucking Fae screamed them my way right before she disappeared. Right after her and her brood came to reign judgment down on me for killing her kind.

For my sins.

Sin-Eater snarled them, too. He belongs to Lilith. It's her revenge, and the bastard's gonna keep coming until I stop him, and Lilith will send something else my way until I meet my end. I pull the Expunger from my pocket, staring down at it. Didn't have one of these before. Just gotta get close enough.

Fuck... How could I be so dumb? How? They're right. Everyone's been right about me, including myself. Arrogant. Sloppy. Cutting corners. '*Flying by the seat of my pants*'. Well, I gotta act before it kills anything else. I gotta—

"Nick!" Diana screams, pulling me from my self-inflicted misery.

"I gotta talk to Rose. Ruby. Someone," I mutter, putting the Expunger away and pulling out my cell. But it's got no signal. "Fuck."

"He's here, Nick!" Diana cries. "He's—"

Ping.

Ping. Ping. Ping.

The insistent blaring of my cell cuts her off as the signal returns.

"Gone," she finishes, frowning down at the sidewalk. "What's happening? Why are you feeling like that?"

"Like what?"

"Rotten."

"I've screwed up, kid. Badly. I know what Sin-Eater is, or who it's linked to at any rate." I shake my head, but then it's my turn to frown. Greaney's car, a black Rolls Royce, took off a minute ago, but one just like it is still sitting there with no sign of moving. He's left someone to tail me? Not doing a good job of keeping it subtle. I glance at Diana. "Come on."

We walk down the steps, my cell ignored, thoughts of calling into my support network and getting them researching *anything* to do with the fae, with Lilith, and anything regarding sin in that realm gone clean out of my mind. There's no movement in the car, though the fully opaque windows block my view inside. Gotta take a peak. Standing before the door, I grab the handle.

"Nick..." Diana breathes, the sounds of the city dim. The ghosts crowding the sidewalk fading from view. "I can't feel anything from that car. It's like when—"

"Sin-Eater's fed," I finish, pulling open the driver's seat door. "You were right, kid. It's killed again."

One of Greaney's goons stares up at me, face a gray, crusted mask of fear. His dead eyes peer into mine, judging me for not putting this shit together quickly enough. Another death on my hands, even though he's a sinner. Another corpse added to the ledger. Diana presses her face into my side, and I wrap an arm around her, absorbing her coldness.

This isn't gonna stop till I put an end to Lilith, or she puts an end to me. I have to find her, and I gotta be prepared. Not just with Excalibur. Not just with an Expunger and consecrated bullets. Knowledge, I gotta have more fucking—

"Nick Holleran?" Shit. The goddamn cops. "Hands where we can see them."

I turn at the sound of Lori's call, raising my hands, but I'm roughly shoved face first against the side of the Rolls Royce, my arms twisted behind my back, handcuffs cutting into my wrists.

"You're under arrest, you sonofabitch," Henry snarls, spinning me around. "Three dead. All in your vicinity. You might have got your friends to lie about you last night, but you haven't got an alibi this time. You're standing over a corpse, and this is the third one, all linked to you. No one else has gone near this vehicle. We've been watching. No one but you."

He frisks me, pulling my cell, my Ruger, the rings, and my Expunger away.

"Evidence." He grins. The cat who got Hell's largest, juiciest mouse that happens to be filled entirely with cream.

Diana's glowing, her hair lifting to the sides, her arms outstretched, fingers trembling. Ghosts flee from the sidewalk.

"I didn't do this!" I call, staring right at her. "But I'm gonna come quietly. No trouble from me, or anyone, right? It's for the best. We can sort all of this out."

"I'd save that kind of talk for your lawyer," Lori growls, gun trained on me. "We don't know how you're doing this, but we're gonna find out."

"Sure," I say, nodding, my gut unclenching as the light fades from Diana. "We just gotta stick together."

"What the fuck are you talking about, you crazy bastard?" Henry shoves me forward, his gun pressed into the small of my back. "Get to the car, nice and easy. No trouble."

Lori's already calling for an ambulance for the poor sonofabitch in the Rolls as they take me away, Diana trailing at my side.

Henry grabs my hair as he pushes me into the back seat, smiling down at me as he checks the cuffs.

"I get my phone call, right?" I ask. "One call?"

"Sure, Holleran, sure. You're going away for a long time. Best make it count."

Car doors slam and Henry goes back across the sidewalk, shaking hands with his partner, grinning at each other like there isn't a stiff rotting in the Rolls. Guess I'm Haven's fat goose, huh? I lean against the headrest, eyes closed, mind whirling. One call. Fuck.

"Do you have a plan, Nick?" Diana asks.

"Sure, when don't I?" I reply, summoning a smile from God knows where. "They can't prove any of this is me. We'll be out of there in no time."

Diana nods, but I know how this works. They're gonna see me rot, unless Sin-Eater kills again somewhere else in the city when I'm behind bars. Another death on my hands. Leaning my head against the window, one thing's clear.

I gotta get out of here. Fast.

CHAPTER FOURTEEN

JAILHOUSE ROCK

Diana hasn't left my side since Lori and Henry drove us from downtown to the precinct, watching quietly as officers laughed while they processed me. And not just laughed. Some called me a killer without a hint of amusement in their eyes.

My already shitty reputation outside of a select few in the Haven City PD has taken a turn for the worse.

I know I'm not a murderer, and it's only a matter of time until Sin-Eater strikes again. That'll prove my innocence, but who's it gonna kill instead? A cop, more likely than not, and cops take that kind of shit to heart. Things will get ugly fast, and they'll blame me, 'cos who else are they gonna turn their anger at? The guy they wrongly arrested in the first place.

Jesus, it's been hours. They've just left me here to stew, and it's working. Rosa's gonna be going out of her mind about me. Goddammit!

No point in screaming or shouting. No one will hear me. The door leading into my wing is soundproofed.

"Who are you going to call, Nick?" Diana asks, sitting beside me on the uncomfortable molded plastic bench that's fixed into the wall. Nothing moves or makes a sound on the other side of the bars. They stuck me in an empty row, right beside the door leading into the precinct. "Rosa?"

I glance at her. To the kid's credit, she didn't call me a freaking idiot for not pulling together all the strands around Sin-Eater sooner. Said we'd all known the facts, and no one had made a strong argument for fae involvement even when Ruby mentioned it. Maybe she's just trying to make me feel a little less sore. Even so, who the knew Lilith had a creature like Sin-Eater in her thrall?

"Yeah, reckon I will. She probably thinks I'm dead already." I flick at my fingernails, a bad habit of mine when I'm nervous or frustrated, but Diana hasn't complained about it yet. Yet. "But we gotta get looking into where we can find Lilith. Reckon wandering around Haven Woods in the dead of night ain't smart. We have to find her home territory."

"If you get out of here."

"I'm getting out. I just hope it's before some other poor sinner bites it." I point at the jail cell bars. "You know what they're made out of? Iron. Fort Knox hasn't got a thing on this cell. I'm safe but it doesn't mean others are."

Diana nods. "You think Rosa could find out the information?"

"She could, but there's a lot to pick through, and we don't even know she's at home. She's probably roaming Haven looking for any sign of us, right?" I sigh, squeezing the bridge of my nose. "Look, we're gonna have to attack this from two directions. I got one call, but I got you, too."

The kid's eyebrows draw down. She isn't gonna like this one fucking bit.

"What do you mean?" Each word's spat out between gritted teeth.

"I'm gonna call Rosa, tell her what's happened and what she needs to do, but we need Ruby on it, too."

"No, Nick."

"Yes, Diana." I point at her. Han Solo telling Threepio to shut the Hell up and listen. "I'm safe here. Sin-Eater just fed, I'm behind iron bars, and even though the sonofabitch flickers in the light it doesn't pass through walls. The Styx is close. I need you to go there, tell Ruby, and come right back. Tell her we'll head over there when I'm out and share notes."

Diana's glowing again, the muscles at the side of her jaw bunching. "No, Nick! I won't leave you!"

"Don't you glow at me, young lady."

Jesus H Christ. Did I really just say that? Young lady? Kid's as surprised as I am. Jaw hanging loose, the light pulsating inside of her dims a little, returning her to the familiar washed-out gray. Gonna put it down as a win and move on.

"Look, we don't have a lot of options. We have to do this, and it's not gonna take you long, right? And weren't you pissed at me for trying to look out for you all the time? Saying you couldn't do this, that, or the other." The lop-sided grin takes its majestic place on my kisser. "Seems like I learned the lesson but you ain't, kid."

"It's not the same," she mutters, bottom lip almost protruding.

"It is. Sometimes you just gotta trust. I know you can do this; you just have to believe I'm making the right call."

"Even if it's putting you in danger?"

I reach out and grab her shoulder, giving it a squeeze. "Kid, I don't want anyone else dying because of me. I'm sick of reacting. We gotta go on the attack, and I mean to start right now. Even if I'm behind bars."

Diana shakes her head, no doubt deciding on which argument she's gonna use to talk me down, but then she nods. It's a reluctant one, no doubt, but it's a nod.

"Okay, Nick. I'll be back soon." She grins, then gives me a pat on the cheek. "Don't go anywhere."

Fuck me. I'm a bad influence. I knew it.

She disappears right through the wall, leaving me alone for the first time in days. Since all this started. It *is* different now. Then I put myself in harm's way in a dumb attempt to protect everyone else around me, and no short amount of arrogance played into that. Me thinking I could handle anything sent my way 'cos I talked to Lucifer one time, and I got Nephilim and Charon tailing me.

Well, now I don't. They gave me a weird kinda safety net, even if the Ferryman wanted me dead. Both of them are AWOL, and it's been made painfully clear I don't know shit about Hell. The only reason I'm still alive is through pure dumb luck, and because of my friends. Right now, I'm relying on them. Hoping they'll pull through for me. It's only right I treat 'em as the capable women they are. I'm no knight in shining armor, and they don't need one, either.

Even if I *did* wield Excalibur for a sliver of time.

Wonder where it is? Lori or Henry probably have the rings in their office, poring over it as well as the rest of my shit. None of it incriminates me, and nothing points to me creating an alibi for last night. They know they haven't got a thing that'll stick except for a healthy amount of suspicion and coincidence, but there's enough circumstantial evidence to keep me behind bars for a while yet. Probably until after Christmas.

I cradle my head. Tired. Weary. Been a Hell of a few days. My head spins a little. Shit, must be more tired than I thought...

I hear it before I see it. The sound of the flickering light bulb piercing my ear drums. No, I ain't that tired. It's not natural. Opening my eyes, the light in my cell and the corridor outside are going crazy. I get to my feet, the scent of strawberries filling the jail cell.

It's here. Sin-Eater.

"These fucking bars best work," I mutter, staggering over to them, limbs weak, thoughts coming slow as my brain creaks with weariness. "Please fucking work."

Peering through the bars, I see nothing, then the bulb dies again, plunging the whole row into darkness and complete silence.

Beside my cell, the door creaks before it closes again.

"Hello?" I call, grabbing the bars. Some of the weakness seeps out of me, sudden regained strength obliterating it, the touch of iron beneath my fingers battling Sin-Eater's effect on me.

"This isn't me! You might wanna get out of here. Fast!"

No sooner do I shout the last word, the bulbs spurt back into life, and I fall on my ass in shock.

Sin-Eater leers at me from the other side of the bars. It tilts its head, studying them, a grimace on its scalded, fucked-up face, before turning its violet eyes on me.

"Why don't you come and touch the bars again? They'll give you some strength. I know how I sap away a person's vitality. Call it an appetizer before the main." A gurgling giggle escapes its throat. "Come now... What is it Dullahan calls you? Fateless?" He lifts a finger and wags it slowly from side to side. "Everyone has a fate. Even if he can't see it. Yours is to die."

As tempting as grabbing a hold of the bars is, I'm not that stupid, no matter what some might say. It puts me within his reach. Wiggling off my boot and pulling the sock off, I plant my toes against the iron legs of the cell's bed, instead. Fuck him. I grin as the weariness and brain fog ebbs away.

"Clever." Sin-Eater looks anything but impressed. "I must say, I did not expect such trouble from you."

"I'm full of surprises, asshole," I snarl, staring up at it from the ground. Not the position I'd like to be in, but beggars and all that. "Like I know who you're working for."

"I don't work for Lilith." Sin-Eater's violet eyes turn a shade darker as it reads my thoughts.

"No? You appeared after my last run in with her, after the kid went supernova. You both speak Irish, bleed purple, carry the scent of strawberries." I nod at the bars. "Don't like iron, either."

"I said I did not work for her," Sin-Eater snarls. "Not that I am not of her realm, and she has enslaved me. For now. But I was there first, Nick Holleran, and I will exist long after she is a speck in the Void."

"Then why are you hunting me? Or are you a lying sack of shit as well as being a killer?"

Sin-Eater giggles again. High-pitched and wet. "She has control over me. An ancient matter, one she should not use on the likes of you, but I have come to understand you have a particular talent in vexing reality itself."

She's controlling him and she shouldn't be? That's an angle I can exploit.

"Tell me where she is. I can get her to call if off, stop this fucking madness!" I force myself to meet those horrible glowing eyes. Imploring the creature to see reason. "You don't wanna do all this just because of me? Who am I? Some schmuck in a fucking world full of them. You don't need some psycho holding your leash!"

Sin-Eater tilts its head to the side, mouth hanging loose in a half-grin, its violet eyes shining. What I wouldn't give but to reach through those bars and pull it against the iron, but I can't give it the chance of touching me. I've seen what it can do.

"Now, now, Nick Holleran. You are not *that* clever. The thoughts of a sinner are clear to me, and my how you have sinned. Revenge. Hiding the sins of others and letting all those people wonder just what happened to their loved ones. Tut-tut. What a bad child you were." I glare back at it. No one knows about that night. No one. I left Portland without saying a word. Don't even let myself think about it. Sin-Eater's grin widens. "The truth is, I am hungry. Starving. Lilith kept me locked away for centuries, and time works differently in her domain. One day there is a week here. You may be beneath me, but the soul of any sinner is delicious, and this hunt is filling my belly. For that I thank you."

"You're not going to stop? Not even if I can help you?"

"I do not want your *help*!" Sin-Eater giggles. "I want this chase to last as long as it can. Keep pushing me away, I only grow stronger each time your little 'supernova' Malignant attacks me, and each time I feed. Perhaps I will gather such strength to break Lilith's chains and the rules which govern nature! Even the innocent will fear me then, for even those who have not sinned yet have the capacity to do so. Why wait for them to act? Your precious Rosa... Yes. There's sin in her future, to be sure. Perhaps she will be mine, too."

"You fucking try it," I snarl. "You go anywhere near her and—"

The door leading into the cell area creaks open, cutting me off. Even Sin-Eater turns to look at it, grinning.

"Alright, Holleran, time for us to talk. I want you to explain what the hell these things are before you get your phone call," Henry Butler barks, letting the door close behind him, plastic bags with my possessions in his hands, as well as the keycard for the cell door. He stares down at me, and for a moment, I wonder what's crossing his mind. I'm laying down, one boot on, one off, my toes curled around one of the bed legs. If he didn't think I was crazy before… "Jesus fucking Christ, Holleran."

I stare at him, then at Sin-Eater. It sniffs the air, its grin turning feral.

"A sinner." It giggles. "Oh, I *do* hunger."

"Henry, get the fuck out of here!" I scream, scrambling to my feet. "Now!"

But it's too late. Henry does a double-take, like he's only just noticing someone else in the corridor. Fuck, he can *See*! Somehow, Sin-Eater's revealing itself to him, tearing through the veils of reality before it devours his fucking soul.

And all I'm gonna be able to do is watch.

"What the fuck?" Henry screams, color draining from his face as he finally understands the truth of it all. The truth I've warned him about. Some horrific way to see reason.

An entity so powerful it's changed Henry's perception before it drains his soul. I'd say you learn something new every day, but, for once, this ain't the time to be pithy.

Sin-Eater drops on all fours, lower jaw detached at the hinges again, hanging low, and it pounces at Henry, driving him into the wall. His hands fly wide, the plastic bags flying everywhere, the twin rings of Excalibur creating a heavy thud, and Sin-Eater pushes Henry to the ground, straddling him, its bottom jaw locking onto his chin.

The keycard. It's by the cell!

Diving for it, I stretch my hands through the bars just as Henry starts screaming, his legs kicking, my fingertips brushing the Haven City PD lanyard. Gritting my teeth, I stretch further, but no dice. Too far.

"Holleran!" Henry manages to scream before Sin-Eater's maw covers his face. "Help me!"

I stretch again, growling in frustration, and then I see it. No, I feel it. A breeze against my bare foot.

My fucking boot!

Turning, I grab it, holding it by the laces and cast it toward the keycard, knocking it closer to me. I've got it! I toss the boot at Sin-Eater for good measure, but it bounces off him without interrupting the feeding frenzy.

God loves a trier.

Getting to my feet, I slam the keycard against the lock and stagger forward as the door swings open, casting about at the plastic bags until I see what I want to see.

The Expunger.

Grinning, I swipe the bag, tear it open, and turn on Sin-Eater.

"Hey, fuck face? Feed on this, you son of a bitch!"

I toss it, nonchalant-like, knowing what's gonna happen as soon as the little disc so much as touches the monster, ready to send it out of reality as its matter unravels.

But it doesn't work like that. Not like how I'm expecting it should.

The Expunger lands on Sin-Eater's back, and it pulls off from Henry's face, hissing and screaming as steam rises from its back. But it doesn't start unraveling. The creature's still all-too whole.

"Iron!" It hisses, spinning around. The Expunger falls to the ground, and it snarls. "You think that would have worked on *me*? It is created from the fae, you fool!"

"It's worked on everything else," I mutter, backing away,

extremely aware I no longer have the protection the iron bars give me.

Sin-Eater grins, leaving Henry's twitching body alone. Reckon it's realized I'm out in the open, too. It wanted to extend the chase before, but now I'm here... All bets are off.

"I am *sin*! There is no reality without it, and there is no stopping me with such trinkets made from my own kind!"

It launches itself at me, pushing me onto the ground, its jaws already locked on mine. My limbs turn to rubber, and even though a part of me is aware I'm screaming, my thoughts flee to another place.

A place of sin. *My* sins.

Darkness surrounds me. Thick and massive. Endless. Footsteps sound, but their echo comes from a far-away place like the boots fell minutes before their noise reaches my ears.

Sin-Eater's high-pitched giggle cuts through it all.

'*Sins of the past just gone.*' The creature's purr surrounds me.

Searing red light blooms from the depths. I cover my eyes, turning my head away from the heat of the crimson baking me but a part of me needs to look. Has to. Cracking one eye open, I find myself in the Wheeler basement, Michelle standing in front of her altar, Dean's shade hovering behind her, and me running down the stairs, Ruger in one hand and an Expunger in the other.

I could tell anyone I thought Dean was about to attack Michelle, and it would be true. He was my target, the person I thought had killed Harry from beyond the grave and would do the same to his still-living wife. I could tell anyone I raced down there to protect her, and, partly, I'd be right. Not even that deep down though, I wanted revenge. Desired it. Had to have it for the three bullets Dean Wheeler had left in my chest, for what he'd done to Harry and Maeve. For the torture he'd brought down on Michelle. Cutting at her. Twisting her. The truth turned out to be worse; he'd killed and resuscitated her countless times. I almost admired her for the trap she'd made. One I only sprung through defiance and dumb luck.

The me of months ago charges across the basement, closing the gap on the unmoving Wheeler, and slams the Expunger against his back.

'*Die, you fuck!*' I scream, pushing against it with all my strength, as if I could have rammed it into the heart he didn't have. The heart he never had.

Die. I wanted his death so bad, even though I knew what it would mean for me. Revenge is a sin, no matter what.

The crimson light fades, back to a still darkness. Outside of here, I'm screaming. Thrashing. Thrumming my heels against the floor as Sin-Eater drains my soul of sin, and it doesn't leave much else leftover. I'm done for, but all I can do is watch what I've done.

'*Sins of the distant past.*'

I get to my feet, knowing what I'm gonna see. To be honest, when I died and I started rising to Heaven, my biggest surprise wasn't that Heaven was real, even though that sure came as a shock.

The surprise came from having a place there in the first place.

I'd studied the bible in Sunday School. Had family members preach it at me, which was rich seeing what my old folks did for their kicks. Saying nothing and just walking away from it all, starting a new life in Haven for myself, should have been a sin to keep me in Hell. Those sorry bastards and their families deserved justice. Peace. I could have given it to them, but I didn't want anything else to do with my parents. Not after that.

Crimson light blasts through the darkness, and I walk forward, determined to see this on my feet. It's my old backyard. Seems like Sin-Eater classes this as a sin, too, even if God didn't. Weird.

Tears sting my eyes as I watch myself confront my parents. I wasn't supposed to be there. Pals of mine arranged a camping trip for one of their sixteenth birthdays, but they left without me. Could never call me the popular type, hadn't expected to be invited in the first place. Inviting me was just another way to add more torment. Relationships at home weren't exactly peachy either, so I spent the day alone in Portland with my gear before traipsing home after nightfall, hoping to avoid the questions and permanent tension that flowed from my parents.

I should have called the cops. Should have done *anything* else instead of running away and never going back.

"Don't do it," I breathe, watching my younger self take a halting step forward. "Don't look."

But he won't listen. Curiosity has always been my curse.

My parents remain silent, watching, the shovels in their hands. Pure anger shines in my mom's eyes. The slackness stands out in my old man's face, like he doesn't care what I've found. That he's only gonna add me to it.

'*You shouldn't be here, Nicky.*' My mother hisses, knuckles white as she grabs the shovel. '*You're always turning up where you're not wanted.*'

Bones fill the pit. Dad always kept tarp over it, saying he grew something he never wanted disturbed. Covered the place with pesticide and other things to keep animals away. I never wanted to look at him, let alone get involved in his business, so I avoided it even though my curiosity got me into enough trouble elsewhere. Something about my parents always itched at the back of my brain. Something telling me not everything added up, so I never tried to anger them if I could help it. That night I knew why.

At first I thought they just were serial killers, and I ran for my life, but in later years I discovered the truth. My parents were followers of the old god Moloch. Devoted their lives to it, the pit a testament to their beliefs. Serial killers and worshippers of an evil freak. Some combination.

Black runes stand out on the pale ivory of the skulls of all shapes and sizes. Some are whole, others crushed. Some small, and belonging to children, others larger. And there's a fresh head in there. Flesh still stuck to it. Blood, too. I don't know who it belonged to. Never wanted to know, but it stares at the younger me, a rune seared into its forehead, and I'll never forget the desperate frozen look in its bloodshot eyes.

Younger me falls backwards, scrambling to his feet, already running. He'll never go back. Not even when he heard about the death of his parents. He didn't even shed a tear.

Darkness swoops in one more time, beating away the crimson light.

'*Sins yet to happen.*'

Huh. The creature said he could see them, but couldn't act. Guess it doesn't stop him from feeding on them. This is it. The final stop. Once he's through with this, I'm done. There's a sense of my body straining, grabbing at Sin-Eater's skull, trying to heave him away but it's useless.

Glowing green oozes out of the darkness, and I'm standing in my study, myself and Rosa in the armchairs before me. We don't look that much older. I'm looking out of the window, refusing to acknowledge the tears in her eyes. The angry tears.

'*Why are you doing this, Nick? Why?*'

She rubs at her eyes, her fingers without jewelry. Guess I didn't get around to popping the question after all.

'*It's just... Disappointing, you know? I guess you start thinking you're the same amount of important to someone else, right? And when you think it, you start believing it.*'

'*You're not seriously trying to blame me for this, are you?*' Rosa snaps. '*That's it? That's your play-book? You're scared of commitment and can't let anyone in, even me. But you won't admit that, will you? You'll just lie to me, and lie to yourself?*'

You stupid bastard! Why can't you ever learn?

'*Things haven't been the same since... Well, you know when. We don't talk anymore.*'

Wait. Where's Diana? There's no other noise, no sound from the TV in the other room.

'*That's because you refuse to.*'

'*Now look here—*'

Rosa's sigh is one of those that twists your stomach. The type where the sigh turns into a fist sinking into your gut, a fist that goes deep and keeps on turning until it hits your spine.

'Nick... What can I tell you? You're right. This is over. People just drift apart, some people were never meant to be together, and grief can end things or make it stronger. Looks like the former with us. I've always known this would happen, it's why I swore to myself you'd only have one chance left. I'll get out...'

"No!" I scream at myself as Rosa starts unpicking herself from our life. "You can't do that! Fear. Is that it? Fear of losing her? Fear of letting her in? Well, you're fucking losing her, buddy! You're fucking—"

My head bangs against the wall.

Giving it a shake, I look around, breath flooding into my lungs in a rush. I'm back in the corridor, outside of the cell. Alive.

I'm fucking alive!

And Henry Butler is beating on Sin-Eater. The creature's thrashing, lower jaw slack, disoriented after being disturbed while feeding, almost with its belly full, but I'm as weak as a minute old lamb. It almost had me. Almost.

Sin-Eater screams, swatting at Henry, forcing him off it. I gotta act.

Flopping over, I grab the bar of the jail cell, letting the iron's power wash away my weakness, and my eyes fall on a plastic bag with two rings inside of it. The Expunger didn't work, but Excalibur?

Only one way to find out, slick. I got enough strength in me for this.

I roll, Sin-Eater heaving Henry off of him and spinning, looking for me, it's number one target. It's already had a taste and it prefers its Nick Holleran well-done. But I ain't giving the fucker the chance. Tearing open the bag, I shove the rings of Excalibur onto my index fingers, twisting them so the same icon's front-facing beneath the knuckles. I'm spoiled for choice, but my mind decides for me.

I wanna fight, so sword icon it is.

"Hey, sin for brains!" I call, needlessly as Sin-Eater, on all fours with its bottom jaw hanging loose, is staring right at me. Ready to pounce. "Devour this."

You can take the boy outta the 1980s action flicks...

Balling my hands into fists just as Sin-Eater leaps, I jam them together, the rings of Excalibur touching.

Time slows. I'm a magnet turned the wrong way round, pressing against another, resisting it. A fakir mediating on a bed of nails with my pants pulled down. Energy prickles at every millimeter of my skin, warming me inside and out, lifting my feet off the ground. Levitating just like Diana did in the alleyway. I can't hold it. Can't contain it. It doesn't hurt, it throbs. Heats my blood to an almost uncomfortable level, and my bones and organs rattle, my heartbeat thudding in my ears, drowning out my shouted out '*this*' that still isn't finished.

Light blazes from the rings of Excalibur, just when I think I'm gonna straight up explode. A pure blast of energy, a channeled blazing inferno of white luminosity and it slams into Sin-Eater's chest.

Time returns to normal.

The monster screams. It isn't like the other times it has, shrieks filled with pain and fury. This one has those, but it has something else, too. Fear. The Expunger might not have worked, but Excalibur? No wonder every fucker in England wanted to pull it out of the stone. Er, if that actually happened.

The blast slams Sin-Eater against the wall, pinning it there. My feet touch the ground and, gritting my teeth, hair blowing this way and that from the cacophony of energy, I take a step forward.

"No!" Sin-Eater half-snarls, half-screams. "Stop this!"

Its pale skin tears from its face, turning to dust when it leaves its skull. Excalibur obliterates its red hair, its clothes and bones beneath the failing flesh as it pins it halfway up the wall.

"I'm not stopping until you're fucking dead!" I growl through gritted teeth, taking another step forward, pressing Sin-Eater further against the wall. "You won't hurt anyone again, you piece of shit."

Despite the agony painted across its eaten, devoured face, Sin-Eater gargles out a giggle.

"Fool," it breathes. "There is always sin." It screams. Snarls. A living body of splintered bones with slivers of skin stuck to it. "I cannot be killed, human, and I will return for you and everyone you care for."

"I'll be fucking waiting when you do." Shouting at the top of my lungs, I close the gap between us, ramming my fists against its ruined chest.

The light devours all. My sight. The sound.

And Sin-Eater?

Swaying on the spot, I open my eyes. It's gone. Nothing left on the white wall except for a black stain. Like sin on a once-pure soul.

Staggering backward, my back hits iron and I slide to the floor, legs giving out, head resting against the bars. Strength doesn't return this time. Excalibur took it from me, or maybe it's just general exhaustion after what Hell has thrown at me these last three days. Staring down at the rings of Excalibur, I can't help but grin.

That was fucking *awesome*!

"Is it dead, Holleran?" Henry groans, and I blink, forgetting he's lying on the floor. He struggles to get up, matching my pose across from me. "Is it gone?"

"It's called Sin-Eater, and it's gone," I say, turning my head so it still rests where it is, but I can meet the man's eyes. "For now. You okay, pal?"

"It's going to come back?" Henry asks, face as pale as a full moon. "When?"

"Don't know, but no time soon, I reckon. Need to take the fight to its master." I pat my chest, instincts reaching for a pack of cigarettes that aren't there. Not even wearing a jacket to hold 'em even if I had 'em on me. "You doing okay?"

He meets my eyes. "It's true. Everything you ever said is true."

"Who knew, right?" There's always room for a little snark. I sigh. "Welcome to the fucking team, pal."

"I'm sorry, Holleran. I didn't know. We all had you down as a crank. Everyone. And your past. I know I gave you a hard time but… What the fuck?"

Just as Henry's spilling out an extremely deserved apology, Diana picks the perfect moment to phase through the wall. Just when I thought someone couldn't get any paler. Henry raises a hand, pointing, finger trembling.

"W-w-wha…"

"Relax, she's with me," I breathe, shaking my head. "Diana, Henry, Henry, Diana. Seems like Sin-Eater did such a number on your mind, you really are a part of the team. Hell's a real eye opener, you're gonna love it."

"What happened here?" Diana asks, head swiveling as she takes in the tired middle-aged men and scattered relics. "Sin-Eater?"

"Gone. For now." I groan as I start getting to my feet. "Looks like Grandpa came through for us. I'll tell you all about it on the way over to the Styx."

"Holleran!" Henry calls. "You can't—"

I cut him off with a pointed finger.

"Look, hoss, you've seen a part of the real fucking picture. A sliver of it. That's all. Now, I gotta go make sure the freak that killed Kieran Greaney, my next-door neighbor, and the poor sonofabitch in the Rolls this morning, before nearly killing you *and* me, doesn't come back to finish the job or turn its attention somewhere else." I scoop up my cell, and the still steaming Expunger from the floor as well as my Ruger. "If you wanna keep me here, fine. But then any blood's on your hands if that thing comes back before I walk. Because I *will* fucking walk. Now, you can drop all the charges, give me my coat and hat, and let me on my merry way. Understand?"

Henry meets my stare. Hatred flashes in his eyes, just for a moment. Old habits really do die hard. But he knows what's happened here. Me and him fought together, too. Saved one another's lives, and there's no forgetting that. The hatred ebbs away. Understanding and resolve takes its place.

"Fine," he mutters. "I'm going to have to pull some strings, and my reputation is going to take a hit, but better than being dead."

"That's the spirit," I say, grinning down at him and holding out my hand. He can't help but look Diana's way when I say '*spirit*'. Pun very much intended. Hoisting him to his feet, I pat him on his meaty shoulder. "Look, it's tough acclimatizing to Hell. Fucking brutal, to be perfectly honest with you. Swing by the Styx, the lower level; probably best you don't drive unless you wanna crash your car. Folk there will help you. You're gonna need it."

"Sure, Holleran, sure," he mutters, bending to retrieve the keycard. "Try to look chastened when we're heading through the bullpen, okay?"

I grin. Chastened. I can do that.

"Ah, just a sec," I say as Henry goes to open the heavy door leading out of the cell areas. Thank God for soundproofing otherwise the entire PD might be in on Hell's little secret. Actually, that might not be a bad thing at all... "Forgot something."

I wiggle my bare toes, and go for my boot, head full of thoughts. Where am I gonna find Lilith? What's she got on Sin-Eater, and how long will it take the freak to return?

There's other, more personal matters, too. The future sin he showed me. Is that gonna happen? Am I always gonna fuck up?

And he called Diana a 'Malignant.' Now, that could have just been an insult, but it sounded more ominous to me. Way more. And I didn't see her in my future. Rosa talked about grief. Shit...

Why can't the path ever be straight through Hell, huh? Why? One thing's for sure, though. The rings of Excalibur catch the light as I tie up my bootlaces.

I'm sick of reacting. Sick of being on the defense. From now on, Nick Holleran and friends are going on the fucking attack.

CHAPTER FIFTEEN

IN THE HOUSES OF THE HOLY

Cold sinks its teeth into me as we trudge down the snow-filled sidewalk. The sky really emptied itself during my prolonged stay at Haven City PD's five-star facilities, and looks like there's no end to it. Night's fallen since Henry and Lori threw me in my jail cell, and the streets are packed with the living getting their holiday season tasks completed, and with the dead and denizens of Hell doing whatever it is they do, rain, snow or shine. A pair of demons the size of double-door wardrobes pick their way over on the other side, careful not to jolt a human into seeing them, or disturbing any of the ghosts lost in their memories. A reminder that not all demons are bad news.

Rosa screamed my ear off for a full minute, her words a mashed-up stream of exasperation, anger, relief and disbelief. When she'd fully vented, or just ran out of different ways to call my ass dumb, and found herself in a state to listen to me, she agreed to meet immediately at the Styx with anything she could find on the fae. She threw in more than a couple of sorrys for good measure but she didn't need to. I'd been in that cell for over six hours, and she'd called me over a hundred times, sending just as many texts. Rosa thought Sin-Eater had punched my ticket. Diana's, too. The tears she shed at the end of our call were of relief.

Mine, too. I'm not some macho man afraid of emotions. It was a fucking pleasure to speak to her again, to hear her voice.

Can't wait to hold her. Kiss her. It's been too long. Me being dead was a close-run thing. Too close. Then there's my future sin. I ain't gonna let it come to that. No way, no how.

So, we're all convening at the Styx. Makes sense to me. Ruby's always got sage advice, and the place has its own protection, just in case. Plus, the Mustang's parked that way in case we need to travel anywhere, though I shudder to think of the parking tickets it's sporting.

"Cross over," I say, tapping Diana on the shoulder. Kid's lost in thought.

"Why?" she asks, frowning up at me.

I pause, pointing at a disheveled and seemingly abandoned building across from the Church of St. Michael.

"See that place?"

"Yeah?"

"It's a lair."

"A lair for what?"

"Succubi." It might just be my imagination, but I reckon the gray in her face turns into a more washed-out shade of drab. "Try to avoid it when I can." As we talk, a pale, skinny looking fella looks left and right then heads into the ramshackle building. "Can't say the same for every red-blooded man in Haven, though."

"They'll kill him!" Diana says, glowing slightly.

I squeeze her shoulder. "Not right away. They like their thralls, succubi. Incubi do, too. They have a place across town. They'll keep him alive long enough, kid."

The light inside her fades a little. "We should do something about them."

"Kid, if I've learned anything from the past few days is that Hell has a certain equilibrium and it's mighty dangerous to go messing with it."

"I guess so," she mutters, nodding, and crosses the road when I do. "Nick, isn't that—"

"Suraz," I breathe, picking up the pace.

The goddamned elusive Nephilim, who used to be stuck

to my ass at all times, just slunk into the fucking Church of St. Michael.

"What's a Nephilim doing going into a church?" Diana asks.

"Good question, kid," I reply. "I'm gonna go see. Go ahead to the Styx, would ya?"

"Nick."

"Diana. Don't make me pull out the 'young lady' card again. I'll be fine for a while. Can you feel Sin-Eater at all?" The kid glances around, then shakes her head, sullen. "There you go. Get to the Styx, tell Rosa I'll be right there, and see what you can find on Lilith and the fae realm. That's the aim, and you're great at it. Take charge. The Nephilim going into the church has got my curiosity buzzing, and I wouldn't mind doing a little bit of sneaking. You've got a habit of... making your presence known. Small as it is."

Jesus, I can't even believe there *is* a fae realm. Days ago, I wouldn't have believed it. I heard about different layers, like Dante described, and the Seal, whatever that is, but other realms? Shit's getting weirder all the time.

"Okay, Nick, I'll go," Diana says, but she doesn't look all too happy about it. "Don't do anything stupid."

"Sure, I'll get Suraz to walk me home when we're done." I roll my eyes. "Be seeing you."

Diana gives me an odd look before walking away, and I frown too. '*Be seeing you*'? Starting to sound a little too like Charon for comfort. Wherever the fuck he is. I give the surrounding shadows a quick scan, looking for his boney grin and come up wanting. Diana merges with the press of bodies up ahead, thankfully still on the opposite side of the succubi bordello. Satisfied she's making herself scarce, I turn to the church and take the steps one at a time.

Never enjoyed churches. Even though I didn't believe in their power, or status. Probably why I didn't like 'em. As Marvin Clancy Sr. proved, who was some stuffy, gray-haired man-of-the-cloth to judge me? Especially when they preached from some book that was just a cut above a fairy tale.

But it isn't a fairytale. Just... the Good Book's got some of the details wrong, that's all. Maybe that's by design, or maybe folk got the telling of it funky. Doesn't change that the very basis of what these churches represent is painfully real. Me being me, I used to look down on those pious petitioners, sneering at their faith. Fuck me, right? A little faith ain't no bad thing, says the Nick Holleran of 2024.

Still, the lingering suspicion I got of churches holds. My gut flutters when I take the top step, and I pull in a lungful of air to settle it. With a quick look left and right like the schmoe heading into the incubi lair—why? Who the fuck knows—I take the plunge and cross the threshold.

Pushing through the doors, a raised voice booms in a tongue I don't understand and before I can get my bearings, light stings my eyes. So bright I gotta look away, have to shield them by shoving my face into the crook of my arm. An illumination so strong it singes my skin a little, or maybe that's just my rampant imagination and inclination towards the dramatic. Sue me. The sensation fades, and goosebumps spring up all over my flesh from head to toe.

Pulling my arm away, and giving my head a quick shake, I glance around. Except for Suraz, the church is empty. He's kneeling beside the altar, staring up at a stained-glass window, his fully-grown man-sized greatsword propped against a wall. Don't know why, but I get the impression he's just lowered his arms. Combined with the voice, the light, and the fact a Nephilim's slunk into a House of God, my Spidey-sense is going haywire.

My footsteps echo as I approach the altar. Church isn't so big, and sound likes to travel in these kinds of places, so Suraz glances over his shoulder. Is that... Shame? Fear? Whatever expression Suraz wore, he replaces it with the almost aggressive indifference he usually sports.

"You talking to someone, hoss?" I ask, spreading my arms and glancing around. "Sorry to interrupt."

"Nick Holleran, always appearing where you are least wanted," Suraz growls, golden eyes glittering. The phrase is a little too close to comfort, especially as I just heard my mom saying the exact same thing in a near-death vision not one hour ago. "What do you want?"

Look, personal deep-seated demons, here's the thing. I don't have time to deal with you right now. Why don't you grab a drink at the bar, and we'll settle our differences another time over a few bourbons? I park the memories of mom, and all the fucked-up feelings that come with them.

"Least wanted?" I ask, raising an eyebrow. "Don't see anyone else here?"

Who am I? Robert de Niro? Still, I *don't* see a soul, and I *heard* plenty to suggest all isn't what it seems.

Suraz scowls. "What do you want, I said."

"Talking to God? Is that it?" The lop-sided grin forms, seemingly of its own will. "You and your buddy Morningstar had a tiff and you're running to the great Agony Aunt in the sky for advice?"

That touches a nerve. Such is Suraz's speed, I don't have time to react as he surges to his feet and spins in one movement, closing the gap until he's towering above me, so close my nose is almost touching his chest. The Nephilim's shoulders heave as he sucks in air through gritted teeth, snarling, and down there, in my peripheral vision, his fists flex as he squeezes them.

I may have finally taken my snark too far. It was bound to happen one day.

The End?

Not quite yet. I close my eyes, realizing I haven't got a hope in... Hell... if Suraz can't keep his anger in check.

The Nephilim lets out a cry and I brace myself, flinching. A crunching grind fills the church and then? Blessed silence. I press my hands against my chest and stomach, making sure I'm intact, making sure I'm still breathing. Reckon maybe I am.

"Damn," Suraz mutters, and I risk opening one eye.

A part of the altar lies on the ground, pieces of smooth

marble turned to rubble, and Suraz is rubbing at the side of his left hand.

One day the fact that this smile of mine I figure is so fucking charming only causes more trouble than good is going to cement itself in my brain.

I raise my hands, taking a backward step down the little stairs leading to the now ruined altar. "Can we start again? I didn't mean to cause offense."

Well, would you look at that? I *can* be contrite!

Suraz glares at me, the rage leering through the indifference, and then he shakes his head and sighs.

"I am the one who should apologize, Nick Holleran. I have been failing in my tasks lately, and I took the anger I directed at myself and aimed it at you."

He turns, and there's tiredness eating away at every fiber of him. He sags instead of standing upright, his armor is chipped and filthy in places. New lines and dark circles plague the poor bastard's face, and the conversation I overheard between him and Absin sails back into my mind. The loss, the drugs, the grief he wears has left his sleeve and taken over his entire body.

"Look, I hear you've had a lot on your plate lately. Incursions from the lower levels," I say, then narrow my eyes. "And maybe... Other realms?"

Suraz's eyes glitter. "Other realms. What do you know of such things?"

"Well, lot of interesting shit's been happening to me since you stopped tailing my ass." Suraz flinches each time I cuss. Really? What's God gonna do, smite me down? Sure the big guy's got better things to do than that. "Had a run in with Lilith. You know, Queen of the Fae."

His face twitches. "Nothing you cannot handle. Bring iron."

"Thanks for that, buddy. Seems like Lilith has a few rabbits in her hat. Some ancient things I *really* can't handle."

The Nephilim inhales sharply, meeting my eyes. The weight of his focus slams into me, and I stagger backward, throwing my hands out to steady myself on the pews.

"The Sluagh?" he snarls, teeth bared. "She unleashed the Sluagh?"

I mentally file the name away.

"Never called itself that, slick. Calls itself 'Sin-Eater.'"

Suraz hands turn into fists again, and I reckon the other side of the altar's about to crumble.

"It's still free?" he hisses, perfectly still. Like the stillness before someone explodes into devastating action. "It's in this realm?"

"Managed to send it away for a little while, and I'm planning on calling in on Lilith and giving her a talking to." I raise my hands, the rings of Excalibur catching the low light. "Got me a relic that can make a difference."

Suraz eyes them, shoulders relaxing back into the slump.

"Excalibur. I shall not ask where you got those from," he mutters, and his eyes flick to the stained-glass window. "I do not *want* to know."

From the way he's looking to his behavior and body language, if Suraz wasn't a Nephilim and tough to read, I'd say he had the entire fate of the world on his mind. Reckon I'm right, anyway. This is a soul plagued by demons, and game recognizes game.

"Look, Suraz, I'm gonna level with you." I take a seat before I fall down, the effort of withstanding a Nephilim's focus and fury getting to be too much, and cross my legs, trying to act all nonchalant, like. "Reckon you're meant to be keeping an eye on me, and though I understand why you're not, with all the incursions and lack of help from your partner, the head honcho won't be so happy you haven't been keeping tabs. And there's only one fella who could order you around, right?"

Suraz mutters something under his breath and glances at that damned window again. He ain't arguing, though.

"Lucifer." I pause, just in case the House of God starts

shaking or some shit. Don't know about cussing, but even I'm not comfortable with saying his name in here all of a sudden. "I'm gonna let it slide. I'm gonna be gracious. Not gonna tell if you won't, even though I've had a lousy few days. But I'm gonna want some help from you."

"I cannot fight Lilith or Sin-Eater for you, Holleran. Neither can die. Both are essential to the balance of reality." He shakes his head. "Though her setting it loose changes things..."

"Don't want you to fight 'em, hoss, and I understand all too well about the status quo around these parts. Reckon it's what got me into all this mess in the first place. So, I got some questions and a few favors to ask. Oh, and into the bargain, I won't mention to Lucifer about you being here, and how nervous you are about that window, either." He snarls, but I raise a finger. "Figure I can deal with Lilith in a way she'd understand, so long as I can get to her. So, I wanna know how to get to her realm. Right now. No warnings about how fucking dangerous it's gonna be, no '*be careful where you place your business in Hell, Holleran*', and no goddamned '*One life left*' advice. I know all that, but I gotta do this. She wants me dead, and she isn't gonna stop until I put an end to it or I'm feeding the fucking worms."

Thank you for coming to my TED Talk. Pretty nice speech if I do say so myself.

Suraz pulls his stare away from me, granting some blessed relief. Other details flood my mind now it isn't batting away the Nephilim's massive focus; the smell of incense these churches always have swirls around me, and I'm reminded of how cold it is. Probably cooler than outside, truth be told. I pull my bobble hat a little lower and my coat tighter while an internal struggle rages inside of Suraz. Reckon a Nephilim doesn't like being told what to do unless it's Lucifer doing the telling, and this poor bastard's getting orders left, right, and center at the moment.

"The Morningstar *would* be aggrieved if he found out I had not been following you, even though my other activities have been necessary, and me joining you on an excursion into the fae realm would start a war, no matter what Lilith's crimes have been," Suraz rumbles, staring at his armored feet, his voice low and reluctant. He doesn't wanna agree with me, but at least he ain't so frustrated he's smashing altars. "Do you know Haven Woods?"

Do I know Haven Woods? Wish I didn't. I almost roll my eyes. "Yeah, I know 'em."

"Perhaps not as well as you think, Nick Holleran." Suraz wipes away some of the rubble from the top of the altar. "There is a disused railroad that runs through the forest, into a tunnel that passes underground. To those who do not see, this tunnel has collapsed. It has, but it is passable, though no one tries. Through there you will find Haven's portal into the fae realm. There are other entry points, of course, but that is the closest to here. Let me warn you, humans are not welcome. In truth, only those creatures allowed by Lilith are. Her followers will fight you."

"Best come prepared then, huh?" I reply. A railroad. Reckon I know a guy who might help with that. "Now. Questions. What's a Malignant?"

"The girl..." Suraz replies, shakes his head, then takes a seat on the top of the stairs, propping his elbows on his knees and letting his hands hang loose. His focus hits me again, but it's like he's keeping it in check for my benefit. "Has she..."

Sadness crosses his face, like he's only now realizing she isn't here and he's fearing the worst. Seems like this Malignant term is one well-known to him, and it isn't a massive surprise to pair it with the kid.

"Diana's fine. She's meeting with friends, preparing for our trip into the fae realm." Shit, I can't actually believe I'm saying that but here we are. "Sin-Eater called her that. He and Lilith seem to be pretty afraid of her."

"So they should be." Suraz sighs. "Malignants are not common."

"You knew Diana was one of these things all this time?"

Suraz nods. "I suspected, but I had hoped not. Her sudden Awareness was not a natural thing, and maybe it is because of that she is the way she is, or perhaps it is the girl's nature before death. I do not know."

"Wait. '*Not a natural thing*'? Expand on that, slick."

A grimace eats into his obsidian face. I almost feel sorry for Suraz, but he's been holding secrets about my kid for months, I ain't letting him off the hook.

"You remember the moment she became Aware?"

"Course. Wasn't sure what was gonna tear itself from my body first. My fucking heart or... Hey, let's not talk about that, huh? Not in a church, anyway."

"Lucifer and I watched you, and it was my lord who gave her Awareness. A '*nudge*', is what he called it."

My vision flashes red at the same time a wave of dizziness slams into me. Pain follows, and I realize I've bit into my tongue.

"Why?" I seethe, glaring at Suraz. "Why'd he do that to her, huh? For kicks?"

"I believe he was trying to help you in some way. Or spur you on. You had captured his interest, and your involvement in matters intrigued him. He spoke of your constant involvement in matters, and thought it not a coincidence. When Absin called you unimportant, I disagreed. Lucifer does, too."

"Help me? Do you know what he did to *her*?" I shout, pointing in God knows what direction, my arm trembling. "She had to confront the fucker who murdered her and by that point ending her life was a goddamned mercy. She had to remember all of that! Not to mention finding herself sixty years in the future, without a family, without anything!"

Suraz drops his head. "I cannot speak for Lucifer, but I know this. She has something, Nick Holleran. She has you."

He says it in a whisper, but it's got enough strength behind it to knock the anger outta my sails. Enough truth.

"You're goddamn right she has," I mutter.

"Listen to me, and listen to me well, human. A Malignant is a terrible thing. The power they possess... I believe you have seen the beginning of it?" He glances up at me and I nod. "You humans have developed a weapon. An EMP, you call it. A Malignant is like a Hell version of that and their blast can destroy all kinds of matter. At first it will only affect those of the *Other*, but a power like that cannot be contained. It will bleed over, and it is always devastating. They act on impulse, through fear, and that is always the most dangerous way to exist, especially when one has power. It is one of my tasks to neutralize all Malignants before it is too late."

I glance at his sword, propped up against the wall beneath the stained-glass window, and narrow my eyes. What chance do I have against a Nephilim if it comes to it? As if to remind me, the weight of the rings of Excalibur press against my fingers. If it comes to it, Suraz will find me standing between him and the kid.

"But you haven't with Diana?" I ask, rubbing at one of the rings with my thumb. "Why?"

"Because there is a chance she shall not *become* a Malignant."

"But you said—"

Suraz holds up a shovel-sized hand. "I said she has the power and is on the path. She does not have to walk down it. Malignants are often tortured souls, ones with innate power and greatly abused in life. If that continues in death? If that anguish is not tempered? They walk the path. Your child does not have to go down that route."

The future sin. Diana's absence. The grief. Was that it? She went full Malignant and had to be taken down? Fuck me... I'm not about to let that happen.

"What can I do?" I whisper, forcing myself to meet the Nephilim's eyes. Deep sorrow swims there, heavier than his normal amount.

"Love her, Nick Holleran. Be there for her. Show her the path."

"That simple, huh?"

Suraz sighs. "There is no such thing as simple in Hell, I am afraid."

Never a truer sentence has ever been breathed in life or

death. Rubbing my hands over my face, cares and concerns about anything else blown from my mind, I can only think about the kid. A ticking EMP of Hellish proportions, and I got a glimpse of the future. Well, Charon calls me the Fateless. Gonna make that work in my favor. Screw Sin-Eater and his visions, the ginger-haired freak. I get to my feet. There's work to be done.

"A moment," Suraz calls. "Take all you can into Lilith's domain. She will not go down without a fight, but you cannot kill her. She is one of the Ancients, a primordial building block of reality. We have lost too many of those already, and I am not sure how many more the universe can take before the foundations break."

Interesting. "An Ancient. Guessing that's with a capital 'A'. Reckon there's a few of them I've met; Charon, Sin-Eater, Lilith, Lucifer? God too, though I haven't met him. Yet."

Suraz nods. "And more. Good luck, Nick Holleran. I will be in your debt should you succeed. The Sluagh is not a force to be used for a personal vendetta."

I turn away then pause, my curiosity getting the better of me and, Hell, for once I've enjoyed having the upper hand in a conversation though Suraz has taken that away from me a little. Turning back to him, finger wagging like a prime Columbo, I gaze at the stained-glass window.

"What saint is that?" I ask. "You seem mighty preoccupied with it."

"It is not a saint," Suraz mumbles, glancing at it. "It is an archangel by the name of Metatron."

I raise my eyebrows. "The Scribe of God, huh?"

What? I've read books and like I said, I was forced to go to Sunday School way more than I wanted to. Some of it stuck.

"The very same," Suraz replies, staring at the window. "Be well, Nick Holleran. And Merry Christmas."

"And a happy fucking New Year," I reply, turning away, my footsteps echoing as I leave the House of God, my mind full.

"Nick Holleran," Suraz calls, and it isn't in a tone I can ignore. Nothing he ever growls is. I pause. "I understand that you, above all humans, err towards the cocksure, and no doubt having had an encounter with both Lilith and Sin-Eater that you have survived you think you will prevail again. Bolstered by that relic you carry. Let me tell you this, Sin-Eater may be weaker after you exiled him, but you are about to enter Lilith's domain and the place where she is strongest. Do not underestimate her. If you do, you shall not return. You may not anyway even with Excalibur and every weapon you possess. Win or lose, it solves the issue for me. Once you are dead, Sin-Eater will remain in the Unseen, and I shall be free of watching you and my burden shall be less."

"Gee, thanks, Suraz," I mutter, walking away, my stomach sinking into my boots. "Just when I'd added you to my Christmas card list, too."

Got Lilith's location, with a few rules of engagement to boot. Suraz has given me plenty to think about with Diana too, and me and Rosa have to talk about that as soon as this situation's taken care of, but there's something else.

I push through the doors and glance over my shoulder. Suraz still stares up at Metatron's window like it's the only thing that exists in Hell and all its goddamned realms. I said my Spidey-sense tingled, and it hasn't stopped throughout our whole pow-wow.

Suraz has secrets, and I reckon they're more dangerous than any EMP blast from a teenage Malignant or a trip into the lair of the goddamned Queen of the Fae.

CHAPTER SIXTEEN

CHARIOTS OF IRON

Here we are, Team Fae Fuckers. Me, Rosa, Diana, and Ruby. We're sitting at a table, the Styx quiet again. A few of the regular ghosts drink Paintstripper by the bar, and Rubes leaves to help one of them every now and then. She says holiday week is slow compared to the usual as many of the ghosts pick this time of year to haunt their family lines. Guess December is the month they miss having a pulse the most. I get it. She's helping old Fred the train driver with a drink now, so there's a lull in the conversation while we pore through some books.

I glance at Rosa, smiling as she studies a page, a small frown forming on her forehead. My first order of business when arriving here was to kiss her like it was my last time, and I didn't give a shit about who watched. Just to feel her body pressed against mine, her warmth, the smell of the lavender-scented perfume she wears... I'm not gonna give her up, no matter what my future shows. Fuck the future just like those fucking fae.

She looks up at me, a smile replacing the small frown of concentration. Not had the time to talk to her about the kid, yet. Gonna need her guidance on that.

"Coffee?" Ruby asks, dropping into her seat and pushing a couple of mugs our way. I let the steam warm my face for a second before taking a quick sip. "What's the plan?"

Rosa sighs and closes her book. "I think I've found everything I can about Sluaghs. Their mythology is Irish in origin, like the fae or Tuatha dé Danann, and they're known as the hosts of the unforgiven dead. I guess there's some truth in that. Sin has the unforgiven aspect to it after all."

"Yes, but there aren't many of them like in these myths. In reality, there's only one," Diana murmurs, her book closing without her even touching it. A subtle show of how her powers are developing. I suppress a shiver and try not to think about the word 'Malignant'. "There are links everywhere I've read to the fae realm. To the Wild Hunt, too, which is interesting."

"Maybe there's a similar origin point to all these creatures. Suraz mentioned the term Ancients, right? On the other hand, guess it shows that much of what we know has been written by people sitting behind desks and not by the folk fighting these things. Reckon we gotta change that," I mutter, staring into my coffee. "Any weaknesses?"

"Harry didn't have anything to say on it," Diana replies, her gray hand resting on top of the handbook. "It seems like he had quite a cordial relationship with the fae, despite harvesting their wings, and didn't write much about them. Cordial, Nick. Once this is all settled, you should try it."

If this gets settled. Suraz warned me I'd only witnessed a sliver of Lilith's power, and there doesn't seem to be a way to stop Sin-Eater permanently without resorting to drastic measures. But, and in Hell, there always seems to be a 'but', I can't kill either of the fuckers. That's the easy option gone, though I'm guessing neither are particularly simple to end, anyway.

"Listen to this." Ruby grabs at a printout from an article she found on the Internet. "Could be something. '*The foulest and most feared of the Unseen, the Sluagh had power greater than Death itself. Dullahan and the Sluagh raced to gather souls for reasons known only to them, and who could know the minds of creatures such as they?*' This might explain the power it had over Charon."

I nod. My task was to research anything to do with Ancients. I flunked out, so I'm taking on the role of Group Leader in Team

Fae Fuckers. Which, like with any Group Leader, means sitting here, asking questions, listening, and then taking all credit for any success.

"I found this," Rosa says, pulling out her notepad. She's the type who takes notes when she does research. Lots of notes. "It was on a slip of paper stuck into one of Ruby's books called '*Of Fae and the Other*' by an Earnest Raleigh."

She hands the notebook to me, and I clear my throat.

'*One thing pervades all matters with the fae. Bargains. No matter the creature, no matter their standing in the Unseen, their delight is captured by the promise of a tantalizing notion. Another subject to bear in mind is this; fae are consumed by the extremity of reality. Life, death, sin, sacrifice, retribution, penance, and, above all, redemption. These notions move them, govern them, and sway their decision making. Even, and especially, Lilith. If dealing with the fae, use this knowledge to your favor. K.M.S.*'

"K.M.S.?" I ask. Blank stares meet me. I shrug. "Never met anyone with three initials I liked."

"You don't *know* anyone with three initials," Rosa says, nudging my arm and grinning. "Doofus."

"I used to," I reply. "It's why I avoid them these days."

"Not that it isn't cute, but if you two are done flirting?" Ruby asks, raising an eyebrow. "That reminds me of something else I found. Listen, it ties in with the Wild Hunt angle Diana found, and while it isn't completely accurate, it might have some basis of truth in it. '*The only way to ward off one of the Sluagh or another member of the Hunt is by placing another in its path.*' Do you think it's something we could work with?"

"Willing to use anything at the moment, this has got to stop. Tonight. We're in a better position than we were in a couple of days ago." I spread my hands, the rings of Excalibur catching the light and drawing everyone's eyes. "We got these, and we got knowledge we didn't have before."

"It's slim pickings though, Nick," Ruby says, and I reckon she's speaking for everyone else at the table. More than a little of my mind too, truth be told.

"Look, it's more of a plan than I usually have for these kinds of things," I reply, offering an extremely half-hearted shrug. The words sound lame in my own ears and I'm the one saying 'em.

Rosa's eyebrows climb to her hairline. At least she's keeping quiet.

Can't say so much for the kid.

"That isn't saying a lot, Nick," Diana murmurs, shaking her head. Can't say she's not right.

"Well, I ain't finished yet. Suraz gave us a roundabout location, and I reckon I can find it easily enough but walking through that tunnel into the Unseen? Doesn't seem wise to me." I lean my elbows on the table and flick my head at the bar. "Just so happens we got a train driver from when the railroad running through there was in use. And you know what those old trains are made out of..."

"Iron," Rosa says, grinning.

"And Bingo was his name-o. Told ya, *way* more of a plan than usual." Wriggling my eyebrows, I return her grin. "Be back in a minute."

Only a little stung by the lack of congratulations on my great idea, and it *is* a fucking wonderful idea, I climb to my feet and take a place besides Fred at the bar. By taking the train, we'd be encased in material fae-like creatures find toxic and harmful.

"Reckon you've been listening in, buddy," I say, taking his cup and reaching over to the pumps, I fill it to the brim with Paintstripper. Never been back here, and lookie here. There's different flavors. Ghosts can taste? Really? "So, whaddya say? You know where this tunnel is?"

Fred grins at me, his faded eyes twinkling. "I do, youngster. I do. Curious thing; that railroad's always been off-limits. Abandoned, you might say. Rumor said the tunnel collapsed the first time a locomotive passed through back in the 1860s."

That familiar sinking feeling hits my guts again. "So, there's no way to get a train through there? Rather not walk if there's gonna be an attack."

"Now, hold your damned horses, son, I didn't say that." Fred downs his Paintstripper, wincing as he does, then holds out his cup for more. I happily oblige. "There's an old shunting yard with lines leading onto the one you want. You'd call it a train graveyard nowadays."

"The one over by Haversome and Foster?"

It's out near the city's outer limits. Nice and remote, actually.

Fred nods. "The very same. Happens to be where many of the old iron horses rest. I go take a look over there every now and then. Drove one or two of them myself back in the day. Now, resting there is a grand old Southern Pacific GS-4 class. Goes by the name of 'Falcon'. Made in the 1940s, retired in the 80s. Streamlined and a mighty piece of iron. Get its engine hot enough, and I'd fancy it would work like a charm."

The sinking feelings turned heel and gone straight to giddy excitement, charging through my chest and into my head. And the name's Falcon! Pinch me!

"And can you get the engine hot enough?"

Fred takes a sip and leans back in his chair. Sonofabitch is milking the moment. I'm only half as annoyed as I might be. Been known to do the same myself.

"Well... The engine's been dormant a long time, Mr. Holleran, and you'd need to manually switch all the old tracks, so it gets onto the railroad you'd need. Have to do it in advance too so the locomotive can build up a head of steam if you're aiming to blast through some rocks. We don't know if they're an illusion or not..." He twists in his seat and smiles over at Diana who's got her head buried in one of those books, his jaws working like he's chewing on something. Tobacco? Looks the type, but a ghost doesn't chew *anything*. God knows I understand how hard giving up a nasty habit is. "But your girl over there isn't normal like me. She's special. Known it since the first time I laid my peepers on her. It can be done with a little bit of special, son. I believe it can."

Alright, mode of transportation complete. Now comes the rub.

"Ah, I hate to ask this. We barely know one another, and you don't owe me anything, but—"

"But you don't know the first thing about switching a track, let alone driving an eighty-year-old locomotive." Fred drains his Paintstripper and holds it out to me again, wiggling it, then hocks a wad of invisible tobacco onto the floor. Must have been an old habit of his. Course, there's no tobacco actually there, but I guess you can't teach dead dogs new tricks, huh? "Keep topping this up for me and I'll be your huckleberry. Death's been a little boring of late, and I'd give anything to fire up a Southern Pacific again. If it means saving a few lives in the bargain, then count me in."

I take the mug, filling it again. "Thanks, buddy. You don't know how much I appreciate this."

"Let's not think about settling down with one another just yet, sonny." Fred laughs and slaps his hand on the bar with a shake of his head. "This might be our last day in Hell! Still, it's worth it to climb aboard that grand old steamie one more time..."

His eyes go to a faraway place, and I reckon it's time to get this show on the railroad. Nodding, I get to my feet, and return to the rest of Team Fae Fuckers.

"Good news, we got a way in, riding on a chariot of iron," I say, grinning as I drop into my seat. "Now, to brass tacks. Given it a lot of thought, and—"

"Nick," Rosa cuts in. "If you think for one minute—"

"You and the kid are coming with me." I hold up my hands, the rings of Excalibur shining on my index fingers and stifle a laugh when three jaws drop in response to my declaration. "What? Reckon an old dog can't learn new tricks? Seems to me I got into this predicament through arrogance, a lack of preparation, and lone wolfing it. Well, I'm not doing any of that anymore. I don't want harm to come to any of you, of course not, but the more I try to avoid it, the worse the situations I keep getting into. Then I bring them down on you all, anyway."

Ruby leans forward, eyes narrowed. "Are you the real Nick Holleran? Is he in there?"

"Come on," I growl, folding my arms.

"No, she's right," Rosa adds, her face the picture of seriousness and concern. "I mean, you're talking a lot of sense right now. This isn't right at all. What have you done with my boyfriend?"

"Have you all finished?" I ask, glaring at them. At least the kid kept quiet, but I could do with less of the grin she's wearing.

The women share a glance and nod together, like they're part of a hive mind.

"Okay, like I was saying, I reckon I can do a better job of looking after you all if you come with me." I take a breath. "And you can take care of me better, too. A team. That's what we are, right?"

"Right," Diana says, smiling.

"With that in mind, I'm not stupid." I ignore the choking sound coming out of Ruby and press on. "I got my Ruger, its consecrated rounds, *and* Excalibur. Diana's well, her. I know you can handle yourself, Rosa, and I'm sure with your Aikido you could easily beat *my* ass, but that ain't gonna cut it in Hell. So..."

I pull the rings of Excalibur from my fingers one at a time, and hold them out to her, the relics heavy in the center of my palm.

"Want you to take these," I say, meeting her eyes. Hers are shining, and mine sting just a little. Goddamned emotions. "Like I said, I got other weapons. If you're coming with, you need something, and I can't think of anything better. You'll pick up how to use 'em in no time."

She reaches out for them, and bites her bottom lip. "Are you sure?"

"Sweetheart, it's non-negotiable. You aren't launching an attack on Lilith's realm with nothing but your beauty, stunning as it is."

A tear falls down her cheek as she takes the rings from me, and gasps as she slides them over her index fingers. "They fit!"

"Well, they're magic, right?" I sniff and blink, then scowl when I see Ruby's eyes and Diana's pits fixed on me, their expressions of the romantic and melting kind. "What?"

"Nothing, Nick," Ruby replies, wiping at her eye. "I just didn't think you had it in you."

What's that supposed to mean?

Getting to my feet, and making my voice a little rougher than necessary, I nod at the bar's office. "You got any consecrated clips? Could make a pit-stop if I need to. And, ah, nicotine patches? I really picked the wrong goddamn time to give up the cigarettes."

"I've got some, Nick," she replies, smiling. Rosa's staring at the rings of Excalibur like I just dropped a pair of six-figure jewels on her fingers. "You can have all you need."

"Alright, alright," I say, clapping my hands. "No time like the present. You ready, Fred?"

He raises his Paintstripper then downs it. "One for the road?"

With a sigh, Ruby moves to fill the order before disappearing into the office, no doubt getting me the ammo and patches I need. Just then, a sheepish Henry Butler walks in, eyes staring out of his head like he's just taken his first trip through Hell.

In his case, he really has.

Lori's steering him, scowling but, for once, not on the attack though she looks less than pleased to see me.

"Glad you could join us," I say, waving in Henry's face until he focuses on me and not the specters haunting the bar. "We're just on our way out."

"But you said you'd help me!" Henry stammers, voice high and cracking. "You won't believe what I saw out there!"

"Reckon I would, hoss," I reply as Ruby emerges, sliding my order across the bar. I eagerly collect, including the extra gun she's added to the pile. Might come in handy. "So would everyone else here. She can help get you settled. Tell your partner a few home truths, too."

"I can't believe it," Henry slurs. "I fucking can't believe it."

"You'll get over being dead and coming back to life pretty soon," Ruby replies with a grin, "but Hell will keep surprising you."

"I didn't die," Henry mutters.

Ruby frowns. "What?"

"He didn't die." I rub at the back of my neck. "Think I left that part out. Sin-Eater… I don't know, revealed himself? Or maybe the power he has—and he said its might has fucking grown—forced Henry to *See*, but he didn't quite snuff it."

Henry shakes his head. "Like Holleran said."

"Is that possible?" I ask Ruby.

She shrugs. "We're all learning, Nick. But it makes some kind of sense, doesn't it? An entity that powerful is going to leave an impression, and once your eyes are open, there's no closing them."

I wink at Henry. "Good luck, pal."

"Fuck you, Holleran," he whispers, but his heart ain't in it. I'm a little surprised it's still beating.

Nodding at Rosa and Diana, I make to leave, then pause as Fred downs his drink in one and follows.

"Oh, you might hear some reports of a break in at the train graveyard over on Haversome and Foster. Maybe some talk of an old steam engine chugging out of the place." The lop-sided grin senses that the time is right and takes its rightful place on my kisser. "Tell the PD you'll deal with it and do precisely nothing until you hear from me, got it? We're going after the sons of whores that opened your eyes to a whole new world, friend."

I stride away, taking the stairs two at a time, the lop-sided grin a satisfied one. Having someone like me on the inside of the law ain't no bad thing at all, I reckon. A Christmas gift from the universe, an apology for the shitty time it's shoved down my throat over the last few days.

Letting my hand drop to my Ruger, the spare tucked into the waist of my jeans, I reckon it's time to hand out a few gifts of my own. 'Tis the season, and all that. Ho fucking ho.

CHAPTER SEVENTEEN

THERE'S NO EARTHLY WAY OF KNOWING WHICH DIRECTION WE ARE GOING

21st DECEMBER, 2024

It's gone midnight by the time we approach the train graveyard on Haversome and Foster, stopping only to get all the railroads lined up correctly and clearing any debris from the tracks. Fred reckons it'll be a bumpy ride, but it'll do. Ready to roll.

Had to pinch myself a couple times on the way over when I glanced in my rearview and found two grayed-out ghosts sitting in the Mustang's backseat watching the frosty December night go by.

"Hey," I ask Rosa when I bring the car to a halt. "I reckon there's no way you're not gonna see reality for what it is after this trip. I'm not about to tell you what you can or can't do, but are you sure you wanna do this? Nothing's ever gonna be the same, and that's taking for granted there's even gonna be an after."

She turns my way, those soulful eyes rich and soft. Biting her bottom lip, she leans over and kisses me. I think she's gonna pull away, but she doesn't, and I lean into it. Her fingers run through my hair as we drink in each other's sweetness, oblivious to the rest of Hell for a blessed stretch of time. Our bodies press together, and I want this to last forever.

But it can't.

Pulling her mouth from mine before kissing me one more too-brief time, she leans back, a small smile on those full lips, her pupils larger than before. Fred whistles, and blood rushes up from somewhere lower in my body and into my neck and cheeks, making them a little too hot for comfort. Movement in the corner of my vision tells me Diana's found something mighty interesting to look at outta her window.

Rosa presses her hand against my cheek, one of Excalibur's rings colder than ice. "I'm good if you are, boo."

I can't help but laugh and I kiss her one more time, screw whoever's watching.

"Alright, show us the way, Fred. Our chariot awaits," I say, opening my door and getting out, feet crunching in the thick, unbroken snow. A fence that's frankly seen better days stands in the way of the shunting yard. "Me and Rosa will climb over."

The kid and Fred pass through the fence without a backward glance, and Rosa springs on to it, scampering up. Running a hand across the Mustang's hood, I follow, not nearly as spry. She drops down to the other side, and I shoo her away, making slow progress. Don't want her hanging around and seeing just how ungraceful I am, right?

"Go with them," I breathe, boots slipping against the wet metal. "I'll catch up."

Nodding, she disappears, and I cuss, sweat and scramble to the top of the fence, wobbling as I hoist a leg over and nearly fall from the top before my reflexes remember they're needed and I cling on so my dignity, and bones, remain intact.

Finally, I mount my personal Everest and drop to the ground, bending over and sucking in air. Straightening up, I wipe at my forehead and freeze. Even though the shunting yard is out of use, and these locomotives haven't seen any action in decades, the stench of oil lies thick in the air. Almost thick enough to taste the crud on my tongue.

From out of the shunting yard's darkness, a boney grin

emerges, and with it comes a weird and utterly unexpected sense of relief.

"Where the fuck have you been?" I grate, striding over to Charon. "Was beginning to think you were done with me and I'm as shocked as anyone that I found little goddamn comfort in that."

"I will never be done with you, Fateless. Not until I collect your soul," the Ferryman says in a whisper that sounds like two bags of gravel colliding. "It simply took me some time to return to this moment of reality. The vast, remote Great Divide is—"

"Great and empty," I cut in. Grinning. "Kind of gives it away in the name."

"You have not changed, Fateless," Charon rumbles, but then he pauses, his head tilted to the side under that wide-brimmed hat of his. "Though perhaps you have. You have the scent of magic about you."

Snow picks that particular moment to start falling. It's so fucking cold that even Charon's breath fogs the night air. It's literally colder than death out here!

"A lot's happened since Sin-Eater handed you your boney fucking ass, *Dullahan*."

Charon's mirthless grin widens, the embers of his almost-human eyes burning from the shadows of his hat. Funny, I always thought of him as taller, larger than life, but he isn't much bigger than me. Without his sword, without the shadows draped around him, and after seeing him made someone's bitch, the Ferryman just looks like some skinny loser attending a spaghetti-western convention.

If you don't stare into his eyes, that is. You could catch Charon's silhouette and mistake him for any Clint Eastwood obsessed cinephile, but one look at his face would obliterate the notion before it had time to settle.

"Sin-Eater caught me by surprise, I must admit." Charon doesn't sound like he enjoys admitting anything. "It had been eons since we last tangled, and I acted with a certain amount of sloppiness. Yours is a soul I did not want him to devour."

I blink. Sloppiness. Guess I'm a little more like Charon than I'd care to admit.

"Oh, I'm touched," I say instead, pressing a hand against my still-beating heart. "Really, I am."

"Do not be." The stretched skin across his skull-like face tightens as he grins. "Your soul belongs to me, and one day, I shall take you to the Seal."

"So you keep saying, and for once, I ain't gonna quiz you about this goddamned Seal." I point over to where the others disappeared into the darkness. "Got work to do."

"You are heading into the Unseen?" Charon asks, a thin eyebrow raising on his gnarled forehead. "You take the fight to Lilith?"

"Out of options, hoss. Can sit here and wait for Sin-Eater to come back, fend him off and watch others die until I can't keep it at arm's length any longer, or I can convince Lilith to call off her attack." I shrug. "Only one choice if you look at it that way."

"Look for the heart of her realm, Fateless. I do not rate your chances too highly against another Ancient, but the heart of the Unseen is her weakness, and these iron locomotives would spread poison through her domain."

The shadows surrounding him deepen as the snow continues to fall. Charon says nothing more, his mirthless grin unflinching.

Curiosity gets the better of me. "Can I ask you something? Seeing as I might die soon?"

"You are not ready to understand the Seal, Fateless," Charon replies. "Only when experiencing it can your mind grasp its enormity."

"No, it isn't that, I figured you'd say as much," I say. Rosa's raised voice drifts over to me when she calls my name. Gotta make this quick. "Sin-Eater reckons he's gonna outlast you, that he came first, too. That right?"

The fires in Charon's alien eyes burn a touch fiercer. "It is... Complicated. We are in an eternal struggle but one day there shall be an end and it may not go the way Sin-Eater expects." He gazes off into the sky. "Right now, it is weakened, convalescing in the heart. It would take many years for it to return from the Great Divide if sent there."

Fair enough. Chances of me doing that? Zero. Rosa calls again, voice more urgent.

"Anyway, thanks for the help, pal," I mutter, pressing against one of the nicotine patches stuck to my skin as if it might force more of the substance into my bloodstream. "Catch you later, no doubt."

I turn away.

"Fateless," Charon grates, making me pause. The shadows gather around him, swallowing everything save for his ruined, all-too human face. "Remember, your soul belongs to me. So it is promised. Be seeing you."

"My soul belongs to me, you gnarly Ancient fuck," I growl, scowling as nothing is left behind except for his grin. An undead Cheshire cat from the depths of Hell. Or the Great Divide, as he called it. Who the fuck knows where Charon came from. The Seal? Doubt I'm ever gonna find out.

Shaking my head, I break into a jog, heading after Team Fae Fuckers.

"I'm coming!" I call when Rosa yells again, and find them quickly enough, all standing in front of a pretty impressive, if decrepit, hunk of iron stream train. It's mostly intact, save for a giant hole in its side where some of the plating got torn away.

"What kept you?" Rosa asks, frowning.

"Ran into an old friend. Charon. Just reminding me that," I make my voice all gravely and emotionless, "'*my soul belongs to him,*'. You know, the usual spiel."

Rosa shivers like a herd of elephants stampeded across her grave. "Never do an impression of him again. I have no idea what he sounds like, but that was too creepy."

I shrug. Have to admit, reckon I got it down pretty well.

"So, what's the idea?" I ask, walking toward the locomotive.

It's sitting on the rails. Dormant but ready. "Is this baby ready to go?"

"It just needs fuel," Fred answers, climbing into the cab. "That's where your girl comes in. No fire is going to burn in this firebox again. Not a natural one at any rate."

"Can you show her where it is?" I ask, then nod at the kid. "Go up there with him, I'll be along in a second."

"You want me alone, big guy?" Rosa asks, grinning.

For a moment, I just can't understand how she's so chipper about this situation, about the fact she's about to assault another realm of reality. But then I realize. It's her. She's the strongest person I know. Way stronger than me. I'll never understand how she copes with all this shit without batting one of her pretty eyelids, all I need to know is that she can, and I'll be there for her if she can't. Future me be damned.

I take her hands in mine, smiling at her before studying the rings of Excalibur.

"You ready to use these? They pack a fucking punch."

"Line up the symbols, press the rings together, batten down the hatch. Got it."

"Matching symbols. That's what Greaney said."

Rosa rolls her eyes. "Go get the kid ready, I've got it all in hand."

Fucking excellent pun.

"Sure." I smile, watching her climb into the cab. Go get the kid ready, she says. I've no idea what she's meant to be doing, but sure. I'll go get her ready.

I hoist myself up the cab's ladder. Fred and the kid's standing in front of what I presume is the firebox, deep in a whispered discussion, his jaws still working when he's listening. Does he know he's doing it? Hocks it out often enough, Diana cringes every time he does it. The inside is roomy, not boxy like some of the ones I've seen on TV. It's wide enough for the four of us inside, and could fit plenty more, too. There's a window above the ladder at the side, and there's that chunk of iron plating missing in one of the sides creating an impromptu window, but that's all she wrote. Nodding at me, Fred moves away toward the controls, a wide grin on his face. You could say the dude's in Heaven if it weren't for the obvious.

"Reckon you can do this, kid?" I ask, kneeling beside her. She frowns.

"I don't even know what I'm supposed to do," Diana replies, the corners of her mouth tugging downward, echoing my thoughts. At least there's two of us, huh? The kid's the kind of person who likes to know what's what and having to do *something* to get us going is bothering her big time.

I study her for a moment. The kid's potentially a Malignant, a term I'd never heard of just twenty-four hours ago but fuck me if my life hasn't been flipped on its head over the last few days, anyway. Diana could be an entity powerful enough to make Suraz hesitate. One he'd need to '*neutralize*' if it came to it. But she isn't just that. The kid's a girl. *My* girl. And the power she possesses doesn't need to send her down the treacherous path. I won't let it.

"Kid, all I know is you can do anything you put your mind to." I reach out, and grip her shoulder, ignoring the ice rushing through my hand and into my forearm. "Reckon you were like that when you breathed too, and your talents have only gotten more impressive. Fred over there says we need something special, fire maybe, and I reckon you're the girl to do it."

Diana nods, but her chin dips.

"I'm scared, Nick. All this power, I can feel it inside me. Sometimes I feel so frightened, or even angry. Both at once even! And it just pours out. I don't know it's even happening sometimes, but when I do, when I think I'm going to lose you, or that something bad is about to happen, I'm back in your office, before it *was* your office, and... and..."

I pull her into my shoulder, hugging her tight, gasping as the cold floods through me, but I hold on, even when the ice tightens when Diana hugs me back.

"Kid, it's all gonna be okay. You got me and Rosa on your

side, and we love you." I pull back a little so I can take in her face. "I know you never thought you'd have a dad like me, but you've got it. And I'm not going anywhere."

"Thank you, Nick. I know." She sniffs, then takes a step back, composing herself. "I just need to control what's mine. This train needs fire. That's what I'll do."

Nodding, I stand up and give her room as she focuses on the firebox, her eyebrows drawn tight. Fingers belonging to Rosa find mine, and I grip 'em tight, holding on to their warmth.

"I love you too, Nick," Rosa whispers, reaching up and kissing me on the cheek. "We'll make it. I know we will."

I fucking hope so.

"Course we will," I murmur. "We're Team Fae Fuckers."

"What?"

"Oh, uh, guess I didn't get around to telling y'all the name I came up with." I shrug. "Too late now. It's settled."

"Team Fae Fuckers," Rosa breathes. "I like it."

Damn right.

A glimmer of light catches my eye. It flickers inside Diana as she raises her hand, pointing her palm toward the firebox, face a mask of absolute concentration. It isn't like the light from before when she stood on the verge of going supernova. It builds in her chest, slowly. The muscles in her jaw bunch from gritted teeth, and the light flows into her outstretched arm.

"You want fire?" she bites out. "I can do more than that!"

I turn away as a green column of light blasts from her hand, a roaring sound like a mixture of an inferno and a crashing waterfall accompanying it.

"Weee-hoo!" Fred yells above the din, and the unmistakable honk of a steam engine's horn sounds triumphant.

Raising a hand to shield my eyes, I creak open my eyelids and gasp. Green flames are pouring out of the kid's hands—two of 'em now—filling the firebox with some extra fucking special fire, but that's not all. The power from inside the kid's lancing around the cab, crackling like green lightning, powering all the machinery. Like she's the Emperor working for the good guys. That makes Fred Chewbacca for more reasons than one. Rosa is Leia, of course. Do I really need to say who it makes me? Here's a hint: it ain't Luke Skywalker.

Fred pulls levers, checks gauges and flicks a couple of switches, and the locomotive's headlights illuminate the shunting yard, chasing away the shadows, the heat pouring from the metalwork melting the snow. A squeal fills the air; metal on metal, rust complaining in its impotent fury as it's worn away from a sudden, stubborn indomitable will of a machine that wants to move again.

And the old iron chariot edges forward. Falcon. The Magnesium Falcon. That's one for the scientific folk to figure out.

"It's working!" Fred yells, gray face showing just a hint of red in the cheeks. "The old girl's alive again! Can you believe it?"

"Believe it?" I yell as he pulls on the horn again, the locomotive hollering into the cold December night. "This was your goddamn idea!"

"Didn't know it was gonna work though, did I?"

Now he tells me.

"I have to keep this fire building, Nick!" Diana shouts above the roar of flames. "It can't go out if we want to go faster!"

"Alright, you heard the little lady," I shout, hand dropping to my Ruger. "Fred drives the train. Me and Rosa will do anything we can to keep anything that dares attack us off your backs. And God help whatever sorry bastard tries!"

"We know!" Rosa cries as the locomotive picks up speed. Christ, it's loud in here! "You went over the plan in the car!"

"Well, gee, thanks for taking the wind outta my sails, Rosa. It just felt like a moment."

She slaps me on the ass. "Don't pout, Nick. You're plenty pretty without it."

I make a concerted effort to smooth out my face, and I lean out of the yawning gap in the locomotive's side. Steam rises from the funnel, trailing behind us, as we cut through the city's outer limits, speed building, green bolts of electricity pulsating through the metalwork. Pulling my head back in and glancing to check on the kid, I head over to Fred.

"Hey, can I ask a favor?" I say, eyeing the whistle cords. "May I?"

"Be my guest!" Fred laughs. Dude probably hasn't felt this alive since before his funeral.

Reaching up, I grab the whistle cord and pull, the locomotive bellowing as I do.

"Always wanted to try that," I say, letting go. "Pretty damn satisfying."

"Cute," Rosa says from behind me. "Very cute."

"If you could play music in here it'd be some way to travel, right?" I say, grinning over my shoulder at her.

"It's the *only* way to travel!" Fred calls, affronted.

"It is if you like sticking to the rails." Rosa laughs. "I prefer a little freedom. Like a motorcycle."

I rub the stubble on my chin. A motorcycle? Rosa? Guess you learn something new every day.

"We're approaching the mountain." Fred's shout blows away my thoughts. "Keep that firebox burning, girl!"

I peer out of the window, squinting. Tunnel's coming up pretty quick.

"How fast are we going?" I shout, eyeing the hole in the loco's side.

"Faster than I thought this old girl could go," Fred yells back. "Not really sure. The readouts are going haywire."

It's like we're on the Kessel Run. If he starts talking about parsecs like it's some old train-driver term… Get a grip, Nick!

"Are we going fast enough?"

"We're gonna find out." He glances at me, and nods. "Good luck to you and your lady friend. Me and the little one will be just fine."

Taking a step back, my hand finds Rosa's. She squeezes. Hard.

"No turning back now, huh?" I say, meeting her eyes.

"You're Nick Holleran. Kind of comes with the territory." She bites her lip. "Tell me we're going to be okay."

Fred pulls on the whistle cords, letting the loco wail.

I kiss her, then whisper in her ear, "It's all gonna be okay. Trust me."

"I do," she murmurs.

Hugging her tight, Diana feeding green flames into the firebox, Fred's legs wide like he's a pirate captain on the deck of his ship, I glance outta the front window. The tunnel's wide maw welcomes us, sheer rock piled up inside. Fred yanks on the whistle cords one more time and I count down to impact.

Three.

Two.

I close my eyes.

One.

The locomotive shudders, and I brace myself, ready to throw myself on top of Rosa when the shrapnel and debris starts flying, but I don't fall. Don't hear a peep, either.

"Did we make it?" I ask, face screwed up tight.

"Open your eyes and see, Nick," Rosa breathes, and I do what she says.

Jesus fucking Christ. Toto, we ain't in Kansas no more, friendo.

I race over to the gap in the loco's side, Rosa with me, gawping. There's no railroad beneath us, there isn't a tunnel, and we're not in a Hell I recognise. We've passed through to the other side. Another realm.

The Unseen.

A sickly purple/green sky stretches as far as my sight reveals, a silver moon, twice the size of the one I'm used to, hanging amongst yellow stars. Below the Falcon arrowing through mid-air and the diseased sky, stretching for miles, lies a forest filled with blackened, ragged, twisted trees, impossibly tall, the branches stretching for the train's tracks. Mountains rear in the distance, their tops disappearing into the purple/green hue, so large Everest would quake in their shadow. Reckon I know why Sin-Eater had the scent of strawberries and fresh grass, too. It fills the tight air, atmosphere close enough to pop. Like a storm's coming.

"Nick?" Rosa whispers. "I can see it."

I laugh. Can't help myself. And I can't stop.

"What's so funny?" Rosa asks. She doesn't need to shout any more, the Falcon isn't making a sound even though the flames are still raging in its firebox.

"Before all of this, I thought I was getting a handle on Hell," I reply, shaking my head. "I didn't know jack. Look at this, Rosa. It's incredible, even though it looks like something from the darkest places of Tim Burton's imagination."

"This isn't Hell, Nick. This is something else. Somewhere else. I can see it, Nick. It isn't veiled like Hell is." She squeezes my hand. "Guess we have a lot to learn, huh?"

"Too fucking right," I murmur, then squint. A shadow passed by the silvery moon. A shadow with wings. "Did you—"

"Nick, the trees!" Rosa yells, thrusting a finger towards them.

A stream of flying creatures rises from the branches. I don't need to see 'em up close to know what they are. I know. They're small, they got pointy teeth, nasty dispositions, they eat fucking celery. Last time I met their card they shot me full of tiny little arrows and filled my blood with poison.

And there's more rising to meet us than I've ever seen before in my life.

"Get ready," I shout, pulling my Ruger free and training it on the gap in the side of the loco. Giving it a half-second's thought, I grab the spare, too, and flick the safety off. "Do everything you can, and don't let any of their fucking arrows hit you!"

Before Rosa can reply, a gut-clenching scream erupts from outside, and the shadow of wings comes into view. Last time I saw her, before she almost killed me and Diana blew her away, the Queen of the Fae tempted me with her ways. For a moment, she could have commanded me to dig to Australia, and I'd have tried, scrubbing soil away with my bleeding fingers if it pleased her. But now I see her for what she really is, and she isn't a beauty anymore. She's in her true form, a winged, tailed serpent in semi-human form, a hulking mass driving towards us, murder in her crimson eyes, venom dripping from her bared fangs. The rage in her scream causes the Falcon to vibrate.

"I don't want to hurt you!" I scream through the gap in the Falcon's side. Like I could hurt her. Jesus. "Any of you. I came to talk. To get you to call Sin-Eater off!"

The Queen of the Fae screeches, and her subjects create a chorus of death. She won't talk. Won't listen.

Lilith and her brood have come out to play.

CHAPTER EIGHTEEN

ARE THE FIRES OF HELL A-GLOWING?

"Nick! How in God's name are we meant to fight *that*?" Rosa screams, eyes wider than I've ever seen 'em. "Is that her? Lilith?"

"It is, but in my defense, she looked very different last time I saw her," I yell. "The Falcon's made of iron. She won't touch it, but those little fuckers are small enough to get inside." My pact never to swear in front of the kid is well and truly shot to smithereens. "Concentrate on them, don't let them hit you!"

Lilith roars by the Falcon, screeching at the top of her lungs like the Queen of the fucking Ringwraiths, eyes crimson, razor-sharp fangs glinting under the silver moon, but she doesn't come too close. Yet. Can't say the same for the little pricks in her thrall. The tiny fae, those with the wings needed to create Expungers, the ones I harvested that caused all this mess in the first place, arc toward the gaping hole in the Falcon's side.

And I send a hail of bullets to meet 'em.

Lilith screeches when hot led slams home into her minions, sending purple blood and translucent wings flying as the celery-chomping fucks drop out of the sky. I hammer at the triggers of my guns, spraying rapid fire into the great Unseen, until the roar of gunfire and muzzle flashes die. Out of ammo.

"You're up!" I shout at Rosa, crouching and letting the empty clips slide from my sidearms, scrambling to reload. "Use the rings!"

"Got it!" Rosa yells, twiddling with the jewelry on her fingers. "How about this?"

She slams her hands together, rings touching, and I squint before the bright light flies from her hands.

But nothing happens.

"Fuck!" I shout, just as one of those creepy little fae bastards laughs and sends an arrow my way.

Hopefully someone restocked the antidote to fae venom, 'cos I'm gonna need it. Then the arrow rebounds off solid air.

"What the shit?" I mumble, blinking. That arrow should have stuck me in the shoulder.

"Reload, Nick, hurry up!" Rosa shouts. "The shield symbols. I figured it would protect us, but I don't know how long it will last!"

"Pretty big fucking assumption," I mutter, jamming one consecrated clip into place then another. "Can I even fire through it?"

More of Lilith's brood arc toward the opening, and I raise my weapons, half turning my head just in case the bullets bounce back and hit me. Sure, like shying away a little's gonna stop that, Nick!

Bang. Bang-bang-bang-bang.

I let rip, the bullets flying, knocking the little shits clean out of the sky, and allow myself to grin. We can fire out, they can't get in. Nice.

"Hey!" I shout, letting off another couple of rounds. "We make a pretty good—"

"Nick!" Diana screams. "Behind you!"

The cab's got more than one fucking way in, you dumb bastard.

I spin, firing with one arm pointed aimed at the hole in the side and the other toward the loco's rear, arms vibrating with each bullet fired.

"Rosa, do something! I can't hold 'em off much longer!"

Click, click, click. I'm out.

"Get down!" Rosa yells, slamming her fists together.

Me, Fred, and Diana drop as one, green flames still pouring out of the kid's hands as Rosa spins, fierce gusts of air roaring above me, slamming into the fae coming at us from both directions. They shriek as the fierce wind crashes into them, knocking them into the iron. Their screams take on frenzied and pained pitches as their purple skin sizzles, and the stench of cooking flesh fills the air. Some of them drop to the metal floor, melting into oozing piles of purple mush.

The lady's a professional fae killer.

Rosa drops her hands, staggering, and wipes at her head.

"You okay?" I shout, slamming my clips in place, crouching as I wait for another attack.

"Just a little weak," Rosa replies. "You said it, Nick. Excalibur really packs a punch."

Too fucking right, it does.

"Down to my last clips," I snarl, peering out of the side. Lilith swoops by, hideous twisted face a little too close to comfort as she passes. "Whatever we're gonna do, we gotta do it fast."

"What *are* we gonna do, Nick?" Rosa asks, twiddling with the rings on her fingers. "How are we gonna stop her? Not like your bullets were going to do that anyway."

"We just have to ground her," I say, getting my guns ready. More of the fae are coming. "I've got something cooking."

"It better be good!" Rosa shakes her hands, like a boxer psyching themselves up.

No time to answer, fae come pouring through the gaps, with even more rising from the trees, and I see something behind them. A tower. Tall, golden and shining above the treetops, reaching toward the moon. Reckon it's Lilith's lair. The heart, as Charon called it.

I start firing, fae coming from the side and the rear. Fred yells as some of the little fuckers hurl themselves at the glass windows, trying their damndest to shatter them and they'll succeed if they keep it up. Yeah, by the increased frenzy, I can tell they don't want us anywhere near that tower of gold.

"Nick!" Diana groans, dropping to her knees. "I can't keep this up. It's hurting me!"

"Just a little bit more, kid, hold on, we're almost there!" I bark over the gun fire and fae screeches. "Fred? See that tower? Big and gold, can't miss it. We gotta aim that way!"

"But we're not going in that direction!" he shouts.

"We're in a fucking magical land of myth, legend and murderous goddamned fae flying through the sky!" I yell back. "You'll think of something!"

"Sure, I'll just make a wish," he grumbles, flicking at a bunch of switches, and it might just be my imagination, but I'm sure as shit the train's path bends a little.

I hammer at the triggers, and the bullets don't come. Shrieking, the fae staying out of my range dive for the opening the lack of gunfire provides.

"Rosa, take over!"

I drop as Rosa does her thing. Pure fire pours from her hands, burning our attackers to a crisp. Those already inside fly off in all directions to avoid the flames and slam into the Falcon's interior instead, screeching when the solid iron does its work.

Rosa drops her hands, gasping, the fae gone for now.

And Diana falls face first to the train's floor.

"Kid!" I shout, running over to her, turning her over. She isn't gray anymore. She's almost pure white and she's colder than a Siberian winter. My fingertips burn with ice from touching her. "Can you hear me? Kid?"

"... Tired..." she whispers, eyelids fluttering open. "Need... Rest..."

"You did great, kid. Just great." I prop her against the firebox, the green flames inside already dying. "Stay there, you hear?"

Getting to my feet, I glance at Rosa, then stare outside. Lilith swoops, her screeches filled with grief and anger, her wings sending gusts of wind at us. The loco shakes, lurches, but it's still moving toward the tower, slowing as the green flames in the firebox die, the green lightning lancing around the equipment fading.

"Come on," I breathe, sticking my weapons away and pressing my palm against the Falcon's iron plating. They're no use to me now. Unless I throw 'em at something again. Could throw 'em. Why not? "Make it, goddammit..."

"What's gonna happen when we get to that tower?" Rosa asks, following my stare.

"No idea, but Charon suggested it. Kinda."

"*Kinda*?"

I shrug. "Might be my own interpretation of matters."

"Jesus Christ," Rosa mutters, flinching as Lilith arcs past, her jagged teeth snapping. "If this thing we're riding wasn't made out of iron, we wouldn't last a minute against her."

"She's certainly let herself go over the last few days, that's for sure."

"Yes, you mentioned," Rosa says. "She was less serpenty?"

"And way smaller."

We stagger into each other as she swoops by again. Lilith's flying faster each time, summoning more wind like she's trying to knock us from the air, but we're getting closer to the tower, and her screams are getting more desperate.

"Holleran?" Fred yells, pulling my focus away from the giant, winged, fae Queen with talons, a long tail, and a really angry, all-too-human face. Honestly, I'm gonna have nightmares for weeks. Months. "Below us!"

I race to the front, staring through the cracked front windows, and sigh. It's really all I can do. If anyone had told me a week ago that there even *was* a fae realm, I'd have laughed and avoided speaking to whoever said it for as long as I could and that's me even knowing Hell exists. Now here I am, my girlfriend wielding the rings of Excalibur, flying through a purple/green sky in an abandoned locomotive from the goddamn 1940s with a half fae-dragon thing pursuing us, my teenage ghost-daughter exhausted after powering up said locomotive, and a train-driving spirit pointing frantically at the mass of blackened, gnarly, twisted trees *growing and reaching up toward the train's underbelly.*

You could say my life has taken a really strange goddamned turn.

"What is it, Nick?" Rosa yells.

I sigh again and shake my head. "The fucking trees are kinda growing, and their fucking branches are reaching out to grab at the fucking train 'cos they're probably aiming to drag us to the fucking ground."

Too many fucks? Reckon they're warranted.

"What the—"

An echoing groan from the train's metalwork interrupts whatever words of disbelief Rosa was gonna say. Screeching of iron on steel breaks out, and part of the roof and floor buckle from the pressure of being squeezed like a tin of sardines.

"The branches are squeezing us!" Fred shouts.

"No shit!" I yell back, wincing as I meet Diana's pits, and not because of my ruined self-made pact to never swear in front of her. She's still as white as a wedding dress.

I stagger, crashing against the side then throwing myself to the floor as a branch bursts through the side of the loco, black ichor flying from the bark as it sizzles from the touch of the iron. The attack's killing the trees, but it seems Lilith sees it as the lesser evil. She's determined to stop us reaching the tower. Faebent, you might say.

More branches snake through the gaping hole in the Falcon's side, and Rosa backs away from them, sliding down the far side of the loco's wall, her wild eyes meeting mine.

"I got nothing," I whisper from where I'm crouched on the train's floor. I don't know if she can hear me, but the sudden dawning understanding in her face tells me she understands. "I'm sorry."

She gives her head a fierce shake. "I've got this, Nick. I've got this!"

Twiddling with the rings on her fingers, her jaw set, Rosa charges to her feet, hands moving to meet. She's used Excalibur three times, she can't have the energy for another assault, but even if she did, what the Hell is she gonna do against the Queen of the Fae and a whole forest of evil trees trying to tear us from the sky?

Well, slick, she does what she fucking does, and man is it glorious.

Slamming her fists together, a fiery orange colored sonic wave booms from her hands, spreading out in a circle, rushing by the branches, doing them no harm at first, but then the wave ascends into the sickly sky.

And the shrieking begins.

It isn't human. Not fae, either. It's like the creaking of old wood during a storm, or when timber warps when it's too cold and the frost settles into its marrow. But this isn't coming from one piece of bark. It's the entire forest. A deafening chorus of fear and pain.

Fire falls from the sky like rain and covers the Unseen like a blanket.

Rosa's feet lift from the floor, her hair flying in all directions from the sheer power she's commanding, and the diseased sky spits down droplets of flames, the sparks dropping across the black forest and creating an inferno. Lilith's shrieks take on a frenzied edge as the devouring blaze eats into her, singeing her wings. She drops, darting to avoid the storm of Hellish flame, but she can't go low enough. The entire forest is aflame already.

I don't know how Rosa's doing this, I don't care so long as she's safe, but I do know this. King fucking Arthur would be dancing a merry jig somewhere right now if he knew Excalibur was kicking so much goddamned ass.

The locomotive shoots forward, the last stubborn branches letting go or being torn from their trunks below, and we sail through the air, back on our journey, closing in as the fire falls around us. Together, we've brought the flames of Hell to the Unseen.

Rosa drops and I rush to her side, catching her before she hits the ground.

"Did I do okay, Nick?" she murmurs, eyes closed.

"That was fucking incredible," I breathe. "How'd you do it?"

Without opening her eyes, a small smile spreads across her face, and she raises her hands.

"Mixed the symbols," she whispers. "Figured the wavy ones going up and down were rain and trees wouldn't like fire. We didn't have a lot of options, so I thought I'd give it a go."

"You experimented?" I gasp, eyes wide. "Just when it looked like we were gonna die?"

"Probably the best time to start flying by the seat of my pants, huh? Learned from the best."

"Marry me," I breathe, leaning down to kiss her on the lips. Her fingers find my hair, and we stay together as fire falls around us, mouths entwined.

I pull away, and her eyelids flutter open. "Do you mean that, Nick? You want to do this right here and now? I mean, you *did* give me rings..."

Is she being serious? Am I? Not the most romantic of places, but still, the flames dropping from the sky do have that certain je ne sais quoi...

"You're right, not the time. We'll talk once we survive this," I say, kissing her again. "Deal?"

"Deal."

Lilith's scream of rage spoils the moment. Scrambling to my feet, and pulling Rosa with me, I race to the gap in the side, stones sinking to my boots.

Singed, smoke curling from her ruined wings, her wide-set eyes red with fury, the Queen of the Fae is flying right at us. Like, right at us. Head-first. This is gonna hurt us both.

"Get down!" I yell, throwing myself at Rosa and pushing her to the ground, covering my head with my hands.

Lilith's furious scream turns to one of agony as she slams into the Falcon, the entire vehicle shaking, glass shattering from the impact, metal groaning, the stink of singed flesh filling the air, overpowering the already potent aroma of cooked fae wings. The loco flips in on its side, flinging me from floor to ceiling, Rosa landing on top of me, the air knocked from my lungs, and then we fall again, me doing the same to her.

The Falcon shudders, like after hacking out a rattly cough, then dips.

Falling forward, I scramble to my feet, leaning against the switches next to Fred. He looks at me, speechless, as we arrow towards the blanket of flame below us.

Fuck. Me.

"Kid, you still with us?" I shout, looking over my shoulder.

"Here, Nick," she calls, weak, but on her feet and a little more washed-out gray.

"Rosa?"

She leans against me. "What do you need?"

"Fred, you do whatever you've been doing to steer us towards that fucking tower. If it's because you're wishing it, wish harder," I scream, wind howling through all the holes in the locomotive. "Diana, you use your powers to try and keep us straight as long as possible. We wanna slide right into that fucking thing when we hit the ground. We're inside iron, and Charon says that's the heart of her realm. I aim to fucking poison it." A piece of the loco's side flies off, revealing a giant half-serpent, half-fae plummeting to the ground near her home. "Rosa, use Excalibur to shield us, and all stay close to her. Got it?"

"What are you going to do, Nick?" Rosa asks.

I swallow, my stomach flipping as the Falcon drops a few feet without warning. "Pray to God."

I close my eyes as Rosa slams her fists together just as the locomotive plummets through the flames. Heat sears my skin, and I start screaming. Rosa does too, and I stare wildly around but all I see is smoke. I ain't burning, but it feels like it, the ring's magic protecting us from the worst. Resistance hits the Falcon as we crash through the charred and broken limbs, and Rosa collides into my back. I turn, grab her fists blindly and keep them pressed together. White light beside me beats away the smoke. Diana's turning supernova, her face a grimace.

"Get ready for impact!" Fred cries and, still holding Rosa's fists, I pull her close, bowing and leaning my head on her shoulder.

"I love you," I shout so she can hear me over the howling, the screeching, the metallic scraping and groaning.

Then, with a deafening screech, slam and thud, I'm thrown from my feet and the world turns dark.

CHAPTER NINETEEN

SHOT THROUGH THE HEART

I cough before I open my eyes. Then cough again. My vision isn't worth a damn anyway, it's all fuzzed up and blurry. The smoke filling the locomotive doesn't help matters either. The crackle and pop of fire fills the air.

"Everyone okay?" I croak, groaning as I turn over. Feel like a sack of potatoes freshly mashed. *Everything* hurts. "Are at least two of us still breathing?"

Reckon I am, and a quick check of my body tells me I still have two arms and two legs.

"Nick?" Rosa calls above the crackle of fire. "I think I'm okay."

A hot, wet sensation moves across my forehead. Reaching up, I wipe at it, and my fingers come away bloody.

"Shit," I mutter, sitting up and staring around.

Can't see Diana or Fred, but the Falcon's a mess. The entire front section is crumpled and twisted, and there's an extra hole in the side now. One big enough to walk right on through. A wall of fire greets me on the other side.

"Nick, you're bleeding!" Rosa staggers over to me, and I smile at her. Apart from the soot covering her face, she seems fine. Her t-shirt is ripped, and I pull her close to check for injuries, but thankfully her skin is smooth and unmarred.

"Reckon I banged my head when we crashed," I mutter,

pain lancing through my skull when Rosa grabs it, peering at the wound then into my eyes. "How bad is it?"

"Not the worst," Rosa replies, clearly relieved. She opens her jacket and, with a snarl, tears away the bottom half of her t-shirt, where it's ripped. I send up a quick thanks to the guy upstairs that she's whole and healthy. Not to mention a quick thinker. "Hold still."

I wince as she ties it around my forehead, then groan when she pulls it tight.

"It's quiet out there," I say when she's done. "If you don't count the roaring fires."

"Where's Diana?" Rosa asks, looking around.

"I'm out here," the kid calls from the other side of the protective iron. "Come and see."

"That way," I flick my head in her direction.

Rosa gets to her feet and pulls me up, holding on to me when I flounder at first, but she lets go when I nod. My ankle screams when I walk forward, twisted more than likely, but I limp on, and out of the locomotive.

Flames surround us. A wall of fire of what used to be trees. The Falcon's nose disappears into the base of the tall golden tower, and I follow its rise, up into the sky. It isn't all gold anymore, and it ain't made of stone, either. It's like a massive, living tree, and tendrils of black snake up from the locomotive poisoning it. Regret and shame fill my chest for a moment, and I shake my head. I didn't want it to come to this. Taking the fight to Lilith and getting her to call her Ancient attack-dog off, yes. Poisoning an entire realm and setting it aflame? No.

Diana and Fred are standing before the tower's base, the bottom entirely pitch now, but Diana's staring in a different direction. She glances at me and points off to the side.

"Look," she whispers. "It's here."

I follow her finger. Golden roots poke through the red colored grass, obsidian poison from the iron staining them, and they lead a short distance away until a group of them push through the soil. They form a kind of throne, but it mostly reminds me of an electric chair. The figure sitting in it certainly hasn't got leave to get up on its own accord. Blackened tendrils strap its arms and legs to the formerly golden chair, and the figure's glowing violet eyes flash when I meet 'em, the wide, out-of-place grin growing wider.

"Sin-Eater," I say, limping over to it. "Fancy meeting you here."

"Your arrival is most unexpected, Nick Holleran. Living up to the Fateless moniker, I see. Lilith was surely surprised." He giggles, his stare drifting. "Most surprised, indeed."

"What's so funny?" I ask, narrowing my eyes. "Charon told me you'd be weak, and I reckon whatever I did to you means you gotta recharge here. But it's poisoning you. It's gonna kill you."

Sin-Eater glares at me, sudden lines eating into its healed face, the scorch marks I put there gone, then the wrinkles fade away as it lets out a high-pitched, wet giggle.

"You still do not understand, do you, Fateless? Do you not heed the words of your betters? Charon." His mouth twists. "The *Nephilim*. I do suppose they are better than you, after all. I am an Ancient. There is *no* way you can kill me. Lilith is, too, and she may have me trapped for now, but her power is fading because of you. You shall have my thanks before I eat your soul."

My eyes narrow. "What do you mean?"

Sin-Eater sighs. "I suppose there is no harm in you knowing, it will not change anything. Dullahan and I battle for souls, him for his precious Seal, and me for my own designs. In my error, I made a bargain with Lilith, oh, eons ago now, and the bargain means I must reside here. Her power nourishes me, but it also chains me to her. You could say I was offered a deal too good to be true and did not read the small print." Sin-Eater tilts his head to the side. "It makes me follow the rules the other Ancients set down, but I grow weary of them, and soon, when I am free, there will be no reason to abide by them. Not even God."

I glance at the poisoned tower, and the blackening roots

leading to him, a fist in my stomach clenching.

"This poison will weaken her power over you, and you're going to take any soul you want, aren't you? Sinners. Innocents. It won't matter." I growl. "As soon as you're free."

"Starting with yours, Fateless. Then your friends, even those already dead." Sin-Eater licks his lips, his tongue forked, and I just wanna sink my knuckles into his face. "It might not be soon, but I am patient. You shall not leave this place, after all. Only Lilith can send you away, and she wishes to see you dead."

Diana's cold fingers wrap around mine, and she tugs me backward. I let her, Sin-Eater leering at us before staring back at the poisoned tower.

Fuck. All I've done by coming here is made matters worse. Instead of just my death, Sin-Eater's gonna spread like a god-damned plague. Unless the other Ancients can stop him. Wait...

"Nick, we have to get the iron out of the heart," Diana whispers, but I can't really concentrate on her words. The research... What did Rosa and Ruby say? "Nick!"

"What?" I say, turning to her, the fires raging around us but coming no closer.

"I said we need to get rid of that iron. This isn't right, no matter what Lilith's done."

She's got a great soul. Malignant my ass.

I smile down at her. "You're more right than you know, kid. Reckon you could get it out?"

She frowns at the ruined Falcon, then nods. "I think so. I'm dead tired, but I think so."

Dead tired. Nice.

A scream from behind us has me spinning, hand dropping to my empty Ruger out of habit.

"*What have you done?*" Lilith screams, staggering through the wall of flames. "*You are killing my realm!*"

Smoke curls from her skin as she shambles toward us, back to her normal size but without her veil of beauty. Purple blood from a hundred or more cuts makes her burned rags cling to her, tears stream from her crimson eyes. Her fingers are curled, the nails on them like razors. She'd like nothing more than to drive them through my guts. Black veins pulse beneath her skin.

I glance at Diana. "Get ready to lift that free, but not yet. I got an idea."

"You will answer for your crimes, Nick Holleran!" Lilith screams, her footsteps leaving the red grass scorched. "You will pay! There is no escape for you!"

Stepping backward, my heel drums up against a piece of iron from the locomotive. Spinning, I grab it, holding it up between me and the approaching Lilith, and edge a little closer to where Sin-Eater's recharging.

"That's what got you into this mess in the first place, Lilith," I shout back. The Queen of the Fae eyes the metal in my hands and slows her advance, but she's completely focused on me. The others don't exist to her. "You tried to kill me in the Haven Woods. You set Sin-Eater free. What did you expect?"

"But you hurt me, human! You hurt all of my kind! I watched you for a long time, taking what you desired, killing without mercy." Lilith sobs, and doesn't a huge part of my fucking heart ache for her. I can see it in her twisted face. Each one of her minion's deaths have hit hard. "You were not like the others. They took only what they needed to keep the—"

"Balance," I finish, nodding, and coming to a stop beside Sin-Eater. It watches me, violet eyes glowing. Grinning. "I get that. There's a balance to Hell, and not just Hell. All of the realms, and that's why I harvested. I ain't gonna pretend I did it in the right way, the way my pal Harry used to, I understand that now. But, Lilith, tell me this. Is unleashing Sin-Eater promoting fucking balance? You hear what he's saying? This sonofabitch isn't gonna stop with just the souls of sinners. It already planned on that before I sent its ass back here."

"What we do is beyond your comprehension." Lilith draws herself up, disdain painted across her face. "How dare you lecture—"

"I *dare* because I know that hunk of iron over there is killing your realm, all your kind, and I know that it isn't right. Didn't want it to happen, but you forced my hand. Balance, right? Poisoning the entire Unseen is the fucking opposite of that, and who the Hell knows what'll happen because of it?" I thrust the piece of iron toward Sin-Eater. "But I know for a fact some others of your kind, the Ancients, are fucking pissed at you, Lilith. And they're not gonna be happy you set this freak free over some vendetta with a schmuck like me."

The crackling flames start to die, leaving charred and oozing trunks in their wake. Creatures limp out of the trees, huddling together. The small winged fae with them and more. Puca huddled together, weeping, their skin turning black. Animals that look like squirrels, but with six legs and two tails, lie down in the crimson grass, their little chests heaving as they struggle to suck in air. Ain't no doubt about it, this place is screwed. All that's gonna be left is my crew, Team Fae Fuckers, standing opposite Lilith with Sin-Eater waiting in the wings and nothing but destruction surrounding us.

It isn't a good feeling, and the name Team Fae Fuckers has taken on a less than awesome meaning.

"Look, Lilith, there's another way around all of this. If you kill me, kill my friends, that iron isn't going anywhere. You can't touch it; your magic doesn't work on it." I meet her eyes. The last time we met, they intoxicated me for a moment. Made me almost forget about Rosa. Now I just feel nothing but pity. "We all make mistakes, and I should know. My actions, my sloppiness and disregard caused all this mess. But if we wait this stalemate out, Sin-Eater's gonna be free, kill us, and that still won't solve the poison in your realm."

Lilith sniffs, wiping at her eyes, then tilts her chin back like the queen she is. "What do you suggest, Nick Holleran?"

You know, in a previous life I was a private detective. Now, you might be forgiven if you're thinking my skills have gotten rusty from all these spirits with vendettas, Devil Worshipers,

Nephilim, Ancients and fae I've been rumbling with lately, not to mention my frequent lapses in intelligence, but they haven't. See, I'm not bad in a scrap, and I seem to have a knack at staying mostly alive, but my real skill set lies in being able to piece together a jigsaw, even if a lot of the pieces ain't showing the right way, and for sensing an opportunity.

And boy, do I sense one. I remember what the women in my life talked about back in the Styx and, adding it to the pow-wows I've had with Charon and Sin-Eater, I reckon I see a way out of this.

I just gotta hope it works. And keep my fingers crossed that Rosa and the kid don't intervene first, as they're not gonna like what I'm about to say. Not one bit.

The pieces are these: Bargains. Grand acts of important notions like redemption and sacrifice, the stuff that fae go ga-ga over. Then there's more Machiavellian aspects like playing one Ancient off another, and the debate as to who my soul actually belongs to between these fuckers. The hunk of iron sticking out of the heart of Lilith's realm is my ace in the hole.

Glancing over my shoulder, I nod at Diana, then meet Rosa's eyes. She's got her hands with the rings of Excalibur ready to go, but I hope she isn't gonna need them. Smiling, I throw her a wink, then turn back to Lilith.

Here we go. If I still smoked, now would be the time to light one up.

"Seems to me, Lilith, that getting that iron out of your way so your realm can recover is down to me. One of my friends over there can do it. You know, the one who blasted you away the other day."

"The Malignant," Lilith snarls, fear flashing in her eyes. My stomach flips. I hope to Christ the kid didn't hear her say that, but kids have a knack of hearing anything to do with them no matter the circumstances.

"You know who I'm talking about," I reply, giving her a level stare. "We can take that iron out, but I'm not doing it unless you let us all go. Me, the kid, Rosa and Fred there. Transport us back to Hell, back to Haven, and we'll take the iron with us. You can recover, Sin-Eater's still under your thrall, and we can go about our lives."

Sin-Eater giggles. "Fools. She loses her power over me. I shall be free no matter what. It is just a matter of time!"

I glance at him. Shadows build where the fires die.

"But what about all the dead, Nick Holleran?" Lilith snarls, taking a step forward. I raise my iron shield a little, reflexes taking over. "Do they not deserve satisfaction? And what do I say to my fellow Ancients when I have nothing to show for my actions? At least your death would go some way in balancing the ledger and explaining my actions. Without your death I have unleashed chaos."

This is it. Here's the rub. Lilith's engaged, the bargaining in action, but she wants more. I get her point-of-view, I do. Breathing in deeply, I nod, and send my silent prayers in a different direction than God's. No, not a prayer. More like a plea.

"In exchange for all of the fae lives I've taken, Sin-Eater can have my soul at the moment of my death." My eyes lock onto Lilith's when I make my proclamation. Unflinching. Rosa screams. Diana joins her. The Queen of the Fae smiles. I ignore them and turn to the creature, its violet eyes flashing with delight. Moment of my death. Didn't say the cause and Sin-Eater and Lilith know it. She just has to send me to Haven. "Let's make it official. An oath. I, Nick Holleran, the Fateless, do swear that—"

The shadows rush forward and from it emerges my fucking hero, sword in hand.

Charon. He listened to my prayers after all!

"The Fateless' soul belongs to *me*!" he roars, voice an avalanche of stone, throwing an arm out at the locomotive. A piece of iron tears from the side and slams into Lilith. She squeals, steaming, as it pins her to the ground. "No one shall touch him but I!"

Sword flashing, Charon sweeps at the golden/black roots

connecting to the chair Sin-Eater's sitting on. Another piece of iron tears from the Falcon and flies toward Sin-Eater, wrapping itself around him. The Ferryman falls onto the creature, the shadows building. Sin-Eater doesn't giggle now. It screams in rage until the sound cuts off into silence.

The shadows roll away leaving nothing behind. No chair. No Sin-Eater, and no Charon.

Nodding, I approach the downed Lilith. She squeals, struggling under the iron plate. I toss mine to the side, and stand before her, staring down at the beaten Queen of the Fae.

"Nick, you are a fucking pain in the ass," Rosa murmurs next to me. I turn. The whole gang's here, looming over Lilith. "Did you know he'd come?"

I shrug, then turn back to Lilith. "Heard something recently, and thought it would come in handy. Went like this: '*The only way to ward off one of the Sluagh or another member of the Hunt is by placing another of similar aspect in its path.*' Now, Charon's got a real hard-on over my soul. I'm talking a boney tent pole like you wouldn't fucking believe. Reckon that solves the Sin-Eater issue."

"But you promised!" Lilith screeches, her creatures wailing behind her. Sympathy pangs erupt in my chest, but I push them away. I gotta do this. "You said you would—"

"Reckon Sin-Eater's gonna be in whatever this Great Divide is for a long time, sweetheart. Doesn't take a genius to figure out what's gonna happen with that iron, does it? Charon said it's weak and I reckon he's building Sin-Eater a prison. Plus, if I ain't mistaken, I didn't finish my promise, didn't even *say* promise, and you're trapped under a sheet of iron, your realm getting sicker by the second."

"Nick," Diana warns, an edge to her voice.

I hold up a hand.

"Here are my terms. You send me, Rosa, Diana and Fred back to the Haven trainyard on Haversome and Foster, and we'll bring the locomotive with us. You don't come after me, or any of my friends, family, or loved ones again. Even after death. Eternally, right?" I bend a little lower, meeting her eyes. "And I also promise you this: for the rest of my days, I will fucking ensure no one harvests the fae wherever and whenever I can. I will fight to protect you and your kind. My actions set all this in motion, and I wanna make up for it, but I got a lot to live for, you understand? I still need wings and fae blood for Expungers, for balance remember, some creatures in Hell need putting down, but I'm sure we can come to an agreement. A fae doesn't need to be dead to shed some wings and a little drop of blood. These are the things I swear. Do you agree?"

Nick Holleran, defender of the fae. Has a nice ring to it. We'll just overlook all the fire, death, and poison I've left in my wake. Look, folk can change, alright, and Lilith *did* set an Ancient soul-devouring asshat on me.

Lilith squeezes her eyes shut, sending tears flooding down her cheeks.

"I agree," she gasps. "I agree with your terms. All of them, Nick Holleran. I swear it. Just get this thing of me and that horrible metal out of the heart. Please!"

I turn to Diana. "You're up, kid."

Bending over, I grab the sheet of metal and hurl it away, then help Lilith to her feet for good measure. Might as well start our new business arrangement on a good footing. White light builds inside the kid's outstretched arms, and the Falcon rattles and shakes.

"I'm sorry, Lilith. For everything," I say, glancing at her, Rosa's hand in mine.

"I do not need your apologies, Nick Holleran. I just need you to keep to your end of the bargain." She turns to the sickly green and purple sky. "I do not like you. I never will, but a bargain is a bargain made, and I will see to it that you keep your end. The storm builds in Hell and all realms, and it will break sooner than later. It will affect us all."

"So folk keep telling me," I mutter. "Taking its sweet time. Reckon time's a little funky to you Ancients."

She grimaces. Whether that's because of my smart ass or the poison still spreading through her realm, I'm at a loss. Let's call it fifty-fifty. "I am talking in a way you would understand, human. A year. Maybe two. Is that soon enough for you?"

"Plenty soon."

White light spreads from inside Diana as the Falcon rattles and shakes, pulling itself clear inch by inch. Her going supernova's starting to get mighty familiar.

"I must add, I did not just act out of hatred toward you, Nick Holleran," Lilith whispers, eyes fixed on the kid. "I did it out of fear. Malignants are not to be trifled with, but her power? I have not felt its like in eons. I thought removing you from the table might deal with her. That she would spend her power in rage in Hell, and my revenge would be complete."

She sighs and lurches when the locomotive lifts into the sky, free of the golden tower, Diana underneath it, her feet dangling above the ground as she levitates, a blaze of brightness in a dark world.

"Be careful of your girl, Nick Holleran," Lilith murmurs. "You know what she is, and what she will become. Be seeing you."

Be seeing you. Is this the official goodbye of the Ancients? I pull my eyes away from Diana as Lilith claps her hands together, and the world turns white.

I stagger as my feet slam onto the ground, and I throw myself forward at the crash of metal from behind me.

Cold sweeps over my body as I slide across the snow. It's beneath me, and it's falling all around me and the completely ruined locomotive that's literally a bucket of bolts with slivers of metal clinging to it on wheels. The Falcon's flown for the first and last time.

We're back. It worked. It fucking worked!

"Are we all here?" I ask, scrambling to my feet.

Rosa crashes into me, knocking me back into the snow, kissing my face over and over.

"You clever bastard!" she cries, pulling her lips away from me for a second. "I'm not going to lie, for a moment there I thought we weren't going to make it."

"Me neither," Diana calls, but she's not smiling. I know why. She heard what Lilith said about her. Knows I've kept something from her. Fuck.

"You did great, kid," I say, gently pushing Rosa off me and getting to my feet, brushing away the snow. "You too, Fred."

He stands with his hands on his hips, staring at the ruined locomotive. "A night to remember for sure. I could use a drink."

Fred turns and shakes my hand, adding to the overall frosty feeling I got running all over me.

Then my cell buzzes and pings. Glancing down at it, I see all the missed calls and messages coming in. Mostly they're all from Ruby, but there's some from Henry Butler, a couple from Lori Gavin, and one or two from a number I don't recognize. Reckon I know who it is, though. Russell Greaney keeping tabs.

"Diana?" Rosa says, staring at the kid. "I can see you! I couldn't in the fae realm!"

"Hello," the kid says, bowing her head.

Rosa crosses over to her and tilts her head up. Ignoring the cold, she kisses her on the forehead and smiles. "Diana, you're beautiful. I'm so happy to see you at last. To hear you."

Something powerful. The kid... She did what Sin-Eater did to Henry, or maybe the might of the Unseen has altered Rosa's perception, and altered it forever. She's... Rosa's like *me.* Heat floods my chest, a heat warm enough to melt an ice cap.

The kid sobs, then they're hugging one another, and I reach up to swipe something out of my eye then frown down at my cell.

"Shit," I mutter. "It's 4am."

"What's so weird about that?" Fred asks, smiling down at

the two most important people in my life hugging one another.

"It's 4am on Christmas Eve. We were gone for three days."

Fred laughs, and I shake my head, before crossing over to Rosa and Diana and turning their embrace into a group hug, then wave our train driver over, too, ignoring the ice seeping through me as he joins our huddle.

We did it. Team Fae Friends fucking did it.

And nothing's ever going to be the same again.

CHAPTER TWENTY

SERVICES RENDERED
24th DECEMBER, 2024

Not gonna lie, I'm dead tired. Beat. But there's no resting for me. After driving back into Haven, and taking Rosa and Diana home, and Fred to the Styx, I headed to my office. Had to respond to all the folk thinking I was dead, and tell them of our trip into the Unseen but, more importantly, it's Christmas Eve, and I hadn't gotten Rosa's gift. Called in a few favors, and I'm just waiting for it to be finished, so I'm kicking back in my office with a glass of whisky and some music. A collection of Buddy Holly tunes blare out of my speakers as I smile out at the snow-filled sidewalk beneath me, taking this opportunity Hell has given me to take stock. Buddy Holly's *It Doesn't Matter Anymore* is plenty Christmassy for a guy like me. Hey, I'm not all about 90s rock and grunge, you know.

Lately, I've bumbled through things. Had all manner of folk come to my aid when I needed it without playing a part in it; Lucifer, Suraz. This time, with the help of my team, I figured a way out myself. Preparation, relics, research. A man could get used to such things when traversing Hell and all the realms. Wonder how many realms?

Relics. The rings of Excalibur are sitting on my desk. I haven't worn them since Rosa gave 'em back to me. She told me her fingers can still feel their weight, though. After effects? There's so much we don't know.

After catching up with the increasingly heartfelt messages I received, I left my cell alone. Course, there were some texts and calls I didn't get back to. It's partly why I'm hanging out alone in my office and not at the Styx. When the single rap of knuckles sounds at my door, I turn my chair and lower the volume of my tunes. Ready to face my visitor. I had a feeling Russell Greaney would find me.

"My people told me you'd surface, boy," he says, striding into my office, eyes hard. He takes one look at the empty seat across from me, and his mouth twists before he sits in it. Immaculate as ever apart from his crooked teeth. "Ye could have at least had the courtesy to return my calls." He takes in the gash across my forehead and the bruises that have appeared throughout the day. "Ye look like shit."

"I was in the Unseen, slick, taking care of business." I pull over a spare glass and fill it with whisky then push it over to Greaney. Refilling my own, I raise it. "Merry Christmas."

Scowling, he takes the glass and raises it ever-so slightly in return. "And a Happy New Year. Enough of that. The creature. Is it dead?"

"There's no killing it, hoss. It's an Ancient, and I don't have the means. Reckon you don't either." His face clouds over. "However, where it's gone, it won't be coming back any time soon."

"Where?" Greaney hisses.

"Into the Great Divide in a prison of iron," I reply. "Can you live with that?"

The Irish Don leans back, eyes fixed on mine. For once, I don't look away. I'm in control here. Me. This is my office, and the shit I've seen? The shit I've done? I'm not gonna let this prick have any kind of hold on me.

He raises the whisky to his lips and takes a sip. "I believe I can live with that, yes."

"Then that brings our transaction to an end, pleasure doing

business." I glance at the rings of Excalibur. "They came in mighty handy."

Greaney barks out a laugh, but I'm quicker. Before his fingers reach them, I snatch them up and hold them in my hand.

"What do ye think ye are doing, *boy*?" he spits.

"Before we left the Unseen, Lilith told me a storm is building, one that's gonna break out in Hell and all the realms. It ain't the first time I've heard that. As much as it pains me, I reckon we're gonna be seeing a lot of one another, and this whole experience has proven I need to run a more robust operation. We're gonna work together, you and I, but you don't own me." Pulling open my desk drawer, I drop the rings into it, and pull out the ten-thousand dollar check Greaney wrote for me half a decade ago. The one I never cashed. "You have no power over me anymore. None."

Holding the check up, I rip it in half, watching his eyes the whole while. He doesn't look away when I tear it into smaller pieces, or when I drop it into the trash can and throw a lit match in there after it.

But he smiles.

"I'm keeping the rings as payment for finding and dealing with your son's killer, Mr. Greaney," I say, closing the drawer. "Merry Christmas. Close the door behind you on the way out."

The smile fades, a shrewd expression replacing it as he tilts his chin back. Then he nods.

"Merry Christmas, Mr. Holleran. I thank ye for your services, and ye are right. We will be seeing lots of one another from this day on."

Greaney gets to his feet and heads to the door. Before reaching it, he pauses, and glances over his shoulder.

"Can I ask ye a question, sonny?" he asks, a single eyebrow raised.

"Shoot."

"What do ye do when you've met the Queen of the Fae,

Death, the embodiment of sin, Nephilim, and Lucifer himself? Where do ye go?"

I take a moment and fill my glass before taking a long sip.

"You sure as shit don't go back to being an atheist, hoss."

Smiling, Greaney leaves without another word, slamming the door behind him, and I sink into my chair, downing the rest of my whisky, hands trembling. Another battle won. Pouring myself another drink, I let another shaky breath loose from my lungs and smile as I watch the check burn into cinder and ash.

Merry Christmas, Nick. It's gonna be a Hell of a New Year.

CHAPTER TWENTY-ONE

A CHRISTMAS IN HELL
25th DECEMBER, 2024

Rosa sprang a surprise this morning, before we even opened any of our gifts, though the kid comes first. Rosa says me, the big kid, will get mine after dinner. Only fair I do the same for her. So, the surprise; Ruby called over, Fred too, poor guy has no living family to haunt, and Ruby has no one save those in the bar. Both came at her invitation to spend the day with us. Just in time for breakfast, though Fred, understandably, ain't eating much.

"You ready for your presents, Di?" Rosa calls.

We're all sitting in the den by the Christmas tree, one tastefully decked out in traditional red, white, and green decorations. Well, traditional by Coca Cola's standards, but anyway, I digress.

The kid's holed herself up in the study. No doubt adding to her knowledge of Hell and the other realms.

"Coming!" she calls, and, in a flash, she's here, grinning at Rosa. Honestly, those two being able to talk without Rosa dying or having a close call is present enough for me.

"They're all yours, kid," I say, pointing at a pile under the tree. I let Rosa take a lead on this one, and I reckon she picked well.

Diana smiles at me, kinda, then dives at her pile, wrapping paper shredding. Ruby laughs, coffee in hand, while Fred beams down at her. Rosa's crying, so I make my way over to her and wrap an arm around her shoulders.

"Merry Christmas, sweetheart," I say, kissing her on the cheek. "And thank you."

"For what?" Rosa asks as the kid squeals in delight at a pristine vinyl copy of *A Hard Day's Night* by The Beatles. We've sure had a few of those lately.

"Everything," I reply. "Just about everything."

The day has been almost perfect. The food's been amazing, the drink flowing, the company great, and the kid enjoyed her gifts. Not only did she get the missing Beatles vinyls she wanted for her collection, she also scored the rest of Tolkien's larger works that she hasn't read yet, encyclopedias of world mythology, and a framed picture of all the maps from the books she likes. Oh, and another subscription to a streaming service we didn't already have. Kid watches a lot of TV. She doesn't sleep, after all.

Rosa's carried off the job of host well. I offered to help, of course, but she swatted me away more than once. She said she wanted to keep busy. Truth be told, she hasn't stopped doing *something* since returning from the Unseen. She ain't left the house yet, no doubt warming herself up for a real trip through Hell when she's ready for it, but Rosa had her face almost pressed to the Mustang's window on our trip through Haven, the color drained from her face when she saw the city for what it really is. Reckon we'll have a discussion soon, but I'm willing to wait. It's Christmas, and it's been a mighty swell day, pain in my ankle, forehead and just generally everywhere aside.

But it hasn't been perfect. Diana's avoiding me beyond being polite. That kinda smile she gave me when opening her presents spoke volumes.

"Hey, I think it's time for our presents, don't you?" Rosa whispers in my ear. Everyone's in the den watching *Big Trouble in*

Little China, as promised, wine and Paintstripper in folk's hands. Diana's watching too, but she isn't really paying attention.

"Sure, been waiting all day," I say, grinning despite my misgivings over the kid. "You wanna do it here?"

"In the study, come on," she replies, and leads the way. She looks awful cute in a Christmas sweater. So cute she even got me wearing one, Rudolph's bright red bobbly nose protruding off my stomach.

Study's perfect, my gift for her is in there, hiding under the desk.

"You first!" Rosa almost shouts, eyes shining as soon as I walk in, thrusting a large, soft package in my hands. "Open it, come on!"

Tearing open the wrapping paper, I frown at what I see folded up inside, then I grin.

"Ah, Rosa, you shouldn't have!"

"Do you love it? You hate it, don't you?" she babbles as I let the garment unfold. It's a fucking authentically cool black leather duster jacket. It must have cost a fortune! "I can take it back, I have the receipt. It's okay. I get it, you hate it."

"Rosa," I say, leaning over and kissing her deeply. "I love it. It's perfect. Thank you. It's automatically my favorite jacket. No question."

"You really mean it?" she asks, grinning.

"I do." I hang it up off the coat hanger on the door, the rich leathery smell thick as the material creaks in a mightily pleasing way. "Now it's your turn."

To level with you, I thought about getting her an engagement ring, but it's corny, right? Proposing on Christmas Day, and we haven't even mentioned my impromptu '*marry me*' since we returned. Maybe it was right in that particular moment, but we've only been properly together for a handful of months, and I don't wanna scare her away. I'll bring it up in the new year. Scout's honor.

Stooping, I pull a rounded parcel from beneath the desk,

and sit down, telling her to take a seat, too.

There's gonna be some preamble.

"Look, as you know I left it late, but I also didn't know I was gonna lose three days in the Unseen, either." I hand her the package. "I never knew you wanted something like this, and it's cool with me, but you ain't having one without what's in here."

Frowning, Rosa gazes at the parcel and unwraps it carefully. There's no tearing at it like me.

Then she laughs, and pulls out the motorcycle helmet I had designed for her. An envelope drops out of it, and she catches it.

"Lessons," I say, "and when you pass, I'll get you a motorcycle of your choice. I hope you like the helmet. It's custom, had it made yesterday."

Tears leak from her eyes as she turns the helmet around. Colored black on the whole, it shows a scene of fire falling from a green and purple sky. On the back there's a pretty fucking good depiction of the rings of Excalibur, the symbols for fire and rain showing.

"Just so you can remember the moment you saved all our asses," I whisper. "Is it okay?"

Placing it on the desk, Rosa throws herself into my lap, hugging me tight before our lips find one another's again. We kiss for God knows how long, the taste of red wine on her mouth and tongue but I'm not complaining.

"I love it, and I love you," she murmurs at last. "It's so you. Trying to look after everyone, but it's the new you, too. It's like you're saying, '*go do this crazy thing*' and helping me with it, trying to keep me safe."

"I do try to smooth out my edges, you know," I reply, kissing her again. "Every day is a lesson."

"Speaking of," Rosa says, kissing me once more then moving back to her chair. "You should go talk to Diana before the day's over, and there's no time like the present. I know there were other issues at hand, but she's hurting about this Malignant thing."

Sighing, I get to my feet. "I know. Gonna do it now."

As I leave the study, I see the kid pass the front door. She'd been listening to us, no doubt feeling our emotions and it drew her close. I duck back inside the study and grab my new duster, grinning at Rosa. She smiles back, but I pause. She's sitting in the exact place in the vision Sin-Eater showed me when he tried to drain my soul.

"You okay?" she asks, looking up from her helmet.

"Peachy," I say, then follow Diana, shrugging into the jacket. Fits perfectly.

I close the door behind me, coming to a stop beside the kid. Darkness has already fallen, and the sounds of music drift over the neighborhood. Christmas decorations sparkle and twinkle as the snow falls and builds on the ground.

"Pretty, ain't it?" I murmur, glancing down at her.

"Nick, what's a Malignant, and why didn't you tell me?"

I sigh. "You haven't searched for it?"

"No, because I wanted to hear it from you first."

She doesn't look at me, and stares out at the night instead, but I reckon she doesn't see any of it.

"Look, I was gonna tell you after we dealt with Lilith and Sin-Eater. Honest. Reckon you can tell if I'm lying by the way I'm feeling." She gives a half-nod. "I didn't want you to worry, but, yeah, Suraz filled me in about it after Sin-Eater said it. He isn't sure why you're the way you are, but it's down to your power. What you can do, and most ghosts can't."

"It's the way I've been acting, isn't it?" she whispers. "Blowing away Lilith. What I did to you. Twice."

"It's the other stuff too, kid. You know, the saving our asses, the frankly awesome stuff you're capable of." I turn to her, my hand on her shoulder. "Look, you have the potential to turn Malignant. *Potential.* No guarantee you'll go that way, and I'm gonna do everything I can so it doesn't. But you have to remember this, kid, you're a good person. You're kind. You're loving, and you're surrounded with people who love you, okay? We'll get through this together. Like a family."

Sin-Eater's future vision flashes in my mind again. The one without Diana in it. The talk of grief.

"What happens if I *do* go Malignant?" she asks in a low voice, her pits meeting my eyes. "What does it mean?"

I sigh, squeezing the bridge of my nose. Not gonna lie to her. "Suraz likened it to a Hell version of an EMP blast. Said you'd be highly dangerous."

"Oh."

"It's just potentially, kid. We've all got it in us to be nightmares. Look at me? I was the fae's bogey man, practically, but I'm changing my ways. We can decide. It's free will, right? Focus on the good you have around you. The people who love you, and that isn't just me. Rosa, Ruby. Hell, Fred, too. From what I can gather, Malignants are those who see nothing but darkness. You're not that, kid."

She turns on her heel, heading back inside the house, then pauses. "We best make sure that it won't happen then, won't we. Thank you for telling me, Nick."

She disappears through the door, and I have no idea if our little talk went well or not.

"Well, at least she knows," I mutter to myself.

"Yes, the problems just add to one another, do they not, Fateless?"

I almost leap straight through my new jacket when Charon's gravelly voice whispers in my ear.

"Fuck, you're actually trying to kill me now?" I growl, hand on my chest. "Jesus."

"Sin-Eater is taken care of. I must admit you acted in a much smarter way than I gave you credit for," Charon replies, his grin mirthless. Then his eyes give me the quick up and down. "Nice duster."

"Thanks," I reply, folding my arms against the cold. It's always colder when this bozo's about. "You just dropping by to say Merry Christmas?"

"No, I come with a warning, Fateless, as a favor for your

assistance in my battle with Sin-Eater." He fixes me with those eyes filled with the souls of millions. "I told you before you had the hint of magic about you. Now it is a cloak. You have used it, and you have taken a glimpse at the wider state of reality. Other realms are open to you."

"Doesn't sound so bad," I mutter, hankering for a cigarette.

"Those realms, and their occupiers, will come and find you too, Fateless." He glances up at the black sky. "The storm moves ever closer, and Sin-Eater will return one day. Be seeing you."

I shiver as Charon fades into the darkness, the snow falling all the heavier. Hell. Other realms and a wider reality. Ancients, demons, Nephilim, creatures, and ghosts. The approaching storm. I snort and turn away, heading back into my house.

Together, we'll build a network. We know more than we did a week ago, and now my eyes are open to the wider world. Again. It's almost like it was when I first was able to *See,* but this time I'm not gonna spend a few years floundering around. The storm's coming, Hell's waiting, and other realms loom.

But not today.

Warmth wraps me in an embrace, and Rosa smiles over her shoulder as she walks back into the den, hand-in-hand with Diana. For one evening, Hell and all the differing and divergent battling realms can exist without me. It's time for wine, snacks, *Big Trouble in Little China* and a nice, long time in bed. For once, Hell can wait.

Nick Holleran's out of office.

"*Don't talk to me about other worlds, separate realities, lost continents or invisible realms.*

I know where I belong. Heaven is home. Utopia is here. Nirvana is now."

— Edward Abbey

THE END

NICK HOLLERAN WILL RETURN IN
"A SHADOW OVER HAVEN"

A NOTE FROM THE AUTHOR

At one point, when I was writing about Nick, Rosa, Diana, and Fred flying through the fae realm in a dilapidated steam train whilst being chased by a ... mischief?... of fae and Lilith in dragon form, I thought I might have gone too far.

But then I was having way too much fun to do it any differently.

'One Life Left' is the Nick Holleran book I'd always wanted to write. I'm still quite a new author, and this series has had a rather troubled beginning, but this book is the one I always had in mind for the series: a marriage of the hard-boiled P.I. and the fantastical or, as some of my readers say in their reviews, 'Dresden Files meets Supernatural with a dose of Hellblazer and a modern twist'. When I came up with this world, I had a sandbox in mind that I could play within a set of defined rules. Nick could tangle with fae, or vampires, or demons and angels, or serial killers, or even wizards and witches, so long as it felt real to the world. This book is really the first to reveal the strangeness looming at the edges of Haven, and I truly hope you all had as much of a blast reading it as I did writing it.

Thanks must go to my constant beta readers Nikki De-Keuster and Chris Hewitt for their advice, thoughts, and enjoyment when reading this. As I said, especially at one point, I thought I may have gone too far, but my team's reaction to the madness I'd cooked boosted my confidence. To Shona Kinsella too for coming in to edit this one, and doing such a brilliant job.

And I couldn't have gotten through the many long months of 2023 without the friendship of Bella Pagan or Adrian Fletcher, and my Friday night TTRPG crew of Peter Hutchinson, Jenny Hannaford-Jennings, Vinjii, and Luke Winch. Though, throughout it all, my little boy Ollie was there, asking for me to include a steam train in the story.

He now prefers cruise ships...

Nick Holleran will return, and soon. As will his friends, and the stories of the future are just as much about Rosa, Diana, Ruby, Suraz, and Charon as they are about Nick. In fact, I'm planning on writing the next book imminently. I hope you'll be here for it, and thank you all for reading so far. I appreciate every second you've all spent in Haven.

Be seeing you,
Dave
(November 2023)

David Green is a writer of the epic and the urban, the fantastical and the mysterious.

With his character-driven dark fantasy series Empire Of Ruin, or urban fantasy noir Hell In Haven starring Haven's only supernatural PI Nick Holleran, David takes readers on emotional, character-driven, action-packed thrill rides that leaves a reader needing their next fix.

Hailing from the north-west of England, David now lives in County Galway on the west coast of Ireland with his wife and train-obsessed son.

When not writing, David can be found wondering why he chooses to live in, and write about, places where it constantly rains.

Follow David Linktr.ee/davidgreenwriter

More from Eerie River

Eerie River Publishing is a leader in independent horror, dark fantasy, and dark speculative fiction.

We are dedicated to publishing anthologies, collections, and novels from some of the best indie authors around the world. Our goal is to become a go-to resource for horror, dark fantasy and dark speculative readers, and to provide a safe space for authors to share their stories.

Interested in becoming a Patreon member?
By joining our patreon, you will be supporting our artists and authors, who work hard to produce high-quality and original content for your enjoyment. You will also get access to exclusive perks, such as early releases, behind-the-scenes updates, bonus material, and more. If you love dark fiction and want to support independent publishing, please consider becoming a patron today. Thank you for your interest and support.

www.patreon.com/EerieRiverPub.

To stay up to date with all our new releases and upcoming giveaways, follow us on Facebook, Twitter, Instagram and YouTube.

linktr.ee/eerieriver

EERIE RIVER PUBLISHING
NOVELS
Dead Man Walking
Devil Walks in Blood
The Darkness In The Pines
At Eternity's Gate
Beyond Sundered Seas
Path of War
In Solitudes Shadow
The Void
They Are Cursed Like You
SENTINEL
NOTHUS
Miracle Growth
Infested
Helluland
A Sword Named Sorrow
Storming Area 51

ANTHOLOGIES
AFTER: A Post-Apocalyptic Survivor Series
Elemental Cycle: Four Book Series Blood Sins
It Calls From Series
Blood Sins
Last Stop: Whiskey Pete
Elemental Series
Of Fire and Stars
From Beyond the Threshold

DRABBLE COLLECTIONS
Forgotten Ones: Drabbles of Myth and Legend
Dark Magic: Drabbles of Magic and Lore

COMING SOON

Rotten House
Chasing the Dragon
The Naughty Corner
Tarot Anthology
The Earth Bleeds at Night

EMPIRE OF RUIN
1
IN SOLITUDE'S
SHADOW
DAVID GREEN

EMPIRE OF RUIN
2
PATH OF
WAR
DAVID GREEN

HELLULAND
A NOVEL
A GIFT
AWAKENING.
A LEGEND
REVEALED.
C.R. LINDSTRÖM

Printed in Great Britain
by Amazon

48987316R00148